I Never Knew
I Had a Choice

By Gerald Corey:

Theory and Practice of Counseling and Psychotherapy
A Manual for Theory and Practice of Counseling and
Psychotherapy

By Gerald Corey and Marianne Schneider Corey:

Groups: Process and Practice

I Never Knew
I Had a Choice

Gerald Corey

California State University, Fullerton

in collaboration with Marianne Schneider Corey

Brooks/Cole Publishing Company

Monterey, California
A Division of Wadsworth Publishing Company, Inc.

Printed in the United States of America

10 9 8 7 6 5 4 3

Library of Congress Cataloging in Publication Data

Corey, Gerald F.
    I never knew I had a choice.

    Includes bibliographies and index.
    1. Humanistic psychology.   2. Self-perception.
3. Emotions.   4. Interpersonal relations.   I. Corey,
Marianne Schneider, 1942-   joint author.   II. Title.
BF204.C67   158   78-6702
ISBN 0-8183-0263-0

Photos on pages 15, 16, 28, 93, 115, 172, 219, 227, and 359 by Richard Kuhlenschmidt. Photos on pages 24, 102, 123, 158, 194, 250, 253, 284, and 319 by Helen Nestor. Photo on page 108 by Robert Llewellyn/Freelance Photographers Guild. Photo on page 128 by Freelance Photographers Guild. Photo on page 114 by Bernie Rubalcaba. Photo on page 195 by Karen Preuss. Photo on page 208 by William Tuohy/Freelance Photographers Guild. Photo on page 221 by Dr. Robert E. Hager/Freelance Photographers Guild. Sculpture on page 276 by Dr. Richard Fox; photo courtesy of the author. Photos on pages v and 337 courtesy of the author. Back cover photo by Karl Schneider.

Acquisition Editor: *Claire Verduin*
Production Editor: *John Bergez*
Interior and Cover Design: *Jamie S. Brooks*
Illustrations: *Tom Durfee*
Typesetting: *Holmes*

In memory of my friend Jim Morelock,
a searcher who lived and died with dignity
and self-respect,
who struggled and questioned,
who made the choice to live his days fully
until time ran out on him at age 25.

Preface

I Never Knew I Had a Choice is designed as a resource for college students of any age who wish to expand their self-awareness and to explore the choices available to them in significant areas of their lives. The topics discussed include: the effects our schooling has on us; our views of ourselves and of human nature; our struggle to achieve autonomy; the roles that work, love, sexuality, intimacy, and solitude play in our lives; the meaning of loneliness, death, and loss; and the ways in which we choose our values and philosophies of life. This is a personal book, because throughout I encourage readers to examine carefully the choices they have made and how these choices affect their present level of satisfaction. It is also a personal book inasmuch as I describe my own concerns, struggles, decisions, and values in regard to many of the issues raised.

I wrote this book for use in college courses dealing with the psychology of adjustment, personality development, personal growth, and self-awareness. My experience has been that active, open, and personal participation in courses like these can lead to expanded self-awareness and greater autonomy in living. Some of the unique problems and challenges associated with teaching such a course are discussed in the Instructor's Manual that I have written to accompany the text.

The book itself is designed to be a personal workbook as well as a classroom text. Each chapter begins with a *Self-Inventory* that gives readers the chance to focus on their own present beliefs and attitudes. Within the chapters, sections called *Time Out for Personal Reflection* provide an opportunity to pause and reflect on the issues raised. Additional *Activities and Exercises* are given at the end of each chapter that can be done both inside and outside of class. Each chapter also contains a *Suggested Readings* list; most of the books listed are available in paperback editions. The final chapter provides a consumer's guide to professional resources for those who wish to continue their personal learning through some form of counseling or group experience.

Although my own approach may be broadly characterized as humanistic and existential, my aim has been to challenge readers to recognize and assess their own choices, beliefs, and values, rather than to convert them to a particular point of view. My basic premise is that a commitment to self-exploration can create new potentials for choice—a premise that has grown out of my own experience in counseling, group work, and college teaching. Most of my clients and students are relatively well-functioning people who desire more from life and who want to recognize and remove blocks to their personal creativity and freedom. It is for people like these that I've written *I Never Knew I Had a Choice.*

I want to acknowledge the contributions of several people to this book. Most significantly, my wife, Marianne Schneider Corey, has been a true collaborator with me on this project; her ideas and criticisms have contributed to every chapter. I also want to express my deep appreciation for the insightful suggestions given to me by friends, associates, and reviewers. Among the reviewers were M. Michael Klaber, University of Hartford; George McWilliams, Ventura College; and Dru Spiro, Lincoln Land Community College. In addition, the following people not only read the manuscript carefully but also gathered for a weekend at my home in Idyllwild to discuss the manuscript in detail: John Brennecke, Mt. San Antonio College; Patrick Callanan, Mt. San Antonio College; Lani Carney, Cypress College; Alan Dahms, Metropolitan College, Denver; Logan Fox, El Camino College; Todd Gaffaney, Cerritos College; Chuck Lee, Orange Coast College; and Velma Walker, Tarrant County Community College. Friends and former students who also took part in this weekend conference and offered many valuable ideas included Merri Chalenor, Randy Corliss, Jim Morelock, Karen Palmer, and Linda Weber.

I also want to thank Terry Hendrix and Claire Verduin of Brooks/Cole for the encouragement and challenge they provided throughout the writing, and I especially want to express my appreciation to John Bergez for his sensitive and insightful editing. I also owe debts of gratitude to my close friend and colleague J. Michael Russell of California State University at Fullerton, for our many provocative discussions concerning the issues raised in this book, and to William Lyon of Chapman College, who encouraged the move to Cal State Fullerton that ultimately led to the writing of *I Never Knew I Had a Choice.*

Last, but surely not least, I thank my daughters, Heidi and Cindy, for the lessons they continue to teach me and for their patience in tolerating a busy father for many months. I am also grateful to Heidi for her help in alphabetizing the Index.

Gerald Corey

Contents

Part 1

Foundations
of
Choice

*"One thing that I can see now that I did not see
before is that I have a choice—that things
do not have to stay the way they are and that
I can change my life if I want to. I never knew
I had a choice!"*

Chapter 1

Introduction

As we recognize that we are not merely passive victims of our circumstances, we can consciously become the architects of our lives. Even though others may have drawn the blueprints, we can recognize the plan, take a stand, and change the design.

A person who had been a client of mine in individual therapy for close to a year said one day "One thing that I can see now that I did not see before is that I *have a choice*—that things do not have to stay the way they are and that I can change my life if I want to. *I never knew I had a choice!*" This remark captures the central message of this book: we are *not* passive victims of life, we *do* make choices, and we *do* have the power to change major aspects of our lives as we struggle toward a more authentic existence.

Some of the choices that will be examined in this book are these:

- We can become independent persons with our own unique identities, or we can remain dependent on others to mold and shape us.
- We can remain children, emotionally speaking, or we can work toward becoming psychological adults.
- We can become aware of early decisions that we made about ourselves and about life, or we can remain blind to the many ways in which we continue to be influenced and limited by our past.
- We can make new decisions that will change the course of our lives, or we can cling to old decisions without ever reexamining their validity.
- We can recognize our need for love, even though we might experience fears in opening ourselves to loving; or we can choose not to risk trusting ourselves in loving relationships.
- We can make sexuality a meaningful and enriching part of our experience, or we can choose to deny our sexuality or to experience only mechanical sex in which we and others become objects instead of persons.
- We can create meaningful, committed relationships, or we can avoid intimacy and commitment.
- We can choose to learn about ourselves from our lonely experiences, or we can avoid fully experiencing the lonely periods in our lives.
- We can recreate ourselves by finding time alone in which to discover new facets within, or we can flee from time alone for fear of feeling empty and lonely when we have only ourselves.
- We can take our mortality as a challenge to live each day as fully as possible, or we can deny the reality of death and its meaning for us.
- We can actively search for a purpose in living and thus give meaning to our work and our play, or we can avoid asking ourselves what the point of our lives really is.
- We can carve out our own meanings and values, or we can let others tell us what we should value.

One of the basic assumptions of this book is that, although we do possess freedom to make choices, this freedom comes with a degree of anxiety; indeed, the more freedom we have, the more anxiety we are likely to experience. Nevertheless, as we recognize that we are not merely passive victims of our circumstances, we can consciously become the architects of our lives. Even though others may have drawn the initial

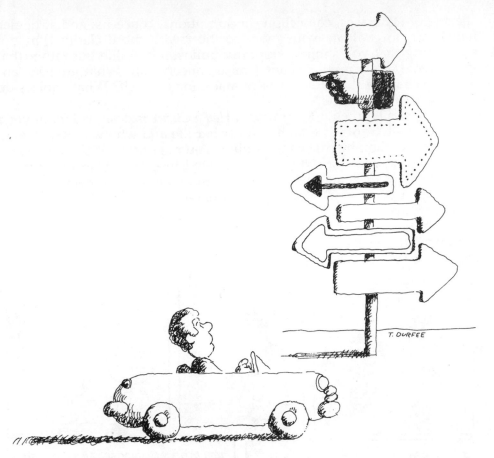

T. DURFEE

blueprints, we can recognize the plan, take a stand, and change the design. This book is intended to stimulate your thinking about changes *you* want to make and encourage you to carry them out.

In developing the various chapters of this book, I talked with both students and instructors in courses such as Psychology of Personal Growth at many community colleges. A theme that frequently came up during these discussions was that students selected such a course because of their interest in discovering more about themselves and their relationships with others. Most of them were looking for a *practical* course, one that dealt with real issues in everyday living and that would provide an impetus for their own personal growth. Accordingly, I have focused on helping you to recognize blocks to your creative and productive energies, to find ways of removing these obstructions, and to make conscious choices about the ways in which you might want to modify your attitudes and behavior.

Another dimension of my approach in this book concerns the self-disclosures I've made about my own life. It seemed fitting to write this book in a personal style and to openly share with you how I have come to certain of the beliefs and values I write about. I hope that my sharing of my biases, convictions, assumptions, concerns, and struggles helps you to evaluate your own position with more clarity. I'm not suggesting that you should adopt my philosophy of life but rather that you should ask how the issues I raise concern *you*. What are *your* answers? What are the choices *you've* made for yourself? What choices do you want to make now?

Basically, then, *I Never Knew I Had a Choice* is designed for anyone who seriously wants to examine his or her life and who wants to live by choice rather than by past conditioning. You might say "Well, surely this includes everyone, for who isn't interested in growing, learning more about himself, or being the master of her fate rather than being directed and shaped by others?" Yet there is a degree of uncomfortableness, and even fear, associated with discovering ourselves. Many people may prefer to remain unaware, to allow others to choose for them, and to be content with the status quo. Consequently, I ask you to think about the price involved in expanding your awareness and choosing for yourself.

Are you comfortable with yourself now? Do you see any risks involved in taking the time and making a personal commitment to explore various aspects of your life? Are you reluctant to recognize problem areas, for fear that you'll feel overwhelmed if you begin to question your life? These are important questions, and, since personal awareness and growth cannot be forced on us, it is vital that you decide whether you genuinely want to do all that is involved in self-exploration.

My Philosophical Orientation and Assumptions

Anyone who writes about human concerns and values has a basic viewpoint or philosophy that determines his or her approach, even if that philosophy is not stated explicitly. Since this is a book about personal choices, it's especially appropriate that I share openly with you my basic assumptions and philosophical orientation.

Fundamentally, my approach in *I Never Knew I Had a Choice* is humanistic and personal; that is, I emphasize the healthy and effective personality and the common struggles that most of us experience in becoming autonomous. I especially emphasize accepting personal responsibility for the choices we make and consciously deciding whether and in what ways we want to change our lives. This emphasis is in keeping with the existential-humanistic viewpoint in psychology, whose proponents assume that we have a strong drive toward health and psychological wholeness and that we are motivated to become all that we are able to become. Both my own thinking and the theoretical approach I take in my professional work have been greatly influenced by people who have contributed to this tradition in psychology, including Carl Rogers, Abraham Maslow, Fritz Perls, Sidney Jourard, Clark Moustakas, and Rollo May.

Throughout this book, I have drawn upon both my personal experience and my professional work with students and clients in counseling. I have used these experiences to highlight the issue of human choice and to develop the theme that freedom of choice is not something that is given to us but something that we must actively achieve for ourselves. As Harry Browne (1973) argues in his book, *How I Found Freedom in an Unfree World*, it is a great mistake to assume that we cannot change or become free until others give us permission to. Instead, Browne insists, we must retain final "permission rights" for ourselves. In doing so, however, we should not expect that others will necessarily change also. We don't have the power to change others, unless they themselves want to change. Moreover, we can easily get hung up by focusing on all the ways we wish others in our lives would change, instead of working on changing ourselves. If we wait for others to become different, or if we blame others for the fact that we're not as happy as we'd like, we diminish our power to take full control of our own lives.

Although this book deals with questions in what is often called "the psychology of adjustment," I have an uneasy feeling about this common phrase. My thinking is geared to personal *growth, awareness, and choice,* and to the courage we must have if we are honestly to face our struggles as we try to take charge of our lives. In contrast, the term *adjustment* is frequently taken to mean that there is an ideal norm that people should be measured by. This notion raises many problems; for example, you may ask: What is the desired norm of adjustment? Who determines the standards of "good" adjustment? Is it possible that the same person could be considered well adjusted in our culture and poorly adjusted in some other culture?

A further bias I have against the "adjustment" concept of human behavior is that often those who claim to be well-adjusted are the ones who have settled for a complacent and dead existence, one that has neither challenge nor excitement. My hope is that we can create our own definitions of ourselves as persons, rather than being primarily ruled by other people's norms or expectations. Although I believe that it is unwise to merely "do your own thing" in an irresponsible manner, I also believe that we can consider the good of others and still retain our integrity by making our own choices in life.

Instead of talking about *adjustment,* then, I prefer to talk about *growth.* A psychology of growth rests on the assumption that growth is a lifelong adventure, not some fixed point at which we arrive. In order to continue to grow, we have to be willing to let go of some of our old ways of thinking and being in order to make room for new behavior. During your reading and studying, you might try to become alert to ways in which you've stopped growing, to your fears of doing what is necessary to grow, and, most important, to the degree of personal growth you're willing to invest in.

Some Suggestions for Using This Book

I hope you'll treat this book, and the course, in a personal way. Rather than merely reading *I Never Knew I Had a Choice* as a textbook or thinking about how the issues I raise apply to others, you may profit most by attempting to apply this material to yourself. With this in mind, I'd like to suggest some guidelines for you to consider.

1. Each chapter begins with a self-inventory. These inventories are designed to get you to think and to involve yourself personally with each topic. You might want to bring your responses to class and discuss your views or compare them with those of others. If you're reading this book alone, you may wish to have a close friend or your spouse answer some of the questions, and then share the results. You may also find it useful to re-take the inventories after you finish studying each chapter.

2. In many of the chapters, examples are drawn from everyday life. You might think of how you relate to these examples. How does each example apply to you?

3. I suggest that, rather than reading simply to learn facts, you take your own position on the issues I raise. As much as possible, put yourself into what you read.

4. Questions and exercises are inserted into the main part of the chapters. Since these exercises are designed to help you focus on specific and concrete topics, it can be most valuable for you to take the time to do these exercises as you read. Actually writing down your responses in the text will help you begin to reflect and think about how each of these topics applies to you.

5. At the end of each chapter, there are additional activities and exercises suggested for both in-class and out-of-class practice. I present many of these activities, so that you'll have a range from which to select those that are most meaningful for you. As you finish each chapter, I suggest reading all the exercises and then deciding on a few that you would most like to do.

6. One activity that I suggest throughout the book is that of keeping a journal. You might purchase a separate notebook in which to write your reactions to each topic or to do more extensive writing on some of the exercises. Many students have claimed that the time they took to write in their journals was most productive, because it gave them a written account that they could read at various times. Later, you can look for patterns in your journal; doing so can help you identify some of your critical choices and areas of conflict. Frequently, I give concrete suggestions concerning things you might include in your journal, but the important thing is for you to decide what to put in your journal and how you want to use it.

7. Many students who examine the kinds of personal topics discussed in this book develop an interest in reading related books and going into some topics in greater depth. For this reason, I give a list of selected books for each chapter. The lists are annotated to give you an idea of the potential usefulness of each book for you. I'm convinced that reading good and thoughtful books is one excellent way for us to challenge the meaning of our lives, to expand our self-awareness and understanding of others, and to discover guidelines for reflection.

8. As you work with the ideas in this book, I hope that you'll keep in mind that growth and change entail risking and a willingness to experience some anxiety. Mistakes can be significant learning experiences, and I doubt that we can gain very much if we're unwilling to explore for fear of making them. Making mistakes usually isn't fatal, and it can be an essential part of growing.

The writing of this book has been a source of both joy and pain. It was a difficult and challenging book to write, because I was forced to look at my own life and how the issues I raise apply to me. Moreover, despite the support and encouragement of others, the writing of a book like this one can be a lonely venture. After all, in courses that I teach, I can engage in dialogue with my students and get their ideas and reactions to what I say, but in a book the conversation is decidedly one-way. Nevertheless, I'd very much like to know how you are affected by *I Never Knew I Had a Choice*, and I hope that, if you want to, you'll write and tell me your impressions and reactions. I'd also be very interested in finding out how you'd like to see this book changed. What topics most affect you? Least affect you? What are your suggestions for changes in the book, including deletions and additions? If you'd like to write, address your letter to me in care of Brooks/Cole Publishing Company, Monterey, California 93940.

Suggested Readings

At the end of each chapter, I list several books that are relevant to the topic of that chapter. The following are some books that deal with many of the general themes discussed in *I Never Knew I Had a Choice*. You might want to select several of them for supplementary reading.

Arkoff, A. (Ed.). *Psychology and Human Growth.* Boston: Allyn & Bacon, 1975. A book of readings on topics such as problems in identity, body image, sex-role image, achievement, aggression, sex, anxiety, defense, growth, death, love, marriage, family life, and work.

Bach, R. *Jonathan Livingston Seagull.* New York: Macmillan, 1970. A moving story about a seagull in search of freedom and autonomy. He continued to do things that others said he could never do.

Brennecke, J., & Amick, R. *The Struggle for Significance* (2nd ed.). Beverly Hills, Calif.: Glencoe, 1975. A book that deals with most of the topics covered in this book, written in an interesting, personal, and thought-provoking style.

Browne, Harry. *How I Found Freedom in an Unfree World.* New York: Avon, 1973. The author points out many ways in which we aren't free and, at the same time, makes a case for how we can achieve freedom in an unfree world. The central message is that we shouldn't wait for someone else to give us permission to change; we can achieve freedom if we focus on changing ourselves and avoid changing others.

Daniels, V., & Horowitz, L. *Being and Caring.* Palo Alto, Calif.: Mayfield, 1976. A very well-written self-development book that deals with the themes that we are responsible for finding our own way and that with awareness we can create our own world. The authors discuss issues of awareness, acceptance, self-honesty, living with feeling, being and sharing, and centeredness.

Greenwald, J. *Be the Person You Were Meant to Be.* New York: Dell, 1973. The core of this book deals with behavior and relationships that are either "nourishing" or "toxic." It is an invitation to look at your life-style to decide on ways in which you might want to change.

Kangas, J., & Solomon, G. *The Psychology of Strength.* Englewood Cliffs, N.J.: Prentice-Hall, 1975. This is a guide to the fulfillment of your human potential. It describes the process of being strong in relation to yourself and to others as you meet the challenges and crises of life.

Lair, J. *I Ain't Much, Baby - But I'm All I've Got.* New York: Doubleday, 1972. A very personal account of one man's struggle to find meaning in his world. Lair emphasizes that we have choices that lead to either constructive or destructive living. His choice to drastically change his life was made in a hospital bed while he was recovering from a heart attack. He writes about self-acceptance, trust, love, sexuality, death, spirituality.

Lair, J. *I Ain't Well - But I Sure Am Better.* Greenwich, Conn.: Fawcett, 1975. A continuation of his earlier book, this book reveals the author's methods for continuing the search for personal and spiritual growth. He emphasizes the importance of genuine and deep friendships in his "mutual-need therapy."

Lyon, W. *Let Me Live!* North Quincy, Mass.: Christopher Press, 1975. This is a book that will probably capture your interest and make you think. Its theme is that we get from life what we deserve. Topics include: a view of the world and life, "you make me sick, so let's get married," love, sex, meaning, "therapy-therapy," autonomy, femininity, masculinity, and becoming your own parent.

May, R. *The Courage to Create.* New York: Bantam, 1975. This book is a collection of lectures by Rollo May on the theme of the courage to choose and create—a potential that May believes is in all of us.

Pirsig, R. *Zen and the Art of Motorcycle Maintenance.* New York: Bantam, 1974. This is both a story of a father and son on a journey of self-discovery and a philosophical treatment of many issues relating to the quality and meaning of life.

Stevens, J. *Awareness: Exploring, Experimenting, Experiencing.* Moab, Utah: Real People Press, 1971. The theme of this book is how we can explore and expand our self-awareness. The bulk of the book consists of experiments that can be done by yourself.

Education and
Personal Learning

*If you could go back and relive your school years,
how would you want them to be different?*

Pre-Chapter Self-Inventory

As I explained in Chapter 1, the purpose of the pre-chapter self-inventories is to help you focus on your attitudes and beliefs about the issues that will be discussed in the chapter. I recommend that you take these inventories rapidly by giving your initial reaction to each statement. There are no correct or incorrect answers, since the inventory is an aid in identifying *your* beliefs. You might want to take each chapter's inventory again after you've read and studied the chapter, to determine whether you've changed your thinking on any items.

For each statement, indicate the response that most closely identifies your beliefs and attitudes. Use this code: A = I strongly agree; B = I slightly agree; C = I slightly disagree; D = I strongly disagree.

_C_   1. Most of my teachers have had a significant, positive impact on me.

_C_   2. During my elementary and high school years, I was an eager learner.

_A_   3. I tend to rely on the authority of the teacher more than on my own judgment.

_B_   4. The primary purpose of education is to give me factual knowledge.

_B_   5. My educational experiences have made me a more curious person.

_C_   6. Basically, I am an intrinsic learner; that is, I learn because of the satisfaction that learning itself brings, not because of external rewards or incentives.

_A_   7. The fear of failing has interfered with my learning.

_A_   8. My school experiences have dealt with issues that were personally meaningful to me.

_A_   9. In the course of my education, I have been given ample freedom to pursue significant topics and problems, and this freedom has helped me to choose more wisely.

_B_   10. I consider myself successful as a student.

_A_   11. If an instructor grants me freedom to learn and trusts me, I generally can handle this freedom constructively.

_A_   12. I have the power to effect significant changes in my own education.

_B_   13. I tend to be a teacher-pleaser; that is, I usually do what's expected, without questioning it.

_A_   14. I'm responsible for making my learning meaningful, and I can do so by becoming committed and involved in the process of my learning.

_A_   15. I generally decide for myself what I want to get from a course.

B __ 16. I'm willing to take risks in most of my classes.
A __ 17. If a class is apathetic, the lack of interest is the responsibility of the students as well as the instructor.
A __ 18. I feel excited by most of my classes.
B __ 19. Most students would rather complain about what they don't like about their classes than invest energy in working toward a change.
B __ 20. Most of the students I encounter feel enthused about learning.

Introduction

I believe that you can get the most out of this course if you develop an active style of learning in which you raise questions and search for answers within yourself. Since this kind of personal learning might be different from most of your past experiences in school, it's appropriate at this point for you to review your own experiences as a learner and to think about the effects your education has had on you. Later on in this chapter, I'll suggest some specific ways in which you can become an active and involved learner.

The Effects of Education on Us

In this section, I take some strong positions on what I think schooling often does to us. For this reason, I want to state my bias at the outset and to describe the experiences that have contributed to my thinking on this subject.

For the most part, school for me during childhood and adolescence was a meaningless and sometimes painful experience. In addition, my educational experiences (from grammar school through graduate school) in many ways taught me to be a passive learner. I believe that my education taught me that pleasing the teacher is more important than pleasing myself; that accepting the opinions of an authority is more valuable than becoming a questioner; that learning facts and information is more valuable than learning about oneself; that learning is motivated by external factors; that there is a right answer to every problem; that school life and out-of-school life are separate; that the sharing of personal feelings and concerns has no place in the classroom; and that the purpose of school is mainly to cultivate the intellect and present basic skills, not to encourage people to understand themselves more fully and make choices based on this self-awareness.

My work as an educator has further strengthened my bias against schooling as it is usually practiced. I have taught students in high school, junior college, undergraduate and graduate programs in psychology and human services, graduate programs in education for people preparing to become teachers, and university-extension courses for practicing teachers. My work with these people has shown me that many students are no longer excited by education or learning of any type. I see them as being afraid of making mistakes, overly concerned with what the instructor expects, inhibited by others in the class, and frequently bored and uncommitted to investing themselves in a personal way, even in classes that deal with highly personal material. And not all of these students are products of traditional education. Some of them have experienced unstructured education, and some have been given more freedom than they could handle. Some have had very few demands placed on them to learn any factual material. The point is that schools, regardless of their approach, are often not perceived as exciting places to be or as places where we can learn about life and explore our values, feelings, and personal experiences.

Although I've encountered problems with my own schooling and with the schooling my students have had, I continue to work in education, because I believe that we can change systems from within. Being part of an institution gives us the power to work for change in a constructive way. Moreover, I don't want my critical remarks about traditional education to leave the impression that I think all traditional education is evil or that traditional teachers are necessarily bad for children. My daughter Heidi, who is now in the fourth grade, has a rather traditional teacher at this time, and she is enjoying school more now than she has in a long while. She is also learning more, and I credit this to the influence of her teacher, Mr. Satter. She likes him, and she senses that he likes children. She responds well to the structure that he provides and appreciates the fact that he does have expectations and demands. He believes that learning basic skills is important; he teaches facts; he encourages children to explore projects that are personally meaningful; and, although he believes that structure is important, at the same time he values the social and personal aspects of learning. He cares about children and wants them to learn. He is gentle, patient, and understanding. He also understands that every child is different, and he is sensitive to children as persons.

I am not, therefore, making a case for an educational program that deals exclusively with what the learners want. I do think that it is essential to learn basic skills, but I also think that academic learning of content is most fruitful when it is combined with the personal concerns of the learners.

In the courses I teach on the university level, I have certain standards and expectations. In fact, I have the reputation of being very demanding, and many students avoid taking my classes because they think that I have unrealistically high expectations and demand too much reading and written work. It's true that I expect my students to do quite a bit of writing, mostly in the form of reaction or position papers in which they can express their own feelings, thoughts, and values. I do encourage them to read many books that deal with the issues related to the course. However, my major goal in most of my courses is to encourage students to examine personal issues, and I find that it is possible to combine cognitive or intellectual learning with the more personal kind of learning that involves feelings, values, belief systems, and the personal experiences of the students.

Whatever your own school experiences have been like, it's important to think about them, because school is a powerful shaper of our attitudes and personalities. Understanding the effects our schooling has had on us in the past and continues to have on us as adults puts us in a better position to consciously modify those effects.

Reviewing Your Own School Experience[1]

The questions on the following pages are intended to help you review your own school experiences. I hope that you'll try to determine how some of your present values and beliefs are related to these experiences. If you like the kind of learner you now are, or if you have had mostly positive experiences with school, then you can build upon this positive framework as you approach this course. You can continue to find ways of involving yourself with the material you will read, study, and discuss. If you feel cheated by a negative educational experience, you can begin to change it. *You* can make this class different by applying some of the ideas provided in this chapter. Once you become aware of those aspects of your education that you don't like, *you* can decide to change your style of learning.

Were You a Teacher Pleaser?

One effect of much of traditional education is to teach us the importance of pleasing the teacher. We soon discover that, if the teacher is pleased, we're rewarded with approval, tokens, good grades, and so on. The sad part of this learning is that the desire to please *ourselves* becomes unimportant. The more we strive to please others, the more we lose a sense of urgency about working for our own approval. Of course, this is true both in and out of the school setting.

- What were some ways in which you learned to prize pleasing the teacher over pleasing yourself?
- Is it important for you to please others, particularly those in authority? What happens to you if you can't please others?

[1]Adapted from *Teachers Can Make a Difference*, by G. Corey. Copyright 1973 by Charles E. Merrill Publishing Company. Used by permission.

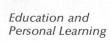

Were You a Questioner?

In my own schooling, I learned that the teacher had the authority and that it was wrong to question it. I've found that I'm not alone in this regard. For many of us, obedience has been a prime virtue. The trouble is that blind obedience keeps us from thinking openly and critically. Instead of encouraging us to be active and curious searchers, the attitude of "never question authority" leads us to passively do what we're told. Since we learn that it's more desirable to be led by others than to initiate our own learning, we acquire a passive, receptive, and reactive style. Moreover, we tend to extend this passive stance to our behavior outside the confines of the classroom.

In their book, *Teaching as a Subversive Activity*, Postman and Weingartner (1969) propose that teachers should attempt to cultivate a new kind of learner—one who becomes an expert at "crap detecting." Instead of merely being concerned with the "information-dissemination" business, they argue, teachers should encourage children and adolescents to be "subversive" by encouraging them to ask "Why are we doing this?" They make an important point: "Once you have learned to ask questions—relevant and appropriate and substantial questions—you have learned how to learn, and no one can keep you from learning whatever you want to or need to know" (p. 23).

- How active were you in your learning? Did you dare to question the authority of the teacher?
- Do you now see learning as something to be done passively?
- Do you now ask substantive questions of life?
- In what ways are you "subversive"? Do you see yourself as able to "detect crap"?
- What are some specific issues that you have critically questioned recently?

Unfortunately, much of conventional education seems to be based on the premise that people won't learn unless there is a carrot at the end of the stick. Yet infants and small children work eagerly at new tasks simply for the intrinsic pleasure of learning how things work or making a new discovery. It is clear that they are motivated by the sheer joy that comes from making their own discoveries.

In *How Children Learn,* John Holt (1967) indicates that children learn because learning is a basic human need and also because it's fun. Healthy children do manifest a curiosity, and a need to explore and figure things out for themselves. The unschooled child doesn't need competition, threats, bribes, tokens, or other external motivators. Unfortunately, schooling often stamps out this native curiosity, and we begin to ask "Why should I learn, unless what I learn will be on a test or help me get a job?" For too many students, learning ceases to be fun, self-initiated, and sustained by their own internal motivation.

- What kinds of learning tasks do you do for the fun of it?
- Are your motives for learning mostly external or internal? Would you go to school merely for the enjoyment and the meaning it provides?

Were You Caught Up in the Right-Answer Syndrome?

A pervasive myth that many of us acquire as a part of our schooling is that for every problem there is one correct answer. We soon learn that, if we're to survive in school (and in life, too), we'd better produce these "right answers." Soon we come to expect that there are solutions to almost every problem imaginable.

As a result of accepting this myth, we begin to search for solutions and answers outside of ourselves. We learn to distrust our own judgment, feeling, and sense of direction. We begin to look more and more to others to show us the correct way. We experiment less and become less willing to take chances. To avoid making mistakes, we become more adept at academic game playing by learning strategies for figuring out what is expected of us. Ultimately, we're no longer able to discriminate between *our* values and *others'* values, for they become merged indistinguishably.

In *How Children Fail,* Holt (1964) asserts that most children fail to learn in school, and they fail because they are afraid, bored, and confused. He argues that most children in school are afraid of failing or being labeled "stupid"; hence, they are reluctant to gamble. This fear, he argues, inhibits real learning.

- What kinds of "right answers" have you accepted?
- Are you afraid to take risks in your learning?

Was Your Learning Real or Apparent?

One striking thing that occurs to me as I review my own experiences as a learner is that much of what I "learned" could best be labeled *apparent learning,* as opposed to *real learning.* Apparent learning lacks real impact; it takes place when we learn something only because others expect us to. This is a common malady among both children and adolescents today, many of whom feel that their school life has little to do with real life. Thus, school becomes a place where they perform tasks and pursue goals that others determine and that are consequently without personal meaning for them. In contrast, *real learning* occurs when we can apply knowledge to specific problems, when we can get involved and excited, and when there is a personal value in our learning.

In *Education and Ecstasy,* George Leonard (1969) proposes that *every* child could learn the basics of reading, writing, and calculating in less than one-third of the time it now takes. His position is that schools are geared to prevent real learning: "Perhaps half of all learning ability was squelched in the earliest elementary grades, where children found out that there exist predetermined and unyielding 'right answers' for everything, that following instructions is what really counts, and that the whole business of education is mostly dull and painful" (p. 120).

- Can you think of some examples of apparent learning that you underwent in school? What effect did this apparent learning have on you?
- What kinds of real learning can you cite in your life? Did it take place inside or outside of school?
- What can you remember learning in elementary and secondary school that had a direct bearing on real life? What do you still use now as a result of that learning?

Was Your Self Included in Your Schooling?

From my own work in the public-school system, I've concluded that schools are generally less concerned with the goals, perceptions, values, and feelings of the learners than they are with the curriculum. In my own schooling, learning about imports and exports, capitals of countries, historical events, parts of speech, the times tables, catechism responses, and other bits of information was given top priority. Many of us learned that our feelings and concerns were not key issues in education; indeed, we were taught, either directly or indirectly, to keep these unimportant matters out of the classroom.

This preoccupation with our intellectual side to the exclusion of our emotional side is, in my judgment, one of the most damaging aspects of traditional education. As A. S. Neill, the founder of Summerhill, has commented, what's wrong with most education is that it takes place from the neck up. According to Neill (1964), if children are just allowed to develop naturally and to experience their feelings, the intellect takes care of itself. What happens now is that schools turn out too many people like the intellectual "half man" Harold Lyon (1971) describes in *Learning to Feel - Feeling to Learn.* Years of conditioning have taught us that emotions cloud clear thinking, that feelings are best denied, and that what *we* think and feel ultimately is unimportant. Consequently, many of us have even become numb to our own feelings; when we're asked what we feel, we usually reply by saying what we *think.*

Another aspect of this process is that children and adolescents are too often viewed and treated as objects instead of as persons. Thus, they are labeled "mentally gifted," "culturally deprived," "unmotivated," "behavior-disordered," and so on. And too often teachers see children and adolescents as empty vessels to be filled or as objects to be molded and manipulated for their own good.

- Can you recall feeling like a person of value during your school years? If so, what contributed to this feeling? If you felt more like an object than a person, what was this like?
- Did you feel free to express your feelings in school? Were you ever encouraged to do so? What are some of the things you might have liked to have said that you kept to yourself?

- Was school a place of joy for you? Did you fear going to school?
- To what degree did your schooling address issues that were vitally related to your self?

23

Education and Personal Learning

Did Your Schooling Teach You to Be Honest or Dishonest?

Many educators who give lip service to the ideals of honesty, integrity, and trust nevertheless often display a basic dishonesty. Too few teachers, for example, express their own feelings and thoughts regarding issues related to their values or take personal positions on controversial and sensitive topics. By the same token, too few teachers encourage their students to develop and express their own views. Thus, instead of trust and honesty, many of us have learned that we are not to be trusted.

The same lesson is taught in other ways as well. It is for this reason that Leonard (1969) describes most schools as unfit places for learning; in his opinion, they resemble jails more than learning centers. He claims that schools are designed to prevent thinking and creativity and to emphasize control and conformity. Schools, he asserts, are places where children learn to sit still, form orderly rows, take instructions, and feel guilty about their natural impulses. Holt (1969) agrees, maintaining that teaching and learning are often secondary to the supreme function of babysitting. He charges schools with giving lip service to democracy while imposing upon children a form of "practical slavery." Holt contends that "schools are bad places for kids" and that children are smarter, more curious, more eager, and less afraid *before* starting school than they are afterward.

- In what ways has your education taught you to be honest or dishonest? Do you see your schooling as dishonest?
- How much freedom for your own learning are you now able to handle?

Some Summary Comments

When I've given talks on my views of education to college classes, some students have protested that their school experiences were not as negative as those I've depicted and that I am unduly critical of what schools do to learners. Even a couple of the professional educators who read this manuscript commented that I was a bit too negative and that I should consider toning down my writing on this subject and balancing my criticisms with more positive statements. Well, I have carefully reconsidered, and I still feel strongly about what I've written. I continue to be very much a part of professional education, precisely because I believe that teachers *can* make a significant, positive difference and that schools *can* be places where meaningful learning occurs. Moreover, there are many educators who are providing a very different climate from the one I've described. I remain convinced, however, that there are real problems in formal education and that we need to look at them honestly.

Whether or not you agree with some or all of my comments on this subject, I hope they have encouraged you to review what your own school years were like for you and to see what connections there may be between these experiences and your present view of yourself. School teaches us a lot more than facts and information. It also teaches us about ourselves—our potentials, our limitations, our impact on others, and the way others see us. Many adults continue to struggle with things they learned about themselves through interactions with their teachers and fellow students. You might let yourself relive imaginatively some of the highlights of your own school experience. What do you most remember about school? What are some pleasant memories? When did you feel the most competent and successful? Who were some of your close friends? What teachers had the greatest impact on you? Was their influence positive or negative? What were the teachers like who did reach you? If you could go back and relive your school years, how would you want them to be different? What were some frightening or sad experiences for you? Can you recall and relive any events that were particularly painful? Did you generally feel like a "winner" or a "loser"? What were some of your failures? How did you handle them? How do you think that you are affected today by the successes and failures you experienced? What was missing from your school experiences? What kind of relationships did you have with the other students? Were you popular?

These questions are only suggestions to get you started. You

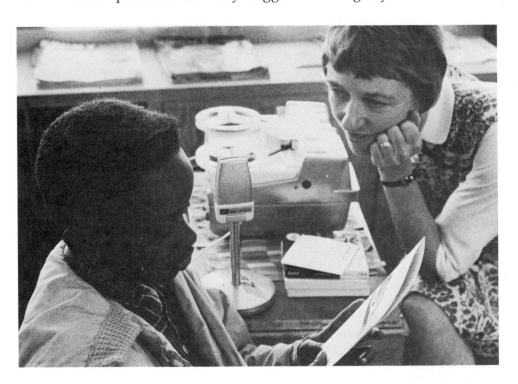

might even try a fantasy. I have often asked students to imagine that they have stored up on videotape all their grammar school and high school experiences. I have asked them to allow themselves to replay these events, as though they were looking at a film, and meanwhile to try to recapture some of the feelings they had about themselves. This is an exercise that you can do on your own, and you might write a few notes about what the experience was like for you. You may want to bring your notes to class and share your reliving of your school years.

Time Out for Personal Reflection

The following questions are designed to help you focus on your past and present experiences as a learner and on the effects these experiences have had on you. In taking this inventory, respond quickly by giving your initial reaction. Indicate your response by circling the corresponding letter. *You may choose more than one response for each item,* or, if none of the responses fit you, you can write your own response on the blank line provided.

1. How would you evaluate your elementary school experience?
    a. It was a pleasant time for me.
    b. I dreaded going to school.
    c. I feel that it taught me a lot about life.
    d. Although I learned facts and information, I learned little about myself.

    e. _____

2. How would you evaluate your high school experience?
    a. I have mostly favorable memories of this time.
    b. I got more from the social aspects of high school than I did in terms of learning.
    c. I remember it as a lonely time.
    d. I was very involved in my classes.

    e. _____

3. How do you evaluate your present college experience?
    a. I like what I'm getting from my college education.
    b. I see college as an extension of my earlier schooling experiences.
    c. I'm learning more about myself as a result of attending college.
    d. I'm here mainly to get a degree; learning is secondary.

    e. _____

4. To what degree do you see yourself as a "teacher pleaser"?
    a. In the past, I worked very hard to gain the approval of my teachers.

b. I'm now more concerned with pleasing myself than I am with pleasing my teachers.

c. It's very important to me to please those who are in authority.

d. Good grades are more important than what I learn.

e. _____

5. To what degree have you been a questioner?

 a. I generally haven't questioned authority.

 b. I've been an active learner, and I've raised many questions.

 c. Basically, I see myself as a passive learner.

 d. I didn't raise questions earlier in my schooling, but now I'm willing to question the meaning of what I do in school.

 e. _____

6. Have you been externally or internally motivated?

 a. I've been motivated primarily by competition and other forms of external motivation.

 b. I've generally learned things mainly because of the satisfaction I've gotten from learning.

 c. I see myself as having a lot of curiosity and a need to explore.

 d. I've generally learned what I thought would be on a test or what would help me get a job.

 e. _____

7. To what degree are you a confident learner?

 a. I'm afraid of making mistakes and looking foolish.

 b. I often look for the "correct way" or the "one right answer."

 c. I trust my own judgment, and I live by my values.

 d. I think that there can be many right answers to a problem.

 e. _____

8. To what degree has your learning been real and meaningful?

 a. School has been a place where I've learned things that were personally meaningful.

 b. School has been a place where I've mostly performed meaningless tasks and pursued meaningless goals.

 c. I've learned how to apply what I've learned in school to my life outside of school.

 d. I've tended to see school learning and real life as separate.

 e. _____

9. To what degree have feelings been a part of your schooling?

 a. School has dealt with issues that have been related to my personal concerns.

 b. I've believed that what I felt had no place in school.

c. The emphasis has been on the intellect, not on feelings.
d. I've learned to distrust my feelings.

e. _____

10. How much freedom have you experienced in your schooling?
    a. Schooling has taught me how to handle freedom in my own learning.
    b. I've found it difficult to accept freedom in school.
    c. I've experienced schools as places that restricted my freedom and did not encourage me to make my own choices.
    d. I've experienced schools as sources of encouragement to make and accept my own choices.

    e. _____

Some Suggestions for Using and Applying This Inventory

Now that you've taken this inventory, I have some suggestions for applying the results to yourself. I recommend that you look over your responses and then decide which of the following questions might be meaningful follow-up activities for you.

1. How would you describe yourself as a learner during your elementary school years? During your high school years? As a college student?
2. What effects do you think your schooling has had on you as a person?
3. If you don't like the kind of learner you've been up until now, what can you do about it? What kinds of changes would you like to make?
4. What were some of the most important things (both positive and negative) that you learned *about yourself* as a result of your schooling?

When you've completed your review of your school experience, you might consider (a) bringing your responses to class and sharing them, and/or (b) using your journal to write down memories of school experiences that have had an impact on you and to keep an ongoing account of significant events in your present learning.

Choosing a New Learning Style

In the preceding section, I encouraged you to take a critical look at your past learning patterns and at the ways in which you might now be continuing patterns that you established earlier. If you've become aware of ways in which you've failed to exercise your power as a learner, you can decide on being a more active learner now.

What is most important is that you take responsibility for your own learning. Students who fail to see their own role in the learning process could use my criticisms of education to support a stance of helplessness. However, I don't want to give anyone a convenient ax to grind. I have little sympathy with those who maintain an apathetic attitude toward their own learning while doing nothing but complaining about their boring teachers and their irrelevant classes. If you're dissatisfied with your education, I hope you'll look at yourself and see how much you're willing to invest in order to make it more vital. Are you just waiting for others to make your learning meaningful? How much are you willing to do to change the things you don't like? Are you accepting your share of responsibility for putting something into the learning process?

Many students who complain among themselves seem very unwilling to take any risks in approaching their instructors and talking about their feelings. Consequently, I encourage students to refrain from making excuses why they "can't" approach their instructors and to have the courage to express their views directly. I encourage you to do the same.

I'm sure that you can think of other ways in which you can assume responsibility for changing those aspects of your education that you want to change. Regardless of the format or structure of a course, you can actively search for ways of becoming personally involved in the issues it deals with. For example, in this book, many personal topics are discussed that have a direct bearing on your life. Whatever the limits set by your instructor, you will have many opportunities to decide on the degree to which you'll become involved in these issues. Whether the class is conducted primarily as a lecture, a lecture/discussion, or an open-ended group, you can decide to be only marginally involved or to actively apply these topics to yourself. During a lecture, you can raise many of your own unanswered questions and think about your daily behavior. The central issue is not the structure of the classroom situation but the decisions you make concerning your commitment to take an honest look at your own life.

Personal learning. Throughout this book, I encourage you to make your learning in the course both personal and meaningful. Making your learning personal doesn't mean that you should divulge your secrets or become an open book for others to look at; nor does it mean that you must turn your class into a therapy or encounter group. It *does* mean coming to a new understanding of yourself, and that involves questioning your assumptions about how you live.

One way to begin to make your learning in this course more meaningful is to think about your reasons for taking this course and your expectations concerning what you will learn. The following "Time Out" may help you focus on these issues.

Time Out for Personal Reflection

1. What are your main reasons for taking this course?

   It was required & I also am interested in anything involving psychology.

2. What expectations do you have concerning what this course will be like? Check all the comments that fit you.
   - ✓ I expect to talk openly about issues that matter to me.
   - ✓ I expect to get answers to certain problems in my life.
   - ✓ I hope that I will become a more fulfilled person.
   - ✓ I hope that I will have less fear of expressing my feelings and ideas.
   - ___ I expect to be challenged on why I am the way I am.
   - ✓ I expect to learn more about how other people function.
   - ✓ I expect that I will understand myself more fully by the end of the course than I do now.

   List other specific expectations:

   _____

   _____

   _____

3. What do you *most* want to accomplish in this course?

How to UNDERSTAND MYSELF ALL THE TIME & HOW I FUNCTION AS A TOTAL PERSON.

4. What are you willing to invest in order to become actively involved in your learning? Check the appropriate comments.

___✓___ I'm willing to participate in class discussions.
___✓___ I will read the material and think about how it applies to me.
___✓___ I'm willing to question my assumptions and look at my values.
___✓___ I'm willing to spend some time most days reflecting on the issues raised in this course.
___✓___ I'm willing to keep a journal and to record my reactions to what I read and experience.

Mention any other things you're willing to do in order to be actively involved.

_____

_____

_____

Getting the Most from Your Course: Some Guidelines for Personal Learning

To a large degree, you will get from the experience of this course whatever you're willing to invest of yourself in the class; so it's important that you clarify your goals and the steps you can take to reach them. The following suggestions may help you become active and involved as you read the book and participate in your class.

1. *Preparation.* You can prepare yourself for your classes by reading and thinking about yourself outside of class. Completing the exercises and doing the activities in this book can help you to sharpen your focus on the specific things you want from your course.

2. *Dealing with fears.* Personal learning entails experiencing some common fears. Some of these fears are: the fear of discovering terrible things about yourself; the fear of the unknown; the fear of looking foolish in front of others; the fear of being criticized or ridiculed; the fear of talking out in front of others; and the fear of taking an honest look at yourself.

Besides these fears, you might experience fears concerning others as you approach this course. For example, you might feel intimidated by the authority of the instructor. If you elevate your instructor to an unrealistically high position, he or she is likely to become somewhat threatening to you. You might fear what the other students will think of

you if you participate in class. You might wonder whether you have
anything valuable or interesting to contribute or whether you'll be accepted if you express certain values.

It's natural to experience some fear about participating personally
and actively in the class, especially since this kind of participation may
involve taking risks you don't usually take in your courses. What is
critical is how you deal with any fears you experience. You have the
choice of either remaining a passive observer or recognizing your fears
and dealing with them openly, even though you might experience some
degree of discomfort. Facing your fears takes both courage and a genuine
desire to increase your awareness of yourself, but by doing so you take a
first big step toward expanding the range of your choices.

3. *Deciding what you want for yourself.* Only you can decide
whether you want to know yourself more fully or whether you're content
with what you know about yourself now. If you do make the decision to
invest yourself in the course, then I cannot overemphasize the importance of deciding on your own concrete goals. If you come to class with
only vague ideas of what you want, the chances are that you'll be disappointed. You can increase your chances of having a profitable experience
by taking the time and effort to think about what problems and personal
concerns you're willing to explore.

4. *Risks.* If you make the choice to invest yourself fully in the
course, you should be prepared for the possibility of some disruption in
your life. You may find yourself changing as a result of the thought and
effort you devote to this book and to the class. It can be a shock to
discover that those who are close to you might not appreciate your
changes. They may prefer that you remain as you are. Thus, instead of
receiving their support, you might encounter their resistance to many of
your changes.

5. *Establishing trust.* You can choose to take the initiative in establishing the trust necessary for you to participate in this course in a meaningful way, or you can wait for others to create a climate of trust. Often
students have feelings of mistrust or other negative feelings toward an
instructor yet avoid approaching the instructor to discuss the issue
openly. One way to establish trust is to seek out your instructor and
discuss any feelings you have that might prevent you from participating
fully in the course. The same applies to any feelings of mistrust you have
toward other class members. By expressing your feelings, you can actively help establish a higher level of trust.

6. *Self-disclosure.* Disclosing yourself to others is one way to come
to know yourself more fully. Sometimes participants in self-awareness
courses or experiential groups fear that they must relinquish their privacy
in order to be active participants. However, you can be open and at the
same time retain your need for privacy by deciding how much you will
disclose and when it is appropriate to do so. Of course, you have the
options of not revealing yourself or revealing only safe aspects of yourself.

7. *Expressing your feelings and thoughts.* Too often people assume that others know them intuitively. The fact is that others don't know what we think and feel unless we tell them directly. In your class there may be times when you experience feelings of boredom, anger, joy, closeness, or disappointment. You can decide whether it's appropriate to keep these feelings to yourself or to share them with others in your class. For example, if you do some work in small groups and you find that you are persistently bored, your expression of your boredom could help your group assess the meaningfulness of their interaction.

8. *Being direct.* You can adopt a style of being direct in your communication. You'll be more direct if you make "I" statements than if you say "you" when you really mean "I." For example, instead of saying "You can't trust people with what you feel, because they will let you down if you make yourself vulnerable," substitute "I" for "you." In this way, you take responsibility for your own statement. Similarly, it will help your communication if you develop the habit of making eye contact and speaking directly *to* a person, rather than speaking *at* or *about* the person.

9. *Questioning.* If you want to get the most from your interactions in class, I suggest that you avoid adopting a style of asking questions of others. Continually asking questions can lead to a never-ending chain of "whys" and "becauses." Moreover, questioning can be a way of avoiding personal involvement. I have seen people in a class or group push others to be personal by asking them many personal questions, even though they were not willing to become personally involved themselves. Questions keep the questioner safe and unknown; it's more honest and more productive to make personal statements.

10. *Listening.* You can work on developing the skill of really listening to what others are saying without thinking of what you will say in reply. The first step in understanding what others say about you is to listen carefully, neither accepting what they say wholesale nor rejecting it outright. *Active listening* (really hearing the full message another is sending) requires remaining open and carefully considering what others say, instead of rushing to give reasons and explanations.

11. *Thinking for yourself.* Only you can make the choice whether to do your own thinking or to let others do your thinking and deciding for you. Many people seek counseling because they have lost the ability to find their own way and have become dependent on others to direct their lives and take responsibility for their decisions. If you value thinking and deciding for yourself, it is important for you to realize that neither your fellow students nor your instructor can give you answers.

12. *Self-fulfilling prophecies.* You can avoid limiting your ability to change by letting go of ways in which you've categorized yourself or been categorized by others. If *you* start off with the assumption that you're stupid, helpless, or boring, you'll probably convince others as well. For example, if you see yourself as boring, you'll probably present yourself in such a way that others will respond to you as a boring person.

If you like the idea of changing some of the ways in which you see yourself and present yourself to others, you can experiment with going beyond some of your self-limiting labels. Allowing yourself to believe that a particular change is possible is a large part of experiencing that change. And, once you experience *yourself* differently, others might experience you differently too.

13. *Practicing outside of class.* One important way of getting the maximum benefit from a class dealing with personal learning is to think about ways of applying what you learn in class to your everyday life. You can do this by keeping a journal and by writing personal reactions to your experiences in and out of class. You can make specific contracts with yourself (or with others) detailing what you're willing to do to experiment with new behavior and work toward the changes you want to make. By practicing new behavior, you can make the experience of this class a catalyst for you to put your new insights into action.

Assessing your own readiness to change. At this point, it would be worthwhile to pause and assess your readiness for taking an honest look at yourself. Right now you may or may not feel motivated to examine the issues explored in these chapters. You may feel that you don't need to explore these topics, or you may see yourself as being not quite ready. If you do feel some hesitation, I hope that you'll leave the door open and give yourself and the course a chance. I've had many students who entered a self-development and experiential course mainly for the units, only to leave feeling very excited and committed to go further. If you open yourself to change and try the techniques I've suggested, you may well experience a similar sense of excitement and promise.

Chapter Summary

In this chapter, I've encouraged you to review your school experiences and to make an inventory of the ways in which your present attitudes toward learning have been influenced by these past experiences with school. Although I've discussed some of the negative aspects of schooling, I've stressed that becoming aware of the effects schooling has had upon you gives you the power to choose a new learning style.

A major purpose of this chapter has been to challenge you to examine your own responsibility for making your learning meaningful. It's easy to lash out at impersonal institutions if you feel apathetic about your learning. It's more difficult and more honest to look at *yourself* and ask such questions as: When I find myself in an exciting class, do I get fully involved and take advantage of the opportunity for learning? Do I expect instructors to entertain and *teach* me, while I sit back passively? If I'm bored, what am I doing about it?

Even if your earlier educational experiences have taught you to be a passive learner and to fear taking risks in your classes, once you become aware of this influence, you acquire the power to change your learning style. In this chapter, I've asked you to decide how personal you want your learning to be in the course you're about to experience, and I've suggested several guidelines to help you personalize your own learning.

List some of the major ideas in this chapter that had the greatest impact on you. You might write down statements that captured your own experience and also some that you disagreed with.

DEALING W/ FEARS

SELF DISCLOSURE

RISKS

Activities and Exercises

1. Recall the one teacher in your life who had the most significant impact on you—either positive or negative. Briefly describe the effect this teacher had on you.
2. Make a list of the fears or anxieties you experience in regard to school. For example, do you fear expressing your opinions because you wonder what others will think? Do you fear authority and seek to please? Do you worry about maintaining passing grades? After you've listed your fears, write down some specific things you can do to deal with them.
3. In your journal, keep a record of specific situations that you feel you handle in a nonassertive manner—particularly those that occur in class. Keeping such a record will increase your awareness of *how* and *when* you behave in nonassertive ways. You should also write down how you'd like to handle these situations more assertively. When you do behave assertively, record these instances too. Finally, be sure to include how you feel when you behave assertively and nonassertively.
4. The following are exercises that you can do at home. The exercises are intended to help you focus on specific ways in which you behave assertively or nonassertively. I've drawn the examples from typical fears and concerns often expressed by college students. Study the situations by putting yourself in each one and deciding how you might typically respond. Then keep an account in your journal of actual instances you encounter in your classes.

a. *Situation.* You'd like to ask a question in class, but you're afraid that your question will sound dumb and that others will laugh.
   Issues. Will you simply refrain from asking questions? If so, is this a pattern you're willing to continue? Are you willing to practice asking questions, even though you might experience some anxiety? What do you imagine will happen if you ask questions? What would you like to have happen?

b. *Situation.* You feel that you have a hang-up concerning authority figures. You feel intimidated, afraid to venture your opinions, and even more afraid to register a point of view opposed to your instructor's.
   Issues. Does this description fit you? If it does, do you want to change? Do you ever examine where you picked up your attitudes toward yourself in relation to authority? Do you think they're still appropriate for you?

c. *Situation.* You and most of the other students think that your instructor is very boring. He goes strictly by the book and lectures from your textbook. However, it isn't worth it to you to change to another instructor, because the change would mess up your schedule.
   Issues. What options do you have if you stay in the class? Are you condemned to tolerating boredom for a semester? Are you content to tell yourself that there's really nothing you can do, since all the power belongs to the instructor? Are you willing to go to your instructor during office hours and tell him how you experience the class? Do you have any ideas or suggestions for making the class more lively?

d. *Situation.* In your psychology class, there are a few students who dominate the discussion time. They go on with long-winded stories, they continually make their own points, and they are irritating you and most of the class. The instructor doesn't deal with the situation.
   Issues. Have you experienced this kind of situation? What alternatives do you see yourself as having? Might you openly tell these persons in class that you would appreciate it if others had a chance to express themselves? Would you confront them privately?

e. *Situation.* There is a great deal of hostility in your class; the class members show little respect for one another. You feel somewhat overwhelmed by this hostility.
   Issues. Would you tend to withdraw, or would you deal openly with your feelings about this hostility? What can you do when you're aware that somebody treats another class member with disrespect? What fears do you have about confronting the tensions you sense in the room? What steps might you take to confront it?

f. *Situation.* Your instructor seems genuinely interested in the students and the course, and she has extended herself by inviting you to come to her office if you have any problems with the course. You're having real difficulty grasping the material, and you're falling behind and doing poorly on the tests and assignments. Nevertheless, you keep putting off going to see the instructor to talk about your problems in the class.

Issues. Have you been in this situation before? If so, what kept you from talking with your instructor? If you find yourself in this kind of situation, are you willing to seek help before it's too late?

5. In your journal, write down other situations that relate to being assertive or nonassertive in your classes. For each situation, describe how you see yourself responding. List all the options you can think of. If you decide that you're willing to take definite steps toward becoming more assertive, begin with the class in which you feel the most safety. In your journal, keep an account of what you do and of the results. You shouldn't expect to change your learning style immediately; be patient with yourself, but do practice, and do make an effort to try new behavior even if you feel some discomfort.

Suggested Readings

Brown, G. *Human Teaching for Human Learning: An Introduction to Confluent Education.* New York: Viking, 1971. This excellent book provides an introduction to "confluent education." Brown describes a variety of effective techniques that can be used to bring together the intellectual and emotional aspects of learning. He gives examples of how humanistic education has worked for elementary and secondary teachers.

Corey, G. *Teachers Can Make a Difference.* Columbus, Ohio: Charles E. Merrill, 1973. In this book, I examine what schooling does to a learner and suggest humanistic alternatives to traditional education. The focus is on the teacher as a person, and the theme is that teachers hold the key to any significant change in education. I also give some guidelines for evaluating your own educational experience.

Hendricks, C., & Fadiman, J. (Eds.). *Transpersonal Education: A Curriculum for Feeling and Being.* Englewood Cliffs, N.J.: Prentice-Hall, 1976. This book focuses on forms of education for the whole person. The discussion is aimed at helping both teachers and students understand themselves better and provide a more personal dimension to classroom learning.

Holt, J. *How Children Fail.* New York: Dell, 1964. In this book, Holt provides a critical evaluation of strategies that children learn for coping with fear and failure in school. He also describes the ways in which schools fail children.

Holt, J. *How Children Learn.* New York: Dell, 1967. This is an excellent book for elementary school teachers. It deals with games, talking, reading, sports, math, art, and so on. Holt argues that children are naturally curious and have a built-in will to learn and that we can trust them to do so.

Holt, J. *The Underachieving School.* New York: Dell (Delta), 1969. Holt gives a biting critique of what schools do to learners, along with some proposals for constructive change. Some of the chapter titles are: "Schools Are Bad Places for Kids," "Teachers Talk Too Much," "The Tyranny of Testing," "Making Children Hate Reading," and "Education for the Future."

Lembo, J. *Why Teachers Fail.* Columbus, Ohio: Charles E. Merrill, 1971. Lembo's topics are: destructive institutional processes, the inquiry process, characteristics of competent teachers, improving teachers' competence, and the conditions of successful school learning.

Leonard, G. *Education and Ecstasy.* New York: Dell (Delta), 1969. Leonard analyzes the limitations of the traditional school and calls for schools that maximize human potential. The principal theme of this very interesting and readable book is that learning should be a joy.

Lyon, H. *Learning to Feel—Feeling to Learn.* Columbus, Ohio: Charles E. Merrill, 1971. Lyon deals with the problem of the intellectual half-man and provides guidelines for humanizing education. Chapters 4 and 5 are rich sources of humanistic techniques that can be applied to classroom situations. The book includes an excellent bibliography on humanistic education.

Neill, A. S. *Summerhill: A Radical Approach to Child Rearing.* New York: Hart, 1964. Here is a book that you cannot read passively. It is an easy-to-read but challenging and stimulating work that deals with the free school, child rearing, sex education, religion, and other aspects of child development. A must for anyone dealing with children.

Postman, N., & Weingartner, C. *Teaching as a Subversive Activity.* New York: Dell (Delta), 1969. Here is a book that should be on the library shelf of every teacher. Its theme is that teachers ought to teach students how to think critically. The book is filled with thought-provoking ideas and concrete suggestions concerning ways in which teachers can make some changes within the walls of their classrooms.

Rogers, C. *Freedom to Learn: A View of What Education Might Become.* Columbus, Ohio: Charles E. Merrill, 1969. Rogers calls for freedom instead of stifling, authoritarian approaches to education. Methods for creating a climate of freedom are discussed.

Chapter 3

Three Ways
of Understanding
Ourselves

*How much freedom do you believe you have?
Are you the passive product of your
environment, your past development, and your
heredity, or are you an active agent in shaping
your own existence? Are you responsible for the
quality of your life?*

Pre-Chapter Self-Inventory

This chapter's self-inventory is designed to help you focus on how you see human nature. How much choice do you see yourself as having? Do you think that you're determined by outside forces to the extent that freedom is merely an illusion? To what extent do you think your personality is the product of early childhood experiences? I believe that asking questions like these is a necessary part of gaining an in-depth understanding of ourselves.

Remember, all the pre-chapter self-inventories are designed to clarify your own thinking and help you formulate your viewpoints; thus, there are no correct or incorrect answers. After you finish this chapter, you might look over your responses to see which of the three psychological viewpoints discussed is the closest to your own beliefs. Also, you might attempt to select key ideas from each of the three views and thus develop your personal view of human nature. Another way to make this inventory meaningful for you is to ask yourself: How is my actual, day-to-day behavior influenced by my assumptions and beliefs about human nature?

For each statement, indicate the response that most closely identifies your beliefs and attitudes. Use this code: A = I strongly agree; B = I slightly agree; C = I slightly disagree; D = I strongly disagree.

_____ 1. We define our own identities as persons by the choices we make.

_____ 2. Freedom of choice is really an illusion.

_____ 3. What makes us unique and distinct from animals is our capacity for self-awareness.

_____ 4. Much of what we do is really motivated by reasons we're unaware of.

_____ 5. We cannot escape experiencing some anxiety when we realize the uncertainty of our existence.

_____ 6. Our environments are the primary shapers of our lives.

_____ 7. I experience a sense of responsibility that comes with freedom.

_____ 8. We're basically determined by internal drives and internal conflicts; we really have little choice in our daily behavior.

_____ 9. I must find my own way in life and accept personal responsibility if I hope to become mature.

_____ 10. Psychological defenses are necessary to protect us against anxiety and psychological threat.

_____ 11. I sometimes hang on to the past in order to justify my unwillingness to take responsibility for my present actions.

_____ 12. Most of what we do is a direct result of being rewarded for certain behavior.

_____ 13. I sometimes avoid taking risks that are necessary for living fully in the present because of my fears that terrible things will occur if I take these risks.

_____ 14. We can change any behavior we want to by changing the environment.

_____ 15. I often raise questions such as: Who am I? What do I want from life? What gives my life purpose and meaning?

_____ 16. What occurred during the first five years of my life greatly influences the person I am today.

_____ 17. The meaning in my life is not given to me by others; I must actively create my own meaning through my choices and actions.

_____ 18. Most of my present problems and conflicts have their roots in the experiences of my early childhood.

_____ 19. I strive to become all that I am able to become.

_____ 20. Anxiety can be a stimulus for growth.

Introduction

My purpose in this chapter is to spell out some of the theoretical preferences that are a basic part of *I Never Knew I Had a Choice.* In keeping with the tone of the rest of the book, I present the three major psychological approaches to human nature—psychoanalytic, behavioristic, and existential-humanistic—in a personal style. My approach has been guided by such questions as: What do I find of value in each approach? What concepts do I actually use and apply in my work with students and clients? How has each of these approaches contributed to my own understanding of people? How has each one given me some tools for assisting people in understanding and working through their struggles? How are these theories meaningful to me in my personal life? What does each theory say about our ability to make choices?

Although I find valuable concepts in all three psychological positions, my clear preference is for the existential-humanistic approach. This perspective provides an optimistic picture of human beings; it addresses itself to the issue of choice; and it provides me with a useful model for understanding conflict and decision making. However, the psychoanalytic and behavioristic perspectives also provide me with insights and tools that I apply in my counseling practice, and I have found some ways of integrating all three theoretical approaches.

In addition to clarifying my own position, I hope to motivate you to think about your personal perspective on the issue of choice. How much freedom do you believe you have? Are you the passive product of your heredity, your environment, and your past development, or are you an active agent in shaping your own existence? Are you responsible for the quality of your life? Dealing with these questions is of the utmost

importance if you are to get the most from the rest of the chapters, so I encourage you to formulate your own viewpoints on the questions raised by each of the three theories I discuss. You may well find that you can take some ideas from each perspective, for each has its own unique contributions to make to our understanding of ourselves.

The Psychoanalytic Way of Understanding Ourselves

I first encountered Freudian psychoanalysis as a junior psychology major, in a course called "Theories of Personality." Half of the course was devoted to psychoanalysis, and I recall thinking that concepts such as the Oedipus complex, castration anxiety, penis envy, the boy's sexual longing for his mother, and the girl's sexual longing for her father were mystical, farfetched, and almost comical. Since then, my observations of my own children and my experiences in many hours of therapy with groups and individuals have convinced me of the validity of some of the classical Freudian concepts. I don't mean to say that I accept the totality of Freudian psychoanalysis, for I do object to Freud's deterministic view of humans and to his pessimism. However, there are a number of psychoanalytic concepts that I find most useful and that I've incorporated in my therapeutic work. I do pay attention to the effects of early childhood development on a person's current problems, for example, and I fully believe that we can change and make choices only to the extent that we become aware of previously unconscious influences. I find the concepts of *anxiety* and *ego defenses* to be most useful. The tool of using dreams as an avenue to self-understanding is another asset. These aspects of psychoanalysis will be discussed in this section.

Personality Development

One of the most significant contributions of the psychoanalytic approach is the idea that all of us pass through stages of psychological and psychosexual development. According to this viewpoint, our personal, sexual, and social development are largely based upon our experiences during the first five years of life. During this time, we go through three stages of development (which Freud termed *oral, anal,* and *phallic*), and our later personality development hinges on how well we have resolved the demands and conflicts of each of these early stages. I have found evidence to support this assumption in my counseling practice, in the sense that most of the problems that people wrestle with in adulthood seem to have some relationship to unresolved conflicts dating from their early childhood years. In the next chapter, I'll discuss the three Freudian stages in more detail; here I want to give a general overview of the psychoanalytic approach.

According to psychoanalytic theorists, we experience a number of critical conflicts before we begin school, and we are presented with several developmental tasks. One task is to develop a sense of trust in the world, which requires that we feel loved and accepted. If love is absent, we will suffer during later years from an inability to trust ourselves and others, a fear of loving and becoming intimate, and low self-esteem. I've seen many adults who have wanted to change such tendencies. They may fear rejection, or they may think that they have little to offer, or they may come to believe that they must continually meet others' expectations if they are to be loved. My work has demonstrated to me that it is very difficult to experience intimate relationships if we have not felt loved and wanted during the first years of life. Let me hasten to add that I don't take a fatalistic view that we're doomed if we didn't get our quota of love. I've seen many people reexperience their childhood feelings of hurt and rejection through some form of counseling; in this way, they have come to understand that the fact that they didn't feel loved by their parents doesn't mean that they are unlovable or that others find them unlovable now. With awareness, we can open ourselves up and begin to trust.

A second task of early childhood is learning how to recognize and deal with negative feelings, such as hostility, anger, rage, and aggression. Perhaps you can think of a time in your own childhood when you were extremely angry with your parents, or perhaps you've seen a small child exclaim "I hate you, and I wish you were dead! You're mean and I don't ever want to see you again!" A parent might respond with "Don't you *ever* talk to me like that. You should be ashamed of yourself!" If children consistently receive messages that *they* are bad for having such *feelings*, they may repress "bad" feelings out of fear of being abandoned by their parents. In this way, they learn to dissociate themselves from feelings such as anger, for they learn that *they* are unacceptable when they have these feelings.

You might think of how this applies to you. Can you allow yourself to feel and directly express your anger? Many students and clients I've worked with have learned to erect a false front to hide their negative feelings. In fact, many of them have real difficulty even experiencing their negative feelings, let alone *expressing* them.

A third significant developmental task is forming a sex-role identity. Before children enter school, they begin to decide how they feel about themselves in their roles as boys and girls. Children exhibit a natural curiosity about sexual matters, and very early in life they form attitudes toward their sexuality and sexual feelings, their bodies, and what they think is right and wrong. Many adults suffer from deep feelings of guilt concerning sexual pleasure or feelings. Some have learned that their sexual organs are disgusting; others have traumatic memories associated with sexual intercourse. I have become convinced that much sexual dysfunctioning in adulthood has its roots in early conditioning and experiences.

Again, I want to emphasize that, although I believe that the events of the first five years of our lives have a significant influence on our later behavior, I don't accept the notion that we are determined by these events. If I did not believe in the possibility of overcoming our early conditioning, I could not in good faith be a psychotherapist. In any event, I have seen many people learn new values, come to accept new feelings and attitudes, and overcome much of their past negative conditioning.

I have also seen many people steadfastly hang on to the past as an excuse for not taking any action to change in the present. I'm convinced that we can't change in a positive direction if we refuse to stop blaming others for the way we are now. Statements that begin "If it hadn't been for . . .," are too often used to justify an immobile position. For example, I've heard people say "If it hadn't been for the fact that I was adopted and had several foster parents, I'd be able to feel loved now, and I wouldn't be stuck with feelings of abandonment." "If only my parents had done more for me, I could feel a sense of security and trust." "If only my parents had done less for me, I could have grown up independent." "If only my parents had given me a healthy outlook on sex, I wouldn't feel so guilty now about my sexual feelings."

I remember one client who used to blame his mother for everything. Because she had dominated his father, he felt that he could not trust any woman now. If he couldn't trust his own mother, he reasoned, then whom could he trust? At 25, he saw himself as fearing independence, and he blamed his mother for his fear. He refused to date, and he tried to convince himself that he did so because his mother "messed up my life by making me afraid." He continually wanted to use his therapy sessions to dwell on the past and blame his present problems on what his parents had and hadn't done. Through counseling, he became aware that his dwelling on his past and his focusing on others were ways he avoided assuming responsibility for his own life. After actively questioning some of his beliefs about women and about himself, he decided that not all women were like his mother, that he didn't have to respond to women in the way his father did, and that he could change his life now if he was willing to accept the responsibility for doing so.

It may often be important to go through a stage of experiencing feelings of anger and hurt for having been cheated in the past, but I think it is imperative that we eventually claim for ourselves the power we thus continue to give to the people who were once significant and essential in our lives. Unless we recognize and exercise the power we now have to take care of ourselves instead of waiting for others to direct us, we close the door to new choices and new growth.

The Unconscious and Choice

In my judgment, one of Freud's greatest contributions was the concept of the *unconscious*. From his clinical experiences with numerous patients, Freud concluded that problems of personality and behavior could be traced to the functioning of unconscious processes. This idea— that our behavior is strongly influenced by internal dramas taking place entirely outside of our awareness—has had a revolutionary impact on our understanding of ourselves.

According to Freud, consciousness is a thin slice of our total experience. Just as the greater part of an iceberg lies below the surface of the water, an unconscious store of painful memories, forbidden desires, and other material too threatening to accept remains hidden from our conscious view. However, even though we are unaware of this repressed material, it does motivate our behavior and influence our actions.

If much of our behavior is therefore the result of unconscious motivation, how much choice do we really have? Are we condemned to being blindly driven by forces and influences beyond our awareness and control? Personally, I accept that many of us appear to make conscious choices when in fact we are motivated by factors that are inaccessible to us. Such influences may help to determine our selection of a mate or a vocation, as well as other key decisions. I do not accept, however, that we must be passive victims of the unconscious. There are ways of uncovering many of our unconscious motives and thus assuming the power to exercise choice.

One way of making the unconscious accessible is to learn to understand the meaning of our dreams. In psychoanalytic practice, dream analysis is an important procedure for uncovering unconscious material and gaining insight into unresolved problems. Indeed, Freud himself called dreams "the royal road to the unconscious." During sleep, our defenses are lowered, and repressed feelings surface. Unconscious wishes, needs, and fears are expressed—some of them so unacceptable to the dreamer that they are expressed in disguised or symbolic form rather than openly and directly.

Dreams have two levels of content: the *latent content* and the *manifest content*. The *latent content* consists of the disguised, hidden, symbolic, and unconscious meanings. Because they are so painful and threatening, the unconscious impulses that comprise the latent content are transformed into the more acceptable *manifest content*, which is the dream as it appears to the dreamer. In psychoanalytic dream analysis, the therapist uncovers the meanings disguised in the symbols of dreams and interprets them for the clients.

Although I value Freud's insights into the nature of dreams, my approach in working with my clients' dreams is rather different from that of a psychoanalyst. Instead of interpreting the dreams *for* my clients, I prefer to have them become all the parts of their dreams and then give their own meaning to the dreams. This approach to dream work, which comes from Gestalt therapy, is described in detail in Perls' *Gestalt Therapy Verbatim*. In a previous book, I gave the following summary[1] of this technique:

> In psychoanalysis dreams are interpreted, intellectual insight is stressed, and free association is used as one method of exploring the unconscious meanings of dreams. The Gestalt approach does not interpret and analyze a dream. Instead, the intent is to bring the dream back to life, to re-create the dream, and to relive the dream as though it were happening now. The dream is not told as a past event but is acted out in the present, and the dreamer becomes a part of his or her dream. The suggested format for working with dreams includes making a list of all the details of the dream, remembering each person, event, and mood in the dream, and then becoming each of these parts in the dream by transforming oneself, acting as fully as possible and inventing dialogue; since each part of the dream is assumed to be a projection of oneself, one creates scripts for encounters between various characters or parts; all of the different parts of a dream are expressions of one's own contradictory and inconsistent sides. Thus, by engaging in a dialogue between these opposing sides, one gradually becomes more aware of the range of one's feelings.

You might try writing down your dreams and keeping a record of them in your journal. You might then take some of your dreams and use the Gestalt method just described to work with your dreams and to try to understand what your dreams are telling you.

The Ego Defenses and Anxiety

Another dimension of the psychoanalytic view that I have come to respect is its description of the way we develop defenses to protect ourselves from threatening material. According to this view, anxiety results when unconscious material cannot be held in check. For example, I counseled a woman who experienced panic when she began to allow herself to feel her sexual feelings. She had been very controlled and had claimed that she couldn't "let herself go" with her husband. As she began to understand the "father" inside of her who constantly urged her to be proper and to act "like a lady," she loosened up and gave up some of her control. Then she was struck with guilt, and she began to feel evil and nasty. She could hear her father's warnings: "Watch out for men; they only want to see how far they can go with you" and "I know that you'll *never* do anything to make me feel disappointed in you!" Her control, then, was her defense against feeling guilty. As she ex-

---

[1]From *Theory and Practice of Counseling and Psychotherapy*, by G. Corey. Copyright © 1977 by Wadsworth Publishing Company, Inc. Reprinted by permission of the publisher, Brooks/Cole Publishing Company, Monterey, California.

perimented with relinquishing this control, she felt overwhelming anxiety. She needed to learn how to function without having to exercise excessive self-control in order to avoid feelings of guilt.

Most of us use a variety of defenses to ward off anxiety and potential threats to our self-esteem. When I didn't get a position that I'd applied for at a university, I convinced myself that my failure had nothing to do with my qualifications but that it was due to university politics. When that argument failed to soothe my wounded pride, I tried to tell myself that I really didn't want the job anyway, because it would have entailed a lot of administrative busywork.

I also recall using a defense against emotional pain earlier in my life. When I was an adolescent, I fell madly in love with a girl I'd met only briefly, on a boat ride to Catalina Island, near Los Angeles. Despite the brevity of our encounter, I took a three-day trip by Greyhound bus from Los Angeles to Colorado to visit my "first love." When I got there, I felt quickly brushed off; I think she barely remembered me! Although I felt deeply hurt, I didn't allow that hurt to stay with me for very long. Instead, I told myself that I'd had a good experience and that it had taught me a valuable lesson. Besides, I quickly assured myself, she wasn't so special after all, and there were other pebbles on the beach.

The main thing that most defenses have in common, when they function as defense mechanisms, is that they generally operate on an unconscious level; that is, they operate outside our awareness and tend to deny or distort reality. Nevertheless, defenses can be appropriate means of coping, and to some degree we all need them. For instance, one young man I worked with recalled bitter and frightening battles between his mother and father. He recalled that he had been too young to leave and that he had feared that his father might kill his mother during one of his rages. He had defended himself by becoming numb and shutting off his feelings. Had he not reacted in this way, he might have experienced great stress, to the point of emotional breakdown. The problem when he came to see me was that he continued to numb himself and to feel very little. Since this defense was no longer necessary, he could reexamine the appropriateness of shutting off his feelings in order to survive.

I see many people wearing suits of armor to defend themselves, even though there is no enemy and nothing to defend against. My work has shown me time and time again that people can choose to drop pretenses and to make themselves vulnerable by revealing themselves to selected people. I'm not advocating being totally open and defenseless with everyone and in all situations, but I do believe that too many of us conceal ourselves when we don't need to. If we so choose, we can begin to let those people that we care about know more of us, and we can minimize our distortion and denial of reality. I've come to believe that excessive defenses and personal growth are incompatible. If we have a basic sense of security, we can be less defensive and more open to seeing reality as it is, instead of as we wish it would be.

The Psychoanalytic Perspective: A Summary

Sigmund Freud's development of the psychoanalytic viewpoint represents one of the first systematic efforts to understand and describe how and why humans behave as they do. This theoretical system is at once a model of personality development, a philosophy of human nature, and a method of psychotherapy.

The Structure of Personality: Id, Ego, and Superego

Our behavior is assumed to result from the interaction of three systems: the id, the ego, and the superego. These are names for psychological processes and should not be thought of as manikins that separately operate the personality; the personality functions as a whole rather than as three discrete segments.

The *id* (the *biological* component of personality) is the original system of personality; a person is all id at birth. The id is the primary source of psychic energy and of instinctual drives, which are of two types: *sexual* and *aggressive*. These drives are basic to humans; they account for why we behave as we do.

The id lacks organization; it is blind, demanding, and insistent. A cauldron of seething excitement, the id cannot tolerate tension, and it functions to discharge tension immediately and return to a state of balance. Ruled by the *pleasure principle*—which is aimed at reducing tension, avoiding pain, and gaining pleasure—the id is illogical, amoral, and driven by one consideration: to satisfy the instinctual needs in accordance with the pleasure principle. The id never matures but remains the spoiled brat of our personalities.

The *ego* (the *psychological* component of personality) has contact with the external world of reality. The ego is the executive of personality; it governs, controls, and regulates. You might think of the ego as the "traffic cop" for the id, superego, and external world; its principal job is to mediate between our instincts and the surrounding environment. Ruled by the *reality principle*, the ego does realistic and logical thinking and formulates plans of action for satisfying needs. The ego is the seat of intelligence and rationality that checks and controls the blind impulses of the id.

The *superego* (the *social* component of personality) is the moral, or judicial, branch of personality. The superego is a person's moral code; its main concern is whether an action is good or bad, right or wrong. It represents the ideal, rather than the real, and strives not for pleasure but for perfection. It represents the traditional values and ideals of society as they are handed down from our parents to us. It functions to inhibit the id's impulses, to persuade the ego to substitute moralistic goals for realistic ones, and to strive for perfection. The superego, then, as our internalization of the standards of parents and society, is related to psychological *rewards* (feelings of pride and self-love) and *punishments* (feelings of guilt and inferiority).

The interplay among the three systems of id, ego, and superego is of primary importance in determining our behavior. Internal conflicts can be explained by the competition between the demands of the id and the superego. When we are unable to resolve these conflicts, various kinds of personality and behavioral problems result.

Self-Destructive and Aggressive Tendencies

Freud held that we have self-destructive tendencies and death instincts within us, in addition to our instincts for life and survival. Although these notions may seem difficult to comprehend in the abstract, some examples drawn from everyday life may clarify them. If you look at some people you know, you may find that some of them behave in self-destructive ways. Some of these behaviors include: ignoring their health and abusing their bodies; continually hurting themselves or having accidents; frequently making choices that lead them to feel miserable; ignoring warnings of physicians to change their life-styles because they are killing them; abusing alcohol or drugs; attempting or committing suicide.

In addition to self-destructive tendencies, Freud believed that we have *aggressive* tendencies that we ordinarily must repress because their expression is socially forbidden or disapproved of. Aggressive tendencies are related to the death instincts, inasmuch as in aggression we strike out at others. We have only to watch the news each day to find numerous examples of violence and aggression; consider also the aggression that *is* socially sanctioned and approved of, such as violent sports or the use of violence by law-enforcement personnel or the military.

Freud's View of Human Nature

What is the role that choice plays in our day-to-day behavior? Are we the captains of our souls, or are we the victims of past experiences and blind internal forces?

The orthodox Freudian view of human nature is basically pessimistic and deterministic. According to this view, we are in continual conflict with our own repressed experiences and driving instincts. We must do constant battle with id and superego, and we must continually guard against strong aggressive and self-destructive tendencies within us.

Freud emphasized the determining role of instincts, which are biological in origin, and either sexual or aggressive in nature. We are basically determined by the desire to gain pleasure and avoid pain; however, we are also driven by both life and death instincts. Ultimately, the life instincts are subservient to the death instincts, for Freud claimed that the goal of all life is death; life is but a roundabout way to death.

Time Out for Personal Reflection

This Time Out is designed to help you apply the ideas of the psychoanalytic perspective to your own behavior and personality development. Check each of the following statements with which you agree:

_____ 1. I am primarily motivated by the pursuit of pleasure and the avoidance of pain.

_____ 2. By nature, I'm irrational, in the sense that I need controls to keep my impulses in check.

_____ 3. Unconscious factors are undoubtedly the major motivators of my daily behavior.

_____ 4. The early years of my life were so critical that I cannot really change because of the things that happened to me before I was 5.

_____ 5. By nature, I am basically aggressive.

What parts of the psychoanalytic theory do you think apply to you?

_____

_____

_____

_____

_____

The Behavioristic Way of Understanding Ourselves

As a philosophy, the behavioristic approach assumes that all behavior is learned; in other words, we are shaped by social and cultural conditioning. For many years, I discounted the possibility that behavioristic psychology had any contributions to make to an in-depth understanding of human beings. In looking back, I now see that I was overreacting to John Watson's *radical behaviorism*, which allowed no room for choice and freedom as explanations of human behavior. Radical behaviorism rejects the concept of the person as a free agent who shapes his or her own destiny. Instead, the environment is held to be the shaper of our lives. Watson asserted that he could take any healthy infant and make that infant into anything he desired—doctor, lawyer, artist, beggar, thief—through environmental shaping. This kind of assertion led me to believe that all behavioristic practices reduced human beings to mere organisms or objects that passively react to various environmental stimuli. The implication seemed to be that we are all puppets manipulated by environmental strings or shapeless pieces of putty waiting to be given form by outside forces.

About two years ago, I began to be more open to looking at useful and practical applications that were based on behavioristic principles, and I began reading works by contemporary behaviorists. To my surprise, I found that I was already using a number of therapeutic techniques that were behavioristically based. I found, for example, that I focused on early learning patterns and tried to help clients see how they had learned certain behaviors and attitudes and how they could learn new ones. More than I'd realized, I had been employing the classic behavioristic technique of *reinforcement* (giving some type of reward for desired behavior) as a way of encouraging clients to change, for my values, comments, and behavior were influential in determining the direction in which clients would move. The more that I read about specific applications of behaviorism to clinical practice, the more I discovered that there could be a bridge between behaviorism and humanism.

Consequently, although I used to see behaviorism and humanism as incompatible, I now believe that there are many areas of actual practice in which the two approaches can merge fruitfully. I like the concept of "humanistic behaviorism" that David Watson and Roland Tharp (1977) describe. They contend that behavioristic techniques can be used to realize the values of humanism and that a combination of the best attributes of both approaches is the result (pp. 79–80). Therefore, despite some sharp philosophical differences between these approaches, there are areas of convergence with respect to practical applications.

Before I describe some applications of the behavioristic approach, I would like to outline briefly B. F. Skinner's contribution to modern behaviorism, with special emphasis on Skinner's view of the role of choice and freedom in our daily behavior. Skinner is a central figure in the development of contemporary behaviorism. Like John Watson, he is considered a radical behaviorist, because he stresses that we are controlled by environmental conditions. The following is a brief overview of Skinnerian behaviorism as it applies to personal and social issues.

Basic Issues in Skinnerian Behaviorism: A Summary Overview

The following brief discussion of B. F. Skinner's views has been adapted from Robert Nye's *Three Views of Man*. The issues to be considered include Skinner's views of: (1) human nature, (2) personality development, (3) maladjustment and therapy, (4) society's role, (5) the study of behavior, and (6) the control of human behavior.

Basic Human Nature

Skinner views humans as functioning in much the same way as machines—that is, in a lawful and predictable way. Skinner rejects both the notion of an "inner person" and such constructs as self-determination, choice, autonomy, and freedom to create our destinies. Our behavior is to be explained in terms of forces in the environment rather than internal states. Individuals have an equal potential for positive and negative tendencies; they are essentially shaped and determined by their sociocultural environments. All human behavior is learned and is determined according to the principles of reinforcement.

Skinner's approach is aimed at explaining how external factors shape behavior. Since he considers humans to be programmed by the environment, he sees such human traits as love, aggression, jealousy, cooperation, competition, and so on developing mainly as a result of the external conditions that operate on individuals.

Personality Development

Skinner does not deal specifically with the topic of personality, for he considers "personality" nothing more than a label for certain aspects of behavior. "Personality" consists of a person's behavioral repertoire, which results from reinforcements of the person's responses to external stimuli. Thus, no stages of personality development are described; the focus is rather on the interaction of individuals and their environments. The reinforcement that occurs in the present may be as important as past occurrences in determining behavior.

Maladjustment and Therapy

Unlike the psychoanalysts, Skinner does not look to unconscious conflicts as explanations of behavioral problems; rather, he stresses the environmental variables that produce maladaptive behavior. For example, excessive punishment or the reinforcement of undesirable behaviors can lead to problems in living. Like all behavior, maladaptive behavior is learned, and what has been learned can be unlearned through new conditioning that reinforces new and more effective behavior patterns.

Society's Role

In his novel, *Walden Two* (1960), and in a nonfiction work, *Beyond Freedom and Dignity* (1972), Skinner describes the utopian society that he believes would result from systematic application of learning principles to pressing social problems (such as pollution and overpopulation). According to Skinner, the main role of society is to design a program of systematic reinforcements that will increase the chances of human survival by encouraging the "correct" behaviors. Since humans are malleable, behavioral engineering can foster behaviors that are both personally and socially advantageous.

The Study of Human Behavior

Skinnerian psychology is based on the experimental method of gathering information about behavior. Skinner avoids speaking about theories of other abstract constructs, stressing instead the importance of clearly stated *operational definitions* (definitions that describe things in terms of how they work). He advocates a precise study of cause-and-effect relationships between environmental factors and observable behaviors. This kind of study can best be done in carefully controlled laboratory situations. For this reason, Skinner did most of his experimental work with pigeons and rats in laboratory conditions. He then generalized his findings to cover broader applications of learning.

The Control of Human Behavior

Skinner clearly states that human behavior is controlled. We are all involved in controlling and in being controlled, and scientific investigation can highlight the processes of control and can be used to improve human functioning. Thus, Skinner suggests that government and education, by using scientific principles, could enhance our ability to solve problems and to live more effectively.

In Skinner's view, there is no place in psychology for the assumption that our behavior is governed by individual choice. Further, he suggests that talking about choices and other subjective issues distracts us from the intelligent pursuit of knowledge that is necessary for human survival. References to values and choices cloud the issue by drawing us away from a careful study of the environmental conditions that produce behavior.

It should be noted, however, that Skinner's view of humans is not pessimistic; nor does he see us as victims compelled to play a passive, robot-like role. He claims to have an optimistic view, for he contends that, even though our behavior is determined, we can control our future. How? If we fully understand how external factors operate on us, we can control their influence by manipulating many aspects of our environment. Skinner thus ends up with the paradox that humans can change their environmental conditions, even though these external conditions shape human behavior.

Now that I've described a few of the serious issues presented by Skinner's view of human nature, I'd like to deal with the lighter side of Skinner's approach. A close friend of mine, Patrick Callanan, finding himself bored in a graduate psychology class one day, sketched a poem called "I Dreamed I Was a Skinner Rat." I'd like to share it with you.

I dreamed I was a Skinner Rat,
Large and sleek with little fat;
I ran the maze with skill and ease,
Fed with pellets of high-class cheese.

I looped the loop and pressed the bar;
I was the smartest rat by far;
I was his prize, his pride and joy;
He surely loved me, I was his toy.

But then one day a funny thing
Changed my program—I had a fling
With a gorgeous sexy female rat—
It blew my program and that was that.

I was distressed and they distraught;
I ruined the flow chart they so much sought;
There was no use in keeping me;
I had climbed the mountain, I now was free.

So this is the story I wish to tell,
Skinner and such fellows can go to hell,
I would rather be with my cutey fox
Than spend my life in a Skinner Box.

This is the first publication of this poem. Permission to reprint must be obtained
from the publisher and the author, Patrick Callanan.

Time Out for Personal Reflection

1. In order to become more aware of the role that reinforcement plays in
   your everyday actions, rate the importance in your life of each of the
   following reinforcers, using the following code: 1 = extremely important in determining my actions; 2 = somewhat important in determining my actions; 3 = not very important at all in determining my actions.

   _____ a. gaining recognition and approval from others
   _____ b. making plenty of money
   _____ c. enjoying good food
   _____ d. having others notice me
   _____ e. winning in competitive enterprises
   _____ f. deriving personal satisfaction from tasks well done
   _____ g. being with people I enjoy
   _____ h. achieving and producing

2. What aspect of behaviorism do you think *most* applies to you?

_____

_____

_____

3. What aspect of behaviorism do you think *least* applies to you?

_____

_____

_____

4. How do you respond to the behavioristic position that you are basically determined by your social conditioning and by learning—that you have little freedom in actively shaping your life by making choices?

_____

_____

_____

_____

5. Mention some areas of your life over which you presently feel you have little control.

_____

_____

_____

_____

6. Write down some key environmental influences on the choices you make. To clarify what these environmental influences are, respond to the following questions:

   a. Whom in your life are you most afraid to respond to?

   _____

   b. Whose opinions do you most value? Do you check out your decisions with these people? Are you willing to challenge their views?

   _____

   _____

   _____

As I mentioned earlier in this chapter, I have found it valuable to combine behavioral techniques and humanistic goals. In their excellent book, *Self-Directed Behavior: Self-Modification for Personal Adjustment*, Watson and Tharp (1977) present a model that is based on behavioristic concepts and learning principles but that has the goal of assisting people to manage their own lives more effectively by increasing their self-directed behavior. Their book is an example of how a general theory of behavior may be applied to the development of a systematic set of skills designed to help people make specific changes in behavior and thus achieve a greater degree of control over their own lives. Similarly, *Toward a Self-Managed Life-Style*, by Williams and Long (1975), gives a systematic approach for increasing choice and control in such practical areas as health problems, career planning, the management of anxiety, and interpersonal effectiveness. In the remainder of this section, I'll discuss the behavioral techniques that I have found most valuable in my work in individual and group counseling.

Systematic Steps Leading to Self-Directed Change[2]

The following is an adaptation and modification of the systematic model for self-directed change presented by Watson and Tharp (1977). I use this model in my counseling practice with both individuals and groups.

1. *Select your goals.* (In counseling applications, the client, not the counselor, selects the goals.) What do *you* want for yourself? How do you want to be different?

2. *Translate your goals into target behaviors*—that is, the behaviors you need to change or acquire in order to reach your goal. What specific behaviors would you like to increase? What behaviors do you want to decrease? How might you reach your goal?

3. *Observe your behavior* by focusing your awareness on what you're doing. Keep a record of your behavior. You might carry in your pocket a small notebook to keep track of behaviors (and feelings associated with them) you want to change.

4. *Develop a contract.* Formulate a plan for change. After you've increased your awareness of a particular behavior pattern, you can devise a plan for change. This involves, first, negotiating a working contract, and, second, actually doing things to effect a change. These two steps comprise the action phase of the program.

[2]Adapted from *Self-Directed Behavior: Self-Modification for Personal Adjustment*, 2nd Edition, by D. L. Watson and R. G. Tharp. Copyright © 1977 by Wadsworth Publishing Company, Inc. Used by permission of the publisher, Brooks/Cole Publishing Company, Monterey, California.

5. *Arrange to get information and feedback.* If you want to know how effective your new behavior is, it's essential to get feedback and think about it. Is your changed behavior working for you?

6. *Revise your plan of action as needed.* The more you learn about yourself and the impact you have on others, the more you can refine your plans. As you practice looking at your own behavior, you can develop more effective plans for change.

A Case Illustration

The following illustration will help make the outline I've given more concrete. I used the model I've described with a client whom I'll call Roger. Initially, Roger had a great deal of difficulty focusing on *what* he wanted to change. He sought counseling because he felt inferior and frightened, and because he didn't like himself. One of his goals that we worked on for a long while was to reduce his self-deprecating remarks. He would continually put himself down, calling himself stupid and berating himself for being such a "clod."

Another of Roger's goals was to return to college. He had dropped out after his first year, because he had been convinced that he was too stupid to learn. Eventually, he did reapply to the same community college he had left five years before. After being accepted, he began by carrying a light load. Since he wanted to feel better about himself, I thought that it was crucial that he take some definite steps to increase his self-respect. At the same time, taking a full load might have set him up for failure, which would have given him additional ammunition to bombard himself with; so we both decided that it would be more realistic to start with a couple of classes the first semester. Roger selected two courses that particularly interested him: the psychology of personal adjustment and American government.

I suggested to Roger that he keep a small spiral notebook in his pocket and that he observe certain behaviors that we were working on changing. For example, he had real fears about going to class. He feared being called on and not knowing the answer, and he feared looking like a fool in front of his peers. He would tell himself that he was too dumb to go to college. I asked him to write down a few of the sentences he tended to repeat to himself, such as: "I'm really dumb." "It would be terrible if I made a mistake." "Everybody is looking at me, and I'm sure they think that I'm a jerk." I asked him to record each time that he told himself one of these self-defeating sentences. In this way, he became increasingly aware of how often, and in what situations, he would put himself down. During our sessions, we discussed the observations he'd made of himself during the past week.

As Roger began to get a clearer picture of his self-defeating behaviors, we formulated a plan for change. Roger did several things. He learned self-relaxation, which he practiced for about 20 minutes each day. He then began to use relaxation exercises before he entered threatening situations, such as taking a test, approaching an instructor, or being involved in other interpersonal situations. He also attended a one-day assertion-training workshop, because he wanted to learn how to express directly both positive and negative feelings. We then worked with many of the situations that he practiced in his assertion workshop. For instance, he needed to confront the mechanic who had charged him a hefty fee to "repair" his engine, which still didn't work. I became the mechanic who tried to give him the brush-off, and Roger acted out the way he intended to deal with him. I gave him feedback, pointing out areas of strength and things he could do to be more direct and to avoid backing down on his legitimate demands.

Roger had a great deal of difficulty in relating effectively with people. Although he definitely wanted to feel more comfortable and confident in social situations, he would typically shy away and keep to himself. I suggested that he attend one of my weekend personal-growth groups, where he could begin to apply what he was learning in his individual counseling sessions to interactions with others in a relatively safe, supportive, and structured group situation. At the outset of the group session, he made a contract to initiate contacts with others in the group. During the breaks he did go up to others and begin talking to them. This was new behavior for him; his old style would have been to sit alone in a corner and not bother anyone. Then we worked in the group with how he felt when he walked up to people and began a conversation. He was given a lot of positive feedback by the members for his willingness to get involved and do things that were difficult for him. He was also assured that people liked him and saw good qualities in him. They were not bored when he spoke, and his worst fears about how others might respond to him never materialized.

In the group, Roger also learned new behavior by *modeling*—that is, by imitating certain behaviors of another male member whom he respected. Another behavioristic technique that we employed was that of *rehearsal*. Roger wanted to approach his boss and ask him for a change of schedule at work so that he could begin to take a full load of courses. Before attending the group session, Roger had felt that he didn't want to risk making his boss unhappy and that he didn't want to put anyone out. During the workshop, Roger focused more on his legitimate needs, and he came to the conclusion that he deserved this consideration. He began by playing the role of his boss (saying how the change in schedule would be most inconvenient), while another group member played Roger's role. Then they switched roles, and Roger firmly and clearly stated his position. Roger thus had a chance to rehearse the application of his new learnings to this difficult situation. He had the opportunity to get feedback and to improve his effectiveness. Then he actually went out and applied his new style in real life.

This example illustrates how I use many behavioral techniques to help people discover their own power by increasing their self-initiated and self-directed behavior. The use of these techniques is not at all inconsistent with a humanistic orientation; in fact, it is a bridge that links the behavioristic and humanistic approaches.

In summary, the specific behavioral techniques that I have found valuable in working with people include: specifying one's own goals; defining target behaviors that must be changed to reach these goals; becoming increasingly aware of behavior; keeping a record of certain behaviors; developing a plan for change; using action-oriented techniques such as role playing, rehearsal, experimenting with new behavior, and getting feedback, reinforcement, and support; using relaxation training and assertiveness training. I'll now describe in more detail the techniques of relaxation training and assertiveness training.

Relaxation Training

Relaxation training is a behavioral technique that I find useful in many situations. Students can learn to use self-relaxation as a part of their self-directed plans. For instance, many students suffer from excessive anxiety when they take tests, when they participate verbally in class, or when they are involved in interpersonal situations. I know that I frequently work for hours without stopping and often catch myself running and accelerating my pace when I feel under pressure to do many things at once. For me, it's a real problem just to recognize that I'm tense and that I need to take some personal space and time to relax.

Let me describe an exercise in self-relaxation that you can do by yourself. You can practice relaxation in many situations, and doing so can help you assume control of your own behavior, instead of being controlled by situations that produced tension within you. For a period of at least a week (and preferably much longer), engage in relaxation training for approximately 20 to 30 minutes daily. The purpose of the self-relaxation exercise is to teach you to become more aware of the distinction between tension states and relaxation states. A further objective is to reduce unnecessary anxiety and tension and to induce bodily relaxation.

Self-relaxation is best learned in a quiet setting and in a prone position. The strategy for achieving muscular relaxation is to repeatedly tense and relax various muscle groups. Begin by tensing a specific set of muscles for several seconds and then relaxing those muscles for several seconds. In this procedure, you should cover all the major muscles by using about two tension/release cycles per muscle group. For the purpose of deepening your relaxation, auxiliary techniques such as concentrating on your breathing and imagining yourself in peaceful and personally relaxing situations can eventually be added to the self-relaxation procedure.

The following are some guidelines for your relaxation exercise. Make sure that you're in a peaceful setting and in a relaxed position. Tighten and relax the various parts of your body, beginning with your upper extremities and progressing downward to your lower extremities.

- Clench your fists tightly—so tightly that it hurts. Let go of the tension and relax.
- Stiffen the lower part of one arm. Tense it. Feel the tension. Let go of the tension.
- Tense the upper part of the arm. Tighten it until it begins to hurt. Relax it.
- Repeat the last two steps for your other arm.
- Wrinkle up your forehead. Wrinkle it tighter and tighter. Then relax and smooth it out. Picture your entire forehead and scalp becoming smoother and more relaxed.
- Raise your eyebrows as high as you can. Hold this position. Relax.
- Close your eyes as tightly as you can. Feel the tension. Close them even tighter, and feel that tension. Let go, and feel the relaxation around your eyes.
- Wrinkle your nose as tightly as you can. Relax.
- Clench your jaw, and bite your teeth together hard. Feel the pressure. Increase the tension in your jaw. Let your jaw and mouth become increasingly relaxed. Enjoy this relaxation.
- Smile in an exaggerated way, and hold it. Let go. Purse your lips as tightly as you can. Tighten your mouth muscles and feel the tension in your entire face. Let go of the tension. Relax.
- The exercise progresses with the neck, shoulders, and upper back; then the chest, abdomen, and lower back; then the rest of the body, down to the toes; and finally the entire body. During the entire exercise, keep your eyes gently closed. Cover all the major muscle groups. For each group, tense the muscles for several seconds and then relax them. Note the difference between the tension and relaxation states, and repeat the tension/release cycles at least once or twice for each muscle group.

With practice, you can become aware of tension in every part of your body, and you can learn to relax all the areas of your body, separately or together, without first having to tense them. Ultimately, the goal is to teach you to control your tension states by choosing to switch to a deep muscular-relaxation state.

Assertiveness Training

Another behavioral technique that I value and use frequently in both counseling and classroom settings is assertiveness training. The popularity of this approach indicates that there are many of us who could get more from life if we learned how to clearly express what we need and want. I see a lot of people restricting their choices because of their fears of asking directly for what they want, expressing their own feelings and thoughts, or expressing negative feelings when they experience them. In this section I'll briefly discuss what assertiveness training is and what it is not, whom it is for, and how it works.

What is assertiveness training? The titles of popular books on assertiveness training give us a sense of what it is. Alberti and Emmons (1975) urge us to *Stand Up, Speak Out, Talk Back,* while Fensterheim and Baer (1975) tell us *Don't Say Yes When You Want to Say No.* Similarly, Smith (1975) voices the common complaint *When I Say No, I Feel Guilty.* The theme of all these books is basically the same: You can come to understand your rights and express them, you can break away from a self-limiting way of life, you can learn how to express both your negative and positive feelings, you have a right to have your own opinions and preferences, and you can say no when you want to.

It's important to distinguish between being assertive and being aggressive. Being *assertive* means recognizing your right to have your own feelings, thoughts, and opinions and learning how to express them in a way that isn't designed to alienate others. Being *aggressive* means attacking others, blaming them for your problems, putting them down, and threatening them. The goal of assertiveness training is to teach us how to be assertive in asking for what we want and in sticking to our realistic demands without being aggressive.

Whom is assertiveness training for? Assertiveness training is particularly suitable for people who have trouble feeling that it is appropriate or right to assert themselves in interpersonal situations. More specifically, it can be helpful for the people who (1) cannot express anger or irritation, (2) tend to be overly polite and to allow others to take advantage of them, (3) find it difficult to say no, (4) find it difficult to express affection and other positive feelings, or (5) feel they don't have a right to have their own feelings and thoughts.

How does assertiveness training work? Assertiveness training uses role-playing techniques. For example, suppose that you feel put down whenever you participate in a particular class. Your teacher makes sarcastic remarks, and you're left feeling that what you said is unimportant or foolish. You could decide not to participate anymore, or you might just sit back and feel hostile and never say anything about the matter. On the other hand, you might decide to talk directly with this instructor in private and express how you feel about his or her remarks. If you were in an assertiveness-training group, the trainer (leader) or another member might play the role of your instructor. You could then say to this person the things you want to say to your instructor. If you had trouble behaving assertively, the trainer or another member could model an assertive style, and you could then practice again. You could also switch roles, first playing the instructor and then playing the student.

You'd then get feedback on how you come across. If you were presenting yourself in a harsh manner, for example, this could be pointed out to you. In short, the process of role-playing gives you an opportunity to identify specific behaviors that you want to change and provides a format for practicing new and more effective behaviors. It also allows you to gain insight into your style through the feedback others give you. With the help of this feedback, you can then change the ways in which you express yourself.

Assertive behavior is practiced in the role-playing situation first, then in real-life situations. If applying assertive behavior in real life is too threatening, you can create an imaginary situation and practice it there first. For example, suppose that you'd like to speak out more in class. However, week after week goes by, and you still find yourself sitting quietly, wanting to say what you think but feeling paralyzed. You might think to yourself: "What I've got to say isn't important," or "Others can say it better than I can," or "Who am I to have a conviction?" You might fear that you'd sound stupid or that the instructor would criticize you. To change this nonassertive behavior, you could begin by using the relaxation technique described in the preceding section. Then you could imagine yourself in the classroom situation and go through all the motions of participating. Next, you might begin in small ways to apply your new behavior in your classes. For example, you could make a contract to ask at least two questions during each class session. Or, if you fear talking with your instructor, you could decide to approach him or her after class, even if only for a minute. Gradually, you could take on more demanding tasks as you build confidence in your ability to express yourself.

Since most of us can benefit from assertiveness training, I recommend that you select one of the popular books listed in the Suggested Readings for this chapter and that you begin to apply these principles to your participation in this class. You can also apply the concepts I've discussed to other areas of your life, particularly at work and in close personal relationships.

The Existential-Humanistic Way of Understanding Ourselves[3]

The approach to the study of human behavior that I find most meaningful and exciting is the existential-humanistic viewpoint. I have come to embrace many of the concepts of this perspective in both my professional work and my personal life. Of the three approaches discussed in this chapter, I consider this to be the one that most directly deals with the central issues facing us today as we try to find our mean-

[3]Adapted from *Theory and Practice of Counseling and Psychotherapy,* by G. Corey. Copyright © 1977 by Wadsworth Publishing Company, Inc. Used by permission of the publisher, Brooks/Cole Publishing Company, Monterey, California.

ing in a technological and computerized society. These central concerns, which I see both my clients and students struggling with, involve our ability to choose how we will define ourselves and how we will relate to the world. Some of the options that seem open to us are:

- We can choose to expand our awareness, or we can choose to limit our vision of ourselves.
- We can become self-determining, or we can allow our environment and others to determine us.
- We can discover our own uniqueness, or we can submerge our identity in a blind conformity.
- We can choose to isolate ourselves, or we can choose to find meaningful relationships with others.
- We can give our lives meaning, or we can live empty, directionless lives.
- We can choose to recognize the anxiety that comes with our freedom to create ourselves, or we can attempt to escape from anxiety and thus limit our chances for growth.
- We can make the most of the time we have by accepting the fact that we will eventually die, or we can hide from the fact of death because of the anxiety it provokes.
- We can strive to fully actualize our potential, or we can settle for functioning with only a fraction of our potential.

These key choices that I observe people struggling with are also central themes in the existential-humanistic perspective of human nature. Personally, I still struggle with most of these issues. At times I'm willing to settle for the level of awareness I possess, instead of choosing to reach for more. At times I seek out others to make my decisions for me, so that I won't have to bear the burden of being responsible for myself. I had great fears of death at one time in my life, for myself and for others. Although I still have not resolved all these issues, I do think that I am losing some of my morbid fears of death. My life is generally meaningful, although there are many times when I question the ultimate purpose of what I am doing and times when I feel a sense of emptiness. I often struggle over the choice of whether to accept whatever growth I have achieved or to open myself to new risks and ventures. In short, I find that the existential-humanistic approach deals squarely with concerns that are central to my life.

Central Themes of the Existential-Humanistic Viewpoint

In this section, I will discuss seven key propositions that I have formulated as a result of my reading of the most significant writers in the existential-humanistic tradition. These writers include Abraham Maslow,

Carl Rogers, Viktor Frankl, Sidney Jourard, and Frederick Perls. In addition, this branch of psychological thought has many of its roots in the writings of European philosophers such as Jean-Paul Sartre, Martin Heidegger, Karl Jaspers, and Sören Kierkegaard. The propositions I've formulated seem to me to cut across the individual differences among these thinkers, and they express the themes that I find most significant in the existential-humanistic viewpoint.

  Proposition 1: *As human beings, we can think and make choices, because we are capable of self-awareness.* A corollary to this proposition is that the greater our awareness, the greater our possibilities for freedom.

  The capacity for self-awareness separates us from other animals and provides the foundation and framework for our choice making. The view of existentialists is that we are not merely pawns of fate; even though we are subject to deterministic forces of conditioning in our environment and limited by our genetic endowment, we are still able to make choices based on our awareness of these limiting factors.

  The more consciousness we possess, the more alive we are as persons. As Kierkegaard put it, "The more consciousness, the more self." In addition, because of our self-awareness, we can become aware of our *responsibility* to choose.

  Thus, to expand our awareness is to increase our capacity to fully experience human living. At the core of human existence, awareness discloses the following to us:

  - We are finite; we do not have forever to actualize our potentials.
  - We have the potential to take action or not to take action.
  - We have some liberty to choose what our actions will be, and therefore we can create our own destinies.
  - We are basically alone, yet we have a need to relate ourselves to others; we are separate from, yet related to, other beings.
  - Meaning is not bestowed on us automatically but is produced by our searching and our creating of a unique purpose.
  - Existential anxiety is an essential part of living; as we increase our awareness of choice potentials, we also increase our responsibility for the consequences of these choices.
  - We can experience conditions of loneliness, meaninglessness, emptiness, guilt, and isolation, for awareness is the capacity that allows us to know those conditions.

  Proposition 2: *We are self-determining; that is, we possess the freedom to choose among alternatives. Because we are essentially free, we must accept the responsibility for directing our lives and shaping our destinies.*

  A central existential theme is that our existence is a "given"—we are thrust into the world—but how we live and what we become are the result of our choices. Although *existence* is given to us, we create our own *essence*.

Many existentialist writers have expressed this theme. Sartre expresses it in his words "I am my choices." Theologian Paul Tillich remarked "Man becomes truly human only at the moment of decision." The philosopher Nietzsche described freedom as "the capacity to become what we truly are." Similarly, Kierkegaard's phrase "choosing one's self" implies that we are responsible for our own lives; or, as Jaspers said, "We are deciding beings." It is clear, then, that the existential approach puts freedom, self-determination, willingness, and decision making at the very center of human experience. If consciousness and freedom are stripped from us, we no longer exist as humans, for it is precisely those capacities that give us our humanness.

Freedom is the capacity to take a hand in our own development and to choose among alternatives. To be sure, freedom has limits, and choices are restricted by outside factors; but we are not simply bounced around like billiard balls. As Rollo May (1961) stated, "No matter how great the forces victimizing the human being, man has the capacity to know that he is being victimized and thus to influence in some way how he will relate to his fate" (pp. 41–42).

The existential psychiatrist Viktor Frankl continually emphasized human freedom and responsibility, and his own experiences in a concentration camp demonstrate that, even in a situation of extreme powerlessness, people can remain free to choose, at the very least, their attitude toward that situation and thus to master it in some degree. As Frankl (1963) put it, "Life ultimately means taking responsibility to find the right answer to its problems and to fulfill the tasks which it constantly sets for each individual" (p. 122).

Proposition 3: *We have the need to find and preserve the central core that gives us a unique identity, and, at the same time, to go outside ourselves by relating to others and to nature.* A corollary of this proposition is that a failure to relate to others and to nature results in loneliness, alienation, estrangement, and depersonalization.

Each of us has a strong need to discover a self—that is, to find our personal identities. But finding out who we are is not something we do automatically. It takes courage to challenge our values, to decide for ourselves, and to break away from values that are imposed on us from without. We can decide to give up the quest for self-definition by allowing some authority or organization outside of ourselves to decide for us and, in essence, to define us. We can submerge ourselves within a group and thus take on the identity and values of the group. Alternatively, we can each decide to discover our own core and to learn how to live from the inside. The trouble with many of us is that we have tried to find directions, answers, values, and beliefs in the important people in our lives. Rather than trusting ourselves to find our own answers to our conflicts, we sell out by becoming what others expect us to be. In this way, our being becomes rooted in their being, and we become strangers to ourselves.

The existentialists postulate that aloneness is part of the human condition. However, we can derive strength from the experience of looking to ourselves and experiencing our separateness from others. Our sense of aloneness comes when we realize that we cannot depend on anyone else for our own confirmation—that is, that we alone must give a sense of meaning to our lives, we alone must decide how we will live, we alone must find our own answers, and we alone must decide whether we will be or not be. Unless we have identities as individuals, we are unable to relate genuinely and meaningfully to others. We have to be able to stand alone before we can truly stand beside another.

There is a paradox in the proposition that humans are existentially both alone and related, but this very paradox describes the human condition. We depend on relationships with others for our humanness. We have a need for intimacy and a need to grow with others. We also have a need to be significant in another's world, and we each need to feel that another's presence is important in our world. When we are able to stand alone and find our own strength within ourselves, our relationships with others are based on our fulfillment, not on our deprivation. If we feel personally deprived, however, we can expect little but a clinging and parasitic relationship with someone else.

Proposition 4: The struggle for a sense of significance and purpose in life is a distinctively human characteristic; human beings are by nature seekers of meaning and personal identity.

Existentialists propose that we inevitably struggle with creating meaning and purpose in our lives and that in doing so we raise questions such as: Why am I here? What do I want from life? What gives my life purpose and meaning? Life, they contend, is not meaningful in itself; rather, we must create meaning. Indeed, we must struggle and search to find a sense of meaning, even though life may appear meaningless and even absurd. Some existentialists even assert that meaninglessness and absurdity are the wellsprings of our creativity. The very absurdity of life allows us to create our own meaning in the world.

Viktor Frankl (1963) assumes that the "will to meaning" is the human individual's primary striving. Frankl contends that there are a variety of ways of finding meaning: through suffering, through work, through loving, and through doing for others.

Proposition 5: Anxiety is a basic part of human living.

For existentialists, anxiety is not necessarily pathological; nor is it something that always needs to be cured, for it can be a strong motivational force toward growth. Anxiety is the result of our awareness of our responsibility for choosing.

Anxiety can stimulate growth in that we experience anxiety as we become more aware of our freedom and of the consequences of accepting or rejecting it. When we approach a decision that involves reconstructing our way of living, our anxiety can be a signal that we're ready for change.

What causes anxiety? Ultimately, anxiety comes from our awareness that we are finite beings—that we must die. Our awareness of our eventual nonbeing produces *existential anxiety*. It forces us to take account of how well we are living life and how much we are fulfilled as humans. Anxiety also results from our recognition that ultimately we are alone.

Proposition 6: Being aware of death is a basic human condition that gives significance to living.

Existentialists do not view death altogether negatively. For them, the ability to grasp the concept of the future and of the inevitability of death is a distinctively human characteristic. Moreover, the realization of our eventual nonbeing gives meaning to our existence, because it makes every act count. Life has meaning precisely because it must end. If we had an eternity in which to actualize our potentials, no urgency to do so would exist. Since we are finite beings, death jars us into taking the present seriously.

Because some of us are afraid of facing the reality of our own deaths, we might attempt to escape the awareness of this reality. However, when we try to flee from the confrontation with nothingness, we pay a price. As May (1961) put it, "The price for denying death is undefined anxiety, self-alienation. To completely understand himself, man must confront death, become aware of personal death" (p. 65). Frankl (1963) concurs, saying that death gives meaning to human existence. For Frankl, it is not *how long* we live that determines the meaningfulness of our lives but *how* we live.

Proposition 7: As human beings, we strive for self-actualization; that is, we strive to become all that we are able to become.

Each of us has an inborn urge to become a person—that is, a natural tendency to develop our uniqueness and singularity, to discover our personal identities, and to strive for the full actualization of our potential. To the extent that we fulfill our potential as persons, we experience the deepest joy that is possible in human experience.

Although the tendency to become self-actualizing is a natural one, the process of becoming is not automatic. Since we realize that growth can be painful, we experience a constant struggle between our desire for the security of dependence and our desire to experience the delights and pains of growth.

Self-actualization was a central theme in the work of Abraham Maslow (1968, 1970, 1971). Maslow used the phrase "the psychopathology of the average" to highlight his contention that merely "normal" people may never extend themselves to become what they are capable of becoming. Further, he criticized the Freudian orientation for its preoccupation with the sick and crippled side of human nature; if we base our findings on a sick population, Maslow reasoned, we will have a sick psychology. Thus, he believed that too much research attention is given to the study of anxiety, hostility, and neuroses and too little to the study of what we might become, to joy, creativity, and self-fulfillment.

In his quest to create a humanistic psychology that would focus on our potential as human beings, Maslow studied what he believed were self-actualizing persons and found that they differed in important ways from so-called "normals." Some of the characteristics that Maslow found in these people were: a capacity to tolerate and even welcome uncertainty in their lives, an acceptance of themselves and others, spontaneity and creativity, a need for privacy and solitude, autonomy, a capacity for deep and intense interpersonal relationships, a genuine caring for others, a sense of humor, an inner-directedness (as opposed to the tendency to live by others' expectations), and the absence of artificial dichotomies within themselves (such as work/play, love/hate, weak/ strong).

Carl Rogers (1961), a major figure in the development of humanistic psychology, has built his entire theory and practice of psychotherapy on the concept of the "fully functioning person," which is much like Maslow's notion of the "self-actualizing" person. According to Rogers, most people ask basic questions such as: Who am I? How can I discover my real self? How can I become what I deeply wish to become? How can I get behind my facades and become myself? Rogers found that, when people give up their facades and accept themselves, they move in the direction of being open to experience (that is, they begin to see reality without distorting it), they trust themselves and look to themselves for the answers to their problems, and they no longer attempt to become fixed entities or products, realizing instead that growth is a continual process. Such people, Rogers claimed, are in a fluid process of continually challenging and revising their perceptions and beliefs as they open themselves to new experiences.

In contrast to those students of human behavior who assume that we are by nature irrational and destructive of ourselves and others unless we are socialized, Rogers exhibits a deep faith in human beings. He sees people as naturally social and forward-moving, as striving to become fully functioning, and as having at their deepest core a positive goodness. In short, people are to be trusted; and, as they are basically cooperative and constructive, there is no need to control their aggressive impulses.

We can summarize some of the basic ideas of the existential-humanistic approach by means of Maslow's model of the self-actualizing person. Maslow describes self-actualization in his book, *Motivation and Personality* (1970), and he also treats the concept in his other books (1968, 1971). The following chart summarizes Maslow's view of the characteristics of self-actualizing people.

Overview of Maslow's Theory of Self-Actualization

Self-Awareness

Self-actualizing people are more aware of themselves, of others, and of reality than are non-actualizing people. Specifically, they demonstrate the following behavior and traits:

1. Efficient perception of reality
   - Self-actualizing people see reality as it is.
   - They have an ability to detect phoniness.
   - They avoid seeing things in preconceived categories.
2. Ethical awareness
   - Self-actualizing people display a knowledge of what is right and wrong for them.
   - They have a sense of inner direction.
   - They avoid being pressured by others and living by others' standards.
3. Freshness of appreciation
   - Like children, self-actualizing people have an ability to perceive life in a fresh way.
4. Peak moments
   - Self-actualizing people experience times of being one with the universe; they experience moments of joy.
   - They have the ability to be changed by peak moments.

Freedom

Self-actualizing people are willing to make choices for themselves, and they are free to be and to express their potentials. This freedom entails a sense of detachment and a need for privacy, a creativity and spontaneity, and an ability to accept responsibility for choices.

1. Detachment
   - For self-actualizing people, the need for privacy is crucial.
   - They have a need for solitude, to put things in perspective.
   - They have an ability to be objective—to accept life as it is.
2. Creativity
   - Creativity is a universal characteristic of self-actualizing people.
   - Creativity may be in any area of life; it shows itself as inventiveness.
3. Spontaneity
   - Self-actualizing people don't need to show off.
   - They display a naturalness and lack of pretentiousness.
   - They act with ease and grace.

Basic Honesty and Caring

Self-actualizing people show a deep caring and honesty with themselves and with others. These qualities are reflected in their interest in humankind and in their interpersonal relationships.

1. Sense of social interest
   • Self-actualizing people have a concern for the welfare of others.
   • They have a sense of communality with all other people.
   • They have an interest in bettering the world.
2. Interpersonal relationships
   • Self-actualizing people have a capacity for real love and fusion with another.
   • They are able to love and respect themselves.
   • They are able to go outside themselves in a mature love.
   • They are motivated by the urge to grow in their relationships.
3. Sense of humor
   • Self-actualizing people can laugh at themselves.
   • They can laugh at the human condition.
   • Their humor is not hostile.

Trust and Autonomy

Self-actualizing people exhibit faith in themselves and others; they are independent; they accept themselves as valuable persons; and their lives have meaning.

1. Search for purpose and meaning
   • Self-actualizing persons have a sense of mission, of a calling in which their potential can be fulfilled.
   • They are engaged in a search for identity, often through work that is a deeply significant part of their lives.
2. Autonomy and independence
   • Self-actualizing people have the ability to be independent.
   • They resist blind conformity.
   • They are not tradition-bound in making decisions.
3. Acceptance of self and others
   • Self-actualizing people avoid fighting reality.
   • They accept nature as it is.
   • They are comfortable with the world.

Adapted from *Motivation and Personality*, by A. H. Maslow. Copyright © 1970 by Harper & Row, Publishers, Inc. Used by permission.

Time Out for Personal Reflection

1. The existential-humanistic perspective assumes that we are basically the product of our choices. List three important choices you have made during your life.

   a. _____

   b. _____

   c. _____

2. What effects do you think any *one* of the decisions you've listed has had on your life today?

   _____

   _____

   _____

3. Describe some conflict regarding a choice that you are now facing (or have faced recently). How do you generally make your decisions?

   _____

   _____

   _____

4. List some aspects of the existential-humanistic viewpoint that you feel most apply to you.

   _____

   _____

   _____

   _____

Chapter Summary

My central purpose in this chapter has been to highlight the aspects of the psychoanalytic, behavioristic, and existential-humanistic perspectives that I most value and use in my professional work and in my personal life. I have also discussed how these theories give us a framework for understanding the choices we make. I have maintained that, even though our capacity to choose is limited by unconscious motivations, past experiences, social and cultural factors, and genetic endowment, we can still exercise choice within the framework of these limitations and even overcome them to a degree by heightening our awareness of their effects on us. Although my theoretical preference is for the thinking of the humanistic psychologists, I've indicated that I have been influenced by the psychoanalytic and behavioristic approaches as well and that existential-humanistic goals can fruitfully be merged with psychoanalytic and behavioristic methods.

I hope that you will think of the practical applications of these three perspectives and that you will apply some of the concepts to the understanding of your own behavior. You can also use these concepts as you think about the issues raised in the rest of the book. In the next chapter, many of the concepts that I've discussed will be applied to issues in human development.

Now list some of the ideas in this chapter that you most want to remember.

Activities and Exercises

The Psychoanalytic Perspective

1. In your journal, write an account of the first five years of your life. Although you might think that you can't remember much of this time, the following guidelines may help in your recall:
   a. Write down a few key questions that you would like answered about your early developmental years.
   b. Seek out your relatives, and ask them some of these questions.
   c. Collect any reminders of your early years, particularly pictures or family movies.
   d. If possible, visit the place or places where you lived and where you went to school.
   e. Attempt to answer your own questions briefly.
   f. Construct a chart showing key influences on your own development during these early years.
2. Rewrite your past the way you *wish* it had been. Think of all the things you wanted (and allow yourself to have them in fantasy), and remember situations that you wish had been different. After you reconstruct your past the way you'd like it to have been, write a brief

account of how you think your life would be different today if you had experienced *that* past instead of the one you actually have experienced.

3. Record your dreams in your journal. If you're interested in dreams, read Hall's *The Meaning of Dreams* and Perls' *Gestalt Therapy Verbatim* (see the Suggested Readings section of this chapter). You might try Perls' suggestions for doing Gestalt work on your own dreams. Record reoccurring dream patterns in your journal. What are your dreams telling you?

4. Observe a child (of a friend, relative, or neighbor) who is between the ages of 1 and 5. What do you notice in this child's behavior that either confirms or disconfirms the psychoanalytic concepts related to development during the first five years of life? You might also talk with the child's parents and ask them about some relevant developmental patterns.

The Behavioristic Perspective

1. Try to observe ways in which your daily life is controlled by others. List the affected areas of your life and some of the methods of control in your journal. Then write down any areas in which you have freedom to make choices, even though your freedom is partially limited by other people and by circumstances.

2. Apply the model for self-directed behavior that I described to some changes you're willing to make in your life. For example, you might want to change your health habits. Begin by specifying your goals and the concrete behavioral changes you want to make. For instance, your program might include eliminating smoking, reducing your consumption of alcohol, losing 10 pounds, and doing 15 minutes of physical exercise and 20 minutes of relaxation training each day. Then observe the relevant behavior in your daily life, and record such items as how often you smoke and under what conditions. After looking over a week's records, decide on a plan of action, and keep an ongoing account of your progress in your journal. In this way, you can begin to make changes in a systematic way and thus take increasing control of your own behavior.

3. For about a week or so, pay attention to instances of reinforcement in your day-to-day life. Look for things that you do that are associated with some kind of reward or incentive for you. What are the incentives in your daily behavior? Do they include getting affection from others? Giving yourself approval when you do things you like? Getting money or some other tangible thing you value? Avoiding punishment or criticism? The purpose of this exercise is to focus your awareness on the role that reinforcement plays in shaping both your behavior and the behavior of those you come into contact with.

4. Discuss your views on using behavioral concepts (mainly the use of learning principles of reinforcement, reward, and punishment) as they apply to social issues. Consider your position on these questions:

   a. Should the government give a tax rebate to those who purchase small cars that use less gasoline?
   b. Should the government impose an extra tax on those people who buy cars that get less than 15 miles per gallon of gas?
   c. Should people be guaranteed a minimum annual wage, whether they work or not?
   d. Do you think that the fear of getting a speeding ticket is an effective device for keeping speeds down to 55 mph on the freeways?
   e. Do you think that capital punishment is an effective way to reduce the incidence of murder?
5. Some additional ideas for your journal: Try the relaxation exercise given in this chapter, and write about the levels of relaxation and tension you experience in a given week. Keep a record for a week of how well you're asserting yourself, and write down any situations you encounter in which you'd like to change your behavior. Write down how you feel when you behave assertively and nonassertively.

The Existential-Humanistic Perspective

1. Think of a choice that you have made in your life that has had a profound impact on you. In your journal, write about the ways in which making this choice has affected you. In what ways did making this choice enhance or diminish your ability to make future choices?
2. Now that you have studied three different ways of understanding yourself, which aspects of psychoanalysis and behaviorism do you think can be integrated with the existential-humanistic approach? Which aspects of each theory do *you* find most helpful with respect to understanding the choices that are available to you? What parts of each theory do you find most meaningful?
3. Review the seven existential-humanistic propositions listed in the chapter, and in your journal write brief comments on how each of these applies to you. Consider questions such as: What are you now doing to increase your awareness of yourself? How do you avoid your own freedom? In what ways do you deal with anxiety in your life? What are some of the things in your life that give it meaning?
4. In your journal, discuss how free you really feel at this time in your life. Do you make your own choices on important issues, or do you manipulate others to make these decisions for you? I suggest that you keep a specific record for at least a week of the choices you make each day. What influences you to make your choices? In what situations do you avoid making decisions?

General Readings: Theoretical Perspectives

Corey, G. *Theory and Practice of Counseling and Psychotherapy.* Monterey, Calif.: Brooks/Cole, 1977. An overview of eight theoretical perspectives as applied to the counseling process. There are separate chapters devoted to the psychoanalytic, behavioristic, and existential-humanistic positions.

Nye, R. *Three Views of Man: Perspectives from Sigmund Freud, B. F. Skinner, and Carl Rogers.* Monterey, Calif.: Brooks/Cole, 1975. An excellent, brief summary of the perspectives of Sigmund Freud, B. F. Skinner, and Carl Rogers. Nye compares, contrasts, and criticizes psychoanalysis, behaviorism, and humanism as forces in psychological thought.

Schultz, D. *Theories of Personality.* Monterey, Calif.: Brooks/Cole, 1976. Schultz gives a clear and concise summary of neo-Freudian, behavioristic, and humanistic theories of personality and views of human nature. An excellent overview.

The Psychoanalytic Perspective

Baruch, D. *One Little Boy.* New York: Dell (Delta), 1964. This is a fascinating account of one boy's feelings and problems and of how his personal conflicts originated in the family dynamics, as revealed through play therapy. The book gives the reader an appreciation of the kinds of struggles most children experience in their relationships with their parents.

Brand, M. *Savage Sleep.* New York: Bantam, 1968. An excellent novel that dramatizes the psychoanalytic approach to the treatment of psychotic patients.

Green, H. *I Never Promised You a Rose Garden.* New York: New American Library (Signet), 1964. This story of a 16-year-old schizophrenic girl dramatizes her flight from reality into an imaginary world. The book does a good job of showing the reader the inner world of a psychotic and the relationship the patient has with a psychoanalytically oriented therapist.

Hall, C. *A Primer of Freudian Psychology.* New York: New American Library (Mentor), 1973. This is a very useful and clear overview of Freudian psychoanalysis.

Hall, C. *The Meaning of Dreams.* New York: McGraw-Hill, 1966. A highly interesting and readable treatment of dreams, as viewed from the psychoanalytical perspective.

Perls, F. *Gestalt Therapy Verbatim.* Lafayette, Calif.: Real People Press, 1969. Although this book represents an existential-humanistic orientation rather than a psychoanalytic one, it contains some useful information on how to work with dreams.

The Behavioristic Perspective

Alberti, R. E., & Emmons, M. L. *Stand Up, Speak Out, Talk Back.* New York: Pocket Books, 1975. A popularized version of guidelines for assertion training, with many examples of assertive and nonassertive behavior as applied to daily life.

Craighead, W. E., Kazdin, A. E., & Mahoney, M. J. *Behavior Modification: Principles, Issues, and Applications.* Boston: Houghton Mifflin, 1976. A comprehensive textbook that deals with ethical issues, applications of behavior modification, and the practical uses of the approach to control smoking, weight gain, alcohol consumption, drug abuse, and so on.

Evans, R. *B. F. Skinner: The Man and His Ideas.* New York: Dutton, 1968. An overview of many of Skinner's contributions to psychology that focuses on key issues in behaviorism. This book is written in dialogue form.

Fensterheim, H., & Baer, J. *Don't Say Yes When You Want to Say No.* New York: Dell, 1975. A practical and easy-to-read guide to learning how to assert your rights in work, marriage, sexual relationships, social situations, and family life.

Sherman, A. *Behavior Modification: Theory and Practice.* Monterey, Calif.: Brooks/Cole, 1973. This excellent treatment of the basic concepts of behavior modification gives the reader an overall grasp of how the approach actually works.

Skinner, B. F. *Walden Two.* New York: Macmillan, 1960. This novel depicts a utopian society based on the principles of operant conditioning.

Skinner, B. F. *Beyond Freedom and Dignity.* New York: Bantam, 1972. This book deals with human nature from a behavioristic viewpoint. It focuses on such issues as behavior technology in society, freedom, dignity, punishment, and values.

Smith, M. *When I Say No, I Feel Guilty.* New York: Bantam, 1975. This easy-to-read and practical guide can be applied in a personally meaningful way to everyday situations that require assertive skills.

Watson, D. L., & Tharp, R. G. *Self-Directed Behavior: Self-Modification for Personal Adjustment* (2nd ed.). Monterey, Calif.: Brooks/Cole, 1977. Based on behavioral principles, this book is aimed at assisting readers to achieve more self-determination and control over their own lives. It provides exercises for developing skills in self-analysis and concrete information on how to achieve the goals desired.

Williams, R., & Long, J. *Toward a Self-Managed Life-Style.* Boston: Houghton Mifflin, 1975. This book presents a model for self-control methods in such diverse areas as weight control, smoking and drinking control, study skills, career planning, personal problems, and interpersonal skills. Easy to read, it is designed for people who wish to use behavior-modification techniques in changing their own behavior.

The Existential-Humanistic Perspective

Bühler, C., & Allen, M. *Introduction to Humanistic Psychology.* Monterey, Calif.: Brooks/Cole, 1972. This easy-to-read book gives brief sketches of some key concepts of humanistic psychology.

Greening, T. *Existential-Humanistic Psychology.* Monterey, Calif.: Brooks/Cole, 1971. This collection of essays on humanistic theory and application deals with encounter groups, education, psychology, and society from an existential viewpoint.

Evans, R. *Carl Rogers: The Man and His Ideas.* New York: Dutton, 1975. Done in interview style, this book gives a good overview of Rogers' ideas on psychotherapy, education, contemporary psychology, and basic issues in humanistic psychology.

Frankl, V. *Man's Search for Meaning.* New York: Washington Square Press, 1963. (Pocket Books edition, 1975.) Frankl discusses many key existential themes, including self-determination, freedom and responsibility, and the meaning of life.

Koestenbaum, P. *Managing Anxiety: The Power of Knowing Who You Are.* Englewood Cliffs, N.J.: Prentice-Hall (Spectrum), 1974. This is a self-help book with exercises and activities. It deals with pain, consciousness, meaninglessness, death, guilt, and other existential themes.

Maslow, A. *Toward a Psychology of Being* (2nd ed.). New York: Van Nostrand Reinhold, 1968. A classic in humanistic psychology, this book deals with growth and motivation, creativity, values, and the self-actualizing person.

Maslow, A. *Motivation and Personality* (2nd ed.). New York: Harper & Row, 1970. In this book, Maslow gives a detailed report on the personality characteristics of self-actualizing people. The model of self-actualization is a concept that can be applied to living fully and reaching for one's potential.

Maslow, A. *The Farther Reaches of Human Nature.* New York: Viking, 1971. This is a good overview of Maslow's ideas on self-actualization, creativeness, values, society, education, and psychology.

May, R. *Existential Psychology.* New York: Random House, 1961. This book evaluates the role of existential psychology. Leaders in the field of humanistic psychology, including Maslow, May, Rogers, and Allport, are contributors.

May, R. *Man's Search for Himself.* New York: New American Library (Signet), 1953. This is a thought-provoking book for those interested in expanding their self-knowledge. It deals with loneliness, anxiety, the predicament of modern man, the experience of becoming a person, the struggle to be, freedom, choice and responsibility, religion, and meaning in life.

Rogers, C. *On Becoming a Person.* Boston: Houghton Mifflin, 1961. In this book, Rogers applies his views of the good life, the process of psychotherapy, and human nature to education, therapy, family life, and the living of a full life.

Part 2

Personal Struggles and Life Choices: Key Themes

Maturity is not some fixed destination at which we finally arrive; it is rather a direction in which we can choose to travel.

Chapter 4

Autonomy and
Personality Development

*The achievement of personal autonomy is an
ongoing process. . . . Each period of life has its
own challenges and meanings, and we
continue to develop and change
as we encounter new stages of life.*

Pre-Chapter Self-Inventory

For each statement, indicate the response that most closely identifies your beliefs and attitudes. Use this code: A = I strongly agree; B = I slightly agree; C = I slightly disagree; D = I strongly disagree.

_____ 1. I hold most of the same values, attitudes, and beliefs that my parents hold.

_____ 2. My current life-style is very close to that of my parents.

_____ 3. In most areas of my life, I try to live up to the expectations that significant people have of me.

_____ 4. Most of my friends live by their own expectations rather than by the expectations that others have of them.

_____ 5. An autonomous person is one who has rejected most of his or her parents' values.

_____ 6. I'm capable of looking at my past decisions and then making new decisions that will significantly change the course of my life.

_____ 7. "Shoulds" and "oughts" often get in the way of my living my life the way I want.

_____ 8. I'm an independent person more than I am a dependent person.

_____ 9. I basically trust both myself and others.

_____ 10. To a large degree, I've been shaped by the events of my childhood and adolescent years.

_____ 11. Struggles and crises are necessary for personal growth.

_____ 12. When I think of my early childhood years, I remember feeling secure, accepted, and loved.

_____ 13. I have trouble recognizing and expressing "negative" feelings, such as rage, anger, hatred, jealousy, and aggression.

_____ 14. I had desirable models to pattern my behavior after when I was a child and an adolescent.

_____ 15. In looking back at my early school-age years, I think that I had a positive self-concept and that I experienced more successes than failures.

_____ 16. I went through a stage of rebellion during my adolescent years.

_____ 17. My adolescent years were lonely ones.

_____ 18. For the most part, the life choices we make during our early adult years are irrevocable.

_____ 19. I remember being significantly influenced by peer-group pressure during my adolescent and early adult years.

_____ 20. Most people experience a crisis as they approach middle age.

_____ 21. The older we get, the more restricted our choices become.

_____ 22. I have fears of aging.

_____ 23. Most old people don't have much to live for.
_____ 24. If I've successfully mastered the tasks of childhood through middle age, I'll feel productive during the later years of my life.
_____ 25. I expect to experience a meaningful and rich life when I reach old age.

Here are a few suggestions for using this self-inventory:

- Retake the inventory after reading the chapter and again at the end of the course, and compare your answers.
- Have someone who knows you well take the inventory for you, giving the responses he or she thinks actually describe you. Then you can discuss any discrepancies between your sets of responses.
- In your class, compare your responses with those of the other class members, and discuss the similarities and differences between your attitudes and theirs.

Introduction

This chapter lays the groundwork for much of the rest of the book by focusing on our lifelong struggle to achieve psychological emancipation and autonomy. The achievement of personal autonomy is an ongoing process, not something we arrive at once and for all. Indeed, the central message throughout this book is that we must continually make choices concerning the kinds of persons we want to be and that the choices we make, or fail to make, determine the course and meaning of our lives.

As I discussed in the last chapter, our attitudes toward love, sex, intimacy, loneliness, death and dying, and meaning—the themes I'll be discussing in the chapters to come—are largely shaped by our experiences and decisions during our early years. However, each period of life has its own challenges and meanings, and we continue to develop and change as we encounter new stages of life. Before going on to discuss these specific themes, therefore, I want to look at the developmental stages that comprise a complete human life, from infancy through old age. I'll begin by elaborating on the ways in which early learnings affect us and the ways in which we can challenge these learnings and begin to become more autonomous.

Early Learnings and the Process of Maturing

As infants and children, we depend upon our parents or parent substitutes for our very survival. During these formative years, it's natural for us to adopt our parents' values. Since we want our parents' love and approval, we tend to evolve toward what we think they expect us to become, and in this way we gradually form our picture of who we are.

The process of maturing demands that we make conscious decisions concerning the degree to which we will incorporate our parents' values as a part of our way of life. This conscious evaluation is quite different from being unconsciously controlled by our parents because of our need for approval and security, our guilt, and our reluctance to assume responsibility for the direction of our own lives. To become autonomous, we must begin to challenge the impact of our early learning, and to do that we need to understand the nature of this early learning and how it affects us.

Recognizing Early Learnings and Decisions

During our early years, we receive many direct and indirect messages concerning who we are and what we are expected to become. I find concepts from Transactional Analysis (TA) to be useful in gaining a more precise picture of how we learn these messages and how they affect the decisions that constitute the design of our lives. Developed by Eric Berne and extended by Claude Steiner, TA assumes that we can learn to think and decide for ourselves once we understand the nature and impact of these early messages.

The concept of *life scripts* is an important contribution of TA. Life scripts are made up of both parental teachings and the early decisions we make as children. Often, we continue to follow these scripts as adults.

Scripting begins in infancy with subtle, nonverbal messages from our parents. During our earliest years, we learn much about our worth as persons and our place in life. Later, scripting occurs in both subtle and direct ways. Some of the messages we might hear include: "Always listen to authority." "Don't act like a child." "We know that you can perform well, and we expect the best from you, so be sure you don't let us down." "Never trust people; rely on yourself." "You're really stupid, and we're convinced that you'll never amount to much." Often these messages are sent in disguised ways. For example, our parents may never have told us directly that sexual feelings are bad or that touching is inappropriate. However, their behavior with each other and with us might have taught us to think in this way. Moreover, what parents *don't* say or do is just as important as what they say directly. If no mention is ever made of sexuality, for instance, that very fact communicates significant attitudes.

According to TA theory, our life scripts form the core of our personal identities. Our experiences may lead us to such conclusions as: "I really don't have any right to exist." "I can only be loved if I'm productive and successful." "I'd better not trust my feelings, because they'll only get me in trouble." These basic themes running through our lives tend to determine our behavior, and very often they are difficult to unlearn. In many subtle ways, these early decisions about ourselves can come back to haunt us in later life.

A couple of examples may help to clarify how early messages and the decisions we make about them influence us in day-to-day living. In my own case, even though I now experience myself as successful, for many years of my life I felt unsuccessful and unworthy. I haven't erased old tapes completely, and I still experience self-doubts and sometimes question my worth. I don't think that I can change such long-lasting feelings by simply telling myself "Okay, now that I'm meeting with some success, I'm a successful person." It may be necessary to deal again and again with feelings of being insecure and unworthy. In fact, even striving for and attaining success can be a compulsive way of denying basic feelings of inadequacy. In short, although I believe that I can change some of my basic attitudes about myself, I don't think I can ever get rid of all vestiges of my early learnings. In general, although we need not be determined by old decisions, it's wise to be continually aware of manifestations of our old ways that interfere with our attempts to develop new ways of thinking and being.

A second illustration of how we can be affected by the early decisions we make concerns a woman I'll call Pamela. Pamela is 38 years old, and she has been divorced three times. She finds it very difficult to take anything for herself or to experience needing anything from anyone. Instead, she has continually sought ways of being a "giver." She has told herself that she must be strong, that she mustn't allow herself to depend on others, and that she mustn't cry or experience grief. Yet Pamela isn't satisfied to continue living in this way, for she has felt lonely and resentful much of the time. She has typically picked men whom she has viewed as weak—men who could give her nothing but whom she could take care of, thereby satisfying her "giving" needs. She sees the dishonesty in her belief that she was so unselfish; she has become aware that she has been motivated more by her own need *to be needed* than by her concerns for others. Gradually, she has become aware that her parents used to tell her things like: "Always be strong. Don't let yourself need anything from anyone, and in that way you'll never get let down." "Keep your feelings to yourself; if you feel like crying, don't do it in front of others." "Remember that the way to win approval and affection is to do things for others. Always put others before yourself." Pamela's behavior was determined by these values until she became aware that she could change her early decisions if she so chose.

Let's look more closely at the nature of the early messages (often called *injunctions*) that we incorporate into our life-styles. First of all, I want to stress that these injunctions aren't just planted into our heads while we sit by passively. By making decisions in response to real or imagined injunctions, we assume some of the responsibility for indoctrinating ourselves. Thus, if we hope to free ourselves, we must become aware of what these "oughts" and "shoulds" are and of how we allow them to operate in our lives.

Here are a few of the more common injunctions. As you read them, think about how they apply to you.

- Don't be the person you are.
- Don't think.
- Don't grow.
- Don't be sexy.
- Don't change.
- Never show weakness.
- Be perfect.
- Don't express negative feelings.
- Work up to your potential.
- Never say anything unkind.
- Don't get too close to anyone.
- Don't succeed.
- Don't fail.

I encourage you to add your own injunctions to this list and to think about how they affect your life every day. For instance, I sometimes find an old injunction popping up when I'm on a vacation. I might hear an inner voice warn "Be thrifty and practical." In response, I might justify extravagance on the grounds that I've worked hard and therefore have earned certain luxuries; besides, if I relax, I can go back to work more effectively. It would be better to spot the message and learn to challenge it when it interferes with my endeavor to live in a satisfying way. I need to learn how to talk back to the inner voice that keeps me from having fun.

I use the term *inner parent* to refer to the attitudes and beliefs we have about ourselves and others that are a direct result of things we've learned from our parents or parental substitutes. I see the willingness to challenge this inner parent—or "inner custodian," as Sheehy (1976) refers to it—as a mark of autonomy. Since being autonomous means that we are in control of the direction of our lives, it implies that we have discovered an identity that is separate and distinct from the identities of our parents and of others. We haven't really achieved autonomy if our actions are dictated by an unquestioned inner parent.

Many of us, however, are reluctant to give up our inner parents, and we keep them alive and functioning in many ways. By doing so, we become incapable of directing ourselves. Some of the ways in which we can cling to our parents and other significant figures are:

- Choosing to live at home because it's more secure than having to leave and establish our own way of life.
- Making decisions that are primarily motivated by a need to please our parents rather than by a need to please ourselves.
- Attaching ourselves to a substitute parent, such as some hero, guru, or model.
- Marrying a person who is an extension of our mother or father in the hope that he or she will take care of our unmet needs.
- Striving to become perfect parents, thus making up for all that we never had as children.
- Clinging to the irrational notion that we haven't exhausted all the possible ways of pleasing our parents, and continuing to search and search in the hope that someday we will find a way to make them proud of us.

Although becoming autonomous involves challenging our inner parents, it doesn't necessarily involve rejecting all or most of our parents' values. Some of our early decisions may have been growth producing, and many of the values we incorporated from our parents may be healthy standards for guiding our behavior. No doubt our past has contributed in many respects to the good qualities we possess, and many of the things that we like about ourselves may be largely due to the influence of the people who were important to us in our early years. What is essential is that we look for the subtle ways in which we have psychologically incorporated our parents' values in our lives without a conscious and deliberate choice.

How do we learn to recognize the influence that our parents continue to have on us? One way to begin is by talking back and engaging in dialogue with our inner parents. In other words, we can begin to notice some of the things we do and some of the things we avoid doing, and then ask ourselves why. For instance, suppose you avoided enrolling in a college course because you'd long ago branded yourself "stupid." You might tell yourself that you'd never be able to pass that class, so why even try? In this case, an early decision that you'd made about your intellectual capabilities would prevent you from branching out to new endeavors. However, rather than stopping at this first obstacle, you could challenge yourself by asking "Who says that I'm too stupid? Even if my father or my teachers have told me that I'm slow, is this really true? Why have I bought this view of myself uncritically? Let me check it out and see for myself whether it's really true."

In carrying out this kind of dialogue, we can talk to the different selves we have within us. For example, you might be struggling to open yourself to people and trust them, while at the same time you hear the inner injunction "Never trust anybody." In this case you could carry on a two-way discussion between your trusting side and your suspicious side. The important point is that we don't have to passively accept as truth the messages we learned when we were children. As adults, we can now put these messages to the test.

Becoming Our Own Parents

Achieving emotional maturity involves divorcing ourselves from our inner parents and becoming our own parents. But maturity is not some fixed destination at which we finally arrive; it is rather a direction in which we can choose to travel. What are some of the characteristics of the person who is moving toward becoming his or her own parent? There is no authoritative list of the qualities of an autonomous person, but the following characteristics may stimulate you to come up with your own view of what kind of parent you want to be for yourself and what criteria make sense to you in evaluating your own degree of psychological maturity. For each of these characteristics, ask yourself whether it applies to you and whether you agree that it is a mark of one who is becoming independent. I encourage you to add to or modify this list as you see fit.

1. People moving in the direction of autonomy recognize the ways in which their inner parents control them. They see how they are controlled by guilt or by the promise of love and how they have cooperated in giving parents and parent substitutes undue power in their lives.
2. People moving in the direction of autonomy have a desire to become free and responsible persons who stand on their own two feet and do for themselves what they are capable of doing.
3. People who are moving in the direction of autonomy have a sense of identity and uniqueness. Rather than getting their sense of identity by looking outside of themselves, they find answers within. Instead of asking "What do you expect of me? What will it take for me to win your approval? What should I be and do?" they ask "What can I do that will make me pleased with myself? Who is it that I want to become? What seems right for me? What do I expect of myself?"

4. People moving in the direction of autonomy have a sense of commitment and responsibility. They are committed to some ideals and personal goals that make sense to them. Their sense of commitment includes the willingness to accept responsibility for their actions rather than blaming circumstances or other people for the way their lives are going.

5. The discovery of a meaning or purpose in life is an important mark of independent persons. Although this meaning can be derived from many sources, their lives are characterized by purpose and direction.

Time Out for Personal Reflection

1. Take a few moments to think about some of your "oughts," "shoulds," "ought nots," and "should nots." What are some of the injunctions you've bought? (Some typical examples are: "You should be polite." "Don't be sexy." "Don't get close to others." "You ought to do things perfectly." "You shouldn't trust strangers.") Now, make your own list:

   _____

   _____

   _____

   _____

2. What are some messages you've received concerning the following:

   Your self-worth? _____

   Your potential to succeed? _____

   Your sex role? _____

   Your intelligence? _____

   Your trust in yourself? _____

   Trusting others? _____

   Making yourself vulnerable? _____

   Your security? _____

   Your aliveness as a person? _____

   Your creativity? _____

   Your ability to be loved? _____

   Your capacity to give love? _____

3. What does autonomy mean to you? Add to the list I gave earlier by writing down your own criteria for assessing your level of independence.

_____

_____

_____

_____

4. Think honestly about your own degree of psychological independence. On the left side of the page, write down specific characteristics that indicate independence on your part; on the right side, list some specific traits that indicate dependence or a lack of autonomy.

I am independent in these ways: I am dependent in these ways:

_____   _____

_____   _____

_____   _____

_____   _____

_____   _____

_____   _____

5. Complete the following sentences by giving the first response that comes to mind.

a. To me, being an independent person means _____

_____.

b. The things that I received from my parents that I most value

are _____

_____.

c. The things that I received from my parents that I least like and

most want to change are _____

_____.

d. When I think of my childhood, _____

_____.

e. When I think of my adolescence, _____

_____.

f. What I most remember about my elementary school experiences is _____.

g. What I most remember about my high school experiences is
_____.

h. If I could change one thing about my past, it would be _____
_____.

i. My fears of being independent are: _____
_____.

j. One thing I most want for my children is _____
_____.

k. I find it difficult to be my own person when _____
_____.

l. One "should" that I heard as a child was _____
_____.

m. One "should not" or "ought not" that I heard as a child was
_____.

n. The thing I most would like to change about my life now is
_____.

o. I feel the freest when _____
_____.

6. Look over your responses to the incomplete-sentences exercise. Do you see any patterns? What have you learned about yourself from this exercise?

_____

_____

_____

_____

Stages of Human Development: Introduction

So far in this chapter, I've discussed the importance of gaining an awareness of early messages and decisions in developing a more independent personality. In the remainder of this chapter, I describe the highlights and developmental tasks of the major stages of life. I encourage you to apply this discussion to your own life. As you read, it might be useful to construct a chart of the major events that have occurred in each of the stages of life you've experienced so far. Further suggestions for personal applications are given whenever appropriate.

My discussion of the stages of personality development incorporates elements from Erik Erikson's view of personality development, as well as from Freudian theory and existential-humanistic psychology. Although he was intellectually indebted to Freud, Erikson suggested that we should view human development in a more positive light, emphasizing health and growth. In *Childhood and Society*, Erikson (1964) extended Freud's notion of psychosexual stages of development by defining some of the social tasks of each stage. According to this theory of development, *psychosexual* and *psychosocial* growth occur in parallel fashion; in each stage of life, we face the task of establishing a new equilibrium between ourselves and our social world.

Erikson described human development over the entire life span in terms of eight stages, each marked by a particular crisis to be resolved. When you think of the word *crisis*, you may think of a gigantic problem or catastrophic happening, and then it might seem that Erikson's view has little to do with you. But for Erikson, *crisis* means a *turning point* in life, a moment of transition characterized by the potential to either go forward or go backward in development. At these critical points along our developmental path, we either achieve growth through successful resolution of our conflicts or fail to resolve our conflicts, with the result that we encounter difficulties in later stages. In large part, our futures are shaped by the decisions we make at each of these turning points in life.

In *Passages*, Gail Sheehy (1976) describes some predictable crises of adult life. For Sheehy, these crises are *passages* to new stages of life. She assumes that, to become autonomous and authentic persons, we must be willing to face squarely the struggles posed during life; otherwise, we allow others to define who we are.

In addition to the writers I've mentioned, I've also borrowed some ideas from Berne (1975), Steiner (1975), and Havighurst (1972), and I've blended many of their concepts with the existential-humanistic view by focusing on the choice potentials open to us in each stage of life. Using Erikson's eight stages as a framework for my discussion, I'll focus on the issue of choice and provide examples that illustrate this theme. According to Erikson, the stages of development and the central issues we face in each stage are:

1. Infancy: trust versus mistrust
2. Early childhood: autonomy versus shame and doubt
3. Preschool age: initiative versus guilt
4. School age: industry versus inferiority
5. Adolescence: identity versus identity diffusion

6. Young adulthood: intimacy versus isolation
7. Middle age: generativity versus self-absorption or stagnation
8. Later life: integrity versus despair

Infancy: Trust versus Mistrust

From birth to age 2, a child's basic task is to develop a sense of trust in self, others, and the environment. Infants need to count on others; they need to sense that they are cared for and loved and that the world is a secure place. They learn this sense of trust by being held, caressed, and cared for.

Erikson views infants as forming a basic conception of the social world. If the significant other persons in an infant's life provide the needed warmth, cuddling, and attention, the infant develops a sense of trust. When these conditions are *not* present, the child becomes suspicious about interacting with others and acquires a general sense of mistrust toward human relationships. Although neither orientation is fixed to one's personality for life, it is clear that well-nurtured infants are in a more favorable position with respect to future personal growth than are their more neglected peers.

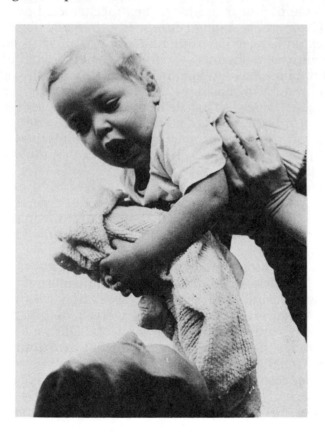

A sense of being loved is also the best safeguard against fear, insecurity, and inadequacy. Children who receive love from parents or parental substitutes generally have little difficulty accepting themselves, while children who feel unloved and unwanted may find it very hard to accept themselves. In addition, rejected children learn to mistrust the world and to view it primarily in terms of its ability to do them harm. Some of the effects of rejection in infancy include tendencies in later childhood to be fearful, insecure, jealous, aggressive, hostile, and isolated.

According to the Freudian view, the events of the first year of life are extremely important for later development and adjustment. Infants who do not get the basic nurturing needs met during this time (known as the *oral stage*) may develop greediness and acquisitiveness in later life. Material things thus become substitutes for what the children really want—love and attention from parents. For instance, a person whose oral needs are unmet may become a compulsive eater, in which case food becomes a symbol for love. Other personality problems that might stem from this period include: a mistrustful and suspicious view of the world, a tendency to reject affection from others, an inability to form intimate relationships, a fear of loving and trusting, and feelings of isolation.

The case of 9-year-old Joey, the "mechanical boy" described by Bettelheim (1967) in *The Empty Fortress,* is a dramatic illustration of how the pain of extreme rejection during infancy can affect us later on. When Joey first went to Bettelheim's school, he seemed devoid of any feeling. He thought of himself as functioning by remote control, with the help of an elaborate system of machines. He had to have his "carburetor" to breathe, "exhaust pipes" to exhale from, and a complex system of wires and motors in order to move. His delusion was so convincing that the staff members at the school sometimes found themselves taking care to be sure that Joey was plugged in properly and that they didn't step on any of his wires.

Neither Joey's father nor his mother had been prepared for his birth, and they had related to him as a thing, not a person. His mother simply ignored him; she reported that she had no feeling of dislike toward Joey but that, "I simply did not want to take care of him." He was a difficult baby who cried most of the time, and he was kept on a rigid schedule. He wasn't touched unless necessary, and he wasn't cuddled or played with. Joey developed more and more unusual symptoms, such as head banging, rocking, and a morbid fascination with machines. Evidently, Joey discovered that machines were better than people; they didn't hurt you, and they could be shut off. During years of intense treatment with Dr. Bettelheim, Joey gradually learned how to trust, and he learned as well that feelings are real and that it can be worth it to feel.

Another case that illustrates the possible effects of severe deprivation during the early developmental years is that of Sally, who is now in her early forties. Sally was given up by her natural parents and spent the first decade of her life in orphanages and foster homes. She recalls pleading with one set of foster parents who had kept her for over a year and then said that they had to send her away. As a child, Sally came to the conclusion that she was at fault; if her own real parents didn't want her, who could? She spent years trying to figure out what she had done wrong and why so many people always "sent her away."

As an adult, Sally still yearns for what she missed during infancy and childhood. Thus, she has never really attained maturity; socially and emotionally, she is much like a child. Sally has never allowed herself to get close to anyone, for she fears that they will leave if she does. As a child, she learned to isolate herself emotionally in order to survive; now, even though she is 42, she still operates on the assumptions that she had as a child. Because of her fear of being deserted, she won't allow herself to venture out and take even minimal risks.

Sally is not unusual. I have worked with a number of women and men who suffer from the effects of early psychological deprivation, and I have observed that, in most cases, such deprivation has lingering adverse effects on a person's ability to form meaningful relationships later in life. Many people I encounter—of all ages—struggle with the issue of trusting others in a loving relationship. They are unable to trust that another can or will love them, they fear being rejected, and they fear even more the possibility of closeness and being accepted and loved. Many of these people don't trust themselves or others sufficiently to make themselves vulnerable enough to experience love.

At this point, you might pause to ask yourself these questions:

- Am I able to trust others? Myself?
- Am I willing to open myself on significant and personal levels—to make myself known to a few selected people in my life?
- Do I basically accept myself as being OK, or do I seek confirmation outside of myself? Am I hungry for approval from others? How far will I go in my attempt to be liked? Do I need to be liked and approved of by everyone? Do I dare make enemies, or must I be "nice" to everyone?

Early Childhood: Autonomy versus Shame and Doubt

Freud called the second year to the end of the third year the *anal stage.* The tasks children must master at this time include learning independence, accepting personal power, and learning skills to cope with negative feelings such as rage and aggression. Their most critical task is to begin the journey toward autonomy by progressing from the stage of being taken care of by others to being able to care for their own physical needs.

In this second stage, children take their first steps toward becoming self-supporting. They take a more active role in taking care of their own needs, and they begin to communicate what they want from others.

During this time, children also face continual parental demands. For instance, they are restricted from physically exploring their environment, they begin to be disciplined, and they have toilet training imposed on them. According to the Freudian view, parental feelings and attitudes associated with toilet training are highly significant for their children's later personality development. Thus, problems in adulthood such as compulsive orderliness or messiness may be due to parental attitudes during this time. For instance, a father who insists that his son be unrealistically clean may find that his son develops into a sloppy individual as a reaction against overly strict training—or that he becomes even more compulsively clean.

Erikson identifies this period as the time for developing a sense of autonomy. Children who fail to master the task of establishing some control over themselves and coping with the world around them develop a sense of shame and feelings of doubt about their capabilities. Erikson emphasizes that during this time children become aware of their emerging skills and have a drive to try them out. Parents who do too much for their children in effect hamper their proper development. They are saying, however indirectly, "Let us do this for you, because you're too clumsy, too slow, or too incapable of doing things for yourself." Young children need to experiment; they need to be allowed to make mistakes and still feel that they are basically worthwhile. If parents insist on keeping their children dependent on them, the children will begin to doubt the value of their own abilities. If parents don't appreciate their children's efforts, the children may feel ashamed of themselves.

Young children also must learn to accept their "negative" feelings. They will surely experience rage, hatred, hostility, destructiveness, and ambivalence, and they need to feel that such feelings are permissible and that they aren't evil for having them. Of course, they also need to learn how to express their feelings in constructive ways.

In many ways, then, early childhood is a time when we struggle between a sense of self-reliance and a sense of self-doubt. Many people I've worked with in counseling have sought professional help precisely because they have a low level of autonomy. They doubt their ability to stand alone, so they depend on others to do for them things they could do for themselves. This applies particularly to some marriages; some people marry so that they will have a mother figure or a father figure to protect them and take care of their needs. Similarly, many of us have grave difficulty in recognizing our negative feelings, even when they are fully justified. We swallow our anger and rationalize away other feelings, because we learned when we were 2 or 3 years old that we were unacceptable when we had such feelings. As children, we might have shouted at our parents "I hate you! I never want to see you again!" Then we may have heard an equally enraged parent reply with "How dare you to say such a thing—after all I've done for you! I don't ever want to hear that from you again!" We soon take these messages to mean "Don't be angry! Never hate those that you love! Keep control of yourself!" And we do just that—keeping many of our feelings to ourselves, stuffing them in the pits of our stomachs and pretending we didn't experience them. Is it any wonder that so many of us suffer from migraine headaches, peptic ulcers, hypertension, or heart disease?

Again, take time out to reflect in a personal way on some of your current struggles in the area of autonomy and self-worth. You might ask yourself:

- Am I able to recognize my own feelings, particularly if they are "unacceptable" to others? How do I express my anger to those I love? Can I tolerate the ambivalence of feeling love and hate toward the same person?
- Do I take care of myself, or do I lean on others to support me? Do I keep myself a psychological cripple by encouraging others to do for me what I can do for myself?
- How assertive am I? Do I let others know what I want, without becoming aggressive? Or do I let myself be manipulated and pushed by others?

The Preschool Age: Initiative versus Guilt

The preschool years (4 to 6 years of age) are characterized by play and by anticipation of roles. During this time, children seek to find out how much they can do. They imitate others; they begin to develop a sense of right and wrong; they widen their circle of significant other persons; they take increasing initiative; they learn to give and receive love and affection; they identify with their own sex; they begin to learn more complex social skills; they learn basic attitudes regarding sexuality; and they increase their capacity to understand and use language.

According to Erikson, the basic task of the preschool years is to establish a sense of *competence* and *initiative*. Preschool children begin to initiate many of their own activities as they become physically and psychologically ready to engage in pursuits of their own choosing. If they are allowed realistic freedom to choose their own activities and to make some of their own decisions, they tend to develop a positive orientation characterized by confidence in their ability to initiate and follow through. On the other hand, if they are unduly restricted, or if their choices are ridiculed, they tend to experience a sense of guilt and ultimately to withdraw from taking an active and initiating stance.

In Freudian theory, this is the *phallic stage,* during which children become increasingly interested in sexual matters and begin to acquire a clearer sense of sex-role identity. Preschool children begin to pay attention to their genitals and experience pleasure from genital stimulation. They typically engage in both masturbatory and sex-play activities. They begin to show considerable curiosity about the differences between the sexes and the differences between adults and children. This is the time for questions such as "Where do babies come from?" and "Why are boys and girls different?" Parental attitudes toward these questions, which can be communicated nonverbally as well as verbally, are critical in helping children form a positive attitude toward their own sexuality. Since this is a time of conscience formation, one danger is that parents may instill rigid and unrealistic moral standards, which can lead to an overdeveloped conscience. Children who learn that their bodies and their impulses are evil soon begin to feel guilty about their natural impulses and feelings. Carried into adult life, these attitudes can prevent people from appreciating and enjoying sexual intimacy. Another danger is that strict parental indoctrination, which can be accomplished in subtle, nonverbal ways, will lead to an infantile conscience. Children may thus develop a fear of questioning and thinking for themselves, instead blindly accepting the dictates of their parents. Other effects of such indoctrination include rigidity, severe conflicts, guilt, remorse, and self-condemnation.

To accept their sexual feelings as natural and to develop a healthy concept of their bodies and their sex-role identities, children need adequate models. In addition to forming attitudes toward their bodies and sexuality, they begin to formulate their conceptions of what it means to be feminine or masculine. By simply being with their parents, they are getting some perspective of the way men and women relate with one another, and they are acquiring basic attitudes toward cross-sexual relationships. They are also deciding how they feel about themselves in their roles as boys and girls.

Our learnings and decisions during the phallic stage pave the way for our ability to accept ourselves as men or women in adulthood. Many people seek counseling because of problems they experience in regard to their sexual identities. Some men are very confused about what it means to be a man in this society. Some are stuck in a stereotype of the masculine role, which for them means never being tender or passionate, never feeling intensely (*thinking* their way through life instead), never crying, and, above all, *always* being "strong." Because they fear that they might not be manly enough, these men often have a desperate drive to succeed financially or to prove their "manhood," or else they measure themselves against some yardstick of what they think constitutes the normal American male. On the other side, there are some biological men who have tried to convince themselves and others that there are simply no differences between themselves and women. Some of these men resist doing anything that might be labeled "masculine," and they hold up as ideal the concept of unisex. And there are men who look to consciousness-raising groups to tell them how they should behave as men.

Of course, such problems are not limited to men. Many women seek some form of therapy because of a sex-role identity crisis. There are women who have submerged their identities totally in the roles of mother and housewife, because they have felt they had no other choice. Others, who want to be wives and mothers, have become aware that they also want something more. Unfortunately, some women have identified themselves completely with some type of women's movement, to the point of losing any independent, unique sense of what it means to be a woman. I don't mean to suggest that consciousness-raising groups for both women and men cannot be useful, but I do believe that some people can use a "movement" to find answers outside of themselves, instead of struggling and deciding upon their own direction.

Again, pause and reflect on some of your own current struggles with these issues.

- Do you have a clear picture of who you are as a woman (man)? What are your standards of femininity (masculinity)? Where did you get them?
- Are you comfortable with your own sexuality? With your body? With giving and receiving sensual and sexual pleasure? Are there any unresolved conflicts from your childhood that get in the way of your enjoyment? Do your present behavior and current conflicts indicate areas of unfinished business?

Summary of the First Six Years of Life

In describing the events of the first six years of life, I have relied rather heavily on the psychoanalytic view of psychosexual and psychosocial development, as originally formulated by Freud and later extended and modified by Erikson. This approach emphasizes the critical nature of the early developmental years in the formation of our personalities. In my work with clients in individual counseling and with relatively well-functioning people in therapeutic groups, I have come to see these early years as a strong influence on our levels of integration and functioning as adults.

When I think of the most typical kinds of problems and conflicts I encounter in my counseling work and in my college classes, the following areas come to mind: inability to trust oneself and others; inability to freely accept and give love; difficulty in recognizing and expressing negative feelings, such as rage, anger, hatred, and aggression; guilt over feelings of anger or hatred toward those one loves; inability or unwillingness to control one's own life; difficulties in fully accepting one's sexuality or in finding meaning in sexual intimacy; difficulty in accepting oneself as a woman or a man; and problems concerning a lack of meaning or purpose in life or a clear sense of personal identity and aspirations. Notice that most of these adult problems are directly related to the turning points and tasks of the early developmental years. I don't think the effects of early learning are irreversible in most cases, but these experiences, whether favorable or unfavorable, clearly influence how we relate to future critical periods in our lives.

If you still wonder about the extent to which normal children really experience the crises I've described, I suggest reading Dorothy Baruch's very moving book, *One Little Boy* (1964). Baruch vividly describes the evolution of a boy named Ken through play therapy, and she makes a strong case that Ken's feelings are typical of most children. In her work with Ken, she drew upon a psychoanalytic perspective and had Ken relive many of the unresolved conflicts of his early childhood. Almost immediately Ken crawled onto her lap and allowed himself to be loved and cared for. During the early stages of play therapy, Baruch created a climate in which Ken could freely give vent to all his feelings. As Ken felt increasingly safe, he began to express pent-up feelings of hostility and rage directed toward both his brother and his father. He built things of clay, and then he destroyed them. He took delight in making bombs and then "destroying" his father. Before his therapy, he had hardly been able to breathe because of severe asthma attacks. As he let go of many of the bottled-up feelings that he had been afraid to experience, he was able to breathe more freely, and many other crippling psychosomatic symptoms decreased.

Ken had developed many fears surrounding sexual matters, and during his play therapy he expressed in symbolic ways his guilt over masturbation, his castration anxiety, and his preoccupation with sex differences. Through the medium of play therapy, he was able to work through much of the unfinished business that presented so many problems in his later childhood. He grew to trust more; he became able to accept love and to express negative feelings without being destructive or feeling guilty; and he began to accept his sexual feelings as natural. He learned the difference between having feelings and acting out all of them. I have found that my students have gained a much deeper knowledge of the events of early childhood by reading *One Little Boy*, and almost all of them report that the book provided a rich and moving experience.

Another book that I highly recommend is Axline's *Dibs: In Search of Self* (1976). Most of my students say they are moved to tears as they read how Dibs struggles and finds himself in his play therapy. Although Axline used a client-centered, nondirective approach in her play therapy (as opposed to Baruch's psychoanalytic approach), we see similar results as Dibs learns to trust and as he expresses his fears. I like the way Axline puts it:

> Dibs experienced profoundly the complex process of growing up, of reaching out for the precious gifts of life, of drenching himself in the sunshine of his hopes and in the rain of his sorrows. Slowly, tentatively, he discovered that the security of his world was not wholly outside of himself, but that the stabilizing center he searched for with such intensity was deep down inside that self [p. ix].

During middle childhood (from age 6 to age 12), children face the following key developmental tasks: to engage in social tasks; to expand their knowledge and understanding of the physical and social worlds; to continue to learn and expand their concepts of an appropriate feminine or masculine role; to develop a sense of values; to learn new communication skills; to learn how to read, write, and calculate; to learn to give and take; to learn how to accept people who are culturally different; to learn to tolerate ambiguity; and to learn physical skills.

For Freudians, this period is the *latency stage,* characterized by a relative decline in sexual interests and the emergence of new interests, activities, and attitudes. With the events of the hectic phallic period behind them, children take a long breathing spell and consolidate their positions. Their attention turns to new fields, such as school, playmates, books, and other features of the real world. Their hostile reactions tend to diminish, and they begin to reach out for friendly relationships with others in the environment.

Erikson, however, disagrees with the Freudian view of this period as a time of latency and neutrality. He argues that the middle-childhood years present unique psychosocial demands that children must meet successfully if their development is to proceed. According to Erikson, the central task of this period is to achieve a sense of *industry;* failure to do so results in a sense of *inadequacy* and *inferiority.* The development of a sense of industry includes focusing on creating and producing, and on attaining goals. Of course, the commencement of school is a critical event of this time. Children who encounter failure during the early grades may experience severe handicaps later on. A child with early learning problems may begin to feel worthless as a person. Such a feeling may, in turn, drastically affect his or her relationships with peers, which are also vital at this time.

Helen's case illustrates some of the common conflicts of the elementary school years. When Helen started kindergarten—a bit too early—she was smaller than most of the other children. Although she had looked forward to beginning school and tried to succeed, for the most part she felt overwhelmed. She began to fail at many of the tasks her peers were enjoying and mastering. School-age children are in the process of developing their self-concepts, whether positive or negative, and Helen's view of her capacity to succeed was growing dimmer. Gradually, she began to avoid even simple tasks and to find many excuses to rationalize away her failures. She wanted to hide the fact that she was not keeping up with the other children. She was fearful of learning and trying new things, so she clung to secure, familiar ways. She grew increasingly afraid of making mistakes, for she believed that everything she did had to be perfect. If she did some art work, for instance, she would soon become frustrated and rip up the piece of paper

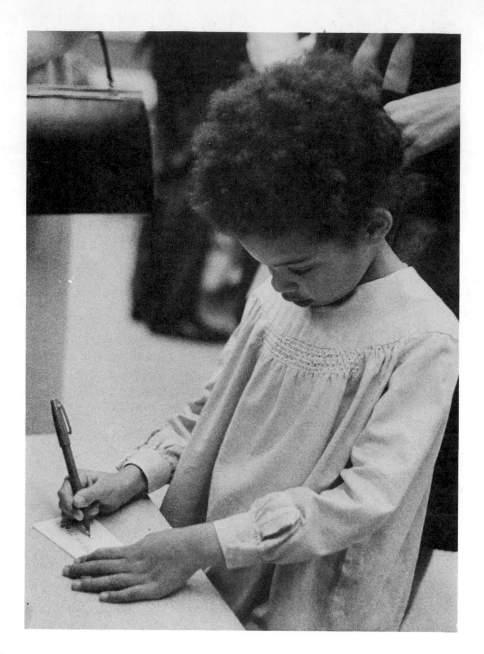

because her picture wasn't coming out exactly as she wanted it to. Basically, Helen was afraid of putting her potential to the test, and she would generally freeze up when she had to be accountable for anything she produced. Her teachers gave her consistent feedback: "Helen is a sensitive child who needs a lot of encouragement and direction. She could do much more than she does, but she quits too soon, because she feels that what she does isn't good enough."

Helen grew to resent the fact that some of her teachers were not demanding much of her because they didn't want to push her. Helen then felt even more different from her peers, completing the vicious circle. Despite her will to try and her desire to succeed, she was prevented from venturing out by her fears of gambling and making mistakes. When she was in the third grade, she was at least a grade level behind in reading, despite the fact that she had repeated kindergarten. As she began to feel stupid and embarrassed because she couldn't read as well as the other children, she shied away from reading aloud. Eventually, she received instruction in remedial reading in a clinic, and this attention seemed to help. She was also given an intelligence test at the clinic, and the results were "low average." The reading staff and those who tested Helen were surprised, for they saw her as creative, insightful, and much brighter than the results showed. Again, Helen froze up when she felt that she had to perform on a test.

Helen's case indicates that the first few years of school can have a powerful impact on a child's life and future adjustment to school. Helen's school experiences colored her view of her self-worth and affected her relationships with other children. However, although her initial experiences were difficult ones, Helen was not doomed to a life of functioning below her real potential. With the concern of her teachers and parents, much was done to help her break out of this negative cycle.

Time Out for Personal Reflection

Reflect on your childhood years, and then take the following self-inventory. Respond quickly, marking "T" if you believe the statement is more true than false for you as a child, and "F" if it tends not to fit your childhood experiences.

_____ 1. As a child, I felt loved and accepted.

_____ 2. I basically trusted the world.

_____ 3. I basically felt that I was an acceptable and valuable person.

_____ 4. I didn't need to work for others' approval.

_____ 5. I felt I was liked by my peers.

_____ 6. I made the transition from home to school well.

_____ 7. I didn't experience a great deal of shame and self-doubt as a child.

_____ 8. Elementary school was a positive experience for me.

_____ 9. I had adequate models as I was growing up.

_____ 10. I felt that it was OK for me to express negative feelings.

_____ 11. My parents trusted my ability to do things for myself.

_____ 12. I believe that I developed a natural and healthy concept of my body and my sex-role identity.

_____ 13. I assumed a degree of initiative during my early school years.

_____ 14. I had friends as a child.

_____ 15. I felt that I could talk to my parents about my problems.

Look over your responses. What do they tell you about the person you now are? If you could live your childhood over again, how would you like it to be? Record some of your impressions in your journal.

Adolescence: Identity versus Identity Diffusion

The years from 12 to 18 constitute a stage of transition between childhood and adulthood. For most people, this is a particularly difficult period. In many ways, it is a paradoxical time: adolescents are not treated as mature adults, yet they are often expected to act as though they have gained complete maturity; they are typically highly self-centered and preoccupied with their subjective worlds, yet they are expected to cope with the demands of reality and to go outside of themselves by expanding their horizons.

Adolescence is a time for continually testing limits, and there is usually a strong urge to break away from dependent ties that restrict one's freedom. It is not uncommon for adolescents to be frightened and lonely, but they may mask their fears with rebellion and cover up their need to be dependent by exaggerating their degree of independence. Although young people are becoming increasingly aware of the extent to which they are the products of their own families, it seems extremely important for them to declare their uniqueness and establish a separate identity. Much of adolescents' rebellion, then, is an attempt to determine the course of their own lives and to assert that they are who and what *they* want to be, not what others expect them to be.

In this quest to define themselves, adolescents may tend to dismiss completely anything their parents stand for, because they are insecure about not achieving their own sense of uniqueness unless they do. It would be better to recognize that our parents, our family, and our history are a part of us, and that it's unrealistic to think that anyone can completely erase this influence. Instead of totally rejecting parental influences, young people could learn how to incorporate those values that could give their lives meaning, to modify those values that they deem in need of change, and to reject the ones that they choose not to live by. Those who go to the extreme of attempting to be totally different from their parents are really not free, because they are investing a great deal of energy in proving themselves and, by their overreaction, are continuing to give their parents undue importance in their lives.

According to White and Speisman (1977), adolescence is a time for integrating the various dimensions of one's identity that have been achieved in the past (pp. 21–22). As infants, we must learn to trust ourselves and others; as adolescents, we need to find a meaning in life and models in whom we believe. As toddlers, we begin to assert our rights as independent people by struggling for autonomy; as adolescents, we make choices that will shape our future. As preschoolers, we engage in play and fantasize different roles; as adolescents, we commit ourselves by assuming new roles and identities. As schoolchildren, we try to achieve a sense of competence; as adolescents, we explore choices concerning what we want from life, what we can succeed in, what kind of education we want, and what career may suit us.

In many ways, adolescents must confront dilemmas similar to those faced by older people in our society. Both age groups must deal with the problem of finding a meaning in living, and both must cope with feelings of uselessness. Just as older people may be forced to retire and may encounter difficulty in replacing activities such as work, young people frequently feel that they are useless to society. They have not yet completed the kind of education that will give them entry to many of the careers they might want to pursue, and they generally haven't had the chance to acquire the skills necessary for many occupations. Instead, they are in a constant process of preparation for the future, in the hope that, if they successfully complete high school and college, then they might have access to their desired careers. Even in their families, they may feel unneeded. Although they may be given chores to do, many adolescents do not experience much opportunity to be productive.

Adolescence is a critical period in the development of personal identity. For Erikson, adolescents' major developmental conflicts center on the clarification of who they are, where they are going, and how they are going to get there. A failure to achieve a sense of identity results in *identity diffusion*. Adolescents may feel overwhelmed by the pressures placed upon them; if so, they may find the development of a clear identity a difficult task. They may feel pressured to make an occupational choice, to compete in the job market or in college, to become financially independent, and to commit themselves to physically and emotionally intimate relationships. In addition, they may feel pressured to live up to the standards of their peer group. Peer-group pressure is such a potent force that there is a danger that adolescents will lose their focus on their own identities and conform to the expectations of their friends and classmates. If the need to be accepted and liked is stronger than the need for self-respect, adolescents will most likely find themselves behaving in nongenuine ways, selling themselves out and increasingly looking to others to tell them what and who they should be.

A further strain on adolescents' sense of identity is imposed by the conflict between their sense of expanding possibilities and the objective narrowing of options. Adolescents are in many ways at their peak emotionally and physically, and their conceptions of their roles and of what they might become are expanding. At the same time, however, society narrows their options for action. As White and Speisman (1977) put it:

> While adolescents are telling themselves they can be anything they want to be, society is telling them, in very different terms, what they must do and who they must be if they are to succeed or even survive. Just when their thought broadens to include new perspectives and expectations, reality narrows the choices [p. 20].

The question of options is made even more urgent by the myth that the choices we make during adolescence bind us for the rest of our lives. Adolescents who believe this will be hesitant to experiment and test out many options. Too many young people yield to pressures to decide too early what they will be and what kind of serious commitments they will make. Thus, they may never realize the range of possibilities open to them. To deal with this problem, Erikson suggests a *psychological moratorium*—a period during which society would give permission to adolescents to experiment with different roles and values so that they can sample life before making major commitments.

Adolescents are also faced with choices concerning what beliefs and values will guide their actions; indeed, forming a philosophy of life is a central task of adolescence. In meeting this challenge, young people need adequate models, for a sense of moral living is largely learned by example. Adolescents are especially sensitive to duplicity, and they are quick to spot phony people who tell them how they *ought* to live while they themselves live in very different ways. They learn values by observing and interacting with adults who are positive examples, rather than by being preached to.

A particular problem adolescents face in the area of values concerns sexual behavior. Adolescents are easily aroused sexually, and everywhere they turn, whether in the media or in real life, they are saturated with sexual stimuli. At the same time, our society formally frowns on engaging in most types of sexual behavior before marriage. The resulting conflict can produce much frustration, anxiety, and guilt. Even apart from moral values in regard to sexuality, adolescents need to assess anew issues related to their sex-role identities. What is a woman? What is a man? What is feminine? What is masculine? What are the expectations we must live up to, and where do they originate? Wrestling with these difficult questions is part of the struggle of being an adolescent.

With all of these tasks and conflicts, it isn't surprising that adolescence is typically a turbulent and fast-moving period of life, and one that is often marked by loneliness. It is a time for making choices in almost every area of life—choices that, to a large extent, define our identities. The identities that we have developed during adolescence, while not necessarily final, have a profound effect on how we relate to future turning points throughout our adult lives.

Time Out for Personal Reflection

1. Indicate whether each of the following statements fits your experience during adolescence by marking them "T" or "F."

     _____ a. I look back and see my adolescent years more as a time of joy than as a time of pain.

     _____ b. I was able to achieve psychological emancipation as an adolescent.

     _____ c. I resisted merely giving in to group and peer pressure and instead made my own decisions for the most part.

     _____ d. As an adolescent, I challenged many values and beliefs.

     _____ e. During my adolescence, I had a sense of who I was and who I wanted to become.

     _____ f. I accepted my body and my sex role.

     _____ g. I felt the freedom to experiment in order to decide what I wanted to do with my life.

     _____ h. I had some close friendships.

     _____ i. I felt accepted and trusted by my parents.

     _____ j. I felt accepted by most of my peers.

2. If you could live your adolescent years again, what would you *most* like to change?

_____

_____

_____

3. How do you think your adolescence affected the person you are today?

_____

_____

_____

Young Adulthood: Intimacy versus Isolation

The period of young adulthood extends from about the ages of 18 to 35. According to Erikson, we enter adulthood after we master the adolescent conflicts over identity and role confusion. However, our sense of identity is tested anew in adulthood by the challenge of intimacy versus isolation.

One characteristic of the psychologically mature person is the ability to form intimate relationships. Before we can form such relationships, we must be sure of our own identities. Intimacy involves a sharing, a giving of ourselves, a relating to another out of strength, and a desire to grow with the other person. Failure to achieve intimacy can result in isolation from others and a sense of alienation. The fact that alienation is a problem for many people in our society is evidenced by the widespread use of drugs and by other ways in which we try to numb our sense of isolation. On the other hand, if we attempt to escape isolation by clinging to another person, we rarely find success in the relationship.

Whereas adolescence is a time of extreme preoccupation with internal conflicts and with the search for identity, young adulthood is a time for beginning to focus on external tasks, such as developing intimate relationships, getting established in an occupation, carving out a lifestyle, and perhaps marrying and starting a family. In *Passages*, Sheehy (1976) says that the tasks of this period are both enormous and exhilarating. During this time we create a dream, and this vision of ourselves generates tremendous energy and vitality. She indicates that the "trying twenties" are characterized by an effort to do what we "should." Our "shoulds" are defined mainly by the media, by our family models, and by peer-group pressures. Some of these shoulds might be: "I should get married." "I should have children." "I should better myself by completing college." "I should be working to get ahead in the organization." "I should be saving money for a house."

Sheehy stresses that one of the terrifying aspects of the twenties is the conviction that the choices we make at this time are cast in cement. For instance, we might choose to "do nothing"for a time, or to go to graduate school, or to get married, or to get established in a career. Whatever we choose, we often fear that we will have to live with our choice for the rest of our lives. According to Sheehy, this fear is largely unjustified, for major changes are almost inevitable. As she puts it: "But since in our twenties we're new at making major life choices, we cannot imagine that possibilities for a better integration will occur to us later on, when some inner growth has taken place" (p. 86).[1] However, she does indicate that, although our choices aren't irrevocable, they do set the stage for the choices we'll make later on.

Sheehy claims that we become impatient with living a life based on "shoulds" when we enter our thirties. Both men and women speak of feeling restricted at this time and may complain that life is narrow and dull. Sheehy asserts that these restrictions are related to the outcomes of the life-style choices we've made during our twenties. Even if these personal and career choices have served us well during the twenties, in the thirties we become ready for some changes. This is a time for making new choices and perhaps for modifying or deepening old commitments. This process, which may involve considerable turmoil and crisis, relates to our desire for more out of life. We may find ourselves asking "Is this all there is to life? What do I want for the rest of my life? What is missing from my life now?" Thus, a woman who has primarily been engaged in a career may now want to spend more time at home and with the children. A woman who has devoted most of her life to being a homemaker may now yearn to extend her horizon by getting established in a career. Men may do a lot of questioning about their work and wonder how they can make it more meaningful. If a man has been an "organization man" for a number of years, he might now consider breaking out of this mold by establishing his own business or changing careers. Single people may consider finding a partner, while those who are married may experience a real crisis in their marriage, which may be a sign that they cannot continue with old patterns.

At this point, I'd like to describe my wife Marianne's evolution during her young adulthood, because I think that her struggles have been similar to those of many other women. Until she was 19, Marianne

[1]This and all other quotations from this source from *Passages: Predictable Crises of Adult Life*, by Gail Sheehy. Copyright © 1974, 1976 by Gail Sheehy. Reprinted by permission of E. P. Dutton & Company, Inc. and Bantam Books, Inc.

lived in a small farm town in Germany. When she was 10 years old, she made a decision to go to the United States someday. At 19, she came to this country as a foreign-exchange student at Whittier High School, where we met in a senior English class that I was teaching. After much struggle, Marianne had already made one critical decision—to leave her country; a second major decision, which was even more difficult, was to marry a foreigner and live in her new country.

Marianne then made the choice to continue her schooling; as it turned out, she studied for the next 13 years. At one point she thought that it would not be possible for her to go to college, but she did go to junior college, then to college and university, and matriculated in 1975 with a master's degree in counseling. This represented a significant change for her, since, when she had first come to this country, she hadn't seen advanced education as a real possibility for her. In Germany she had been needed to work on the farm and take care of her parents' restaurant, which they operated in their home. Moreover, her upbringing had been marked by very traditional values and expectations. She had had a strong indoctrination about becoming only a wife and mother; higher education had not been a part of this design. However, she began to question this expectation and to see many possibilities for adopting a new role as well as broadening her existing role.

Marianne and I now have two children, aged 10 and 11. During their early years, Marianne was fulfilling multiple roles as mother, wife, housekeeper, and student. She experienced much conflict between the inner voices that urged her to be a good wife and mother and those that demanded that she be a perfect student. She did attempt to limit herself to being a wife and mother for a short time, but this expedient was not at all satisfying; she wanted the stimulation that college provided. On the other hand, her investment in school often caused her great anxiety as she wondered whether she was doing enough with and for the children. In addition, the realities of taking care of children and a home coupled with the many demands of being a part-time student were exhausting.

At 35, Marianne has now chosen to make our children her first priority, although she is still active professionally on a part-time basis. She teaches a psychology course at a community college, she has a part-time private practice as a counselor, and she and I co-lead groups for couples and week-long personal-growth workshops. In addition, during the last year, she co-authored a book with me on group counseling. It would be extremely difficult for Marianne to give up her professional activities, because she feels nourished by her work. In fact, she is often tempted to devote herself full-time to her profession, but for now she has decided not to do so.

At one time Marianne used to think that the quality of the time she spent at home was more important than its quantity, but she now feels that at times both the quality and quantity of her investment with the children have suffered because of the energy consumed by her schooling and professional life. An extremely difficult moment came for her when her father said "What good does it do to work as a counselor and help other people if you neglect your own nest?" Although she could easily rationalize intellectually that she was not neglecting our children, her father's comment reached her on a gut level. Her discomfort was heightened when our daughters, Heidi and Cindy, made up a song and sang it to her: "My mother is a psychologist, a psychologist is she; all day she talks to children, and at night, when she comes home, she's too tired to talk to me!"

In my work at the university, I've become convinced that many women returning to school experience conflicts similar to Marianne's. Marianne's struggle is not over yet. She feels she will always be confronted with choices simply because she wants the combined roles of mother, wife, and professional, and the demands of these roles often conflict.

Time Out for Personal Reflection

Think about a few of the major turning points in your young adulthood. Write down not more than three turning points, and then state how you think they were important in your life. What difference did your decisions at these critical times make in your life?

Turning point: _____

Impact of the decision on my life: _____

_____

_____

_____

Turning point: _____

Impact of the decision on my life: _____

_____

_____

_____

Turning point: _____

Impact of the decision on my life: _____

_____

_____

_____

The time between the ages of 35 and 60 is characterized by a "going outside of ourselves." It is a time for learning how to live creatively with ourselves and with others, and it can be the time of greatest productivity in our lives. For most of us, it is also the period when we reach the top of the mountain yet at the same time become aware that we must begin the downhill journey. In addition, we may painfully experience the discrepancy between our dreams of the twenties and thirties and the hard reality of what we have achieved.

According to Erikson, the stimulus for continued growth in middle age is the crisis of generativity versus stagnation. By *generativity*, Erikson meant not just fostering children but being productive in a broad sense—for example, through creative pursuits in a career, in leisure-time activities, in teaching or caring for others, or in some type of meaningful volunteer work. Two important qualities of the productive adult are the ability to love well and the ability to work well. Adults who fail to achieve a sense of productivity begin to stagnate, which is a form of psychological death.

When we reach middle age, we come to a crossroads in our lives. We reach the midpoint of our life's journey, and, even though we are in our prime, we begin to realize more acutely that life has a finishing point and that we are moving toward it. In *Passages*, Sheehy calls the time between the ages of 35 and 45 the "deadline decade." During this period, our physical powers may begin to falter, and the roles that we have used to identify ourselves may lose their meaning. We may begin to question what else is left to life and to reexamine or renew our commitments. Sheehy claims that at this time we face both dangers and opportunities. There are many dangers of slipping into deadening ruts and failing to make any real changes to enrich our lives. There are also opportunities for choosing to rework the narrow identities that we used to define ourselves during the first half of our lives.

Sheehy contends that most of us encounter a mid-life crisis. As we approach the second half of life, we realize the uncertainty of life, and we discover more clearly that we are alone. We stumble upon masculine and feminine aspects of ourselves that have previously been masked. We may also go through a grieving process, because many parts of our old selves are dying. This process does allow us to reevaluate and reintegrate an identity that is new and emerging, as opposed to an identity that is the sum of others' expectations. In Sheehy's words, "It is a dark passage at the beginning. But by disassembling ourselves, we can glimpse the light and gather our parts into a renewal" (Sheehy, 1976, p. 30). A few of the events that might occur to contribute to the mid-life crisis are:

- We may come to realize that some of our youthful dreams will never materialize.

- Our children grow up and leave home at this time. People who have lived largely for their children now may face emptiness.
- We might lose our jobs or be demoted, or we might grow increasingly disenchanted with our work.
- A spouse may have an affair or leave for another person.
- A woman may leave the home to enter the world of work and make this her primary interest.
- We may feel that we have failed to achieve the goals that we set out to achieve.

Along with these factors that can precipitate a crisis, we may have the following choices available to us at this time:

- We could decide to go back for further schooling and gear up for a new career.
- We could choose to develop new talents and embark on novel hobbies, and we could even take steps to change our life-styles.
- We can look increasingly inward to find out what we most want to do with the rest of our lives and begin doing what we say we want to do.

In my own life, I have reached middle age; in fact, I'm writing these words on my 40th birthday! As I review the last ten years of my life, I see them as extremely productive and rich. During this decade, my wife and I reared two children and established a home; I made several very important decisions; I spent ten productive years in university teaching; and I am now completing my sixth book. However, I am also asking what kind of life I want with my wife and children during the next decade. Recently we decided to leave the home in the city that we've had since we were married 13 years ago and move to the small mountain community of Idyllwild. Our decision to move came after we asked the questions: Do we want to remain in the smog and congestion of the city? Is the drive to and from work worth it? Where do we want our children to experience their adolescence? What kind of life-style changes do we want to make? Basically, we came to the conclusion that we wanted to simplify our lives, and we saw the opportunity of moving to a small mountain community as a means to this end. Although this move does entail extra driving, it seems worth it to us because of our enjoyment of the peaceful surroundings of the mountains.

I think it's important to stress that I didn't want to wait until I retired to begin to make some of the moves I'm now making. I have also found that, if I get clear on what I really want, many times I'm able to find a way to realize some of my dreams. I've learned that I have often limited myself by being overly practical and by not dreaming unless I felt sure that my dreams were "realistic." I'm learning that it's very possible to actualize dreams and visions that I never thought I could make real.

Time Out for Personal Reflection

If you have reached middle age, think about how the following questions apply to you. In your journal, you might write down your reactions to a few of the questions that have the most meaning for you. If you haven't reached middle age, think about how you'd like to be able to answer these questions when you reach that stage in your life. What do you need to do now in order to have your expectations met?

1. Is this time one of "generativity" or "stagnation" for you? Think about some of the things you've done during this time of life that you feel the best about.
2. Do you feel productive? If so, in what ways?
3. Are there some things that you'd definitely like to change in your life right now? What prevents you from making these changes?
4. What are some questions that you have raised about your life during this time?
5. Have you experienced a mid-life crisis? If so, how has it affected you?
6. What are some losses you have experienced?
7. What are some of the most important decisions that you have made during this time of your life?
8. Are you developing new interests and talents?
9. What do you look forward to in the remaining years?
10. If you were to review the major successes of your life to this point, what would they be?

Later Life: Integrity versus Despair

After about the age of 60, our central developmental tasks include the following: adjusting to decreased physical and sensory capacities, adjusting to retirement, finding a meaning in life, being able to relate to the past without regrets, adjusting to the death of spouse or friends, accepting inevitable losses, maintaining outside interests, and enjoying grandchildren.

According to Erikson, the central issue of this age period is integrity versus despair. Persons who succeed in achieving *ego integrity* feel that their lives have been productive and worthwhile and that they have managed to cope with failures as well as successes. They can accept the course of their lives and are not obsessed with thoughts of what might have been, and what they could or should have done. They can look back without resentment and regret and can see their lives in a perspective of completeness and satisfaction. Finally, they can view death as a natural part of the experience of life, even while living rich and meaningful lives to the day they die.

Unfortunately, some elderly people fail to achieve ego integration. Typically, such people fear death. They may develop a sense of hopelessness and feelings of self-disgust. They cannot accept their life's cycle, for they see whatever they have done as "not enough" and feel that they have a lot of unfinished business. They yearn for another chance, even though they realize that they cannot have it. They feel inadequate, for they feel that they have wasted their lives and let valuable time slip by. These are the people who die unhappy and unfulfilled.

Old age does not have to be something that we look forward to with horror or resignation; nor must it be associated with bitterness. However, many elderly people in our society do feel resentment, because we have generally neglected them. Many of them are treated as members of an undesirable minority and are merely tolerated or put out to pasture in a convalescent home. Their loss is doubly sad, because the elderly can make definite contributions to society. For example, they can take part in child care in day-care centers. This mutual sharing could greatly enhance the lives of children and of older people; the children would benefit from contact with the elderly, and the elderly would find a new purpose in living. Many elderly persons are still very capable of actively contributing to society, yet the prejudice of younger adults keeps them from fully utilizing their resources. Perhaps we are afraid of aging (and death) and "put away" the elderly so that they won't remind us of our future.

I believe that the attitude an older person has about aging is extremely important. Like adolescents, older persons may feel a sense of uselessness because of others' view of them. Then it is easy for them to accept the myths of others and turn them into self-fulfilling prophecies. Some of these myths are:

- Old people can't change.
- All people who retire become depressed.
- Once we retire, there's not much we can do that is productive.
- It's disgraceful for an old person to remarry.
- Old people are not creative.
- An elderly person will die soon after his or her mate dies.
- Old people are no longer beautiful.
- Old men are impotent.
- Old people no longer have any interest in sex.

These are only a few of the myths that can render older people helpless if they accept them. The fact is that old age can be a time when we can review and renew our lives. Let me illustrate this point with an example.

Jane is 76 years old. Her husband died 11 years ago, and she lives alone. She has two daughters and two sons, all of whom visit her regularly with their children. At times she takes care of her grandchildren for a few days, but then she is always anxious to get back to her own routine. For the most part, she enjoys living alone, and she fills her day by working in her garden, doing housework, and going on occasional short trips with her church group or with friends. Jane has many friends and enjoys talking with them on the telephone or having them visit her from time to time. She also enjoys watching some of her favorite television programs in the afternoon and early evening. Jane doesn't see her life as really exciting, but she does look forward to each day, she finds meaning in her daily activities, and she appreciates her memories of the past. She doesn't brood over her past, wishing that things would have been different. Instead, she accepts both her accomplishments and her failures, and she still derives pleasure in being alone as well as in being with those she loves.

Time Out for Personal Reflection

If you haven't yet reached the elderly stage of life, imagine yourself reaching old age. Think about your fears and about what you'd like to be able to say about your life, your joys, your accomplishments, and your regrets. To facilitate this reflection, you might consider the following questions:

- What do you most hope to accomplish by the time you reach old age?
- What are some of your greatest fears of growing old?
- What kind of old age do you expect to experience? What are you doing in your life now that might have an effect on the kind of person you'll be as you grow older?
- What are some things you hope to do during the later years of your life? How do you expect that you will adjust to retirement? What meaning do you expect your life to have when you reach old age?
- How would you like to be able to respond to your body's aging? How do you think you'll respond to failing health or to physical limitations on your life-style?
- Assume that you will have enough money to live comfortably and to do many of the things that you haven't had time for earlier. What do you think you'd most like to do? With whom?
- What would you most want to be able to say about yourself and your life when you become an elderly person?

In your journal, you might write down some impressions of the kind of old age you hope for, as well as the kind of fears you have about growing older.

Chapter Summary

In this chapter, I've tried to clarify some of the principal conflicts and opportunities for choice that characterize each stage of development throughout the entire life span, and I've encouraged you to think about the critical turning points and choices in your own development. I want to stress that there are no neat marks to delineate one stage of development from another. There is a great deal of overlap between stages; moreover, we all experience each period of life in our own unique ways. I've also emphasized that the attainment of autonomy is a task that we are continually engaged in, and I've suggested some guidelines to help you assess the degree to which you're now an independent person.

The experiences and events that occur during each developmental stage are crucial in helping to determine our subsequent attitudes, beliefs, values, and actions regarding the important areas of our lives that will be discussed in the chapters to come: work, love, sexuality, intimate relationships, loneliness and solitude, death and loss, and meaning and values. For this reason, I've devoted considerable attention to the foundations of our life choices. Understanding how we got where we are now is a critical first step in deciding where we want to go from here.

Now write down some of the ideas in this chapter that you most want to remember.

_____

Activities and Exercises

1. Do you believe that you're able to make new decisions? Do you think that you're in control of your destiny? In your journal, write down some examples of new decisions—or renewals of old decisions—that have made a significant difference in your life.
2. Mention some critical turning points in your life. In your journal, draw a chart showing the age periods you've experienced so far and indicate your key successes, failures, conflicts, and memories for each age period.
3. After you've described some of the significant events in your life, list some of the decisions that you have made in response to these events. How were you affected by some of these milestones in your life? Then think about what you've learned about yourself from doing these exercises. What does all of this tell you about the person you are today?
4. Many students readily assert that they are psychologically independent. If this applies to you, think about some specific examples that show that you have questioned and challenged your parents' values and that you have modified your own value system.
5. Talk with some people who are significantly older than yourself. For instance, if you're in your twenties, you could interview a middle-aged person and an elderly person. Try to get them to take the lead and tell you about their lives. What do they like about their lives? What have been some key turning points for them? What do they most remember of the past? You might even suggest that they read the section of the chapter that pertains to their present age group and react to the ideas presented there.
6. To broaden your perspective on human development in various cultural or ethnic groups, talk to someone you know who grew up in a very different environment from the one you knew as a child. You could find out how their life experiences have differed from yours by sharing with them some aspects of your own life. Try to discover whether there are significant differences in values that seem to be related to the differences in your life experiences. This could help you to reassess many of your own values.

Axline, V. *Dibs: In Search of Self.* New York: Ballantine, 1976. This book gives a touching account of a boy's journey from isolation toward self-awareness and self-expression and emphasizes the crucial effects of parent/child relationships on the development of a child's personality. It also describes how play therapy can be a tool for developing an autonomous individual.

Baruch, D. *One Little Boy.* New York: Dell (Delta), 1964. This is a fascinating account of one boy's feelings and problems and how his personal conflicts originated in the family dynamics, as revealed through play therapy. The book gives the reader a sense of appreciation for the kinds of struggles most children experience during early childhood in relationship with their parents.

Berne, E. *What Do You Say After You Say Hello?* New York: Bantam, 1975. Based on Transactional Analysis, this book demonstrates how we learn certain scripts that determine our present behavior. It discusses how we write our life scripts and how we can change them.

Bettelheim, B. *The Empty Fortress: Infantile Autism and the Birth of Self.* New York: Free Press, 1967. Three very interesting case studies are presented that give dramatic testimony concerning what can happen as a result of inadequate parenting during early childhood.

Erikson, E. *Childhood and Society* (2nd edition). New York: Norton, 1964. Using a modified and extended version of psychoanalytic thought, Erikson describes a psychosocial theory of development. He delineates eight stages of human development and the critical tasks of each stage.

Freud, S. *The Sexual Enlightenment of Children.* New York: Collier, 1963. The essays collected in this book show how Freud developed his theory of sexuality and applied it to the sexual fantasies, fears, and experiences of children.

Havighurst, R. *Developmental Tasks and Education* (3rd edition). New York: David McKay, 1972. Havighurst presents a brief description of the developmental tasks from infancy through later maturity.

James, M., & Jongeward, D. *Born to Win: Transactional Analysis with Gestalt Experiments.* Reading, Mass.: Addison-Wesley, 1971. This is a very readable guide to understanding how we develop a sense of whether we are "winners" or "losers." An overview of the principles of TA and a description of Gestalt experiments comprise the core of the book, which deals with stroking, life scripts, injunctions, early decisions, parental messages, parenting, childhood, personal and sexual identity, game playing, adulthood, and autonomy. It is an excellent source for understanding parenting and learning how we are presently influenced by earlier childhood conditioning.

Kalish, R. *Late Adulthood: Perspectives on Human Development.* Monterey, Calif.: Brooks/Cole, 1975. A very readable account of problems facing the older person, with discussion of issues such as the aging process, age and changing self-concept, attitudes toward the elderly, and physical and social environments for the elderly.

Nouwen, H., & Gaffney, W. *Aging: The Fulfillment of Life.* Garden City, N.Y.: Doubleday, 1976. A moving book in which the authors share their thoughts on what aging means to all of us, regardless of our age.

Sheehy, G. *Passages: Predictable Crises of Adult Life.* New York: Dutton, 1976. A very readable and interesting book that focuses on the crises of the various life stages. Excellent cases are presented to illustrate typical struggles as people pass from one stage of life to the next.

Steiner, C. *Scripts People Live: Transactional Analysis of Life Scripts.* New York: Bantam, 1975. One of the best accounts of life scripts is given in this very useful and interesting book.

Troll, L. *Early and Middle Adulthood.* Monterey, Calif.: Brooks/Cole, 1975. Many books on human development fail to include a discussion of middle age. This book deals with the issues, problems, and tasks of this period of life.

White, K., & Speisman, J. *Adolescence.* Monterey, Calif.: Brooks/Cole, 1977. The authors do a good job of defining and describing many facets of the world of the adolescent. Chapters deal with change and identity, values, sex roles and sexuality, and problems of these years. The thinking of Erikson and of Piaget is applied to adolescent development.

Chapter 5

Work

Regardless of how we approach our jobs, those of us who work are bound to be profoundly affected by our work experience. To exercise the maximum degree of choice in our lives, we need to become aware of the effects our jobs have on us and to consider how much these effects depend on our own attitudes and expectations concerning ourselves and our work.

121

Pre-Chapter Self-Inventory

For each statement, indicate the response that most closely identifies your beliefs and attitudes. Use this code: A = I strongly agree; B = I slightly agree; C = I slightly disagree; D = I strongly disagree.

_____ 1. Work affects all aspects of a person's life.

_____ 2. In general, the work I have done has been meaningful to me.

_____ 3. I can choose the kind of career I want to pursue, and, if I'm not satisfied, I can always change things.

_____ 4. Most people wouldn't work if they didn't need the money.

_____ 5. Work is one very important way in which I can express my creativity.

_____ 6. Most people aren't really that happy in their careers.

_____ 7. Most people will change their jobs several times during their lives.

_____ 8. Work is a source of security for me.

_____ 9. It's more important to me to have a secure job than it is to have one that's exciting.

_____ 10. Work is an energizing force in my life.

_____ 11. Work is a source of anxiety for me.

_____ 12. If I didn't have to support myself or my family, I'd quit my job.

_____ 13. Because I'm not skilled in any other job or profession, I can't change jobs.

_____ 14. I *am* my work.

_____ 15. Work structures my time; without my job, I wouldn't know what to do with myself.

_____ 16. The thought of retirement petrifies me.

_____ 17. I really like the people I work with and think of them as my second family.

_____ 18. Generally, a change of jobs will cure job dissatisfaction.

_____ 19. If I'm unhappy in my job, the cause for my unhappiness is most likely within me, not in the job itself.

_____ 20. It's never too early to choose a vocation.

The Place of Work in Our Lives

Work means different things to different people. Many people look at their jobs only as means for acquiring the money they need to satisfy their material wants and desires. Others look at their work as a primary source of satisfaction and enrichment in their lives. For some people, a sense of security is the most important benefit of a job; for others, prestige, status, fulfillment, or companionship may be at least as important. Some people identify with their jobs or work titles; others think of their work only as something they do or have to do, while finding their sense of identity elsewhere.

Regardless of how we approach our jobs, those of us who work are bound to be profoundly affected by our work experience. To exercise the maximum degree of choice in our lives, we need to become aware of the effects our jobs have on us and to consider how much these effects depend on our own attitudes and expectations concerning ourselves and our work.

I'm convinced that most working people ignore the impact their work has on their lives in general. Work is a good deal more than an activity that takes up a certain number of hours each week. If you feel creative and excited about your work, the quality of your life will be enhanced. If you hate your job and dread the hours you spend on it, your relationships and your feelings about yourself are bound to be affected. If you identify yourself with your job, how you feel about yourself will depend to a great extent on how you feel about the work you do. If you're detached from your job or unhappy with it but don't find some sense of meaning and purpose in your nonworking life, you may feel that your life is far from all that it might be. And if you let others' expectations or attitudes determine how you feel about your work, you'll surrender some of the autonomy and power to control your life that rightfully belong to you. Consequently, it's important to discover your own feelings and attitudes about work if you're to exercise real choice in this large part of your life.

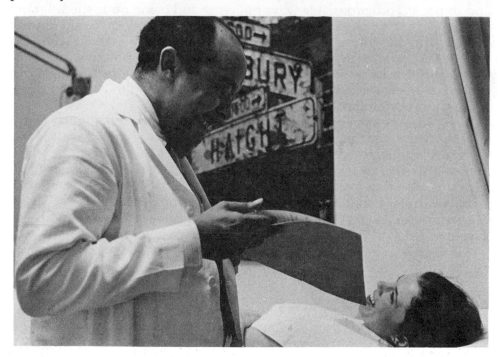

In many ways, I'm fortunate in that my work is very meaningful to me. I find my work projects varied and exciting. They include teaching in both undergraduate and graduate programs in counseling and human services, consulting with professors about in-service programs, doing part-time work in the university counseling center, leading personal-growth groups, and writing books in the areas of my teaching interests. When I assess my work activities, I become aware of how much energy I devote to them and how heavily I depend on them to structure my life. In many respects, my life is my work, and my work is my life. It's frightening to me to consider what my life would be like if I were not working as much as I am.

My work-style has both positive and negative effects on my life. On the good side, I feel creative in my work, I derive a deep sense of personal satisfaction from my projects, and I'm doing them because I want to. I'm not writing books because of the pressure to "publish or perish" but because writing them is one way to express myself personally and professionally. Similarly, if I moonlight in a graduate-school program in counseling, it's not primarily because of the financial rewards but because I like being associated with counselor-education programs at this level. My work is generally fun and a source of vitality, and it gives me a sense of fulfillment and challenge.

Yet there are negative effects too. One disadvantage of my work-style is that I tend to rely too heavily on work as a source of nourishment and to neglect other possible ways of giving and being nourished. I must be careful not to be consumed by my work. Too often I find myself missing the present moment because I'm busy thinking about some future project. Moreover, so much of my life is bound up with work that I find it difficult to really live when I'm not being "productive." During semester breaks or vacations, I feel uneasy unless I'm accomplishing some form of significant work.

Other people are affected by my work-style as well. Often I feel at a loss concerning what to say to someone when I don't talk about work. At times my family suffers from my investment in work, and I cheat myself out of contact with them and with many of the simple joys of life. My daughters have commented "Daddy always has his nose in a book or a pencil in his hand. When is he going to stop writing books?" And Marianne has felt that my enthusiasm for work has interfered with our personal life. Fortunately for me, she and I do a good bit of professional work together, including leading therapy groups and workshops and co-authoring books. The fact that we share a common profession provides for fruitful exchanges between us.

When all is said and done, however, I do feel fortunate in having work that I find meaningful, exciting, and fulfilling. I know that not everyone feels the way I do about work, so some of my struggles in this area may be different from yours. I know that I have choices to make about how I'll structure my life and that I must assess the price I pay for my investment in work. For me, the struggle comes in learning how to really *let go* and forget work at times and still feel that I'm alive and valuable.

Jobs versus Work

Although I derive much satisfaction from the work I'm paid to do, I hope that I'd be able to achieve a sense of productivity and fulfillment even if my jobs did not provide me with the opportunity to do so. In that event, I might think of my *work* or *calling* as something different from my *job*.

This distinction between a *job* and a *work* is made by Robert Strom in his book *Growing Together: Parent and Child Development* (1978). Strom notes that we tend to associate our identities, status, and sense of potency with the activities we're paid for performing. However, many jobs offer little scope for personal creativity or fulfillment, particularly in an increasingly automated society. Moreover, our society seems to be moving in the direction of more and more leisure time, shorter work weeks, and earlier retirement—trends that can make it even more difficult to derive our sense of identity and worth from our jobs. In this situation, one option we have is to find our fulfillment primarily in other activities. In Strom's words:

> If a distinction between job and work were generally accepted, the result would be in everyone's best interest. We could enlarge our inquiry of self and others from "What is your job?" to "What is your *work*?" In other words, "What is your mission as a person, the activity you pursue with a sense of duty and from which you derive self-meaning and a sense of personal worth?" It would be understood that, given the meaninglessness of some jobs, numerous people would necessarily identify their work as something different from their employment. This would release them from the self-delusion and guilt that come from working at a job they abhor but from which they are expected to gain satisfaction [Strom, 1978, p. 234].

The idea that we *are* what we do for a living is so pervasive that society at large may be slow to make the kind of distinction Strom suggests. However, we don't have to wait for others to change their views in order to decide for ourselves how much we will find our sense of meaning and purpose in our employment; nor do we have to despair or become apathetic if, despite our best efforts, we don't find jobs that are meaningful to us. To a great extent, we are the ones who decide how much we contribute to and derive from our jobs. If we feel an emptiness or lack of fulfillment in our lives, it's up to us to create our own meaning, to the extent our circumstances allow, instead of blaming our jobs for failing to provide it.

In the remainder of this chapter, I'll be talking about some of the choices we face in the world of work. Before going on, however, take a few moments to reflect on your own expectations and attitudes concerning work by completing the following Time Out.

Time Out for Personal Reflection

Complete the following sentences by giving your immediate response. After you've finished the exercise, look over your responses to see whether there are any significant patterns. You might also consider asking a friend to look over your responses and then tell you how he or she thinks you view work.

1. If I were absolutely free to choose my occupation, my choice would be _____.

2. When I consider my future career or work prospects, I become ____ _____.

3. The thing that most excites me about work is _____ _____.

4. To me, a person is successful when _____ _____.

5. To me, work means _____ _____.

6. The thing I least like about my job (or about working) is _____ _____.

7. When I think of remaining in the same job for a lifetime, I _____ _____.

8. The kind of career that I think is most rewarding is _____ _____.

9. I think I could find more meaning in my work if I _____ _____.

10. The most significant effect my work has on the rest of my life is ____ _____.

What do you expect from work? What factors do you give the most attention to in selecting a career or an occupation? In my work at a university counseling center, I've discovered that many students haven't really thought seriously about why they are choosing a given vocation. For some, parental pressure or encouragement has been the major reason for their choice of careers. Others have idealized views of what it will be like to be lawyers, engineers, or doctors. Many people I've counseled regarding career decisions haven't looked at what they value the most and whether or not these values can be attained in their chosen vocations. In choosing your vocation (or evaluating the choices you've made previously), you may want to consider which factors really mean the most to you.

Very often job decisions are based on a desire for some type of financial or psychological security. The security a job affords is a legitimate consideration for most people, but you may find that security alone isn't enough to make your job meaningful. On the other hand, the security of a job can actually enhance its meaningfulness. For example, I find that the security of my university position enables me to devote my energies to being creative in my job, instead of having to divert them to needless worry about whether or not I'll have a job. Thus, security is an important consideration for me.

Often people choose a vocation because of the influence of significant persons in their lives. In my own case, I decided to major in psychology largely because of my contact with the instructor of the first psychology class I took in college. His enthusiasm and personal qualities drew me toward this field, and his influence was instrumental in my decision to continue my studies in psychology. Nevertheless, although others might inspire us to move in a certain direction, it seems very

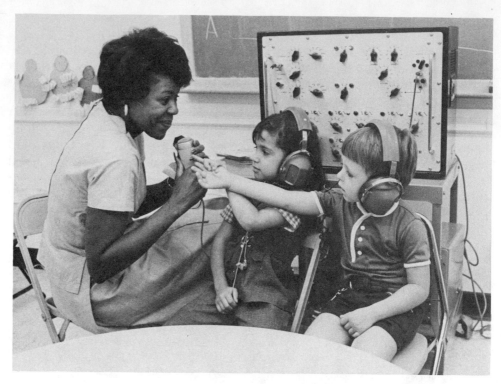

important to me that we consider the appropriateness of that direction *for us* and that our choices remain fundamentally our own.

Other factors that are often considered in connection with vocational choices include the opportunities for challenge and advancement, self-expression, service to others, financial rewards, status, and prestige, to mention only a few. Not everyone has a need to be challenged in their jobs, and not everyone works well under pressure to move upward in a job. Although the opportunity for self-expression is a priority for some people, others may consider it relatively unimportant or may find it outside their jobs. For some people, prestige and status are important considerations; if their jobs failed to provide these things, they would not be happy with them. One common pitfall is that we often allow others to determine what constitutes the "prestige" attached to a particular job. You can decide for yourself what makes a job important. Is it the amount of money you make that defines your status? Is it the opportunity to exceed quotas or to compete and win? Is it the feeling of actually producing something? Is it how hard you work? Is it the opportunity to serve others' needs?

Of course, the factors I've mentioned are only a few of the many considerations involved in selecting a job, vocation, or career. Since so much time and energy are devoted to work, I think it's extremely important to decide for ourselves what weight each factor will have in our thinking. If you value being of service to others and working with people in a personal way, you may be disappointed if you decide on a well-paying job that gives you little opportunity to work with people. If you place a high value on meeting new people and seeing new places, you may regret settling for a more secure position that offers little chance for adventure. In short, *you* are the person who can best decide what you want in your work.

One other consideration is worth mentioning in connection with career choices. One of the reviewers of this book recently called my attention to predictions that there will be five to seven occupational changes in a typical working lifetime during the last part of the century. It therefore seems that, if you're at the beginning of your working life, you can anticipate having a series of different jobs. Thus, it could well be a mistake to think about selecting *one* occupation that will last a lifetime. Instead, it may be more fruitful to think about selecting a general type of work or a broad field of endeavor that appeals to you. With a broad goal in mind, you can consider your present job as a means of gaining experience and opening doors to new possibilities, and you can focus on what *you* want to learn from this experience. It can be liberating to realize that your decisions about work can be part of a developmental process and that your jobs can change as you change. If you see your job choices in this developmental way, you can remain open to making changes and integrating them with other changes in your life-style.

The Dangers of Choosing an Occupation Too Soon

So much emphasis is placed on what we will do "for a living" that there is a real danger of feeling compelled to choose an occupation or a career before we're really ready to do so. The pressure to identify with some occupation begins in childhood with the often-heard question "What are you going to be when you grow up?" (Part of the implication of this question is that we're not grown up until we've decided to *be* something.) If freshman year in high school isn't too early to start worrying about acceptance to college, then no grade is too early to start worrying about acceptance to the right high school! Thus, the pressure is applied at a very early age to decide on what you basically intend to do with your life—before you've really had a chance to sample either the life out there in the world or the life within you.

One of my students decided early in his high school career to major in business administration when he got to college. Joe also decided to follow in his father's footsteps and become a successful accountant. Eventually, he did graduate from college with high grades in his business-administration major. Before graduating, however, he took a few electives in the Human Services program for his own enrichment and in the process discovered the difference between taking courses only because they were required and pursuing courses that excited him personally. As a result, he went on to earn a second bachelor's degree, this time in Human Services. As Joe put it, this second degree was for himself, whereas his first one had been for his father.

Today, Joe is struck by how unaware he was initially of why he was even in college and pursuing the kind of life he once did. It frightens him to think that he could have become an accountant simply because his father had an accounting firm and was pushing him in this direction. Joe realizes that his father had good intentions; after all, as his son, Joe would have had a natural place in his firm and wouldn't ever have had to worry about security. Nevertheless, Joe sees now that these plans were his father's and not his own. So he has made the choice to follow a less certain path and to explore an area that he has discovered is exciting to him. In doing so, he gives up the security of his father's clear design for his future, but Joe envisions other types of rewards.

I admire Joe's willingness to question his motivation for being in college and his courage in making a new decision that was his own. I think it is critically important that Joe realized first that he was being pushed too soon to make his career decision; with this awareness, he was able to make his own choices.

Recently, I hired a young man of 22 to do some painting and carpentry work in my house. Paul went to a community college for a year in the Midwest, but he dropped out because he needed to work to support himself. Then he and a friend decided to travel and experiment with whatever jobs they could find. They traveled over 1000 miles by bicycle, seeing much of the country and doing odd jobs along the way. For a while, they picked apples in the Northwest and really enjoyed that work. Afterwards, Paul wound up in Idyllwild to stay for a time.

Although Paul said that he wasn't really in a hurry to find a job, he found that he soon had plenty of work. He met a carpenter and became an apprentice, and he says that he has never enjoyed work as much as he does now. Previously, most of his jobs have been chores that he performed just to make money. Now he's doing something he likes while learning skills and making living money besides.

Paul has avoided committing himself to a vocation before he's had a chance to experience life, the world of work, and his own interests and capabilities. Some people might see Paul as being aimless and as wasting valuable time, but I respect what he's doing, and I believe that he's really expanding his choices and eventually will find work that will be meaningful to him. Besides, he seems to be having an exciting time living right now, without worrying about preparation for the future.

Joe and Paul are young men who ultimately resisted the pressure to select vocations too early in life. Although different people may make appropriate career decisions at different times, I think it is generally a disservice to young people to pressure them to make crucial life decisions concerning what they want to be "when they grow up." I believe most of us need an opportunity to experiment with a diverse range of occupations, to clarify our interests, and to test our abilities. Although taking the time we need to make choices for ourselves can produce anxiety for all concerned, it can also lead to greater satisfaction in the long run.

Time Out for Personal Reflection

This Time Out is intended to be a survey of your basic attitudes, beliefs, values, and interests in regard to occupational choices. Complete each statement by circling the letters of the response or responses that most apply to you or by writing your own response on the blank line I've provided.

1. Most of the jobs I've had so far
   a. have been very rewarding.
   b. have been unsatisfying.
   c. have primarily been a means to survival.
   d. have been of my own choosing.

   e. _____.

2. For me, the most important consideration in selecting a vocation is
   a. the financial rewards.
   b. the prestige.
   c. the promise of advancement.
   d. the chance to be of service to others.

   e. _____.

3. In choosing a career, I would give top priority to obtaining
   a. a secure position.
   b. a position that would challenge me.
   c. a position that would allow me to work with people.
   d. a position that offers variety.

   e. _____.

4. I think of the financial aspects of a job as
   a. extremely important.
   b. important, but not decisive.
   c. not very important.
   d. one of my least important considerations.

   e. _____.

5. In considering a career, I rank such factors as the status and prestige of the job as
   a. the most important considerations.
   b. very important.

c. somewhat important.
d. of little or no importance.

e. _____.

6. In considering a job, I consider security to be
   a. extremely important.
   b. important, but not decisive.
   c. one of my top five considerations.
   d. one of my least important considerations.

   e. _____.

7. When I think of working, the opportunity to use and develop my creativity and to express myself as a person is
   a. extremely important to me.
   b. important, but not a main factor.
   c. of some value to me.
   d. of little or no importance to me.

   e. _____.

8. In choosing a career, I think of the opportunity to make a significant difference in the lives of other people as
   a. my most important consideration.
   b. important, but not a top priority.
   c. slightly important.
   d. of little or no importance.

   e. _____.

9. I would *most* like a job in which
   a. I could be my own boss.
   b. I could work for others who would assume primary responsibility.
   c. I had a great deal of power and influence.
   d. I could work at my own pace.

   e. _____.

10. I expect that I will probably change my career in my lifetime
    a. six or more times.
    b. four or five times.
    c. two or three times.
    d. no more than once.

    e. _____.

11. I see choosing a career as
    a. a unique kind of decision.
    b. an ongoing process.
    c. a once-and-for-all decision.

d. a matching of my abilities to a specific job.

e. _____.

12. In regard to choosing my own occupation, I believe that
    a. I can be whatever I choose to become.
    b. my choice is severely limited by the job market.
    c. fate will determine what kind of work I do.
    d. my choices, while limited, are nevertheless real and significant.

    e. _____.

13. I think that work satisfaction is related to satisfaction in other areas of my life
    a. to a very high degree.
    b. to a considerable degree.
    c. to some degree.
    d. only to a very slight degree.

    e. _____.

After you've completed this survey, look it over to see whether there are significant patterns in your responses. What can you say by way of summary about your attitudes and values as they relate to selecting a career?

_____

_____

_____

_____

_____

_____

Work and the Meaning of Your Life

Whether or not you've already decided on an occupation or career, it's important to consider what you find or expect to find through work and how work can either contribute to or detract from the meaning and quality of your life. If you expect your work to provide you with a primary source of meaning in your life, and if your life isn't as rich with meaning as you'd like, you might begin to tell yourself "If only I had a job that I liked, *then* I'd be fulfilled." This "If only, then . . ." type of thinking can lead you to believe that somehow the secret of finding a purpose in your life depends on something outside yourself.

In his book *The Doctor and the Soul*, Frankl (1965) contends that "no one occupation is the sole road to salvation." He talks about people who try to deceive themselves by thinking that they *would* be fulfilled now *if only* they had gone into another occupation. Frankl states that, on the contrary, if an occupation doesn't lead to fulfillment, the fault may be in the person rather than in the work: "The work in itself does not make the person indispensable and irreplaceable; it only gives him the chance to be so" (p. 95).

Frankl describes a patient who found her life meaningless and who believed that, if she had a job that fulfilled her, her life would be meaningful. Frankl pointed out to her that her attitude toward her work and the manner in which she did her work were more important than the job itself. He showed her that it is the person who does a particular job that is responsible for any meaning the job has. The way a person approaches a job and the special things he or she does in carrying out that job are what make it meaningful.

As I am typing these words, there is a crew of workers pouring cement in my driveway. The other day I was talking to a young man who was digging a trench in preparation for this cement work, and he told me "I'm really getting tired of digging ditches for a living. Boy, this sure gets old fast. I'd like to get another job, and I'm working on this now." Now it may well be that he will find a job in which he can create more meaning, but it could also be that he is the kind of person Frankl is talking about—the kind who expects the job to provide the meaning. If so, perhaps his new job would get old soon as well. My conversation with this man made me think about Frankl's idea that we are the source of whatever meaning we find in our work; no job automatically brings meaning to us. As Frankl contends, "The capacity to work is not everything; it is neither a sufficient nor essential basis for a meaningful life. A man can be capable of working and nevertheless not lead a meaningful life; and another can be incapable of working and nevertheless give his life meaning" (Frankl, 1965, p. 101).

The Dynamics of Discontent in Work

It is certainly true that, if you're dissatisfied with your job, one recourse you have is to seek a new one. However, change alone might not produce different results. In general, I think it's a mistake to assume that change necessarily cures dissatisfactions, and this very much applies to changing jobs. To know whether a change of jobs would be helpful, you need to understand as clearly as you can why your present job isn't satisfactory to you. Consequently, I'd like to talk about some of the external factors that can devitalize us in our jobs and the very real pressures and stresses our jobs often create. Then I'd like to focus attention on the importance of looking *within ourselves* for the source of our discontent. Often we blame external factors for our unhappiness and, in so doing, fail to look at how our own attitudes and expectations might be contributing to our discontent.

You may like your work and derive satisfaction from it yet at the same time feel drained because of irritations produced by factors that aren't intrinsic to the work itself. Such factors might include low morale among fellow workers, or actual conflict and disharmony with them; authoritarian supervisors who make it difficult for you to feel any sense of freedom on the job; or organizational blocks to your creativity. There are also countless pressures and demands that can sap your energy and lead you to feel dissatisfied with your job, including: having to meet deadlines and quotas; having to compete with others instead of simply doing your best; facing the threat of losing your job; feeling stuck in a job that offers little opportunity for growth or that you deem dehumanizing; dealing with difficult customers or clients; and having to work long hours or perform exhausting or tedious work. A stress that is particularly insidious—because it can compound all the other dissatisfactions you might feel—is the threat of cutbacks or layoffs, an anxiety that becomes more acute when you think of your commitments and responsibilities. In addition to the strains you may experience on the job, there may also be the daily stress of commuting to and from work. You may be tense before you even get to work, and the commute home may only increase the level of tension or anxiety you bring home with you. One real problem for many of us is that our relationships with others are negatively affected by this kind of life-style. If our work drains and deenergizes us, we may have little to give to our children, spouses, and friends, and we may not be receptive to their efforts to give to us.

All the factors I've mentioned can contribute to a general discontent that robs our work of whatever positive benefits it might otherwise have. In the face of such discontent, we might just plod along, hating our jobs and spoiling much of the rest of our lives as well. The alternative is to look at the specific things that contribute to our unhappiness or tension and to ask ourselves what we can do about them. We can also ask what we can do about our own attitudes toward those pressures and sources of strain that we can't influence directly.

In describing his experiences in a concentration camp, Frankl (1963) writes that he experienced little freedom in an external sense: his daily life was highly directed by the guards, who stripped him of every freedom except one—his freedom to choose his attitude toward his situation. Some of his fellow prisoners chose an attitude of resignation; others fought back with whatever means they had; still others took an attitude of hope that someday they would be released. The important point is that how the prisoners experienced their confinement depended to a great extent on the attitude they adopted toward it.

Perhaps we can learn something valuable from this extreme case of powerlessness. Without inviting a comparison between working at your job and being confined to a concentration camp, I do want to suggest that we have some control over the effects difficult circumstances have on us.

One way in which we frequently limit our choice of attitudes toward our jobs is by overemphasizing the *job itself* and other external realities as the cause of our discontent. As long as we project all our troubles outside ourselves, we can make the job or the boss or the customers convenient scapegoats, but we prevent ourselves from looking at what *we* can do to change. Some people, for instance, adopt a perfectionist attitude, blaming their unhappiness on the failure of others to meet their high standards. They may change jobs again and again, hoping that, this time, things will be exactly right, which of course they never are. The trouble is that they are looking outside of themselves instead of at the unrealistically high aspirations they impose on themselves and others. Until they begin to accept that they are contributing to their own discontent, no amount of changing jobs will effect a satisfactory solution.

Meaninglessness in Work

In *Working*, a fascinating report on the everyday lives of working people, Studs Terkel gives a penetrating inside view of the material and spiritual hardships that many workers experience in their struggle to make a living for their families and themselves. He describes scores of interviews with people in many different types of occupations, including a strip miner, a telephone operator, a bookbinder, a garbage man, a spot welder, a bus driver, a car salesman, a mail carrier, an interstate truck driver, a janitor, a waitress, and many others. Many of these first-person accounts are testimonies of the meaninglessness of the workers' lives.

Clearly, many, if not most, working people do not find their jobs personally meaningful or see them as opportunities for self-expression and self-actualization. Thus, many of them do not identify themselves with their jobs, despite the time and energy they must devote to them. To these people, work must simply be made as tolerable as possible. No one can say what an enormous toll this attitude toward their jobs must take on the quality of their lives and their sense of self-respect.

If you find your work meaningless, what can you do about it? What can you do if, instead of energizing you, your job drains you physically and emotionally? What are your options if you feel stuck in a dead-end job?

Admittedly, there are plenty of situations in which there are no easy answers to these questions. Surely, the first step is to challenge the notion that simply changing jobs will bring meaning to your life. No job, however attractive it may seem, provides meaning and fulfillment in and of itself, and any job becomes intolerable if we make it so. Assuming, however, that you've looked for ways to give meaning to your job and that you've examined how you might be contributing to your own dissatisfaction with it, you might consider whether you must resign yourself (at least temporarily) to doing something you don't much like to do, while looking for things to do with the rest of your time that will energize you. Perhaps you wouldn't resent the job so much if you created other sources of meaning and excitement in your life. Perhaps, too, you can redefine the hopes you have of the job itself. Of course, you may also be able to think of the satisfactions you'd most like to aim for in a job and then consider whether there is a job that more nearly meets your needs and what steps you must take to obtain it. You might be able to find ways of advancing within your present job, making new contacts, or acquiring the skills that eventually will enable you to move on. The important thing is to look carefully at how much the initiative rests with *you*—your expectations, your attitudes, and your sense of purpose and perspective.

I'm thinking now of a man I know who used to hate his job and dread going to work, because his days were filled with boredom. He decided to quit his job in the city and move to a mountain community, where he began learning a new trade as a carpenter. For a while, he liked building houses, but eventually this ceased to be a challenge for him. He then followed up on a hobby he had of making cabinets and furniture. With practice, he became an artist in this work, and more and more people came to him for cabinets. He's now establishing himself in the furniture business in the peacefulness of a quiet mountain community that he loves, and he is taking pride in building and creating furniture that has his own personal touch. He could easily have remained in the city, doing a job he hated and all the while convincing himself that he had no other choice. Instead, he stuck with that job until he could make a new move, even though he could not be certain that it would be an improvement. It took imagination, patience, and courage, but he was willing to change his attitude, to take action to change his situation, and to take a risk.

Another person I know is growing increasingly disenchanted with her work as a teacher. She loves antiques, and she often goes antique-shopping with friends. Although antiques are presently her hobby, she's beginning to think of ways of eventually turning her hobby into a career. Until then, she'll continue to teach and to enhance her life through her hobbies and friendships. In this way, she avoids being a victim and retains some control over the role of her job in her life.

In addressing myself to the issue of meaninglessness in work, I think it's important to add that all of us will probably find certain aspects of our work to be boring, or at least unexciting. Every occupation has its tedious and routine chores. For example, although I greatly enjoy most of my work projects, I generally find reading papers to be a chore; I detest making out grades; I never look forward to writing the many letters of recommendation that I write in a semester; and attending meetings gets old for me very fast. I even get bored with some of my classes (or my lectures) once in a while. Even in play and recreation, most of us must learn to tolerate some monotony. I play tenor saxophone in our community swing band, and I very much enjoy playing for groups in the park or at a dance, and I also enjoy the fellowship associated with our weekly band practices. Still, there are times of boredom when I must practice a piece of music over and over or do certain exercises that will keep me in the band. So I see it as vital for me to recognize that some boredom is a part of life but that I have some choice in how I relate to this boredom. Besides, once I recognize the things that are chores for me, I can think of ways to make them more tolerable—or even fun.

Apart from the boredom that might creep into any job, however, there are undoubtedly occupations in which most of the time on the job is merely endured. In *Working*, Terkel documents the quiet desperation experienced by many people in service occupations. He found that certain themes tended to run through his interviews with people in many different occupations: we need to be needed; we need to feel that our work (and we) are of some significance; we need and want to be remembered; we search for "daily meaning as well as daily bread"; we work for "recognition as well as cash." In Terkel's words, "To be remembered was the wish, spoken and unspoken, of the heroes and heroines in this book" (p. xiii).[1] Terkel concludes that merely surviving the day is a victory for many who are among the "walking wounded" in the world of work. As he says, "The scars, psychic as well as physical, brought home to the supper table and the TV set, may have touched, malignantly, the soul of our society" (p. xiii).

---

[1]From *Working: People Talk about What They Do All Day and How They Feel about What They Do*, by S. Terkel. Copyright 1974 by Pantheon Books, a division of Random House, Inc. Reprinted by permission.

In the automated age in which we live, many people feel as if their work could be done better by machines. Indeed, many of the people Terkel interviewed talk about feeling like robots, objects, or machines. They speak in their own way of being depersonalized—faceless, anonymous, interchangeable cogs in a gigantic machine. For example, an 18-year-old telephone operator complains that she is missing any personal touch in her work. People put coins in a machine, and she responds. "You're there to perform your service and go. You're kind of detached" (p. 65). Even though she'd like to be more personal in her job, and even though there are times when she'd like to engage callers in conversations or brief exchanges, she realizes that in her role she can't be much more than a programmed machine. "I'm a communications person," she says with eloquent irony, "but I can't communicate" (p. 66). Instead, she is reduced to repeating a few acceptable and anonymous responses day after day, such as: "Good morning, may I help you?" "What number do you want?" "I have a collect call from Bill; will you accept the charges?" Apart from such standard phrases, she cannot interact with others in a human way without risking her supervisor's disapproval and perhaps her job itself.

Unquestionably, such experiences can be frustrating and dehumanizing. In cases such as this one, the distinction between a job and a "work" may be helpful. If you decide that you must remain in a job that allows little scope for personal effort and satisfaction, you may need to accept the fact that you won't find much meaning in the hours you spend on the job. It's important, then, to be aware of the effects the time spent on the job has on the rest of your life and to minimize them. More positively, it's crucial to find something outside the job that fulfills your need for recognition, significance, productivity, and excitement. By doing so, you may develop a sense of your true work as something different from what you're paid to do; you may even come to think of your job as providing the means for your *work*—that is, the productive activities you engage in away from the job, whether they take the form of hobbies, creative pursuits, volunteer work, the spending of time with friends and family, or whatever the case may be. The point is to see whether things can be turned around so that you are the master rather than the victim of your job. Too many people are so negatively affected by their jobs that their frustration and sense of emptiness spoil their eating, recreation, family lives, sex lives, and relationships with friends. If you can reassume control of your own attitudes toward your job and find dignity and pride elsewhere in your life, you may be able to do much to lessen these negative effects.

It's also worth recognizing that we sometimes allow the prejudices of others to obscure the fact that there is dignity in doing any necessary job. As an example, a waitress interviewed by Terkel speaks of her sense of pride in being a waitress "with class." This attitude—plus the fact that she doesn't perceive her work as menial or demanding—is an important asset to her. What causes her some difficulty is the reaction she sometimes gets from customers. "How come you're *just* a waitress?" they may ask, or "Why isn't a person like you in some other line of work?" Questions like these irritate her, because she believes her work is valuable and that she does it well, and she'd like this fact to be recognized and appreciated by others. Her response to people who take the attitude that her work is menial is "Don't you think you deserve to be served by me?"

Game Playing as a Strategy for Survival

One strategy that some people use to maintain their perspective is to make a game out of their jobs. Game playing, in this sense, doesn't have to be a negative thing. I know a carpenter whose main task is framing houses. He says that he has framed so many houses that he could do it blindfolded. One device he uses to make his work more interesting is to compete with his fellow workers to determine who can frame the fastest. Of course, such a strategy won't make a meaningless job meaningful, but it can make necessary chores less tedious *if* you're finding other sources of meaning in your life.

There are also some games that some people feel they *must* play if they are to keep their jobs. Darlene, an airline stewardess, tells me that she can't let any negative feelings show, even when she thinks a passenger deserves to be confronted. She has been trained to smile regardless of what she feels. If she's angry, she must swallow her anger and smile. If she becomes frightened, she must deny her fear and smile. Her prime mission is to be pleasant. To accomplish it, she must role-play during many of her working hours. This kind of game playing takes its toll on her; she suffers from chronic fatigue, tension, headaches, and stomach problems. Yet she's aware of what she's doing and chooses to continue to play the game, because there are other aspects of her job that make it worthwhile to her to do so.

I've met quite a number of people who are convinced that they have to play a role in order to survive in their jobs—and that they have to keep their jobs in order to survive at all. Some of these people achieve a sense of relief simply by recognizing that they *are* playing a role; in fact, they may then consciously play their roles with gusto. During my college years, I worked as a busboy at a fancy hotel, and I observed the studied acting done by waiters and waitresses. In their encounters with customers, they pretended to be pleasant even when they felt sour; then, as soon as they walked past the double doors into the kitchen, they revealed their true feelings, at times taking delight in mimicking certain customers. They at least knew when they were putting up a front, and as a safety valve they released their true feelings and joked when it was safe to do so.

As I said earlier, game playing is no substitute for finding meaning and purpose in work, but it can be a useful strategy when our work—the activity in which we take pride and from which we derive satisfaction—diverges from what we must do to make a living. It becomes a cynical device only when we are not recognizing or fulfilling our needs for recognition and productive achievement in some other area of our lives.

Changing Jobs or Careers

Life would be simpler if we could see clearly what the outcomes of our vocational choices would be before we made them. However, choosing the right job is probably one of the most complicated decisions we have to make. Certainly, we have the option of changing jobs in order to increase our satisfaction with work, but changing jobs after a period of years can entail even more risk and uncertainty than making our first job selection. Whenever we consider a vocational choice, the key seems to be to become clear about our own expectations and wants.

Again, I'll illustrate by recounting a personal experience. About five years ago, I had a tenured position at a university in a job that I very much enjoyed. The environment was good, I was teaching interesting courses, I liked my association with my students and colleagues, and I felt energized by my work. There were no real drawbacks, and there were many reasons to remain at that university. However, I received an offer to teach at another university in the same state system. The change would entail giving up my tenure, and my future at the state university would be somewhat uncertain. Nevertheless, after struggling with the decision, I decided to make the move. I was attracted by the chance to work in a new program, one that was dedicated to creating innovative courses and designing experimental, interdisciplinary programs. There was the promise (or hope) that I'd be involved in new and challenging projects and that I'd be able to open new vistas. Still, the possibility existed that I would not be retained after the first year, and, by leaving my former university, I closed the door behind me. I realized that I could not go back to my old position again if the new job didn't work out.

Some of the questions I asked myself at the time included the following: When should I stop being hungry for more fulfillment? Should I settle for something that is presently good, if I see a chance for things to be even better? Is it worth it to give up a valued position for one that may be more rewarding when I know that doing so means I cannot return to my former position? There are no easy or pat answers to questions such as these. Clearly, each person's own values must play a big part in the decision-making process. Thus, we each must continually clarify for ourselves the importance we give to such factors as job security, financial gains, possibilities for advancement, opportunities to create and try new things, opportunities to be of service to others, and so on. No one else can measure the personal price we pay for advancement or security; no one else can weigh our willingness to risk one kind of benefit in order to achieve something we want more.

A further illustration is provided by Ralph, a 34-year-old truck driver. Ralph tells me that he knows now that he became a truck driver because he always felt like a loner. He thought that truck driving was one occupation in which he could spend a lot of time alone and not have to deal with people. As he looks back on his decision, he sees that he took the job because he didn't feel that he had the confidence to interact with people. He felt inferior in most areas of his life, but he felt that he could handle trucking. And he adds that he gets some sense of power from driving a huge, noisy truck. However, things are changing within Ralph. He realizes now that he doesn't have to limit his life by staying in an occupation that he doesn't really *want* to stay in. He has resumed college, and he has begun to challenge his self-limiting notion that he was stupid and could never be anything else but a trucker. He says that what he really wants to do is work with adolescents who get themselves into trouble, because he feels a kinship with them. He still drives a truck in order to make a living, but at the same time he is taking steps to prepare himself for a change.

Even though Ralph had done well financially as a trucker, he no longer found his work satisfying. He realized that he had at least three alternatives: he could remain a trucker, he could do some kind of volunteer work in addition to his trucking, or he could prepare himself for another job while keeping his trucking job temporarily. Ultimately, Ralph chose the last option, but the first crucial step was his recognition of his motivations for choosing trucking in the first place. With this awareness, he was able to see clearly that he did want a change and that he had the potential to be something different.

Frequently, people who are not radically dissatisfied with their jobs simply don't feel energized by them either. In such cases, change can become a struggle; things aren't all that bad for them; they're not really suffering, and they could continue what they're doing without being miserable. Thus, Cathy, a 38-year-old high school teacher, finds little meaning in her work after 14 years in a similar job. She considers the pluses to be tenure, a decent salary, summer vacations, and the knowledge that she can do her job well. However, she feels she's growing stale, and she doesn't look forward to her future. She wonders whether things would really be better even if she did change jobs. After all, "Things could be worse."

Cathy's situation illustrates the importance of choosing our attitude toward a given situation. Cathy could simply preserve the status quo, in effect deciding that there's nothing to be done; she could look for ways to rejuvenate her present job; she could look for a new line of work;

she could take a leave of absence; she could keep her job and seek out some meaningful hobbies. In order to make a meaningful decision, however, she needs to look within herself for the reasons for her feelings of staleness and to sort out her priorities. Which does she value more—security or new challenges? What satisfactions does she get from her job, and what is lacking? Does she ask too much (or too little) from her job? Frequently, when we ask questions such as these, it will turn out that our own attitudes are at least as important as what we actually decide to do.

In summary, we don't have to be victimized by our jobs. We're not cemented to our original job decisions for the rest of our lives. The belief that such decisions are binding for a lifetime is frequently the very thing that keeps us victims. As long as we cling to that belief, we reduce the range of options we allow ourselves to consider. It's important to realize that we may be enthused about some type of work for years and yet eventually become dissatisfied because of the changes that occur within us. With these changes comes the possibility that a once-fulfilling job will become monotonous and draining. If we outgrow our jobs, we can learn new skills and in other ways increase our options. Because our own attitudes are crucial, when a feeling of dissatisfaction sets in, it's wise to spend time thinking about what we ourselves want from our jobs and how we can most productively use our talents.

Changing Careers in Mid-Life

The notion that we're stuck with our original career choices is increasingly being challenged, particularly by people in middle age. As I discussed in the last chapter, many people experience a mid-life crisis—a time when they question the meaning of their work, the quality of their relationships, and the direction of their lives. There is a danger at this time in life of slipping into a deadening rut; and there can be the difficult recognition that we may not accomplish all the goals we set for ourselves earlier in life. However, the mid-life crisis can also be a challenge to renew and revitalize our commitments or to branch out in new directions.

The awareness of options can be an important asset at this time in life. Most of the people I know have changed their jobs several times; you might think of the people you know to see whether this pattern fits their experience as well, and, whether or not you've reached middle age, you might ask yourself what your own beliefs and attitudes toward changing careers are. Although making large changes in the directions of our lives is rarely easy, it can be a good deal harder if our own attitudes and fears are left unquestioned and unexamined.

A common example of mid-life change at the present time is the woman who decides to return to college or to the job market after her children reach high-school age. Many community colleges and state universities are enrolling women who realize that they want more fulfill-

ment at this time in their lives. They may still value their work at home, but they are looking forward to developing new facets of themselves.

I'm thinking of one of my students, Nancy, who at age 47 is not at all untypical of many women who are now enrolling in college. Nancy entered college with a lot of mixed feelings. She wanted to meet new people, tap some of her unused resources, take new and challenging courses, and prepare herself for a career in the helping professions. She felt good when she was at school, and a completely new dimension of herself began to blossom as she followed through with her choice to involve herself in activities that were challenging and nourishing for her. She did some field work in the community, working with parents and their children, and she felt excited over the contribution she was making. Despite these positive feelings, however, she frequently felt guilty for not being at home enough and for not being as available to her children and her husband as they wanted her to be at times. For many years she had subordinated her own needs to those of her family. Perceiving her role as one of "doing for" her children, she had lost contact with her identity as a person apart from her identity as a mother. She had nourished and taken care of others, but in the process she had failed to do the same for herself. Now, even though she realizes that she needs to be a person in her own right, she still suffers doubts about her choice and struggles to combine her different roles.

Despite the struggle involved, I respect the refusal of women like Nancy to allow themselves to stagnate. They are making their own choices to do something different, even though they are experiencing some anxiety over establishing a new identity.

This phenomenon is not unique to women. I know of many men who are deciding in middle age to quit jobs they've had for years, even if they're successful, because they want new challenges. Men often define themselves by the work they do, and work thus becomes a major source of the purpose in their lives. If they feel successful in their work, they may feel successful as persons; if they become stagnant in work, they may feel that they are ineffectual in most areas of their lives.

Such is the case with John, a 52-year-old aerospace engineer who finally decided that too much of his identity was wrapped up in his profession. He decided to keep his job in industry as a consultant to various engineering firms while at the same time commencing a master's-degree program in counseling. His interest in counseling stemmed from some marriage counseling he and his wife had received. He had experienced a new realm of feelings, and he decided that he didn't always have to be detached, thing-oriented, logical, and unemotional. Eventually, John received his degree in counseling, and, even though he hasn't switched from engineering to counseling as a profession, it has been important for him to know that he has the qualifications to assume a new career if he so chooses. In this way he experiences more freedom in the world of work, because he knows that he is in engineering because he *wants* to be now, not because he *has* to be.

People like Nancy and John are finding new directions and new dimensions of meaning in their lives because they're willing to question long-standing assumptions about themselves and about work. Although such self-awareness is always relevant and helpful, it is particularly so during mid-life, when we can either renew ourselves or set the stage for a life of doing a job simply in order to survive.

Time Out for Personal Reflection

1. Mention a few of the most important benefits that you get (or expect to get) from work.

_____

_____

_____

_____

2. What kind of work would you most like to be involved in? Why?

_____

_____

_____

3. What kind of work would you *least* like to be involved in? Why?

_____

_____

_____

4. List the aspects that you most look for in selecting a field of work (such as: security, opportunities for self-expression, financial rewards, contact with co-workers, and so on).

_____

_____

_____

5. If you're presently working or have worked in the past, mention *one* thing that you would *most* like to change (or would most liked to have changed) about your work.

_____

_____

_____

6. What non-work activities have you been involved in that you liked because in doing them you felt creative, happy, or energetic?

_____

_____

_____

7. Could you obtain a job that would incorporate some of the activities you've just listed? Or does your job already account for them?

_____

_____

_____

8. What do you think would happen to you if you couldn't work? Write what first comes to mind.

_____

9. Some people experience a good deal of anxiety over making choices dealing with work. Check any of the following factors that you feel create anxiety for you:

_____ I feel that I must make a career choice too early.
_____ I don't know what my abilities are.
_____ Once I make a choice, I think that I must stay with it.
_____ I fear that my choice will be wrong and that I'll be stuck with a miserable job.
_____ I'm afraid that I won't be able to find the kind of work I really want.
_____ I'm afraid that I'll become consumed by my work.
_____ I'm concerned that I'll select a line of work because I've been influenced by others and that I'll be living up to their expectations rather than my own.

10. Mention any other anxieties you are aware of concerning your decisions about work:

_____

_____

_____

11. What specific things do you think you can do now concerning any of the fears you've checked or listed above?

_____

_____

_____

12. If you could quit your job and still have all your needs met, what would you do with your time?

_____

_____

_____

13. Apart from working in the sense of holding a job, what do you see as the primary source of satisfaction or meaning in your life?

_____

_____

_____

14. Think of what you wanted to be when you were a child. There is often a pressure applied when well-meaning friends and relatives ask "What do you want to be when you grow up?" or "What are you studying to be?" Write down your thoughts concerning the degree to which you might *now* be choosing a vocation that you decided upon earlier without critically examining your motivations for continuing with that decision. How appropriate are some of your earlier decisions *now*?

_____

_____

_____

_____

_____

_____

Retirement

Retirement from a job can be traumatic for many people. How can people who have relied largely upon their jobs for meaning or structure in their lives deal with their retirement? Must they lose their sense of self-worth when they are forced to retire? Can they find a sense of purpose and value apart from their occupations?

Personally, I worry about retirement. I have an uneasy feeling about what I'd do with my life if I weren't working, and I fear I'd be lost without my jobs. Thus, the prospect of retirement can be one real disadvantage of making our jobs a major source of our identities as persons.

I remember talking to a woman who was close to 65 and who was feeling abandoned because she was being forced to retire as a junior high school teacher. She loved interacting with the students, and her principal made it clear that she was still a fine teacher and that the children continued to benefit from her. Deeply saddened by what she described as "being put out to pasture," she gradually assumed a hopeless stance and became depressed. Of course, she did have some choice in regard to her response to this situation; instead of remaining depressed, she could have gone on to search for other ways to give of herself, perhaps through some form of volunteer work. The difficulty she had in envisioning any other possibilities for herself illustrates how difficult retirement can be for people who have had meaningful and fulfilling careers. Still, it was unquestionably sad that, because of the school district's policy, her age alone deprived her of the chance to do what she loved doing. As a result, both she and the children were cheated by her forced retirement.

Of course, there are people who initiate retirement for themselves and continue to find meaning in their lives by involving themselves in substitute activities. Lester is an example of this kind of person. Although Lester is formally retired, he says that he continues to work by doing household repairs and remodeling, because he "couldn't stand to do nothing." Although the income he derives from this work is small, he takes satisfaction in the feeling of being needed.

Lester originally had managed a resort before changing jobs during his middle years. Although he had found the work at the resort exciting, he had decided to quit because of his disenchantment with the commercial aspects of the job. He had then taken the risk of accepting a job as chief maintenance man at a hospital. As it turned out, he had liked that job immensely. Lester is an example of a person who chose to make a couple of major job changes before his retirement, which perhaps made it easier for him to refuse to be idle once he did retire. Now he actively creates jobs that not only help people but at the same time give him a sense of being a productive member of the community.

The question of retirement is inseparable from the typical issues and conflicts of later life that were discussed in the last chapter. Like adolescents, older people may experience difficulty in feeling that they are contributing something valuable to society. Unlike adolescents, however, they have had the opportunity to prepare for this time in their lives. What happens to us when we retire depends to a great extent on how well we've resolved the conflicts and issues of the previous stages in our lives. I think it's very unfortunate that so many of us live for the future, deluding ourselves into thinking that we will find what we want, or be able to do what we've always wanted to do, once we retire. We may find that, if we haven't achieved a sense of creativity, identity, and purpose in our earlier years, we'll feel a sense of inadequacy, emptiness, and confusion once retirement arrives. If we haven't defined for ourselves during our years on the job the place work has in our lives and the meaning we find away from the job, we'll be poorly equipped to deal with the questions of meaning and purpose in later life.

In thinking ahead to our own retirement, we can make use of the distinction mentioned earlier in this chapter between a job and a "work." As adults, we can, if we choose, find a sense of identity and purpose in activities other than those we're paid to perform. We can decide during our working lives on the extent to which we identify ourselves and our work with our jobs. If we're alive to these issues during our young and middle adulthood, we'll be in a much better position to handle the experience of retirement.

Very often we're advised to prepare for retirement in a material sense by saving money, investing, and enrolling in some sort of retirement plan. No doubt this is good advice, but it's equally necessary to think of preparing ourselves for retirement in a spiritual or emotional sense. Probably the best way to do that is to work at being aware of the role our jobs play in our lives and the extent to which we find our sense of meaning in them. If we keep in mind the distinction between a job and a work, we may agree with Strom (1978) when he says that, whether a person never holds a job or retires at age 60, "nothing framed by a period shorter than a lifetime can be termed a person's work" (p. 236).

Time Out for Personal Reflection

1. How do you react to the idea of mandatory retirement upon attainment of a certain age (say, 65)? At this time in your life, do you think you'd want to continue working when you reach "retirement age"?

   _____

   _____

   _____

2. Imagine yourself as a retired person now. What are some of the things you expect to do with a typical day or week? How will you make use of your leisure time? Do you want to continue some type of part-time employment? If so, what?

   _____

   _____

   _____

   _____

3. What can you do during your working life to anticipate and prepare for the retirement stage of your life?

   _____

   _____

   _____

   _____

4. Do you know any retired persons? If so, do you think they are leading happy lives? In what ways have they found or failed to find fulfillment in this stage of life?

   _____

   _____

   _____

   _____

What are your present attitudes about retirement? Check each statement with which you find yourself more in agreement than disagreement.

_____ People shouldn't be forced to retire against their wills.

_____ Most people are lost without work.

_____ We need to be educated to make the optimum use of leisure time.

_____ Most people look forward to their retirement.

_____ I believe in saving money during the earlier stages of life so that I'll be secure after I retire.

_____ I see myself as preparing emotionally for the time when I'll retire.

_____ I see myself as preparing financially for the time when I'll retire.

_____ When I retire, I'd like to travel to various parts of the world and experience different ways of life.

_____ I expect retirement to be a lonely and frustrating experience more than a creative and meaningful one.

Chapter Summary

In this chapter, I've stressed that our jobs are important in part because our level of job satisfaction often carries over into the other areas of our lives. I've also stressed that, although work can be an important source of meaning in our lives, it is not the job itself that provides this meaning. The satisfaction we derive from our jobs depends to a great extent on the way in which we relate to our jobs, the manner in which we do them, and the meaning that we ourselves attribute to them. If we find ourselves in occupations that we don't like, and if our opportunities for changing jobs are limited, we still retain the capacity to choose our own attitudes toward our circumstances. Often this realization is a powerful factor that can lead to change.

Perhaps the most important idea in this chapter is that we must look to ourselves if we're dissatisfied with our work. It's easy to blame circumstances outside of ourselves when we feel a lack of purpose and meaning. Even if our circumstances are difficult, this kind of stance only victimizes us and keeps us helpless. We can increase our power to change our circumstances by accepting that we are the ones responsible for making our lives and our work meaningful, instead of expecting our jobs to bring meaning to us.

Now write down some of the ideas you found especially significant in this chapter.

_____

_____

_____

_____

_____

_____

Activities and Exercises

1. Interview a person you know who dislikes his or her career or occupation. You might ask questions such as the following:

   - If you don't find your job satisfying, why do you stay in it?
   - Do you feel that you have much of a choice about whether you'll stay with the job or take a new one?
   - What aspects of your job bother you the most?
   - How does your attitude toward your job affect the other areas of your life?

2. Interview a person you know who feels fulfilled and excited by his or her work. Some questions you might ask are:

   - What does your work do for you? What meaning does your work have for the other aspects of your life?
   - What are the main satisfactions for you in your work?
   - How do you think you would be affected if you could no longer pursue your career?

3. You might interview your parents and determine what meaning their work has for them. How satisfied are they with the work aspects of their lives? How much choice do they feel they have in selecting their work? In what ways do they think the other aspects of their lives are affected by their attitudes toward work? After you've talked with them, determine how your attitudes and beliefs about work have been influenced by your parents. Are you pursuing a career that your parents can understand and respect? Is their reaction to your career choice important to you? Are your attitudes and values concerning work like or unlike those of your parents?

4. If your college has a vocational-counseling program available to you, consider talking with a counselor about your vocational plans. You might want to explore taking a battery of vocational-interest and aptitude tests. If you're in the process of deciding upon a career, consider discussing how realistic your vocational plans are. For example, you can pursue such issues as:

- What are your interests?
- Do your interests match the career you're thinking about pursuing?
- Do you have the knowledge you need to make a career choice?
- Do you have the aptitude and skills for the career you have in mind?
- What are the future possibilities for you in the work you're considering?

5. Here is another suggestion for an interview. If you're presently considering a particular occupation or career, seek out a person who is actively engaged in that type of work and arrange for a time to talk with him or her. Ask personal questions concerning the chances of gaining employment, the experience necessary, the satisfactions and drawbacks of the position, and so on. In this way, you can make the process of deciding on a type of work more realistic and perhaps avoid disappointment if your expectations don't match the way things are in reality.

Suggested Readings

Dunnette, M. D. (Ed.). *Work and Nonwork in the Year 2001.* Monterey, Calif.: Brooks/Cole, 1973. A collection of readings on the future of work in the years ahead, the book includes discussions of work from historical, intercultural, and institutional perspectives.

Frankl, V. *The Doctor and the Soul.* New York: Bantam, 1965. This book has an excellent section on the relationship of work to the meaning of life.

Frankl, V. *Man's Search for Meaning.* New York: Washington Square Press, 1963. (Pocket Books edition, 1975.) In this book, Frankl develops the idea that we are always free to decide on our attitudes toward any set of circumstances—a freedom that has applications to the ways in which we relate to our jobs.

Pirsig, R. *Zen and the Art of Motorcycle Maintenance.* New York: Bantam, 1976. Finding meaning and value in an increasingly technological culture and taking pride in our work are among the themes of this book. Pirsig also has some thoughts about the "gumption traps" that can sap our energy and block our creativity.

Rubin, L. *Worlds of Pain: Life in the Working-Class Family.* New York: Basic Books, 1976. In this sensitive book, the author captures the experience of working-class persons in their work, their marriages, and their leisure time. Her chapters on work and its meaning and the quality of leisure are excellent. She shows how work influences many other important aspects of life.

Strom, R. *Growing Together: Parent and Child Development.* Monterey, Calif.: Brooks/Cole, 1978. Strom's chapter on "Educating for Leisure" discusses the distinction between jobs and work and argues that, although not everyone must have a job, everyone should have work. He also discusses the constructive use of leisure time and has a chapter on "The Future of Grandparents" that is of interest in connection with the problems surrounding retirement.

Terkel, S. *Working*. New York: Avon, 1975. This magnificent book gives penetrating views of what work means to many people in our society, how they deal with feelings of helplessness and meaninglessness, and how their jobs influence the rest of their lives.

Toffler, A. *Future Shock*. New York: Bantam, 1971. This book deals with the rapid rate of change that our society is undergoing and with the effects this accelerated change has on us. "Future shock" has many implications for the world of work.

Chapter 6

Love

We have the choice of deciding whether or not we're willing to gamble that love is worth the risk and to love even though we're afraid.

Pre-Chapter Self-Inventory

For each statement, indicate the response that most closely identifies your beliefs and attitudes. Use this code: A = I strongly agree; B = I slightly agree; C = I slightly disagree; D = I strongly disagree.

_____ 1. Love demands exclusivity. Loving more than one person of the opposite sex diminishes our capacity to be deeply involved with another person.

_____ 2. Genuine love is unconditional, which means fully accepting the other person, without demanding that he or she become something different.

_____ 3. My ability to love others stems from (and is limited to) my love for myself. Unless I love myself, I cannot love others.

_____ 4. It is abnormal to fear losing others' love.

_____ 5. If I experience hurt or frustration in love, the chances are that I won't continue to risk loving.

_____ 6. If I genuinely love another, I'll make myself known and transparent to that person.

_____ 7. Women are more capable than men of achieving intensity and depth in loving relationships.

_____ 8. Our society makes it extremely difficult to express loving feelings toward members of the same sex.

_____ 9. Commitment is essential to authentic loving.

_____ 10. If I sometimes experience indifference toward those I say I love, then I can hardly say I love them.

_____ 11. Most people are at least as afraid of being accepted as they are of being rejected.

_____ 12. Children who don't feel loved by their parents probably won't be able to accept or give love later in life.

_____ 13. I have to take some risks if I'm to open myself to loving.

_____ 14. Jealousy is one sign of love.

_____ 15. True love implies selflessness, in the sense of putting the other person's needs above my own.

_____ 16. In a loving relationship, there is complete trust and a total absence of fear.

_____ 17. Love means simply accepting another person, without challenging him or her to change in any way.

_____ 18. The presence of love in a relationship means that there is continuous excitement and joy with each other.

_____ 19. My ability to experience and express negative feelings (hate, anger, hostility, and so on) toward another is a sign that love does exist between us.

_____ 20. Love implies constant closeness and intimacy.

Introduction

In this chapter, I invite you to look carefully at your style of loving by examining your choices and decisions concerning your ability to give and receive love. Often I hear people claim either that they have love in their lives or that they don't. I make the assumption that the issue is not as clear-cut as this and that we all have the capacity to become better lovers. We can look at the situations that we put ourselves in and that we create for ourselves and then consider how conducive these are to the sharing of love. We can also look at our attitudes toward love. Some of the questions we can examine are: Is love active or passive? Do we fall in and out of love? How much are we responsible for creating a climate in which we can love others and receive love from them? Do we have romantic and unrealistic ideals of what love should be? If so, how can we challenge them? In what ways does love change as we change?

As you read this chapter, I hope that you'll try to apply the issues I discuss to your own experience of love and that you'll consider the degree to which you're now able to appreciate and love yourself. I also hope that you'll review your own need for love as well as your fears of loving and that you may come to recognize whether there are barriers within yourself that prevent you from experiencing the level of love you're capable of.

Our Need to Love and to Be Loved

I believe that, in order to fully develop as persons and to enjoy a rich existence, we need to care about others and have them return this care to us. To me, a loveless life is characterized by a joyless isolation and alienation. Our need for love includes the need to know that, at least in one person's world, our existence makes a difference. If we exclude ourselves from physical and emotional closeness with others, we pay the price of experiencing emotional deprivation.

In my professional work as a counseling psychologist, I've observed that people express their need to love and to be loved in many ways, a few of which are revealed in the following statements:

- "I need to have someone in my life that I can actively care for. I need to let that person know that he makes a difference in my life, and I need to know that I make a difference in his life."
- "I want to feel loved and accepted for who I am now, not for what the other person thinks I should be in order to be worthy of acceptance."
- "Although I enjoy my own company, I also have a need for people in my life. I want to reach out to certain people, and I hope they'll want something from me."
- "It's true that loving and being loved is frightening, but I'd rather open myself up and risk what loving entails than close myself off from this experience."

- "I'm finding out that I'm a person who does need others and that I have more of a capacity to give something to others than I thought I had."
- "I'm beginning to realize that I need to learn how to love myself more fully, for up until now I've limited myself by discounting my worth. I want to learn how to appreciate myself and accept myself in spite of my imperfections. Then maybe I'll be able to really believe that others can love me."
- "There are times when I want to share my joys, my dreams, my anxieties and uncertainties with another person, and at these times I want to feel heard and understood."

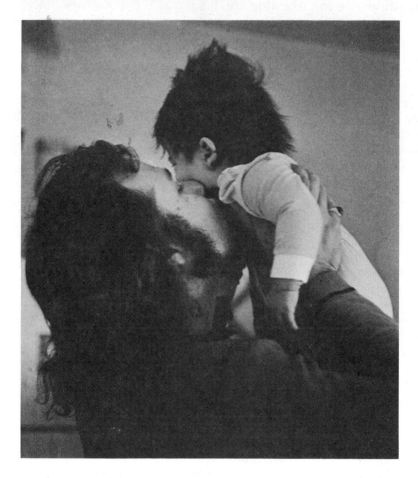

Of course, there are many ways to harden ourselves so that we won't experience a need for love. We can close ourselves off from needing anything from anybody; we can isolate ourselves by never reaching out to another; we can refuse to trust others and to make ourselves vulnerable; we can cling to an early decision that we are basically unlovable. It's important to recognize, however, that *we* make these decisions about love—and *we* pay the price.

Still another way of protecting ourselves is pointed out by Hodge (1967) in *Your Fear of Love.* Hodge maintains that there are two alternatives to being fully open to love. One alternative is to cut ourselves off completely from the experience of love by not allowing anyone to make a difference in our lives. The second alternative is to love with caution by remaining reserved and guarded; in this way, we don't disclose much of ourselves to anyone and thus attempt to protect ourselves from our need for love without cutting ourselves off from love entirely. In whatever way we deaden ourselves to our own need for love, the question is: Is the safety we achieve worth the price we pay for it?

Barriers to Loving and Being Loved

Self-Doubt and Lack of Self-Love

Despite our need for love, we often put barriers in the way of our attempts to give and to receive love. One common obstacle consists of the messages we sometimes send to others concerning ourselves. If we enter relationships convinced that nobody could possibly love us, we will give this message to others in many subtle ways. We thus create a self-fulfilling prophecy, whereby we make the very thing we fear come true because we tell both ourselves and others that life can be no other way.

If you are convinced that you're unlovable, your conviction probably is related to decisions you made about yourself during your childhood or adolescent years. At one time you may have decided that you wouldn't be loved *unless* you did certain expected things, lived up to another's design for your life, and so forth. For example, one such decision is: "Unless I produce, I won't be loved. To be loved, I must produce good grades, become successful, and make the most of my life." Such a decision can make it difficult to convince yourself later on in life that you can be loved even if you're not productive or whatever it is you've decided you have to be in order to be loved.

In my own life, I'm getting a clearer picture of the fears I have concerning others' love for me. During the closing session of a workshop group I was leading, someone exclaimed "Let me love you!" I think the person was telling me that I hold back and don't fully trust another's love for me—that I put up barriers that prevent another person from loving me fully. I'm also aware that I sometimes suffer doubts about the degree of my childrens' or my wife's love for me, yet at the same time I do things that make it harder for them to do so—such as misinterpreting their actions as signs that they don't love me! I'm often afraid of being left out or dismissed, and it's generally very difficult for me to allow myself to feel my hurt at such times.

I know I have other doubts about my lovableness as well. For instance, on one level I *believe* I'm respected by many people for what I *do*; I believe that many of my students, clients, and colleagues do think highly of me. Yet, at times I've wondered: Would I receive this caring if I didn't teach? What would another person find attractive about me if I didn't write books or conduct groups, or otherwise produce through my work? Even though I believe that there is more to me than what I produce, on some emotional level I often feel that *I* would not be lovable if it weren't for my productivity. In fact, many people have told me that my compulsive energy and drive actually put distance between them and myself and that my activities often get in the way of intimacy. In this way, the very thing I feel I *must* do to be loved actually gets in the way of others' loving me.

My point here is not just that we sometimes imagine that *other people* have expectations we must meet in order to be loved, for we often obstruct our ability to love and receive love by *our own* unwillingness to accept what we actually are, as opposed to what we think we should be. For instance, I think it's essential for me to remember that I experience difficulty in feeling worthy apart from my productivity. It's not always easy for me to acknowledge this difficulty to myself, and I have a tendency to distort or overlook it. I can easily convince myself that I *should* have worked this issue out by now, that I really should be beyond this limitation and should think and feel differently. However, my only hope for changing this early decision about my self-worth is to recognize how I actually feel, think, and behave. Once I accept some of my self-limiting attitudes as part of me, I can actively be alert for manifestations of them, and I can challenge their validity.

Thus, a real limitation on our ability to love is the degree to which we are unable to love and appreciate ourselves. I find over and over that, as we begin to learn to appreciate ourselves, we have some basis for actively loving others and accepting their love. A major stumbling block for many people is that they refuse to look at themselves, focusing instead on what they can do to "give" to others. I believe that we can give the most when we recognize our own worth and our own limitations. However, I also want to stress that early decisions about ourselves aren't easy to erase. In many subtle ways, they continue to manifest themselves. Consequently, we must continually challenge the validity of our assumptions and be alert for the obstacles we put in the way of our loving and being loved.

Learning to love and appreciate ourselves. Some people are reluctant to speak of their own self-love, because they have been brought up to think that self-love is purely egocentric. Yet, unless we learn how to love ourselves, we'll encounter difficulties in loving others and in allowing them to express their love for us. We can't very well give to others what we don't possess ourselves; consequently, if we have a low level of self-esteem, or if we're caught in a cycle of self-hate, it's unlikely that we'll be able to genuinely like, prize, value, or care for anyone else. If I can't appreciate my own worth as a person, how can I believe others when they say that they see value in me?

Having love for ourselves doesn't imply having an exaggerated picture of our own importance or placing ourselves above others or at the center of the universe. Rather, having self-love implies having respect for ourselves, even though we're imperfect. It entails caring about our lives and striving to become the persons we are capable of becoming. Once we can respect, appreciate, and care for ourselves, we open up the possibility of respecting, appreciating, and caring for others.

Many writers have stressed the necessity of self-love as a condition of love for others. In *The Art of Loving*, Erich Fromm (1956) describes self-love as a respect for our own integrity and uniqueness, and he claims that it cannot be separated from love and understanding of others. In his beautiful book, *Love*, Buscaglia (1972) claims that to love others we must first love ourselves, for we cannot give what we haven't ourselves learned and experienced. Buscaglia described the loving of oneself as "the discovery of the true wonder of you; not only the present you, but the many possibilities of you" (p. 99).

The question of how we can learn to love ourselves is raised by Marshall Hodge (1967) in his excellent and moving book, *Your Fear of Love*. According to Hodge, we can begin by realizing that it's impossible to become completely self-accepting. Then we can enjoy the fascinating experience of moving in the direction of learning to love and appreciate ourselves, which is a lifelong adventure.

As we grow to treat ourselves with increasing respect and regard, we increase our ability to fully accept the love that others might want to give us; at the same time, we have the foundation for genuinely loving others. I agree with Hodge when he says "Love of one's self is not antagonistic to having satisfying relationships. On the contrary, we are free to love others only as we become free to love ourselves" (p. 221).[1] Mayeroff (1971) agrees, saying in *On Caring*, "If I am unable to care for myself, I am unable to care for another person" (p. 49).[2] To care for ourselves, Mayeroff adds, we need to be responsive to our own needs for growth; we also need to feel at one with ourselves rather than estranged from ourselves. Furthermore, caring for ourselves and caring for others are mutually dependent: "I can only fulfill myself by serving someone or something apart from myself, and if I am unable to care for anyone or anything separate from me, I am unable to care for myself" (p. 48).

---

[1]This and all other quotations from this source from *Your Fear of Love*, by M. Hodge. Copyright 1967 by Doubleday & Company, Inc. Reprinted by permission.

[2]This and all other quotations from this source from *On Caring*, by M. Mayeroff. Copyright © 1971 by Harper & Row, Publishers, Inc. Reprinted by permission of the publishers, Perennial Library.

There are other barriers to love besides a lack of self-love. Despite our need for love, we often fear loving and being loved. Our fear can lead us to seal off our need to experience love, and it can dull our capacity to care about others. Love doesn't come with guarantees; we can't be sure that another person will always love us, and we do lose loved ones. As Hodge (1967) insists, we can't eliminate the possibility that we will be hurt if we choose to love. Our loved ones may die or be injured or become painfully ill; they may simply be mistrustful of our caring. In Hodge's words, "These are painful experiences, and we cannot avoid them if we choose to love. It is part of the human dilemma that love always includes the element of hurt" (p. 266).

We can choose not to accept the risk of loving and thus protect ourselves from being hurt, but, if we do, we pay the price of excluding love from our lives. Loving demands courage, for there are always risks involved. We have the choice of deciding whether or not we're willing to gamble that love is worth the risk and to love even though we're afraid. I like the way Hodge expresses it:

> If we postponed the experience and expression of love until we no longer feared it, we would postpone it forever. Some people do appear to use their fear of love as a perpetual excuse for stalemated living—loving and trembling seem to go together. If we desire love we must learn to love in spite of our fears [pp. 267–268].

There are some common fears of risking in love that I often hear in my work with people. Most of these fears are related to rejection, loss, the failure of love to be reciprocated, and uncomfortableness with intensity. Some of them might be expressed as follows:

- "Since I once got badly hurt in a love relationship, I'm not willing to take the chance of trusting again."
- "I fear allowing myself to love others because of the possibility that they will be seriously injured, contract a terminal illness, or die. I don't want to let them matter that much; that way, if I lose them, it won't hurt as much as if they really mattered."
- "My fear is that love will never be as good as I imagine it to be—that my ideal notions will never be matched in reality."
- "I'm afraid of loving others because they might want more from me than I'm willing to give, and I might feel suffocated."
- "I'm afraid that I'm basically unlovable and that, when you really get to know me, you'll want little to do with me."
- "My fear is that I'm loved not for who I am but for the functions that I perform and the roles that I serve. If I ceased doing these things, I would no longer be loved. It's hard for me to imagine that I'm loved simply for myself."
- "Emotional closeness is scary for me, because, if I care deeply for a person, and I permit her to care about me, then I'm vulnerable."

- "One great fear is that people in my world will be indifferent to me—that they simply won't give a damn about my existence."
- "Often I really don't like myself much of the time, and, if I can't appreciate myself, then how can I expect anyone else to love me?"
- "In many ways it's easier for me to take rejection than acceptance. It's hard for me to accept compliments or to be close and intimate. If people tell me that they want something with me, I feel I've taken on a burden, and I'm afraid of letting them down."
- "I've never really allowed myself to look at whether I'm lovable. My fear is that I will search deep within me and find little for another to love. What will I do if I discover that I'm grotesque, or hollow and empty, or incapable of giving or receiving?"

Time Out for Personal Reflection

1. Who are some of the people who have made the most difference in your life, and in what ways were they important?

   a. _____

   b. _____

   c. _____

   d. _____

   e. _____

2. Who are some of the people you've been significant for, and in what ways?

   a. _____

   b. _____

   c. _____

   d. _____

   e. _____

3. How do you express your love to others? Check the responses that apply to you, and add any other ways in which you show love, affection, and caring.

   _____ a. by telling the other person that I love him or her
   _____ b. through touching and other nonverbal means
   _____ c. by doing special things for the person
   _____ d. by making myself known to the person
   _____ e. by becoming vulnerable and trusting
   _____ f. by buying the person gifts

g. _____

_____

_____

_____

_____

4. How do you express to another person your own need to receive love, affection, and caring?

_____ a. by telling him or her that I need to be loved
_____ b. by being open and trusting

c. _____

_____

_____

5. List some specific fears that you have concerning loving others.

_____

_____

_____

_____

6. List some specific fears you have concerning allowing others to love you.

_____

_____

_____

_____

7. Mention some barriers within yourself that prevent you from fully loving others. (Examples: extreme selfishness, lack of caring, fear of vulnerability, fear of being responsible for another.)

_____

_____

_____

_____

8. Mention some barriers within yourself that prevent others from loving you or that prevent you from fully receiving their love. (Exam-

ples: being overly suspicious, refusing to accept others' love, feeling a lack of self-worth, needing to return their love.)

_____

_____

_____

_____

9. List some qualities you have that you deem lovable. (Examples: my ability to care for others, my sense of humor.)

_____

_____

_____

_____

10. List some specific ways in which you might become a more lovable person. (Examples: increasing my feelings of self-worth, trusting others more, taking better care of my physical appearance.)

_____

_____

_____

_____

11. What did you learn about yourself from these exercises? Are there ways in which you're willing to change? If so, how might you go about it?

_____

_____

_____

_____

_____

_____

Authentic and Inauthentic Love

Stifling "Love"

It isn't always easy to distinguish between authentic love, which enhances us and those we love, and the kind of "love" that diminishes ourselves and those to whom we attempt to give it. Certainly, there are forms of pseudo-love that parade as real love but that have the effect of crippling not only ourselves but those we say we love. Later in this section, I describe my view of genuine love; here, I want to list some signs of what I consider inauthentic love. This list isn't rigid or definitive, but it may give you some ideas you can use in thinking about the quality of your love.

I believe my love is inauthentic when:

- I have an inordinate need to control the other person.
- I cannot allow my loved ones the freedom to decide for themselves but in many ways dictate how they should be in order to be loved by me.
- There are threats attached to my loving.
- I really don't trust the other person or let the other person trust me.
- I refuse to allow the other person to grow and change, because I fear that I won't know how to respond to his or her new self.
- I treat the loved one like a possession.
- I expect or demand that the other person do for me things I'm unwilling to do for myself.
- My expectations are unrealistic.
- I expect the other person to fill my emptiness, while I avoid doing much about filling myself.
- I refuse to make any type of commitment, keeping myself free but at the same time keeping the other person uncertain about my intentions.
- I won't share my thoughts, my feelings, and my soul with the other person.
- I expect the other person to be an open book to me, while I remain closed.

I'm quite sure that all of us can find some of these manifestations of inauthentic love occurring in our relationships, and I don't think that means our love is necessarily phony. For instance, at times any of us might be reluctant to let another person into our private lives, or have excessive expectations, or attempt to impose our agendas upon others "for their own good." What is essential is to be honest with ourselves and to recognize when we are doing things that are not expressions of genuine love, for then we can change these patterns. It is far more dangerous and destructive to refuse to see these attitudes and behaviors and to be unwilling to consider that *at times* our love may be stifling instead of liberating for ourselves and for those we love.

Myths and Misconceptions about Love

There are many myths and misconceptions about love that frequently inhibit our ability to love fully and to receive love from others. In my judgment, some of the more common beliefs that need to be challenged are the following.

The myth of eternal love. I believe that the notion that love will endure forever is nonsense. This idea can deceive us into feeling a sense of security that simply has no basis in reality. There are no guarantees that our love (or another's love for us) will last a lifetime. That would be true only if we never changed. On the contrary, I think that the intensity and the degree of our love changes as we change. We may experience stages of love with one person, deepening our love and finding new levels of richness; there is also the chance that each of us will grow in different directions or outgrow the love we once shared.

The myth that love is fleeting. On the opposite end of the spectrum is the notion that love is strictly temporary and fleeting. I am thinking of one person who found himself to be in love with different women as often as his moods changed. One day he would claim that he loved Sara and wanted to be committed to her in an exclusive relationship, but in a short while he would grow tired of Sara and find himself in love with Peggy and would maintain that he wanted an intense and exclusive relationship with her. For him, love was strictly a here-and-now feeling that lasted only as long as his mood, and he was not really willing to stay in a relationship with any one person for very long. I don't believe that such changeable feelings constitute real love. In most intense, long-term relationships, there are times when the alliance is characterized by deadness, frustration, strife, or conflict. There inevitably are times when we feel "stuck" with a person, and at such times we may consider dissolving the relationship. If our attitude is "I'll stay while things are rosy, but as soon as things get stormy or dull, I'll split and look elsewhere for something more interesting," then it's worth asking what kind of love it is that crumbles with the first crisis. For me, authentic love means recognizing when we're stuck in an unsatisfying place but being willing to challenge the reasons for the deadness and caring enough about the other person to stay and work on breaking through the impasse.

The myth that love implies constant closeness. I feel strongly that most of us can tolerate only so much closeness and that the other side of this need is our desire for distance. I am fond of Kahlil Gibran's words in *The Prophet:* "And stand together yet not too near together: For the pillars of the temple stand apart, and the oak tree and the cypress grow not in each other's shadow."[3]

There are times when a separation from our loved ones can be very healthy. At these times we can renew our need for the other person and also allow ourselves to become centered again. If we fail to separate ourselves from others when we feel the need to do so, we'll surely strain the relationship. I'm thinking now of a man who refused to spend a weekend without his wife and children, even though he said he wanted some time for himself. The myth of constant closeness and constant togetherness in love prevented him from taking private time just for himself. It might also have been that the myth covered up certain fears. What if he discovered that his wife and children managed very well without him? What if he found that he couldn't stand his own company for a few days and that the reason for "togetherness" was to keep him from boring himself?

The myth that we fall in and out of love. A common notion is that we "fall" in love—that we passively wait for the right person to come along and sweep us off our feet. According to this view, love is something that happens *to* us. In contrast, I see love as being *active,* as something we ourselves create. *We* make love happen.

Numerous writers have discussed this concept of love as an activity. Mayeroff (1971) asserts that patience is an important part of loving, for it enables others to grow in their own way and at their own pace. He adds "Patience is not waiting passively for something to happen, but is a kind of participation with the other in which we give fully of ourselves" (p. 17). In *Let Me Live!,* Lyon (1975) writes that love is a *verb* that implies *acts* of loving. Active lovers, he says, are *greedy* in the sense that they want much from life and from love. "To achieve this goal they are willing to gamble. As gamblers, they are ready to play for high stakes by committing themselves first and fully" (p. 80). To Lyon, the "one basic fact of life" is that, in the long run, we get from life and love what we deserve:

> If you choose to fall in love, you will fall—or be pushed—out of love. If you live as an alien, yours will be a life of alienation. If you passively

---

[3]This and all other quotations from this source reprinted from *The Prophet,* by Kahlil Gibran, with permission of the publisher, Alfred A. Knopf, Inc. Copyright 1923 by Kahlil Gibran; renewal copyright 1951 by Administrators C.T.A. of Kahlil Gibran Estate, and Mary G. Gibran.

wait for love to happen to you, you will wait an eternity. But should you reach, grab, seek, act, risk—then you will find that there *is* life after birth [p. 81].

Buscaglia (1972) also criticizes the phrase "to fall in love." He contends that it's more accurate to say we *grow* in love, which implies an activity of choosing: "Love is active, not passive. It is continually engaged in the process of opening new doors and windows so that fresh ideas and questions can be admitted" (p. 69). For Buscaglia, love is like a "continual feast to be nourished upon. It sets an appetizing, attractive, gourmet table, but it cannot force anyone to eat. It allows each the freedom to select and reject according to his taste" (p. 69). In *The Art of Loving*, Erich Fromm (1956) also describes love as an active agent: "Love is an activity, not a passive affect; it is a 'standing in,' not a 'falling for.' In the most general way, the active character of love can be described by stating that love is primarily *giving*, not receiving" (p. 22).[4]

In summary, active love is something that we can choose to share with others. We don't lose love by sharing it but rather increase it. This thought leads me to the next myth.

The myth of the exclusiveness of love. We sometimes think of love as a limited quantity that we must carefully dole out and conserve. In *Love Today*, Herbert Otto (1973) counters this idea with the statement "Deep within some core of our being, most of us recognize that although we are led to believe we have only so much love to offer, *the more love we give, the more we have to give*" (p. 273). Similarly, we may believe that we are capable of loving only one other person—that there is one right person for each of us and that our fate is to find this singular soul. However, I believe that one of the signs of genuine love is that it is expansive rather than exclusive. By opening myself to loving others, I open myself to loving one person more deeply. The need to restrict love to just one person seems irrationally based on our need to feel that we are irreplaceable.

In some senses, though, we may choose to make our love exclusive or special. For example, two people may choose not to have sexual relationships with others, because they realize that doing so might interfere with their capacity to freely open up and trust each other. Nevertheless, their sexual exclusivity does not have to mean that they cannot genuinely love others as well.

Some Meanings of Authentic Love

So far, I've discussed mostly what I think love is *not*. Now I'd like to share some of the positive meanings love has for me.

---

[4]This and all other quotations from this source from *The Art of Loving*, by E. Fromm. Copyright © 1956 by Harper & Row, Publishers, Inc. Reprinted by permission of the publishers.

• Love means that I *know* the person I love. I'm aware of the many facets of the other person—not just the beautiful side, but also the limitations, inconsistencies, and flaws. I have an awareness of the other's feelings and thoughts, and I experience something of the core of that person. I can penetrate social masks and roles and see the other person on a deeper level.

• Love means that I *care* about the welfare of the person I love. To the extent that it is genuine, my caring is not a smothering of the person or a possessive clinging. On the contrary, my caring liberates both of us. If I care about you, I'm concerned about your growth, and I hope you will become all that you can become. Consequently, I don't put up roadblocks to your personal growth, even though it may result in my discomfort at times.

• Love means having *respect* for the *dignity* of the person I love. If I love you, I can see you as a separate person, with your own values and thoughts and feelings, and I do not insist that you surrender your identity and conform to an image of what I expect you to be for me. I can allow and encourage you to stand alone and to be who you are, and I avoid treating you as an object or using you primarily to gratify my own needs.

• Love means having a *responsibility* toward the person I love. If I love you, I'm responsive to most of your major needs as a person. This responsibility does not entail my doing for you what you are capable of doing for yourself; nor does it mean that I run your life for you. It *does* imply acknowledging that what I am and what I do affects you, so that I am directly involved in your happiness and your misery. A lover does have the capacity to hurt or neglect the loved one, and in this sense I see that love entails an acceptance of some responsibility for the impact of my way of being on you.

• Love means *growth* for both myself and the person I love. If I love you, I am growing as a result of my love. You are a stimulant for me to become more fully what I might become, and my loving enhances your being as well. We each grow as a result of caring and being cared for; we each share in an enriching experience that does not detract from our being.

• Love means making a *commitment* to the person I love. This commitment does not entail surrendering our total selves to each other; nor does it imply that the relationship is necessarily permanent. It does entail a willingness to stay with each other in times of pain, uncertainty, struggle, and despair, as well as in times of calm and enjoyment.

• Love means a *sharing with* and an *experiencing with* the person I love. My love for you implies that I want to spend time with you, share meaningful aspects of your life with you, and experience with you what is meaningful in your life.

• Love means *trusting* the person I love. If I love you, I trust that you will accept my caring and my love and that you won't deliberately hurt me. I trust that you will find me lovable and that you won't abandon me; I trust the reciprocal nature of our love. If we trust each other, we are willing to be open to each other and can shed masks and pretenses and reveal our true selves.

• Love means that I am *vulnerable*. If I open myself up to you in trust, then I am also vulnerable to experiencing hurt and rejection and loss. Since you aren't perfect, you have the capacity to hurt me; and, since there are no guarantees in love, there is no real security that your love will last forever.

• Love is *freeing*. Love is freely given, not doled out on demand. At the same time, my love for you is not contingent upon whether you fulfill my expectations of you. Authentic love does not imply "I'll love you when you become perfect or when you become what I expect you to become." Nevertheless, love is not *unconditional*. Although genuine love is not based on whether we live up to each other's expectations, this does not imply that I will be loved and accepted regardless of what I do or who I become. I can destroy or lessen your love for me, just as I can work to enhance it.

• Love is *expansive*. If I love you, I encourage you to reach out and develop other relationships. Although our love for each other and our commitment to each other might preclude certain actions on our parts, we are not totally and exclusively wedded to each other. It is a pseudo-love that cements one person to another in such a way that he or she is not given room to grow.

• Love means having a *want* for the person I love, without having a *need* for that person in order to be a separate identity. If I am nothing without you, then I'm not really free to love you. If I love you, and you leave, I'll experience a loss, and I'll be sad and lonely, but I'll still be able to survive. If I am overly dependent on you for my meaning and my survival, then I am not free to challenge our relationship; nor am I free to challenge and confront you. Because of my fear of losing you, I'll settle for less than I want, and this settling will surely lead to feelings of resentment.

• Love means *identifying* with the person I love. If I love you, I can empathize with you and see the world through your eyes. I can identify with you because I'm able to see myself in you and you in me. This closeness does not imply a continual "togetherness," for distance and separation are sometimes essential in a loving relationship. Distance can intensify a loving bond, and it can help us rediscover ourselves, so that we are able to meet each other in a new way.

• Love is *selfish*. It is a myth that love ought to be selfless, in the sense that, if I love you, I should forget myself and lose myself in you. I can only love you if I genuinely love, value, appreciate, and respect myself. If I am empty, then all I can give you is my emptiness. If I feel that I'm complete and worthwhile in myself, then I'm able to give to you out of my fullness. One of the best ways for me to give you love is by fully enjoying myself with you.

• Love can tolerate *imperfection*. In a love relationship, there are times of boredom, times when I may feel like giving up, times of real strain, and times I experience an impasse. Authentic love does not imply perpetual and ongoing happiness. However, because I can remember what we have had together in the past, I can stay during rough times, by envisioning what we can have together in our future if we care enough to face our problems and work them through.

I would like to conclude this discussion of the meanings authentic love has for me by sharing a few thoughts from Fromm's *The Art of Loving* (1956). I'm fond of Fromm's description of mature love, which for me sums up the essential characteristics of authentic love:

> Mature love is union under the condition of preserving one's integrity, one's individuality. Love is an active power in man; a power which breaks through the walls which separate man from his fellow men, which unites him with others; love makes him overcome the sense of isolation and separateness, yet it permits him to be himself, to retain his integrity. In love this paradox occurs that two beings become one and yet remain two [pp. 20–21].

Is It Worth It to Love?

Often I hear people say something like "Sure I need to love and to be loved, but is it *really* worth it?" Underlying this question is a series of other questions: Can I survive without love? Is the risk of rejection and loss worth taking? Are the rewards of opening myself up as great as the risks?

It would be comforting to know an absolute answer to these questions, but I fear that each of us must struggle to decide for ourselves whether it's worth it to love. It seems to me that our first task is to decide whether we prefer isolation to intimacy. Of course, our choice is not between extreme isolation and constant intimacy; surely there are degrees of both. But we do need to decide whether to experiment with extending our narrow worlds to include significant others. We can increasingly open ourselves to another and discover for ourselves what that is like for us; alternatively, we can decide that people are basically unreliable or not worth the risk and that it's better to be safe and go hungry emotionally. We can also decide how far we choose to trust and how important loving and being loved will be in our lives.

Suppose now that you feel unable to love or to give love, and thus feel isolated, but that you'd like to learn how to become more intimate. You might begin by acknowledging this reality to yourself, as well as to those in your life with whom you'd like to become more intimate. In this way, you can take some significant beginning steps.

In answering the question of whether it's worth it to you to love, you can also challenge some of your attitudes and beliefs concerning acceptance and rejection. I've encountered many people who believe that it isn't worth it to love because of the possibility of experiencing rejection. If you feel this way, you can decide whether to stop at this barrier. You can ask yourself "What's so catastrophic about being rejected? Will I die if someone I love leaves me? Can I survive the emotional hurt that comes with disappointment in love?"

Hodge (1967) claims that, as adults, we're no longer helpless and that we can do something about rejection and hurt. We can choose to leave relationships that aren't satisfying; we can learn to survive hurt, even though it may be painful; and we can realize that being rejected by a person doesn't mean that we are fundamentally unlovable. I very much like the last line in Hodge's *Your Fear of Love*, and I ask you to consider how it may apply to you: "We can discover for ourselves that it is worth the risk to love, even though we tremble and even though we know we will sometimes experience the hurt we fear" (p. 270).

Time Out for Personal Reflection

1. Below are some possible reasons for thinking that it is or isn't worth it to love. Check the ones that fit your own thoughts and feelings.

It's worth it to love, because

_____ of the joy involved when two people love each other.

_____ the rewards are greater than the risks.

_____ a life without love is empty.

It isn't worth it to love, because

_____ of the pain involved when love is not returned.

_____ the risks are not worth the possible rewards.

_____ it's better to be alone than with someone you might no longer love (or who might no longer love you).

List other reasons: List other reasons:

_____   _____

_____   _____

_____   _____

_____   _____

_____   _____

2. What is *your* answer to the question of whether it's worth it to love?

_____

_____

_____

_____

3. Review my list of the meanings love has for me, and then list some of the meanings love has for *you*.

_____

_____

_____

_____

_____

4. What are some questions you have regarding the ideas discussed so far in this chapter? Which ones would you most like to hear the others in your class respond to?

_____

_____

_____

_____

_____

Love and Sexuality

The next chapter is about sexuality. Although I treat the issues of love, sex, and intimacy in different chapters, these topics cannot really be completely separated. I've discussed love first simply to provide the basis for my discussions of sexuality and intimacy. So I hope you'll keep in mind this chapter's issues as you read the next two and that you'll try to make some connections by integrating the ideas of the three chapters and by applying them to yourself. The following exercises should help get you started.

Time Out for Personal Reflection

A Personal Inventory on Love and Sexuality

After you've worked through the following questions and indicated the responses that actually apply to you now, you might want to take the inventory again and give the responses that indicate how you'd like to be. Feel free to circle more than one response for a given item or to write your own response on the blank line. You may want to take the inventory again at the end of the course to see whether, or to what degree, any of your beliefs, attitudes, and values concerning love and sexuality have changed.

1. As far as my need for love is concerned,
   a. I can give love, but it's difficult for me to receive love.
   b. I can accept love, but it's difficult for me to give love.
   c. Neither giving nor accepting love is especially difficult for me.
   d. Both giving and accepting love are difficult for me.

   e. _____

2. I feel that I have been loved by another person:
   a. only once in my life.
   b. never in my life.
   c. many times in my life.
   d. as often as I've chosen to open up to another.

   e. _____

3. When it comes to self-love and appreciation of myself,
   a. I have a healthy regard and respect for myself.
   b. I find the idea of self-love objectionable.
   c. I encounter great difficulty in appreciating myself.
   d. I'm generally able to love myself, but there are parts of myself that I dislike.

   e. _____

4. I love others because:
   a. I want their love and acceptance in return.

b. I fear being alone if I don't.
c. I like the feeling of loving another.
d. I derive joy from giving to another person.

e. _____

5. To me, love is best described as:
   a. giving to another out of my fullness as a person.
   b. thinking more of the other person than I do of myself.
   c. relating to another in the hopes that I'll not feel so empty.
   d. caring for another to the same degree that I care about myself.

   e. _____

6. My greatest fear of loving and being loved is:
   a. that I will have nothing to give another person.
   b. that I will be vulnerable and may be rejected.
   c. that I might be accepted and then not know what to do with this acceptance.
   d. that I will feel tied down and that my freedom will be restricted.

   e. _____

7. In regard to commitment in a loving relationship, I believe that:
   a. without commitment there is no real love.
   b. commitment means I love that person exclusively.
   c. commitment means that I stay with the person in times of crisis and attempt to change things.
   d. commitment is not necessary for love.

   e. _____

8. For me, the relationship between love and sex is that:
   a. love often develops *after* a sexual relationship.
   b. sex without love is unsatisfying.
   c. the two must always be present in an intimate relationship with another person of the opposite sex.
   d. sex can be very exciting and gratifying without a love relationship.

   e. _____

9. I could become more lovable by:
   a. becoming more sensitive to the other person.
   b. learning to love and care for myself more than I do now.
   c. doing what I think others expect of me.
   d. being more genuinely myself, without roles and pretenses.

   e. _____

10. If I loved a person who did not love me in return, I would:
    a. never trust another love relationship.
    b. feel devastated.
    c. convince myself that I really didn't care.
    d. feel hurt but eventually open myself to others.

    e. _____

11. In love relationships, generally I:
    a. settle for what I have with the other person as long as things are comfortable.
    b. constantly seek to improve the relationship.
    c. am willing to talk openly about things I don't like in myself and in the other person.
    d. am able to express positive feelings but unable to express negative feelings.

    e. _____

12. When it comes to talking about sexuality,
    a. I encounter difficulty, especially with my partner.
    b. I feel free in discussing sexual issues openly.
    c. I usually become defensive.
    d. I'm willing to reveal my feelings if I trust the other person.

    e. _____

13. My attitudes and values toward sexuality have been influenced principally by:
    a. my parents.
    b. my friends and peers.
    c. my church.
    d. my school experiences.

    e. _____

14. I think that social norms and expectations:
    a. encourage the dichotomy between male and female roles.
    b. impose heavy performance standards on men.
    c. make it very difficult to develop one's own ideas about what constitutes normal sexuality.
    d. clash with my own upbringing.

    e. _____

15. I think that sexual attitudes could be improved by:
    a. giving children more information while they are growing up.
    b. teaching principles of religion.

c. increasing people's knowledge about the physical and emotional aspects of sexuality.
d. allowing people to freely discuss their sexual values and conflicts in small groups.

e. _____

Here are a few suggestions of things you can do after you've finished this inventory:

1. You can use any of the items that strike you as points of departure for your journal writing.
2. If you're presently involved in an intimate relationship, you can ask the other person to take the inventory and then share and compare your responses. Your responses can be used as a basis for dialogue on these important issues.
3. You might write down other questions that occurred to you as you took this inventory, and you can bring these questions to class.
4. Your class can form small groups in which to discuss the items that had the most meaning for each person. In this way, you could get the perspective of others in your class.

A Sentence-Completion Exercise on Love and Sex

Complete the following sentences by quickly writing down your immediate response.

1. My greatest fear of love is _____.

2. To me, love without sex is _____.

3. To me, love with sex is _____.

4. To me, sex without love is _____.

5. I need love because _____.

6. I feel most loved when _____.

7. One lovable quality about me is _____.

8. I could increase my ability to love others by _____

_____.

9. I express my love for others primarily by _____.

10. To me, love means primarily _____.

11. If nobody loved me, _____.

12. For me, the greatest risk in loving others is _____.

13. For me, the greatest risk in letting others love me is _____

_____.

14. When I'm with those I love, I _____

_____.

15. When I'm separated from my loved ones, I _____

_____.

Chapter Summary

This chapter has explored some basic issues related to our ability to give and to receive love, including our need for love, our fear of love, barriers to loving and being loved, whether it's worth it to love, early decisions about our own ability to love and to be loved, authentic versus inauthentic love, myths about love, and meanings of authentic love. A few key points to remember are:

1. Loving others and receiving love from them does entail some risk. There are no guarantees in loving.
2. Unless we love ourselves, we cannot really love others. Our ability to care for others is based largely on our ability to care for ourselves.
3. We must each decide for ourselves whether it's worth it to love.
4. By recognizing our attitudes about loving, we can increase our ability to choose the ways in which we behave in our love relationships.

Now list some of the ideas that seemed most significant to you or that you'd most like to remember.

_____

_____

_____

_____

_____

_____

Activities and Exercises

1. Mention some early decisions that you made regarding your own ability to love or to be loved, such as:

   • "I'm not lovable unless I produce."
   • "I'm not lovable unless I meet others' expectations."
   • "I won't love another because of my fears of rejection."
   • "I'm not worthy of being loved."

Write down some of the messages that you've received and perhaps accepted uncritically. How has your ability to feel loved or to give love been restricted by these messages and decisions?

2. Ask several people to give their responses to the question "Is it worth it to love?" Bring these responses to class, and share them with others.

3. For a period of at least a week, pay close attention to the messages conveyed by the media concerning love. What picture of love do you get from television? What do popular songs portray about love? Make a list of some common myths regarding love that you see promoted by the media. Some of these myths might include:

- Love means that two people never argue or disagree.
- Love implies giving up one's identity.
- Love implies constant closeness and romance.
- Love means rarely having negative feelings toward those you love.

4. How much do you agree with the proposition that you can't fully love others unless you first love yourself? How does this apply to you? In your journal, you might want to write some notes to yourself concerning the situations in which you don't appreciate yourself. You might also keep a record of the times and events when you do value and respect yourself.

5. How important is love in your life right now? Do you feel that you love others in the ways you'd like to? Do you feel that you're loved by others in the ways you want to be?

6. Are you an active lover or a passive lover? You might try writing down the ways in which you demonstrate your caring for those you love and then ask them to read your list and discuss with you how they see your style of loving.

Suggested Readings

Buscaglia, L. *Love.* Thorofare, N.J.: Charles B. Slack, 1972. This is a very personal and beautiful book of random thoughts on the meanings of love.

Coutts, R. *Love and Intimacy: A Psychological Approach.* San Ramon, Calif.: Consensus, 1973. A very readable and personal book that deals mostly with how to recognize and how to overcome unrealistic social inhibitions or personal problems that interfere with living and with intimate relationships. Coutts believes that, if love and intimacy needs are satisfied, sexual intimacy will follow.

Fromm, E. *The Art of Loving.* New York: Harper & Row (Colophon), 1956; paperback edition, 1974. Love in all its aspects is the subject of this book. Fromm presents a philosophy of love in a book that can be read several times for new insights.

Gibran, K. *The Prophet.* New York: Knopf, 1923. A rich, poetic treatment of many facets of life, including love, marriage, giving, work, freedom, children, death, friendship, self-knowledge, and so on.

Hodge, M. *Your Fear of Love.* Garden City, N.Y.: Doubleday, 1967. This is a very useful and easy-to-read book that describes how fears originate and how they can prevent us from loving. Hodge gives a personal and down-to-earth treatment of topics such as freedom, anger, sex, manhood and womanhood. He also explores the concept of living to be ourselves, which includes learning to love ourselves and to live spontaneously.

Jourard, S. *The Transparent Self: Self-Disclosure and Well-Being* (2nd ed.). New York: D. Van Nostrand, 1971. Jourard contends that we have many ways of concealing our real selves and that we use masks and roles to keep from being open. He makes a case for the value of being transparent in human relationships. The book includes some excellent essays on love, sex, marriage, and the lethal aspects of male roles.

Lyon, W. *Let Me Live!* (Rev. ed.). North Quincy, Mass.: Christopher, 1975. The author's chapter on love makes a case for learning how to be an active lover. Lyon also deals with other topics, such as sex, masculinity, femininity, and marriage, in an interesting and provocative manner.

May, R. *Love and Will.* New York: Norton, 1969; Dell, 1974. Presenting much insightful material on the core problems of the contemporary person, May discusses paradoxes of love and sex, sex without love, love and death, the relationship of love and will, and the meaning of caring.

Mayeroff, M. *On Caring.* New York: Harper & Row, 1971. This is a sensitive book on the philosophy of caring as a dimension of loving. Mayeroff discusses how caring can give meaning to life and help both oneself and the other person to grow.

Otto, H. (Ed.). *Love Today.* New York: Dell (Delta): 1973. A book of articles on various aspects of love that gives a good overview of issues related to intimacy, creativity, sharing, and all forms of love.

Chapter 7

Sex Roles and Sexuality

I would like to think that we can become more integrated persons who can live with polarities within ourselves and welcome the range and depth of our feelings. My hope is that we will each have the courage to be open to all of our own inner promptings and to decide from within ourselves the qualities we value.

Pre-Chapter Self-Inventory

For each statement, indicate the response that most closely identifies your beliefs and attitudes. Use this code: A = I strongly agree; B = I slightly agree; C = I slightly disagree; D = I strongly disagree.

_____ 1. Men are by nature more sexually aggressive than women and enjoy sex more than women do.

_____ 2. Sex-role definitions and stereotypes get in the way of mutually satisfying sexual relations.

_____ 3. Concern over sexual performance is quite common.

_____ 4. Psychologically healthy people don't experience any guilt over their sexual activities.

_____ 5. If a woman doesn't experience orgasm, it is generally because the man has not been sensitive enough to her needs.

_____ 6. If a man experiences impotence, it is generally because of the woman's lack of appreciation of his manhood.

_____ 7. In a sexual relationship, it is the job of each partner to make the other feel like a woman or a man.

_____ 8. Getting in touch with our sexual attractions and feelings toward others generally leads to overt sexual behavior.

_____ 9. The quality of a sexual relationship is usually parallel to the quality of the partners' relationship in general.

_____ 10. Sexual freedom implies doing whatever consenting adults agree to.

_____ 11. If we want to, we can reeducate ourselves so that we can experience sexual relationships with numerous partners without feeling guilty.

_____ 12. Sexual freedom ought to be counterbalanced by sexual responsibility.

_____ 13. We will probably be no more sexually attractive to others than we are to ourselves.

_____ 14. Discussing sexual wants and needs generally leads to mechanical and unspontaneous sex.

_____ 15. Extramarital sex inevitably causes dissatisfaction in the marital relationship.

_____ 16. Today's generation is really unconcerned about being sexually inadequate.

_____ 17. Most people who are intimate with each other find it relatively easy to talk openly and honestly about the intimate details of sexuality.

_____ 18. The key to improving sexual satisfaction is to master sexual techniques and skills.

_____ 19. Sex without love is unsatisfying.

_____ 20. Most people today rarely experience guilt or shame over sexuality.

Introduction

In this chapter, I encourage you to think critically about sex-role stereotypes and to form your own standards of what it means to be a woman or a man. Since most of us have been exposed to many years of powerful conditioning concerning what a man or a woman should be, it may be difficult to quickly change some of our ingrained attitudes. Nevertheless, we can make a good beginning toward freeing ourselves from limiting roles if we're willing to question our attitudes and if we're truly interested in expanding our consciousness about men and women as persons.

Another goal of this chapter is to introduce the idea of learning how to recognize and openly express our sexual concerns. Too many people suffer from needless guilt, shame, worries, and inhibition, merely because they keep their concerns about sexuality secret, largely out of embarrassment. Moreover, keeping their concerns to themselves can hinder their efforts to determine their own values regarding sex. In this chapter, I ask you to examine your values and attitudes toward sexuality and to determine what kinds of choices *you* want to make in this area of your life.

The Man in Hiding

The All-American Male

I believe that many men in our society live restricted and deadening lives because they have bought some cultural myths of what it means to be a male. Unfortunately, too many men are caught in rigid roles and expect sanctions when they deviate from what is supposedly "manly." In this way they become so involved in the many roles they play that they eventually become strangers to themselves. They no longer know what they are like inside, because they put so much energy into maintaining an acceptable male facade.

What is the stereotype of the all-American male, and what aspects of themselves do many males feel they must hide in order to conform to it? In general, the stereotypic male is cool, detached, objective, rational, and strong. A man who attempts to fit himself to the stereotype will suppress most of his feelings, for he sees the subjective world of feelings as being essentially feminine. Goldberg (1976), Jourard (1971), Deaux (1976), Pleck and Sawyer (1974), and others have discussed these issues and identified characteristics that a man living by the stereotype may attempt to suppress or deny. Among these characteristics are:

- *Dependence.* Rather than admit that he needs anything from anyone, he may live a life of exaggerated independence. He feels he should be able to do by himself whatever needs to be done, and he finds it hard to reach out to others.
- *Passivity.* He feels he must be continually active, aggressive, assertive, and striving. He views the opposites of these traits as signs of weakness, and he fears being seen as weak.
- *Fears.* He won't express his fears, and most likely he won't even allow *himself* to experience them. He has the distorted notion that to be afraid means that he lacks courage, so he hides his fears from himself and from others.
- *His inner self.* He doesn't disclose himself to women, because he is afraid that they will see him as unmanly if they see his inner core. He keeps himself hidden from other men because they are competitors, and, in this sense, potential enemies.
- *Vulnerability.* He cannot make himself vulnerable, as is evidenced by his general unwillingness to disclose much of his inner experiences. He won't let himself feel and express sadness; nor will he cry. To protect himself, he becomes emotionally insulated and puts on a mask of toughness, competence, and decisiveness. He finds it difficult to express warmth and tenderness.
- *Bodily self-awareness.* He doesn't recognize bodily cues that may signal danger. He drives himself unmercifully and views his body as some kind of machine that won't break down or wear out. He may not pay attention to his exhaustion until he collapses from it.
- *Closeness with other men.* Although he may have plenty of acquaintances, he doesn't have very many male friends he can confide in.
- *Failure.* He hides from failure, and he must at all times put on the facade of the successful man. He feels he's expected to succeed and produce, to be "the best," to get ahead and stay ahead. He has to win, which means that someone else has to lose.
- *"Feminine" qualities.* Because he plays a rigid male role, he doesn't see how he can still be a man and at the same time possess (or reveal) traits that are usually attributed to women. Therefore, he is very controlled, shutting out much of what he could experience and leading an impoverished life as a result.
- *A need for or enjoyment of physical contact.* He has a difficult time touching freely. He thinks that he should touch a woman only if it will lead to sex and he fears touching other men because he doesn't want to be perceived as a homosexual.

The Price Men Pay for Remaining in Hiding

What price must a man pay for denying most of his inner self and putting on a false front? First, he loses a sense of himself because of his concern with being the way he thinks he should be as a male. Writing on the "lethal aspects of the male role," Sidney Jourard (1971) contends that men typically find it difficult to love and be loved. They won't reveal themselves enough to be loved. They hide their loneliness, anxiety, and hunger for affection, thus making it difficult for anyone to love them as they really are.

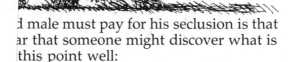

d male must pay for his seclusion is that
ar that someone might discover what is
this point well:

oment, reveal his true self in its nakedness,
of weakness and vulnerability. Naturally,
erritory, he must be continually alert, tense,
s implies that trying to seem manly is a kind
s stress and consumes energy. Manliness,
t a chronic burden of stress and energy ex-
factor related to man's relatively shorter life

e Hazards of Being Male, Goldberg (1976)
tend to die at an earlier age than women
ascular problems more than women do,
girls in school, that men are involved in
d that the suicide rate is higher for males
kes the point that all the statistics that
g male actually constitute a description of the
crises faced by males in our society. He contends that "the male has
become an artist in the creation of many hidden ways of killing himself"
(p. 189) and calls for a "revolution" in male consciousness.[1]

The Emerging Woman and Changing Sex Roles

Like men, women in our society have suffered from a sexual
stereotype. Typically, women have been perceived as weak, fragile, un-

---

[1]From *The Hazards of Being Male,* by H. Goldberg. Copyright 1976 by Nash Publishing
Company. Reprinted by permission.

ambitious, helpless, unintelligent, designed by nature for the role of homemaker and mother, unassertive, noncompetitive, and unadventurous. This rigid viewpoint is in the process of changing as many women actively fight the stereotype of the passive, dependent female.

In comparing the male and female stereotypes, Kay Deaux (1976) notes that the stereotypic woman *is* accorded some redeeming traits. According to Deaux, a cluster of positive traits are usually seen as more characteristic of women than of men:

> These traits generally reflect warmth and expressiveness. Women are described as tactful, gentle, aware of the feelings of others, and able to express tender feelings easily. Men, in contrast, are viewed as blunt, rough, unaware of the feelings of others, and unable to express their own feelings [pp. 13–14].

Nevertheless, Deaux adds, men are generally perceived as having more positive traits than women, and in our society such "male" values as competence and success are more highly prized than the supposedly female qualities of warmth and expressiveness.

How are these sexual stereotypes formed? Deaux cites evidence that boys and girls are conditioned early in life to accept predetermined sex roles. She indicates, for example, that boys are often seen as curious, active, and independent, while girls are seen as lacking in curiosity, having little initiative, and needing help from boys. Not long ago the ones who solved problems and went to work in children's readers were the men, while the women were typically shown in the kitchen. Deaux also cites a study showing how television and magazines influence children to accept sex-role stereotypes. Men usually appear in advertisements and commercials when figures who suggest authority are needed; by contrast, women are usually the principal figures when commercials deal with the use of household products. In summary, Deaux makes the point that "parents and other socializing agents convey certain expectations to their children as to what grown-up men and women are like. These impressions may form the basis of stereotypes that are found much later in life" (Deaux, 1976, p. 20).

Are these stereotypes changing? According to Deaux, if children have good models in the home, and if they see changes in male and female images in the media, the stereotypes may well change in the future, but for now "we must conclude that stereotypes are still alive and doing reasonably well in our culture" (p. 21).

Women in Revolt

Despite the staying power of sexual stereotypes, increasing numbers of women are rejecting limited views of what a woman is expected to be. Women are discovering that they can indeed have many of the traits traditionally attributed to them yet at the same time take a new view of themselves. In particular, many women are in revolt against the pressures put on them to find their satisfactions exclusively or primarily in marriage and the raising of a family. Contending that "earth mother is dead," Goldberg (1976) claims that contemporary women are showing their true identities. They are no longer willing to collude with men in fostering the image of themselves as weak, helpless, and designed primarily to take care of men's needs and the needs of their children.

Goldberg views this assertiveness on the part of women as liberating not only for themselves but for men as well, because it frees men from the need to live up to the macho male image. When both men and women are free of restrictive roles and thus free to be the persons they *could* be, they can develop authentic relationships with one another based on their individual strengths instead of on a game in which one must be weak so that the other can be strong. In Goldberg's words, "When she is she in her genuine, total, strong femaleness and personhood and he is he in his maleness and personhood, they can begin to revel in the realities and joys of an authentic, interdependent, and genuinely fulfilling interaction" (Goldberg, 1976, p. 32).

Although I like the ideal picture of men and women participating as full and independent persons in relationships, I do see a trend that disturbs me. Many women seem so caught up in their revolt against traditional expectations that they have difficulty accepting any of the qualities traditionally attributed to them, regardless of whether the qualities are positive ones that they may in fact possess as individuals. For example, a woman might be embarrassed to admit that she does derive fulfillment from being a homemaker and a mother, even if that happens to be true of her. In short, by going to the extreme of denying any traits that might traditionally be associated with the female stereotype, some women run the risk of losing the independent sense of themselves that they are trying to achieve. I question the degree of freedom achieved by a movement if we allow it to dictate our standards. Although a movement can and should raise our level of consciousness, it seems critically important that each of us choose what we want for ourselves. After all, that's what being liberated really means.

An Increase of Options and Choices

Women today are faced with more options than women in past decades were faced with, but this increase in options brings with it an increase in anxiety. Well-defined roles may be restrictive, but they can also be secure, and many contemporary women experience difficulty when they look inward and attempt to decide what they want. Moreover, many of these women actually feel uncomfortable with choices that will lead to success. They have been conditioned for so long *not* to experience success in the outside world that they have a real fear of succeeding. Deaux (1976) describes research suggesting that, even though women may have a need to achieve, they may also have a motive to *avoid* achieving too much. They have learned to expect negative social consequences if they do succeed. Deaux indicates that the percentage of women who fear success does not appear to be decreasing greatly.

Certainly, to maximize her options, a woman needs to be alert to the danger of keeping herself locked into old roles and denying her talents. She must avoid the pitfall of blaming the dissatisfaction she feels on circumstances outside herself. At the same time, she can recognize that stepping out of old roles can be frightening, and she can try to become aware of what her fears and anxieties are. Just as she can question the traditional female stereotype, she can also question the myth that a successful and independent woman doesn't need anyone and can make it entirely on her own. This trap is very much like the trap that many males fall into and may even represent an assimilation of traditionally male values. Hopefully, a woman can learn that she can achieve independence, exhibit strength, and succeed, while at times being dependent and in need of nurturing. Real strength allows either a woman or a man to be needy and to ask for nurturing without feeling personally inadequate.

The situation in which many women are finding themselves is well illustrated by the following letter, written by a woman in her early forties and used with her permission. It expresses her awareness that she has been what Goldberg calls an "earth mother" to her family and her realization that her confinement to this role has stunted not only her emotional growth but also the well-being of her family. Now she is asserting her need to achieve an identity as a person in more ways than as a wife and a mother. In becoming aware of her options and choices, she has become able to declare that she will pay attention to her own needs as well as to the needs of her family.

Dear John:

It strikes me as humorous that you are getting a "Dear John" letter from your mother. I am tired of playing the role of "mother" and I want to try my wings. When you come home I feel frustrated and trapped back into a role that I am trying to shed. I am determined to be a different person. I no longer am challenged by my role as mother. I've done the best I can, and I am proud of what I have accomplished. But you are all leaving the nest, and I must find and develop other parts of myself so that I can continue to function as a happy, healthy human being.

The battle to change how other people see me is a hard one. My own family is the most resistant to my change. Sometimes I am merely annoyed by their resistance, but other times I feel like a gopher trapped in a hole just waiting for the poison to come and render him helpless. I don't want to be dominated by the family needs. I want to be free to develop the new me. I feel unused potential stirring inside of me, battling to get out, to be expressed. As long as I am the servant keeping everything nice and neat for the rest of you, picking up after you, doing things you don't want to do, I don't have time to develop my own potential.

I can really be SOMEBODY in this world. I am worth more than a chief cook and bottle washer. And I am determined to be much, much more than that. If the rest of you won't allow me to change, then I shall have to dump you. I don't want these anchors dragging me down. I have challenged you to be more than mediocre—to self-actualize yourself. I have willingly sacrificed for you, but now it is my turn. Any help I give you now is destructive to both you and me. To you by not encouraging you to stand on your own two feet; to me by denying my own needs and desires.

I'm not sure exactly where I'm going, but my direction is becoming more focused. I am determined to take the time to find out the best development for me. If you come home this summer, you will have to take care of yourself and not be a burden financially, emotionally or time-wise on me. I'm not sure yet if I will be attending summer school or working or not doing either this summer. But I will be working on where I best fit in this big wide world. I need lots of time to do that. And I am not going to sacrifice myself for the rest of you.

You personally are the biggest complainer about what a lousy mother I am—I don't fill your definition of the role. Too bad! Marry a woman who will, if you can, but don't expect me to be that woman. I can't respect myself when I am that woman. . . . All my life I have been trying to fulfill other people's expectations of what I am. Now I am determined to find out what I am and what I can be. I am going to earn a good salary. I am going to be respected. I am going to be well-known in my field. I am going to think thoughts that other people don't—I already do. I see from my own perspective and put together large patterns and see how different ideas fit together in a way that other people often don't see. Somehow this has got to be useful to me and to the world. I want to find out how.

I am bursting with energy and excitement in this drive to find myself and to free myself from old conventions. I want to be what I *can* be. I am bitter that my family does not want to hear. My change forces all of you to change, and you are afraid. Afraid of the unknown. I am afraid, too. But I am more afraid of staying where I am at. Do you really want me to be a dependent person, like my mother? Or do you want me to be a happy person who can carry her own weight, like Aunt Alice?

The time for change is NOW. I can't wait. My greatest fear is that my family will gang up to pressure me into remaining as the "rescuer"—the one who does what others do not want to do. I love you all. I care about what you think of me. I am afraid I won't have the courage to stand up to all of you and the pressure you put on me. You, my family, bring me the greatest terror and the greatest joy.

Women and Sexual Liberation

Sexual liberation is a part of the liberation of women from significant traditional stereotypes. Increasingly, women are recognizing and expressing their sexual wants and desires. They are freeing themselves of the myths that their role is to be sexually passive or coy and to please their male partners while depending on them for their own achievement of orgasm. In short, they are freeing themselves to say yes when they want to say yes and no when they want to say no.

The widely read *Hite Report*, a nationwide study of female sexuality by Shere Hite (1976), contains much detailed information gathered from over 3000 women, from teenagers to women in their seventies. In this book, women discuss such matters as: what they like and don't like; the experience of orgasm, with and without intercourse; their reactions to what they like and don't like in men; the greatest pleasures and frustrations in their sex lives; the importance of clitoral stimulation; and their views of sexual liberation and sexual slavery. The book contains a wealth of information and can be read with profit by both women and men. One value of such reading is that it can help liberate both sexes from some damaging myths; in addition, it can be a catalyst for discussion between partners about sexual attitudes and practices.

Liberation For Both Women and Men

The increasing liberation of women has also stimulated to some degree the liberation of men. I want to emphasize, however, that both sexes need to remain open to each other and that both men and women need to change their attitudes if they are interested in releasing themselves from stereotyped roles. People of both sexes seem to be in a transitional period in which they are redefining themselves and ridding themselves of old stereotypes; yet too often they are needlessly fighting with each other, when they could be helping each other to recognize that they have *both* been conditioned for many years and that they need to be patient as they each learn new patterns of thought and behavior.

Many women and men want the same thing—to loosen the rigid sex-role expectations that have trapped them. Many men recognize a need to broaden their view of themselves to include capacities that have been traditionally stereotyped as feminine and that they have consequently denied in themselves. Many women are seeking to give expression to a side of themselves that has been associated with males. As men and women alike pay closer attention to attitudes that are deeply ingrained in themselves, they may find that they haven't caught up emotionally with their intellectual level of awareness. Although we might well be "liberated" intellectually and *know* what we want, many of us experience difficulty in *feeling* OK about what we want. The challenge consists in getting the two together!

Alternatives to Rigid Sex Roles

The fact that certain male and female stereotypes have been prevalent in our culture doesn't mean that all men and women in our society live within these narrow confines. Nevertheless, many people have uncritically accepted rigid definitions of their roles, while others just as uncritically reject them; and probably even liberated persons are affected by some vestiges of sexual stereotypes. Fortunately, there seems to be much questioning and challenging of traditional perspectives among many of the college students I come into contact with. For instance, it seems that more and more men are realizing that they can combine self-confidence, assertiveness, and power with tenderness, warmth, and self-expressiveness. The "macho" male doesn't seem to be admired or respected by either the men or the women I encounter on the university campus.

The alternative to living according to a stereotype is to realize that we can actively define our own standards of what we want to be like as women or as men. We don't have to blindly accept roles and expectations that have been imposed on us or remain victims of our early conditioning. We can begin to achieve autonomy in our sexual identities by looking at how we have formed our ideals and standards and who our models have been; then we can decide whether these are the standards we want to use in defining ourselves now.

One appealing alternative to rigid sex-role stereotypes is the concept of *androgyny,* or the coexistence of male and female characteristics in

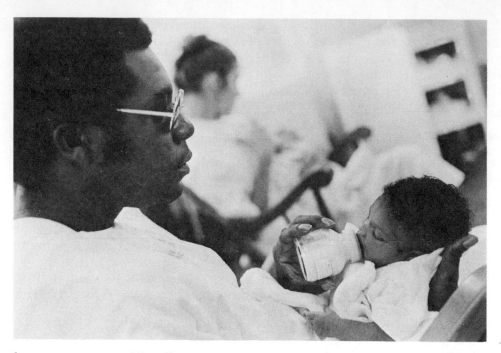

the same person. We all possess some male and female hormones, and many psychologists postulate that we also possess both feminine and masculine psychological characteristics. For example, Carl Jung developed the notions of the *animus* and the *anima*, which referred to the (usually hidden) feminine and masculine aspects within us.

Deaux (1976) cites research indicating that an androgynous person has a wider range of capabilities than a person who lives by sex-typed expectations. For example, an androgynous person can show "masculine" assertiveness or "feminine" warmth, depending on what a situation calls for. For Deaux, androgyny is a promising concept that deserves further attention. One of the central themes of her book, *The Behavior of Women and Men,* is that there are relatively few characteristics in which women and men consistently differ:

> Men and women both seem to be capable of being aggressive, helpful, and alternately cooperative and competitive. In other words, there is little evidence that the nature of women and men is so inherently different that we are justified in making stereotyped generalizations [Deaux, 1976, p. 144].

A similar theme is sounded by Goldberg (1976) in his discussion of alternatives to the stereotyped male. In his view, the free male rejects external definitions of who he "should" be in order to be a man, because he knows that living in this limited way is self-destructive. He learns to listen to his own intuition; he rejects behavior based on guilt; and he

allows himself to be a spontaneous and unpredictable person, because his behavior is not determined by external expectations and pressures. Therefore, he can be active and passive, sometimes tender and at other times tough, sometimes dependent and at other times independent. In short, the liberated male can respond to various situations with a wide range of different behaviors. I like the final lines of Goldberg's book:

> The free male will constantly reaffirm his right and need to develop and to grow, to be total and fluid, and to have no less than a state of total well-being. He will celebrate all of the many dimensions of himself, his strength and his weakness, his achievements and his failures, his sensuality, his affectionate and loyal response to women and men. He will follow his own personal growth path, making his own stops along the way, and reveling in his unique and ever-developing total personhood [Goldberg, 1976, p. 191].

In summary, what Goldberg says of the free male can also be applied to the free female. Although I don't personally favor the concept of unisex, I do believe that persons of both sexes have suffered because of stereotypes that limit the breadth of their experience and behavior. I would like to think that we can become more integrated persons who can live with polarities within ourselves and welcome the range and depth of our feelings. My hope is that we will each have the courage to be open to all of our own inner promptings and to decide from within ourselves the qualities we value.

Time Out for Personal Reflection

1. Complete each of the following sentences by giving your immediate response.

   a. What I most like about women is _____.

   b. What I least like about women is _____.

   c. What I most like about men is _____.

   d. What I least like about men is _____.

   e. One change I'd like to see in women is _____.

   f. One change I'd like to see in men is _____.

   g. I believe most women _____.

   h. I believe most men _____.

   i. The traits I most value in women are: _____

   _____

   _____.

   j. The traits I most value in men are: _____

   _____

   _____.

2. Now look over the responses you've given so far to get some impression of how favorable your assessments of men and women are. What can you say by way of summary about your views of men and of women?

   My view of men: _____

   _____

   My view of women: _____

   _____

3. The following statements may help you assess how you see yourself in relation to sex roles. Place a "T" before each statement that generally applies to you and an "F" before each one that generally doesn't apply to you. Be sure to respond *as you are now,* rather than as you'd like to be.

   _____ I'd rather be rational than emotional.
   _____ I'm more an active person than a passive person.
   _____ I'm more cooperative than I am competitive.

_____ I tend to express my feelings rather than keep them hidden.

_____ I tend to live by what is expected of my sex.

_____ I see myself as possessing both masculine and feminine characteristics.

_____ I'm afraid of deviating very much from the customary sex-role norms.

_____ I'm adventurous in most situations.

_____ I feel OK about expressing both negative and positive feelings.

_____ I'm continually striving for success.

_____ I fear success as much as I fear failure.

Now look over your responses. Which characteristics, if any, would you like to change in yourself?

_____

_____

_____

4. Do some or most of the men you know seem to live by the ideal of the "all-American" male described earlier in this chapter? If so, how do you think they are affected by this way of living? What are the consequences for women when men choose this kind of style?

_____

_____

_____

_____

5. What are some of your reactions to the changes in women's view of their sex role? What impact do you think the women's liberation movement has had upon women? Upon men?

_____

_____

_____

_____

6. What do you think of the concept of androgyny? Would you like to possess more of the qualities you associate with the opposite sex? If so, what are they? Are there any ways in which you feel limited or restricted by rigid sex-role definitions and expectations?

_____

_____

_____

_____

_____

_____

Sexuality and Personal Development

Learning to Talk Openly about Sexual Issues

One might expect that young people today would be able to discuss openly and frankly the concerns they have about sex. In my work with college students, I've not found this to be the case. True, students will discuss attitudes about sexual behavior in a general way, but they show considerable resistance to speaking of their own sexual concerns, fears, and conflicts. I've come to believe that it can be a great service simply to provide a climate in which people can feel free to examine their personal concerns. A particularly valuable technique is to give women and men an opportunity to discuss sexual issues in separate groups and then come together to share the concerns they've discovered. Typically, both men and women appreciate the chance to explore their sexual fears, expectations, secrets, and wishes, as well as their concerns about the normality of their bodies and feelings. Then, when the male and female groups come together, the participants usually find that there is much common ground shared by both sexes, and the experience of making this discovery can be very therapeutic. For instance, men may fear becoming impotent, or not performing up to some expected standard, or being lousy lovers, or not being "man enough." When the men and women meet as one group, the men may be surprised to discover that women worry about having to achieve orgasm (or several of them) every time they have sex or that they, too, have fears about their sexual desirability. When people talk about these concerns in a direct way, much game playing and putting on of false fronts can be dispensed with.

My work with therapeutic groups continues to teach me how much we need to learn how to talk with each other about sexual concerns. Many people suffer from unrealistic fears that they are alone in their feelings and concerns about their sexuality. If we could learn how to initiate open discussion of these issues, we might find that genuine sexual freedom is possible. We could shed many of the fears that needlessly hamper our joy in freely experiencing sex.

At this point, let me describe some of the most typical concerns that are openly aired by both men and women in discussion groups I've participated in. These concerns might be expressed as follows:

- "I often wonder what excites my partner and what that person would like, yet I seldom ask. I suppose that it's important for me to learn how to initiate by asking and also by telling the other person what I enjoy."
- "So often I doubt my capacity as a lover. I'd like to know what my partner thinks. Perhaps one thing that I can learn to do is to share this concern with him (her)."
- "I worry about my body. Am I normal? How do I compare with others? Am I too big? Too small? Am I proportioned properly? Do others find me attractive? Do I find myself attractive? What can I do to increase my own appeal to myself and to others?"
- "Am I responsible if my partner's dissatisfied?"
- "Sex can be fun, I suppose, but often I'm much too serious. It's really difficult for me to be playful and to let go without feeling foolish—and not just in regard to sex. It isn't easy for me to be spontaneous."
- "There are many times when I feel that my spouse is bored with sex, and that makes me wonder whether I'm sexually attractive to her (him)."
- "There are times when I desire sex and initiate it, and my husband (wife) lets me know in subtle or even direct ways that he (she) isn't interested. Then I feel almost like a beggar. This kind of experience makes me not want to initiate any more."
- "As a woman, I'd really like to know how other women feel after a sexual experience. Do they normally feel fulfilled? What prevents them from enjoying sex? How do they decide who's at fault when they don't have a positive experience?"
- "As a man, I frequently worry about performance standards, and that gets in the way of my making love freely and spontaneously. It's a burden to me to worry about doing the right things and being sexually powerful, and I often wonder what other men experience in this area."
- "There seem to be two extremes in sex: we can be overly concerned with pleasing our partners and therefore take too much responsibility for their sexual gratification, or we can become so involved with our own pleasure that we don't concern ourselves with our partners' feelings or needs. I ask myself how I can discover a balance—how I can be selfish enough to seek my own pleasure yet sensitive enough to take care of my partner's needs."
- "Sometimes I get scared of women (men), and I struggle with myself over whether or not I should let the other person know that I feel threatened. Will I be perceived as weak? Is it so terrible to be weak at times? Can I be weak and still be strong?"
- "I frequently feel guilty over my sexual feelings, but there are times when I wonder whether I really want to free myself of guilt feelings. What would happen if I were free of guilt? Would I give up all control?"
- "I worry a lot about being feminine (masculine) and all that it entails. I'm trying to separate out what I've been conditioned to believe about the way a woman (man) is supposed to be, yet I still have a hard time in deciding for myself the kind of woman (man) I want to be. I want to find my own standards and not be haunted by external standards of what I should be and feel."

- "Can sex be an attempt to overcome my feelings of isolation and separation? There are times when I think I'm running into a sexual relationship because I feel lonely."
- "I've wondered whether or not we are by nature monogamous. I know I'd like to experience others sexually, but I surely don't want my mate to have these same experiences."
- "There are times lately when I don't seem to be enjoying sex much. In the past year, I haven't been able to experience orgasm, and the man that I'm living with thinks it's his fault. What's happening? Why am I not as sexually responsive as I used to be with him?"
- "I feel very open and trusting in talking about my sexuality in this group, and I'd very much like to experience this with my partner. I want to be able to be direct and avoid getting involved in sexual games. I need to learn how to initiate this kind of open dialogue."
- "There are times when I really don't crave intercourse but would still like to be held and touched and caressed. I wish my partner could understand this about me and not take it as a personal rejection when for some reason I simply don't want intercourse."
- "I really felt humiliated when I became impotent—I was sure she saw me as unmanly. I'm glad to learn that this is a common experience with other men and that I'm not abnormal."

Learning to Enjoy Sensuality and Sexuality

One reoccurring problem that I've observed in my work with people is the degree to which performance standards and expectations get in the way of their experiencing of both sensual and sexual pleasure, particularly in the case of men. Often men report that they feel a need to perform "up to standard," and they burden themselves with the stress of worrying about what is expected of them. Some men are not content to be themselves but think they must be *supermen*, particularly in the area of sexual attractiveness and performance. They measure themselves by unrealistic standards and may greatly fear losing their sexual power. Instead of enjoying sexual and sensual experiences, they become orgasm oriented. They often place heavy expectations on women to climax as well, in order to reaffirm their view that they are more than sexually adequate. With this type of orientation toward sex, it is no wonder that these men fear two problems in particular: impotence and premature ejaculation.

I like the way Goldberg (1976) deals with the meaning these sexual problems often have. In a chapter entitled "The Wisdom of the Penis," Goldberg says that impotence can really be a message that a man doesn't want to have sex with this particular woman at this particular time; it doesn't necessarily mean that he has lost his power in general. Goldberg makes a strong case that men should have sex only when they are genuinely aroused and excited; otherwise, they are inviting impotence. "The penis," he writes, "is not a piece of plumbing that functions capriciously. It is an expression of the total self. In these days of overintellectualization it is perhaps the only remaining sensitive and revealing barometer of the male's true sexual feelings'' (p. 39). In similar fashion, Goldberg interprets premature ejaculation as the body's way of saying ''I really don't want to do this, but, if I must, let's get it over with as fast as possible.'' In short, if we can learn to pay attention to what our bodies are telling us, they can teach us ways of enjoying a sensual and sexual life. Much the same point is made by Jourard (1971) in writing on the delight and ecstasy that a sexual experience can bring. The body, says Jourard, doesn't lie: ''If she wants me and I don't want her, I cannot lie. My body speaks the truth. And I cannot take her unless she gives herself. Her body cannot lie'' (p. 53).

It should be added that sexual dysfunction can occur for any one of a number of reasons, including, in some cases, physical ones. However, in the majority of cases, a problem such as impotence is due to psychological factors. For example, in addition to the lack of desire to have sex with a certain person at a certain time, impotence may result from feelings of guilt, prolonged depression, anxiety about personal adequacy, or a generally low level of self-esteem. Most men for whom impotence becomes a problem might be well advised to ask ''What is my body telling me?''

Paying attention to the messages of our bodies is only a first step. We still need to learn how to express to our partners *specifically* what we like and don't like sexually. I've found that both men and women tend to keep their sexual preferences and dislikes to themselves instead of sharing them with their partners. They've accepted the misconception that their partners should know intuitively what they like and don't like, and they resist telling their partners what feels good to them out of fear that their lovemaking will become mechanical or that their partners will only be trying to please them. I'm thinking of the man who said that he felt ''very uptight'' because he considered oral sex morally wrong and thought of it as a type of perversion. He engaged in it anyway, without much enthusiasm, because he felt his wife expected it and because he thought that, if he didn't, she would be disappointed in him as a man. It would have been very important for him to have openly expressed his reluctance to her, instead of keeping it a secret.

Often, a woman will complain that she doesn't derive as much enjoyment from sexual intercourse as she might because the man either is too concerned with his own pleasure or is orgasm oriented and sees touching, holding, and caressing only as necessary duties he must perform to obtain ''the real thing.'' Thus, she may say that he rolls over in bed as soon as he is satisfied, even if she's left frustrated. Although she may require touching and considerable foreplay and afterplay, he may not recognize her needs. For this reason, she needs to express to him what it feels like to be left sexually unsatisfied, without attacking him, which only raises his defenses. Hite (1976) makes this point clearly: ''You have to care about yourself and *want* to please yourself, and you have to feel that it is your *right*. You have to do it, whatever it is—or ask for it, very clearly and very specifically'' (p. 302).

Here is an exercise that many sex therapists recommend to clients who want to increase their enjoyment of sensuality and sexuality. The first step is to devote some time to actually *talking* with your partner about what you each like, what feels good, and so on. Then, to avoid the type of goal-oriented sex that is aimed exclusively at orgasm, you might decide *not* to have sexual intercourse, while taking turns in being the receiver and the giver of sensual touching. For example, the woman might be the receiver for five or ten minutes, and during this time her only task is to ask for what she wants, to direct her partner to what feels good for her, and to enjoy the experience. Then she becomes the giver, and he asks for what he wants and gives her feedback. Although this kind of approach might sound simple, it's surprising how many couples have never tried it, and how many people have restricted the pleasure they could give to their partners and receive for themselves, merely because they didn't think it was right to ask directly for what they wanted.

Shame Related to Our Bodies

As children, and even more so as adolescents, many of us learn to associate parts of our body with shame. Small children may be oblivious to nudity and to their bodies, but, as they run around nude and are made the objects of laughter and jokes by other children and by adults, they gradually become more self-conscious about their bodies and tend to hide them. Sometimes the sense of shame remains with people into adulthood. I have talked with many people who have described the anxieties and shame they feel over their bodies and their sexuality. The following brief cases represent some typical difficulties:

- A woman painfully recalls the onset of menstruation. Since no one had really taken the time to prepare her for this event, she became mildly frantic the first time it happened. Her immediate reaction was that she was being punished for having evil thoughts.
- A man finally shares his concern over the size of his penis, which he thinks is small. His anxiety about this has caused him extreme embarrassment when he has showered with other men, and it has inhibited him in his sexual relations with women. He has been convinced that women have been silently laughing at him or have viewed him as sexually inadequate.
- A young, attractive woman relates that she walked stoop-shouldered as an adolescent, trying to conceal her large breasts. She actually felt a sense of shame over being, as she put it, so ''well built.'' Now, as an adult, she frequently feels that men are interested in her only for her physical qualities. She doubts their sincerity in finding her interesting apart from her body.

- A man is convinced that his body is dirty and his impulses vile. He is preoccupied with fears of sinning. He learned early in life to associate shame with his sexual and sensual feelings, and now this attitude prevents him from experiencing his body.

In his book *Existential Sexuality*, Koestenbaum (1974) makes the assumption that our bodies describe our life-styles; in a real sense, if we look at our bodies carefully, we will see that they contain our memories, our past decisions and choices, and our feelings about ourselves. We can see whether we're ashamed of our bodies or try to hide them by studying our bodies and being open to the messages they communicate to us. As we become aware of our bodies and of the shame, guilt, or other attitudes we associate with them, we can challenge our views and decisions and begin to alter our attitudes.

Guilt over Sexual Feelings

Most of us have learned certain taboos about sex and that certain sexual activities are unacceptable. We commonly experience guilt over our *feelings* alone, even if we don't act upon them. Guilt is commonly experienced in connection with homosexual fantasies and impulses, masturbation, feelings of sexual attraction toward members of one's family, feelings of sexual attraction toward people other than one's spouse, enjoyment of sexuality, feelings of sexual adequacy or inadequacy, and too much (or too little) desire for sex.

As is the case with shame concerning our bodies, we need to become aware of our guilt feelings and then to reexamine them to determine whether we're needlessly burdening ourselves with guilt. Even though we intensely fear our feelings, we can and should learn to accept them as legitimate. Moreover, simply having feelings doesn't mean that we're impelled to act upon them.

Not all guilt is unhealthy and irrational, of course, but there is a real value in learning to challenge guilt feelings and to rid ourselves of those that are *unrealistic*. Although we don't have to be brutal with ourselves, we can expect to feel realistic guilt when we violate our own personal ethical standards, without taking on needless guilt as well.

For many of my earlier years, I experienced a great deal of guilt concerning my sexual feelings and fantasies. I believe that my feelings of guilt were largely due to the influence of a strict religious education that took a strong stand on sexual morality. Even though I've consciously struggled to overcome some of this influence, I still experience traces of old guilt. As in so many other areas, I find that early learnings in regard to sex are difficult to unlearn. Consequently, it has been important for me to continue to challenge old guilt patterns that interfere with my sexual and sensual enjoyment, while at the same time developing a personal ethical code that I can live by with integrity and self-respect.

Many people express some very real fears as they begin to recognize and accept their sexuality. A common fear is that, if we recognize or accept our sexual feelings, our impulses will sweep us away, leaving us out of control. It's important to learn that we can accept the full range of our sexual feelings, yet decide for ourselves what we will *do* about them. For instance, I remember a man who said that he felt satisfied with his marriage and found his wife exciting but was troubled because he found other women appealing and sometimes experienced sexual desires toward them. Even though he had made a decision not to have extramarital affairs, he still experienced a high level of anxiety over simply having sexual feelings toward other women. At some level, he believed that he might be more likely to *act* on his feelings if he fully accepted that he had them. In my opinion, he was torturing himself needlessly. I saw it as important that he learn to discriminate between having sexual feelings and deciding to take certain actions and that he learn to trust his own decisions.

In making responsible, inner-directed choices of whether or not to act on sexual feelings, many people find questions such as the following to be helpful guidelines: Will my actions hurt another person or myself? Will my actions limit another person's freedom? Will my actions exploit another's rights? Are my actions consistent with my commitments? Of course, each of us must decide on our own moral guidelines, but it seems unrealistic to expect that we can or should control our feelings in the same way that we can control our actions. By controlling our actions, we define who we are; by trying to deny or banish our feelings, we only become alienated from ourselves.

Ways in Which We Use Sex

Increasing our sexual awareness can include becoming more sensitive to the ways in which we sometimes use sex as a means to some end. For instance, sexual activity can be used as a way of actually preventing the development of intimacy. It can also be a way of avoiding experiencing our aloneness, our isolation, and our feelings of distance from others. Sex can be an escape into activity, a way of avoiding inner emptiness. When sex is being used in any of these ways, it can take on a driving or compulsive quality that detracts from its spontaneity and leaves us unfulfilled. Sex used as a way of filling inner emptiness becomes a mechanical act, divorced of any passion, feeling, or caring. Then it only deepens our feelings of isolation and detachment.

It appears that the pendulum has swung from one extreme to the other. At one time, people typically invested a lot of energy in denying sex while stressing love; now, the ideal for some is to have sex without the attachment of love. As Rollo May (1969) observes, "The Victorian person sought to have love without falling into sex; the modern person seeks to have sex without falling into love" (p. 46). Yet, in my work with many college students, I find that this kind of unfeeling sex isn't what most of them are looking for. Many of those who have experienced it to any significant degree feel increasingly removed from their partners, and from themselves as well.

It might be well to reflect on how sex can be used to either enhance or diminish ourselves and our partners as persons. We can ask ourselves such questions as: Are my intimate relationships based upon a need to conquer or exert power over someone else? Or are they based on a genuine desire to become intimate, to share, to experience joy and pleasure, to both give and receive? Asking ourselves what we want in our relationships and what uses sex serves for us may also help us avoid the overemphasis on technique and performance that frequently detracts from sexual experiences. Although technique and knowledge are important, they are not ends in themselves, and overemphasizing them can cause us to become oblivious to the *persons* we have sex with. An abundance of anxiety over performance and technique can only impede sexual enjoyment and rob the experience of genuine intimacy and caring.

Time Out for Personal Reflection

1. What are your attitudes toward your own body? Take some time to study your body, and become aware of how you look to yourself and what your body feels like to you. Try standing naked in front of a full-length mirror, and reflect on some of these questions:

   - Is your body generally tight or relaxed? What parts tend to be the most unrelaxed?
   - What does your face tell you about yourself? What kind of expression do you convey through your eyes? Are there lines on your face? What parts are tight? Do you force a smile?
   - Are there any parts of your body that you feel ashamed of or try to hide? What aspects of your body would you like most to change? What are the parts of your body that you like the best? The least?

2. After you've done the exercise just described (perhaps several times over a period of a few days), record a few of your impressions below, or keep an extended account of your reactions in your journal.

   a. How do you view your body, and how do you feel about it? ____

   _____

   _____

   b. What messages do you convey to others about yourself through your body? _____

   _____

3. Do you tend to deny your sexuality? If so, in what ways? Check any statements that fit you:

_____ I'm overweight.
_____ I usually wear unattractive clothes that tend to hide my bodily features.
_____ I tend to retreat into my intellect and neglect my body.
_____ I generally don't let myself experience my sexual feelings.
_____ I don't see myself as a sexual person.

4. List some other ways in which you deny your sexuality:

_____

_____

_____

5. Are there any steps you'd like to take toward learning to accept your body and your sexuality more than you do now? If so, what are they?

_____

_____

_____

6. Do you experience guilt over sexual feelings? If so, what specific kinds of feelings give rise to guilt for you?

_____

_____

_____

7. How openly are you able to discuss sexuality in a personal way? Would you like to be more open in discussing your sexuality or sexual issues? If so, what is preventing this openness?

_____

_____

_____

_____

8. What are some personal issues relating to sex that you're willing to discuss in your class group? What are some areas that you would *not* be willing to share or explore?

_____

_____

_____

Developing Our Own Sexual Ethics and Values

During the past couple of decades, a phenomenon has occurred in our society that many people term a sexual revolution. Certainly, there has been an open questioning of society's sexual standards and practices, accompanied by the growing belief that individuals can and should decide for themselves what acceptable sexual practices are. Previously, many people did not have to struggle to decide what was moral or immoral, since they took the standards of sexual behavior from external sources. This is not to say that they were necessarily moral, even by their own standards, for they may have been more secretive about their sexual activities and may also have suffered more guilt than do many people today.

Although I believe that it's desirable for people to bring sexual issues into the open and be able to talk freely without the guilt and shame their parents may have experienced, I also believe that we need to form consistent value systems upon which to base our behavior, including our sexual behavior. The change in sexual attitudes can give us the freedom to be sexually responsible—to determine our own values and govern our own behavior.

For much of the earlier part of my life, I looked outside myself for the answers to sexual issues. Instead of struggling to find values that would be my own, I accepted the guidelines that came ready-made from my church. Although it was comfortable for me at the time, I now see this acceptance of external standards as an avoidance of my responsibility to define my own sexual ethics, as well as an avoidance of the anxiety I would have experienced in attempting to do so. Since then, I've come to recognize the importance of dealing with sexual issues in a way that has meaning for me and that I can live with.

I frequently get the impression that it isn't in vogue to talk about sexual values and ethics; many people seem to prefer to follow their spontaneous impulses without weighing the place of values in their decisions. Of course, designing a personal and meaningful set of sexual ethics is not an easy task. It can be accomplished only through a process of honest questioning. Our questioning can start with the values we presently have: what is their source? Do they fit in with our views of ourselves in other areas of our life? Which of them can we incorporate in our lives in order to live responsibly and with enjoyment? Which do we think we should reject? Achieving freedom doesn't have to mean shedding all our past learnings or values. Whether we keep or reject them in whole or in part, we can refuse to allow someone besides ourselves to make our decisions for us. It can be tempting to allow others (whether

past authorities or present acquaintances) to tell us what is right and wrong and design our lives for us, for then we don't have to wrestle with tough decisions ourselves. Whenever we yield to that temptation, however, we surrender our autonomy and run the risk of becoming alienated from ourselves.

In *Existential Sexuality*, Koestenbaum (1974) describes the journey from "sexual prison" to "sexual paradise," encouraging us never to sell out on our sexual freedom by losing sight of our own power to choose. For Koestenbaum, although sex is a natural urge, the place that sex occupies in our lives and the attitudes we have toward it are very much a matter of free choice. We are free to answer for ourselves such basic questions as: Does sex necessarily have to include love? Can we have love without sex? Are love and sex the foundations for marriage? What is the purpose of sex? Should love precede sex? Many other questions could be added to this list, depending on what issues are central for us. For Koestenbaum, the important point is that these questions cannot be answered objectively by experts or authorities. As he puts it, "Sex seen as a choice, not a need, frees us from the tyranny of 'experts'—moral and medical—returning our bodies and the life of our bodies to the rightful owner: the inwardness residing within each of us" (p. 45). I like the way he expresses the concept of sexual liberation: "It removes the strictures of guilt and opens us up to the spaciousness and grace of our lives. When you realize that the 'whether' and the 'how' of sex is your own decision, you are truly liberated" (p. 45).

Developing our own values means assuming responsibility for ourselves, which for me includes taking into consideration how others may be affected by our choices while allowing them to take responsibility for theirs. I make the assumption that, in an adult relationship, the parties involved are capable of taking personal responsibility for their own actions. Consequently, I think it's difficult to be used or manipulated unless we allow others to use or manipulate us. Generally, we cannot be exploited unless we collaborate in this activity. For example, in the case of premarital or extramarital sex, each person must weigh such questions as: Do I really want to pursue a sexual relationship with this person at this time? Is the price worth it? What are my commitments? Who else is involved, and who could be hurt? Might this be a positive or a negative experience? How does my decision fit in with my values generally?

In summary, it's no easier to achieve sexual autonomy than it is to achieve autonomy in the other areas of our lives. While challenging our values, we need to take a careful look at ways in which we could easily engage in self-deception by adjusting our behavior to whatever we might desire at the moment. We also need to pay attention to how we feel about ourselves in regard to our past sexual experience. Perhaps, in doing so, we can use our level of self-respect as one important guide to our future behavior. That is, we can each ask "Do I feel enhanced or diminished by my past experience?"

Homosexuality as an Alternative Life-Style

Homosexual relationships are becoming the avowed preference of an increasing number of people in our society. Although an in-depth discussion of this topic falls outside the scope of this book, several themes that have been running through this chapter are applicable to the topic of choosing homosexuality as a way of life.

In the past, many people felt ashamed and abnormal because of homosexual preferences, and others frequently categorized them as sexual deviates and as sick or immoral. For these and other reasons, many homosexuals were forced to conceal their preferences, perhaps even to themselves. Today, the gay-liberation movement is actively challenging the stigma attached to this alternative life-style, and those who choose it are increasingly asserting their right to live as they choose, without discrimination. Nevertheless, much of the public continues to cling to stereotypes, prejudices, and misconceptions regarding homosexual behavior.

Just as there are many reasons why people choose heterosexual relationships, so there are many reasons why others choose homosexual ones. In categorizing relationships in this way, we sometimes forget that sex is not the only aspect of a relationship, whether the relationship is between people of the same or the opposite sex. Here I would only urge the same points I've made earlier in this chapter—namely, that whatever choice we make, we need to examine what the bases of our attitudes and choices are, whether our choice is the best choice for us, and whether it is compatible with our own values. Just as I'm concerned that people might choose or reject certain sex roles because of others' expectations, so too I am concerned that people may reject a gay life-style merely because others condemn it or adopt it merely because they are unquestioningly following a liberation movement. For me, what is most important is that we define ourselves, that we assume the responsibility for our own choices, and that we feel that we can live out our choices with inner integrity.

Time Out for Personal Reflection

1. What influences have shaped your attitudes and values concerning sexuality? In the following list, indicate the importance of each factor by placing a "1" in the blank if it was very important, a "2" if it was somewhat important, and a "3" if it was unimportant. For each item that you mark with a "1" or a "2," indicate briefly the nature of that influence.

   _____ parents _____

   _____ church _____

   _____ friends _____

   _____ siblings _____

   _____ movies _____

   _____ school _____

   _____ books _____

   _____ television _____

   _____ spouse _____

   _____ grandparents _____

   _____ your own experiences _____

   Other influential factors:

   _____

   _____

2. Look over the following word list, quickly checking the words that *you* associate with sex.

   _____ fun   _____ dirty   _____ routine
   _____ ecstasy   _____ shameful   _____ closeness

_____ procreation   _____ joy   _____ release
_____ beautiful   _____ pressure   _____ sinful
_____ duty   _____ performance   _____ guilty
_____ trust   _____ experimentation _____ vulnerability

Now look over the words you've checked and see whether there are any significant patterns in your responses. What can you say by way of summary about your attitudes toward sex?

_____

_____

_____

_____

3. Try making a list of specific values you hold regarding sexual issues. As a beginning, you might respond to the following questions:

a. How do you feel about promiscuity?

_____

_____

b. What is your view of sex outside of marriage?

_____

_____

c. How do you feel about homosexuality?

_____

_____

d. Do you think it's legitimate to separate love and sex?

_____

_____

e. How do you feel about having sex with a person you don't like or respect?

_____

_____

f. List other specific values or convictions you have concerning sexual behavior.

_____

_____

4. What are your reactions to those people who choose homosexuality as an alternative life-style?

_____

_____

_____

5. How do you feel about homosexual experiences for yourself?

_____

_____

_____

6. What are your views concerning the gay-liberation movement? Do you believe that the rights of homosexuals have been denied? Do you think that people who openly profess a gay life-style have rights equal to those of heterosexuals and should not be denied a specific job because of their sexual preference alone?

_____

_____

_____

_____

_____

Chapter Summary

In this chapter, I've encouraged you to think about your attitudes and values concerning sexuality and sex roles and to take a close look at where and how you developed these attitudes and values. I've indicated that many of us tend to keep our questions and concerns about sexuality to ourselves and that many of our exaggerated fears and misconceptions can be cleared up if we learn how to discuss sexuality with others. Finally, in asking you to examine the basis of your sex-role expectations, your concept of what constitutes a woman or a man, and your views about sexual behavior, I've stressed the idea that you can decide for yourself what kind of woman or man you want to be, instead of following the expectations of others.

Now think about the key ideas that you would most like to remember, and list them below.

_____

_____

_____

_____

_____

_____

Activities and Exercises

1. Write down some of your major questions or concerns regarding sexuality. You might consider discussing these issues with: a friend, your partner (if you're presently involved in an intimate relationship), or your class group.
2. Write down the characteristics you associate with being a woman (or feminine) and being a man (or masculine). Then think about how you acquired these views and to what degree you're satisfied with them.
3. Select a book on sexuality from the reading list at the end of the chapter, and pick out some sections that you'd like to discuss with a friend or your partner. Read some of these selections together, and discuss how they apply to each of you.
4. Make a list of sex-role stereotypes that apply to men and a list of those that apply to women. Then select people of various ages, and ask them to say how much they agree or disagree with each of these stereotypes. If several people bring their results to class, you might have the basis of an interesting panel discussion.
5. For a week or two, pay close attention to the messages that you see transmitted on television, both in programs and in commercials, regarding sex roles, expectations of women and men, and sexuality. Record your impressions in your journal.
6. In your journal, trace the evolution of your sexual history. What were some important experiences for you, and what did you learn from these experiences?
7. Discuss with some friends various aspects of homosexuality as a lifestyle. What kinds of trends do you see regarding acceptance or rejection of those who choose homosexual relationships? As a starting point for your discussion, you might respond to the following words taken from Patricia Warren's novel *The Front Runner* (1974), which depicts the psychological experience of a homosexual:

> I did not pray to be miraculously changed back into a heterosexual. I prayed for knowledge to know myself, and accept myself totally. Being gay, I now realized, was not merely a question of sex—it was a state of mind. Society had told me I was a disease, but I was now convinced that I had come to homosexuality by natural inclination [p. 33].

Chapter 7

Berne, E. *Sex in Human Loving.* New York: Pocket Books, 1971. This book deals with sexual games, sex and intimacy, and sex and well-being.

Deaux, K. *The Behavior of Women and Men.* Monterey, Calif.: Brooks/Cole, 1976. A very informative work that deals with both stereotypes and self-evaluations of women and men, the book also includes an excellent treatment of the concept of androgyny.

Friedan, B. *The Feminine Mystique.* New York: Dell, 1975. Friedan argues that social change in regard to the way in which women are perceived and treated is a must, and she takes the position that women can affect society as well as be affected by it. Her contention is that both women and men have the power to choose and that in so doing they can make their own heaven or hell.

Goldberg, H. *The Hazards of Being Male.* New York: Nash, 1976. This book is an excellent treatment of the stereotypes of masculinity. The author describes the traps males have fallen into and ways of getting out of them.

Hite, S. *The Hite Report.* New York: Dell, 1976. This book gives the results of a nationwide study of female sexuality. Women of all ages give a subjective view of their feelings about all the aspects of sex, and the author discusses a cultural interpretation of female sexuality. An informative and valuable book for both women and men.

Jourard, S. *The Transparent Self* (2nd edition). New York: Van Nostrand, 1971. The book contains a series of personal articles on love, sex, marriage, the healthy personality, and the lethal aspects of the male role.

Koestenbaum, P. *Existential Sexuality: Choosing to Love.* Englewood Cliffs, N.J.: Prentice-Hall (Spectrum), 1974. A thoughtfully written book that stresses the freedom and responsibility you have to choose your kind of sex and to give meaning to sex.

May, R. *Love and Will.* New York: Norton, 1969; Dell, 1974. This is a powerful book that deals with many aspects of love: the paradoxes of love and sex, love and death, the relation of love and will, the meaning of caring, and our capacity for love.

McCarthy, B., Ryan, M., & Johnson, F. *Sexual Awareness: A Practical Approach.* San Francisco: Boyd and Fraser Publishing Co. and The Scrimshaw Press, 1975. This book emphasizes attitudes and techniques for couples who want to understand and enhance their sexual feelings and functioning. Some of the issues dealt with include: self-expression and experiencing one's sexuality, increasing arousal and sexual response, sexual expression and the concept of sex therapy. The book has exercises for each chapter.

Pengelley, E. *Sex and Human Life.* Reading, Mass.: Addison-Wesley, 1974. This is a well-written and informative book about the physiological aspects of sexuality. It contains information on sexual intercourse, sexual difficulties, sexuality and aging, variations of sexual behavior, and cultural aspects of sex.

Pleck, J., & Sawyer, J. (Eds.). *Men and Masculinity.* Englewood Cliffs, N.J.: Prentice-Hall (Spectrum), 1974. This book includes a series of articles dealing with issues in male liberation. It shows how men in consciousness-raising groups can help one another to go beyond the limits of the male stereotype. The book describes how the male stereotype is learned, how it restricts men, and how men are freeing themselves from traditional roles.

Sheehy, G. *Passages: Predictable Crises of Adult Life*. New York: Bantam, 1976. Sheehy gives some excellent case studies illustrating the struggles of men and women at all ages. She also describes the relationship problems that can arise because of changes in either the man or the woman.

Warren, P. N. *The Front Runner*. New York: Bantam, 1974. This popular novel about homosexual love describes the psychological and physical experience of a gay person and explores struggles and conflicts that many homosexuals experience.

Chapter 8

Intimate
Relationships

*Are you involved in the kinds of intimate
relationships that you want to be involved in?
How can you enhance your intimate
relationships? What is your view of a growing
relationship?*

Pre-Chapter Self-Inventory

For each statement, indicate the response that most closely identifies your beliefs and attitudes. Use this code: A = I strongly agree; B = I slightly agree; C = I slightly disagree; D = I strongly disagree.

_____ 1. An absence of conflict, disagreement, and crisis is one sign of a growing relationship.

_____ 2. It's difficult to have many intimate relationships at one time.

_____ 3. It's a good idea to explore a variety of life-styles besides the traditional type of marriage.

_____ 4. One sign of a good relationship is that both parties remain basically the same.

_____ 5. If I'm involved in a satisfactory intimate relationship, I won't feel attracted to others besides my partner.

_____ 6. Marriage should last forever if we choose the right partners.

_____ 7. If one partner in an intimate relationship expresses a need for privacy or time alone, the relationship must be unsatisfactory in some way.

_____ 8. The traditional form of marriage is obsolete and is bound to give way to alternative life-styles.

_____ 9. One mark of a successful relationship is that each person feels able to survive without the other.

_____ 10. Divorce or termination of the relationship is generally a good solution if a couple is experiencing boredom or difficulties.

_____ 11. Most people would like to find intimacy with one other person.

_____ 12. Wanting too much from another person can cause difficulties in a relationship.

_____ 13. Commitment, in the sense of a willingness to stay with a person in rough times as well as good times, is essential in an intimate relationship.

_____ 14. By its very nature, an exclusive relationship is bound to become dull, predictable, and unexciting.

_____ 15. I know what I'm looking for in a relationship.

_____ 16. It's essential that the partners in a relationship each retain their separate identities if the relationship is to be a good one.

_____ 17. I feel free to choose the kind of life-style I want.

_____ 18. In a meaningful relationship, I forget my needs and devote myself to the other person.

_____ 19. I have what I want in terms of intimacy with others at this time.

_____ 20. I can be emotionally intimate with another person without being physically intimate with that person.

Introduction

Much of this chapter focuses on marriage as one typical form of intimate relationship. Although many students either aren't married or are actively involved in some alternative life-style, there seems to be ample reason to dwell on this type of intimate relationship. Marriage is still one of the most widely practiced life-styles in our society, particularly if the term *marriage* is construed broadly to include the many couples who consider themselves committed to an intense relationship even though they are not legally married as well as those who are creating marriages that are different in many respects from the kind of marriage that has been traditional in our society. I do want to stress, however, that, whether we choose to marry or not, we can be involved in many different types of intimate relationships, and much of what is true for marriage is true for other types of intimate relationships as well. Allowing for the differences in relationships, the signs of growth and meaningfulness are much the same, and so are the types of problems we commonly experience. Consequently, whatever life-style you choose, and whatever intimate relationships you involve yourself in, you can use the ideas in this chapter as a basis for thinking about the role of intimacy in your life.

I've mentioned that there are many types of intimate relationships. One significant type is the kind of relationship that exists between parents and children. Many of the ideas in this chapter can be applied to bettering your relationships with your parents or your children. You can take a fresh look at these relationships, including both their frustrations and their delights, and you can think about how you might initiate some changes.

I'm thinking now of David, who told me about how little closeness he experienced with his father. David saw his father as a "rock," yet he deeply wished that he could be physically and emotionally close to him. David made the difficult decision to talk to his father and tell him exactly how he felt and what he wanted. Instead of the cold rebuff he expected, he found that his father reached out to him and admitted that he, too, wanted to be close but that he felt awkward in asking for it—and that he had feared *David's* rejection!

The type of experience David had with his father could have occurred in any intimate relationship. We can experience feelings of awkwardness, unexpressed desires, and fears of rejection with our friends, lovers, spouses, parents, or children. Thus, many of the suggestions I make in this chapter in regard to couple-type relationships apply also to other significant relationships. In particular, you can use the ideas about growth and change to improve your relationship with your parents or children, especially if you recognize that either you or they have outgrown the relationship you had previously.

Deep and meaningful friendships with persons of either sex are another type of intimacy. In my own life, I feel very fortunate in having three close male friends. With all these men I feel the freedom to be fully myself, which includes being vulnerable, trusting them, caring for them, enjoying my time with them, and knowing that each of the relationships is a two-way street. I believe it's important to think about how free we feel with our closest friends, the respect we give them and the respect we receive from them, and the degree to which we feel enhanced by each friendship. As you read this chapter, I hope you'll reflect on the quality of your friendships and on what you can do to make them better.

The intimacy we share with another person can be emotional, intellectual, physical, spiritual, or any combination of these. It can be exclusive or nonexclusive, long-term or of brief duration. For example, many of the people who have been involved in personal-growth groups Marianne and I have conducted have become very emotionally involved with each other. During the space of a week in which they share their struggles, they develop a closeness with one another that is real and meaningful, even though they may not keep in touch once the week is over. At the same time, I've observed how reluctant many people are to open themselves up emotionally in such short-term situations as a

weekend personal-growth group, because they want to avoid the sadness of parting. They might say "What if we do get close and really care for one another here? I hate to see all this intimacy come to an end when the workshop is over!" Bonds of intimacy and friendship can be formed in a short period of time, however, and subsequent distance in space and time need not diminish the quality of the friendships we form. For example, Marianne and I are very close with a couple who live 500 miles away. Even though we see one another only for several days each year, our contact is meaningful, and we experience a continuity in the relationship when we're together. We don't need to engage in small talk, and we have very personal conversations and intimate moments. To take another example, about a year ago Marianne met a foreign-exchange student from Norway. They had a relatively short time together, but they developed a genuine friendship that they keep alive through correspondence, and both of them have benefited from their exchanges.

Experiences such as the ones I've just described convince me that we only rob ourselves when we avoid intimacy because we know that physical distance or a lack of time will soon intervene.We may pass up the chance to really get to know neighbors and new acquaintances, because we fear that either we or our new friends will move and that the friendship will come to an end. Similarly, we may not want to open ourselves to intimacy with sick or dying persons, because we fear the pain of losing them. Although such fears may be natural ones, too often we allow them to cheat us of the uniquely rich experience of being truly close to another person. I believe that we can enhance our lives greatly by daring to care about others and fully savoring the time we can share with them now.

I'd like to give one more example of intimacy—this time, of an intellectual kind. After I had written the manuscript of this book, my editors at Brooks/Cole sent it to a number of reviewers, both instructors and students, for a careful reading. Then the reviewers and editors joined Marianne and me for a weekend seminar at our home in Idyllwild to discuss the book chapter by chapter. The group was composed of very diverse personalities. Most of the participants were professors who had taught courses in personal growth and adjustment and, in some cases, had written successful books in this field. All in all, I felt before our meeting that our group had the potential for stuffiness and that the seminar might give rise to unproductive arguments and other friction. Instead, the entire group jelled very quickly, and I was amazed at our productivity. We listened carefully to one another and demonstrated genuine respect for one another. We engaged in extremely open, highly stimulating exchanges. Even though most of us had not met previously, a closeness was generated among us by our common task of offering suggestions for the improvement of the book and by our involvement in honest discussions about the issues raised in these chapters. I felt that we all left the seminar feeling high and very close to one another, and the consensus seemed to be that everyone there had gained something from the time we spent together.

As you read the remainder of this chapter, I hope that you'll spend time thinking about the quality of all the various kinds of intimacy you experience in your life now. Are you involved in the kinds of intimate relationships that you want to be involved in? How can you enhance your intimate relationships? What are *you* willing to do to improve your relationships with those who are significant to you? What is your view of a growing relationship? I also hope that you'll think of ways to apply the themes I discuss in connection with couples to the many types of relationships in your life.

The one idea I most want to stress is that you can choose the kinds of intimate relationships you want to experience. Often, we fail to make our own choices and instead fall into a certain type of relationship because we think "This is the way it's *supposed* to be." For example, I wonder how many people marry who in reality might prefer to remain single—particularly women, who often feel the pressure to marry and have a family because it's "natural" for them to do so. Instead of blindly accepting that relationships must be a certain way or that only one type of life-style is possible, you have the choice of giving real thought to the question of what types of intimacy have meaning for you.

Time Out for Personal Reflection

1. What do you look for in a person you'd like to marry or form an intimate relationship with? For each item, put a "1" in the space if the quality is very important to you, a "2" if it is somewhat important, and a "3" if it is not very important.

_____ intelligence
_____ character (a strong sense of values)
_____ physical appearance and attractiveness
_____ money and possessions
_____ charm
_____ prestige and status
_____ a strong sense of identity
_____ expressiveness and tendency to be outgoing
_____ a sense of humor
_____ caring and sensitivity
_____ power
_____ independence
_____ a quiet person
_____ someone who will make decisions for me
_____ someone I can lean on
_____ someone who will lean on me
_____ someone I can't live without
_____ someone who works hard and is disciplined
_____ someone who likes to play and have fun
_____ someone who has values similar to mine
_____ someone I'd like to grow old with

Now list the three qualities that you value most in a person when you are considering an intimate relationship.

_____

_____

_____

2. Why do you think a person might want an intimate relationship with you? Look over the qualities listed above, and then list the qualities you see yourself as having.

_____

_____

_____

_____

3. Identify the kinds of intimate relationships you have chosen so far in your life. If you aren't presently involved in any significant intimate relationships, would you like to be?

_____

_____

_____

_____

_____

4. What do you get from being involved in a significant relationship? Check the responses that apply to you, and add your own on the lines provided.

_____ a feeling of being cared for
_____ a sense of importance
_____ joy in being able to care for another person
_____ excitement
_____ the feeling of not being alone in the world
_____ sharing and companionship

Other:

_____

_____

_____

_____

_____

Meaningful Relationships: A Personal View

In this section, I list some of the characteristics that I judge to be parts of a meaningful couple-type relationship. As you look over my list, you might adapt it to the different kinds of intimacy in your life and add the qualities that *you* think are important in an intimate relationship.

I see intimate relationships as most meaningful when they are dynamic and evolving rather than fixed or final. Thus, there may be periods of joy and excitement followed by times of struggle, pain, and distance. Unless two people have settled for complacency, there are probably not too many long periods of time in which they are the same with each other. As long as two people are growing and changing, both separately and as a couple, their relationship is bound to change as well.

As I look at intimacy from this growth-and-change perspective, the following are some of the qualities of a relationship that seem most important to me.

• *Each person in the relationship has a truly separate identity; they each give and receive without losing their separateness.* I like the way Kahlil Gibran (1923) expresses this thought in *The Prophet:* ''But let there be spaces in your togetherness, and let the winds of the heavens dance between you'' (p. 16).

• *Although each person desires the other, each can survive without the other.* They are not so tightly bound together that, if they are separated, one or the other becomes lost and empty.

• *Each is able to talk openly with the other about matters of significance.* They are willing to make themselves known to each other and to engage in dialogue about the quality of what they have together. They can openly express grievances and let each other know what changes they desire.

• *Each person assumes responsibility for his or her own level of happiness and refrains from blaming the other if he or she is unhappy.* Of course, in a close relationship, the unhappiness of one person is bound to affect the other, but no one should expect another person to *make* him or her happy, fulfilled, or excited.

• *The two people in the relationship are able to have fun and play together; they enjoy doing things with each other from time to time.*

• *The two people in the relationship are able to fight constructively.* It's a myth that ''happy couples'' don't have disagreements and differences. What seems important is that they can bring their differences into the open instead of secretly hanging on to them and letting their resentment grow.

• *If the relationship contains a sexual component, each person makes some attempt to keep the romance alive.* They may not always experience the intensity and novelty of the early period of their relationship, but they can devise ways of creating a climate in which they can experience romance and closeness. They may go places they haven't been to before or otherwise vary their routine in small ways. They recognize when their sex life is getting dull and look for ways to rejuvenate the boring aspects of their life together. In their lovemaking, they are sensitive to each other's needs and desires; at the same time, they are able to ask each other for what they want and need.

• *The two people are equal in the relationship.* People who feel that they are typically the "givers" and that their partners are usually unavailable when they need them might question the balance in their relationships. Also, each person might ask whether he or she feels OK in the presence of the other. In some relationships, one person may feel compelled to assume a superior position relative to the other—for example, to be very willing to listen and give advice, yet unwilling to go to the other person and show any vulnerability or need.

• *Each person actively demonstrates concern for the other.* In a vital relationship, the partners do more than just talk about how much they value each other. The actions they perform show their care and concern more eloquently than any words.

• *Each person is growing, changing, and opening up to new experiences.*

• *Each person finds meaning and sources of nourishment outside the relationship.* Their lives did not begin when they met each other; nor would their lives end if they should part.

• *Each avoids manipulating, exploiting, and using the other.* They each respect and care for the other and are willing to see the world through the other's eyes.

• *Each person is moving in a direction in life that is personally meaningful.* They are each excited about the quality of their lives and their projects. Both of them basically like who they are and what they are becoming.

• *If they are married, they stay married out of choice, not simply for the sake of their children, or out of duty, or because of convenience.* They choose to stay together even if things get rough or if they sometimes experience emptiness in their marriage. They share a commitment to look at what is wrong in their relationship and to work on changing undesirable situations.

• *Each person recognizes the need for solitude and space and is willing to create the time in which to be alone.* Moreover, each recognizes the other's need for private times.

• *Each avoids assuming an attitude of ownership toward the other.* Although they may experience jealousy at times, they do not demand that the other person deaden his or her feelings for others.

• *Each shows some flexibility in role behavior.* They are willing to share chores and activities rather than to refuse on the grounds that a certain activity isn't "masculine" or "feminine." They may even reverse roles at times.

• *They do not expect each other to do for them what they are capable of doing for themselves.* They don't expect the other person to make them feel alive, take away their boredom, assume their risks, or make them feel valued and important. Each is working toward creating his or her own autonomous identity. Consequently, neither person depends on the other for confirmation of his or her personal worth; nor does one walk in the shadow of the other.

• *Each discloses himself or herself to the other.* They need not indiscriminately share every secret, but they are able to share whatever is germane to the relationship. They are each willing to make themselves known to the other in significant ways, which may include sharing joy, expectations, frustrations, dreams, fears, boredom, excitement, and other personal feelings.

• *Each allows the other a sense of privacy.* Because they recognize each other's individual integrity, they recognize each other's right to a sense of privacy and avoid prying into every thought or manipulating the other to disclose what he or she wants to keep private.

• *Each person has a desire to give to the other.* They have an interest in each other's welfare and a desire to see that the other person is fulfilled. Thus, they go beyond thinking only of what the other person can do for them.

• *They encourage each other to become all that they are capable of becoming.* Unfortunately, people often have an investment in keeping those with whom they are intimately involved from changing. Their expectations and needs may lead them to resist changes in their partners and thus make it difficult for their partners to grow. However, if they recognize their fears, they can challenge their need to block their partners' progress. On the other hand, people sometimes hinder their partners' growth by refusing to give them a chance to change or refusing to believe in their ability to do so. They can counter this tendency in themselves by expressing their own desires, without nagging and faultfinding, and by caring enough to challenge their partners when it seems appropriate to do so.

• *Each has a commitment to the other.* The more I work with couples, the more I see commitment as a vital part of an intimate relationship. By commitment, I mean that the people involved have an investment in their future together and that they are willing to stay with each other in times of crisis and conflict. Although many people express an aversion to any long-term commitment in a relationship, I wonder how deeply they will allow themselves to be loved if they believe that the relationship can be dissolved on a whim when things look bleak. Perhaps, for some people, a fear of intimacy gets in the way of developing a sense of commitment. Loving and being loved is both exciting and frightening, and we may have to struggle with the issue of how much anxiety we want to tolerate. Commitment to another person involves risk, and it carries a price, but I believe it is an essential part of an intimate relationship.

In emphasizing the role of commitment in intimate relationships, I don't mean to suggest that all valuable relationships must last a long time or that we must frequently see those whom we have cared for. Many people close the door to the possibility of developing a significant friendship because they feel that they will be "overcommitted" and obligated to call, write, and visit in order to keep the friendship alive. As I said earlier in the chapter, real and meaningful bonds can be formed for a limited period of time, and the experience can be invaluable even if the relationship is not perpetuated in an active way. For instance, even though months have passed since our seminar with the reviewers of this book, I still have very fond memories of the people who were there and of the time we spent together. I have seen some of them since then; others, I haven't seen and may not see again. However, whether or not I continue to have contact with these people, the value of the time we shared is undiminished. I've often thought that we experienced more openness in the space of a weekend than many faculty members ever experience with the colleagues they see month after month. Thus, the intimate moment may be brief and yet be rewarding and lead to much personal growth.

Time Out for Personal Reflection

1. What are some ways in which you see yourself as growing? In what ways do you see yourself as resisting personal growth by sticking with old and comfortable patterns, even if they don't work? To facilitate your reflection, look over the following statements, and mark each one with a "T" or an "F," depending on whether you think it generally applies to you.

   _____ I keep myself attractive.
   _____ If I'm involved in an intimate relationship, I tell the other person what I want.
   _____ I'm willing to try new things.
   _____ Rather than settle for comfort in a relationship or in life, I ask for more.
   _____ If I'm involved in an intimate relationship, I tell the other person what I'm feeling.
   _____ I'm engaged in projects that are meaningful to me.

2. List other ways in which you're growing:

   _____

   _____

   _____

3. List some ways in which you resist personal growth:

   _____

   _____

   _____

4. In what ways do you see the person with whom you're most intimate growing and/or resisting growth?

   _____

   _____

   _____

5. If you're presently involved in a couple-type relationship, in what ways do you think you and your partner are growing closer? In what ways are you going in different directions?

_____

_____

_____

_____

6. Are you satisfied with the relationship you've just described? If not, what would you most like to change? How might you go about it?

_____

_____

_____

_____

_____

7. What did you learn from doing these exercises?

_____

_____

_____

_____

_____

A suggestion for using this Time Out: If you're presently involved in an intimate relationship, have your partner respond to the questions on a separate sheet of paper. Then compare your answers and discuss areas of agreement and disagreement.

Sources of Conflict in Intimate Relationships

During the past few years, Marianne and I have been working with couples in weekend workshops, assisting them to identify sources of conflict in their relationships and encouraging them to decide what kinds of changes they are willing to make with each other. At this point I want to describe some of the common conflicts that seem to surface time and again in our work with couples.

A major problem that arises in intimate relationships is boredom or a sense of predictability. Regardless of how exciting and innovative a person or a couple might be, it seems inevitable that a feeling of staleness will set in at times. When this occurs, the couple can try to avoid confronting their boredom by denying its existence, or they can frankly recognize it and share it with each other. In my own experience, I find that accepting my share of responsibility for my own boredom, as opposed to making my wife responsible for it, gives me a place to begin dealing with it. In general, if I'm not bored with myself, the chances are that our relationship will not *remain* dull, even though we sometimes experience a feeling of stagnation with each other.

In an address he gave a meeting of the American Association of Marriage and Family Counselors, Sidney Jourard described marriage as a dialogue that ends as soon as habitual ways of acting set in. He maintained that people are frequently not very creative when it comes to finding new ways of living with each other and that they tend to fall into the same ruts day after day, year after year. Moreover, many people— whether married or living together—seem to seek only superficial relationships in order to avoid risk. In Jourard's words: "The silent shrieks of pain deafen me. To be married is for many boredom or hell. To be unmarried, legally or unlegally, as many experience it is hell and despair."[1] To this lethal image of marriage and living together, Jourard proposed an alternative, life-giving model. His theme was that "Marriage Is for Life"—not in the sense of having to last a lifetime, but in the sense of giving life to the people involved. As a way of freeing ourselves from deadening ways of living together, Jourard suggested that we might have several different marriages with the same person. We could recognize that, at its best, marriage is a relationship that generates change through dialogue. Instead of being threatened by change, we could welcome it as necessary for keeping the relationship alive.

For Jourard, therefore, we can have a series of marriages with the same person by divorcing ourselves from dead patterns and taking our dissatisfaction as a sign that it is time for new growth. In this way, we may be able to establish a new relationship with the same person. Jourard emphasized that divorce often means that one or the other partner has made a decision not to live in the same manner as before. The meaning of a decision to divorce can thus be similar to the meaning of a suicide, in the sense that people who contemplate suicide often are saying, in part, that they are no longer willing to live in the same way as they have been living. Similarly, the changes that occur in an intimate relationship can lead one or both parties to feel that they are at an impasse and that ending the relationship is the only way out.

My own 13-year marriage has gone through an evolution characterized by periods of security, monotony, experimentation, distance, friction, excitement, crisis, growth, challenge, major turning points, and new decisions. The early years of our marriage were marked by content-

[1]From "Marriage Is for Life," by Sidney Jourard. *Journal of Marriage & The Family,* July 1975, pp. 199–208.

ment and joy, coupled with the struggles both of us had in learning how to live together. In many ways, I married a person who had many of the qualities of my mother, and I allowed and encouraged her to be a mother to me. For her part, Marianne married a person whom she thought had many of her father's qualities, and in some ways she looked to me to affirm her worth, just as she had wanted her father to do. However, Marianne grew tired of "taking care of" me sooner than I became impatient with the way she was. She decided that she wanted me to see and treat her differently, and she told me so. In honesty, I must admit that a large part of me was content with the state of things as they were. My world was shaken when Marianne took the risk of letting me know that she was dissatisfied with the way we were living, and at first I had a hard time understanding why she was unhappy. I now see her initial act of confronting me as a real sign of her care. She cared enough about herself to want more than she was getting, and she cared enough about me to jar me out of my complacency and challenge me to question what I wanted from life.

One pattern that I see in our marriage is that Marianne has consistently demonstrated more interest than I have in our family life, and she has been more willing than I to invest her time and emotional energy in it. In many ways, both of us have accepted that we are different people and that we have different interests and priorities. It has been difficult for Marianne to accept that I have always been more absorbed in my work than she would have liked, but over the years she has become increasingly aware of the importance of obtaining her fulfillment in many ways. She recognizes that, if she depended primarily on me to provide for all of her needs, she would not be satisfied. Consequently, she has created a number of hobbies and interests; she is professionally involved in a part-time private practice; she co-authors books; and she has established several significant friendships.

Recently, we celebrated our 13th anniversary, and Marianne surprised me by arranging for a two-week stay in Hawaii—without our children, and without any manuscripts to work on. We had both become so involved in our move from the city to the mountains and in the demands of our professional lives that we needed the time to do nothing but enjoy each other and assess things. At times like this, we both realize how easy it is to neglect a relationship and become burdened by mundane chores as well as exciting projects, and we learn again how essential it is to take the time to put our lives in perspective.

In our couples' workshops, Marianne and I frequently see conflicts that arise when one person is excited about growing and the other isn't. For example, a woman becomes engaged in her personal growth and in meaningful projects, and she decides that she wants more from all aspects of her life. In her enthusiasm, she wants more from and for her husband. However, these changes may be accompanied by an increase in anxiety; for example, she might be frightened of what her increasing strength will do to her marriage. Thus, she may experience a deep inner conflict: on the one hand, she feels committed to her own growth; on the other hand, she fears that her demands will be threatening to her husband and disrupt or even destroy their relationship. The following example illustrates this kind of conflict.

Sue and Hal dated in high school and married shortly after graduation. During the first few years of their marriage, Sue stayed home, reared children, and generally depended upon Hal to take care of most of her needs. She had few friends, and she didn't cultivate many outside interests. In many respects, Hal fit the picture of the "macho male." He defined himself by competing and succeeding in the business world, and by buying a lavish house. Their relationship was fine, as he saw it, but eventually Sue became disenchanted with her dependence. She initiated marriage counseling, which Hal participated in reluctantly, and she also obtained personal counseling for herself. She made significant new decisions: to get a well-paying job, to go to college part-time, and to be generally more demanding of Hal and less willing to tolerate what she saw as his male chauvinism. Whereas Sue had once been willing to let Hal be the superior one in their relationship, she now began to insist on being treated like a full and equal person.

As a result of these changes, Hal felt a real panic. When Sue became sexually assertive with him on a few occasions, he only felt more inadequate. He believed that men should always be the initiators, while women should merely submit passively. Not knowing how to handle Sue's new assertiveness and strength, he became sexually impotent, and he began to feel that his world was coming apart. He had always defined his power in terms of Sue's dependence on him. Now, if she liked other men and found them interesting and attractive, he reasoned that she must not like him or find him attractive. The more success she enjoyed, the more self-doubt he suffered.

The challenge facing Hal and Sue was to determine whether they could modify some of their long-established patterns and create a relationship in which Sue would be free to become a mature person and Hal could feel confident in his own right. Their predicament was quite typical; I've observed many men who feel threatened when the women they live with exercise power as persons. However, I've also seen men like Hal initially resist any positive changes in their partners and yet eventually come to like and respect them for the courage they manifest in changing.

With this challenge, however, comes risk. For example, although it was true that Hal might eventually have found Sue more attractive because of her growth, he might also have become increasingly defensive and attempted to tighten his control on her thinking and behavior. He might even have left because of his fear. She would then have been faced with a decision. Would she be willing to accept this kind of life? Would she back down and become the person she once was—the person Hal had been comfortable with? Would she remain nominally married while seeking a relationship with another man? Would she push Hal to initiate a divorce, so that he would bear the responsibility, or would she initiate a divorce herself if that was what she wanted?

The case of Sue and Hal illustrates a few of the unknowns and risks involved when one person is eager to change, while the other person wants things to remain the same. Hal and Sue experienced a painful struggle as they tried to decide whether they wanted to remain together and as they tried to clarify what they wanted with each other. Eventually, Hal realized that their original motivations for marrying could be different from their motivations for staying married. Through counseling, he recognized that much of their relationship had been based on Sue's need to have someone take care of her and his own need to be dominant and superior. Ultimately, both Hal and Sue discovered that they could change individually while finding new and different reasons for staying together.

Time Out for Personal Reflection

The following questions are designed for people who are involved in couple-type relationships. If you're not presently involved in such a relationship, you can apply them to whatever relationship is most significant to you right now (for instance, with your parents, children, or closest friend).

1. What are some sources of conflict in your relationship? Check any of the following items that apply to you, and list any other areas of conflict on the lines provided.

      _____ spending money
      _____ use of free time
      _____ what to do about boredom
      _____ investment of energy in work
      _____ interest in others of the opposite sex
      _____ outside friendships
      _____ wanting children
      _____ how to deal with children
      _____ differences in basic values
      _____ in-laws
      _____ sexual needs and satisfaction
      _____ expression of caring and loving
      _____ power struggles
      _____ role conflicts

Other areas of conflict:

_____

_____

_____

_____

_____

2. How do you generally cope with these conflicts in your relationship? Check the items that most apply to you.

_____ by open dialogue
_____ by avoidance
_____ by fighting and arguing
_____ by compromising
_____ by getting involved with other people or in projects

List other ways in which you deal with conflicts in your relationship:

_____

_____

_____

_____

3. Mention one conflict that you would like to resolve, and write down what you'd be willing to do in order to help resolve it.

The conflict is _____.

To attempt a resolution, I'm willing to _____

_____

_____.

4. List some ways in which you've changed during the period of your relationship. How have your changes affected the relationship?

_____

_____

_____

_____

_____

_____

5. To what extent do you have an identity apart from the relationship? How much do you need (and depend) upon the other person? Imagine that he or she is no longer in your life, and write down how your life might be different.

_____

_____

_____

_____

_____

_____

Divorce and Separation

Earlier in this chapter, I mentioned Jourard's concept of establishing new marriages with the same person and suggested that a crisis in a relationship doesn't have to mean that the relationship must or should end. In fact, an impasse or crisis can become a turning point that enables two people to create a new way of life together. If they both care enough about their investment in each other, and if they are committed to doing the work that is necessary to change old patterns and establish more productive ones, a crisis can actually save their relationship and lead to new growth and meaning.

In my work with couples, I've come to realize that people often decide on divorcing without really giving themselves or their partners a chance to face a particular crisis and work it through. For example, a man begins to see how deadening his marriage is for him and to realize how he has contributed to his own unhappiness in it. As a result of changes in his perceptions and attitudes, he decides that he no longer wants to live with a woman in this deadening fashion. However, rather than deciding to simply end the marriage, thinking that this action will bring him a new life, he might allow his partner to really see and experience him as the different person he is becoming. Moreover, he might encourage her to change as well, instead of giving up on her too quickly. His progress toward becoming a more integrated person might well inspire her to work actively toward her own internal changes. This kind of work on the part of both people takes understanding and patience, but they may find that they can meet each other as new and changing persons and form a very different kind of relationship.

Sometimes, of course, ending a relationship is the wisest course. Divorce can then be an act of courage that makes a new beginning possible. My concern is only that too many couples may not be committed to each other to the degree that they will stay together in times of crisis and struggle. As a result, they may separate at the very time when they could be making a new start with each other.

How do two people know when a divorce is the best solution? No categorical answer can be given to this question. However, before two people do decide to divorce or terminate their relationship, they might consider at least the following questions.

• Has each of them sought personal therapy or counseling? Perhaps their exploration of themselves would lead to changes that allowed them to renew or strengthen their relationship.

• Have they considered marital counseling as a couple? Have they attended a couples' group or workshop to explore alternatives for their future? If they do get involved in marriage counseling of any type, are they each doing so willingly, or is one of them merely going along to placate the other?

• Are both parties really interested in preserving their marriage? Perhaps one or both may not be interested in preserving the old relationship, but it is vital that they each want a life together if they are to renew their marriage. I routinely ask both members of a couple in difficulties to decide whether or not they even want to live with the other person. Some of the responses people give include: "I don't really know. I've lost hope for any real change, and at this point I find it difficult to care whether we stay together or not." "I'm sure that I don't want to live with this person any more; I just don't care enough to work on improving things between us. I'm here so that we can separate cleanly and finish business between us." "Even though we're going through some turmoil right now, I would very much like to care enough to make things better. Frankly, I'm not too hopeful, but I'm willing to give it a try." Whatever their responses, it's imperative that they each know how they feel about the possibility of renewing their relationship.

• Have they each taken the time to be alone, to get themselves in focus, and to decide what kind of life they want for themselves and with others?

• As a couple, have they taken time to be with each other for even a weekend? I'm continually surprised at how few couples arrange for time alone with each other. It's almost as if many couples fear discovering that they really have little to say to each other. This discovery in itself might be very useful, for at least they might be able to do something about the situation if they confronted it; but many couples seem to arrange their lives in such a way that they block any possibilities for intimacy. They eat dinner together with the television blasting, or they spend all their time together taking care of their children, or they simply refuse to make time to be together.

• What do they each expect from the divorce? Frequently, problems in a marriage are reflections of internal conflicts within the individuals in that marriage. For this reason, I usually recommend that couples involved in marital counseling also engage in their own personal therapy or counseling. In general, unless there are some changes within the individuals, the problems they experienced may not end with the divorce. In fact, many who do divorce with the expectation of finding increased joy and freedom once they are no longer encumbered with their mates discover instead that they are still miserable, lonely, depressed, and anxious. Lacking insight into themselves, they may soon find new partners very much like the ones they divorced and repeat the same dynamics. Thus, a woman who finally decides to leave a man she thinks of as weak and passive may soon find a similar type of man to live with again, unless she comes to understand why she needs or wants to align herself with this sort of person. Or a man who contends that he has "put up with" his wife for over 20 years may find a similar kind of person unless he understands what motivated him to stay with his first wife for so long. It seems essential, therefore, that each come to know as clearly as possible why they are divorcing and that they look at the changes they may need to make in themselves as well as in their circumstances.

Sometimes one or both members of a couple identify strong reasons for separating but say that, for one reason or another, they are not free to do so. This kind of reasoning is always worth examining, however, since an attitude of "I couldn't possibly leave" will not help either partner to make a free and sound choice. Some of the reasons people give for refusing to divorce include the following.

- "I have an investment of 15 years in this marriage, and to leave now would mean that these 15 years have been wasted." A person who feels this way might ask himself or herself: "If I really don't see much potential for change, and if my partner has consistently and over a long period of time rebuffed any moves that might lead to improving our relationship, should I stay another 15 years and have 30 years to regret?"
- "I can't leave because of the kids, but I do plan on leaving as soon as they get into high school." I often think that this kind of thinking burdens children with unnecessary guilt. In a sense, it makes them responsible for the unhappiness of their parents. I would ask: Why place the burden on them if *you* stay in a place where you say you don't want to be? And will you find another reason to cement yourself to your partner once your children grow up?
- "Since the children need both a mother and a father, I cannot consider breaking up our marriage." True, children do need both a father and a mother. But it's worth asking whether they will get much of value from either parent if they see them despising each other. How useful is the model parents present when they stay together and the children see how little joy they experience? Might they not get more from the two parents separately? Wouldn't the parents set a better and more honest example if they openly admitted that they no longer really chose to remain together?

• "I'm afraid to divorce because I might find that I would be even more lonely than I am now." Certainly, loneliness is a real possibility. There are no guarantees that a new relationship will be established after the divorce. However, we might be more lonely living with someone we don't like, much less love, than we would be if we were living alone. Living alone might bring far more serenity and inner strength. Moreover, whether or not a new relationship can be established depends to a great degree on a person's self-perception. The more people become attractive to themselves, the greater the chance that others will see them as attractive.

• "One thing that holds me back from separating is that I might discover that I left too soon and that I didn't give us a fair chance." To avoid this regret, a couple should explore all the possibilities for creating a new relationship *before* making the decision to dissolve their marriage. However, there does come a point at which a person must finally take a stand and decide, and then I see it as fruitless to brood continually over whether he or she did the right thing.

In summary, we limit our options unnecessarily whenever we tell ourselves that we *can't possibly* take a certain course of action, whether that course of action involves staying with a person or leaving him or her. Before deciding to terminate a relationship, we can ask whether we've really given the other person (and ourselves) a chance to establish something new. By the same token, if we decide that we want to end the relationship but can't, it's worth asking whether we're not simply evading the responsibility for creating our own happiness. Neither keeping a relationship alive and growing nor ending one that no longer is right for us is easy, and it's tempting to find ways of putting the responsibility for our decisions on our children, mates, or circumstances. We take a real step toward genuine freedom when we fully accept that, whatever we decide, the choice is ours to make.

Time Out for Personal Reflection

Complete the following sentences by writing down the first responses that come to mind. *Suggestion:* Ask your partner or a close friend to do the exercise on a separate sheet of paper; then compare and discuss your responses.

1. To me, intimacy means _____.

2. What is most important in making an intimate relationship successful
   is _____.

3. The thing I most fear about an intimate relationship is _____
   _____.

4. When an intimate relationship becomes stale, I usually _____

_____.

5. One of the reasons I need another person is _____

_____.

6. One conflict that I have concerning intimate relationships is _____

_____.

7. In an intimate relationship, it's unrealistic to expect that _____

_____.

8. To me, commitment means _____.

9. I think of commitment in an intimate relationship as _____

_____.

10. My views about marriage have been most influenced by _____

_____.

11. I have encouraged my partner to grow by _____

_____.

12. My partner has encouraged me to grow by _____

_____.

_____

Chapter Summary

In this chapter, I've encouraged you to think about what characterizes a growing, meaningful relationship and to ask yourself such questions as: Do I have what I want in my intimate relationships? Do I desire more (or less) intimacy? What kinds of changes would I most like to make in my intimate relationships? In each of my relationships, can both the other person and I maintain our separate identities and at the same time develop a strong bond that enhances us as individuals?

I think it's important to stress that the picture I've drawn of a growing relationship is not a dogmatic or necessarily complete one; nor will our relationships, however good they are, always approximate it. I've tried to say what I think intimacy is like at its best, and my hope is that these reflections will stimulate your own independent thinking. You can begin by honestly assessing the present state of your intimate relationships, recognizing how they really are (as opposed to how you wish they were). Then you can begin to consider the choices that can lead to positive change in those areas you're dissatisfied with. Throughout this chapter, I've emphasized that we must actively work on recognizing problems in ourselves and in our relationships if we are to make intimacy as rewarding as it can be. Finally, I've stressed that you can choose the kinds of intimacy you want in your life.

Now list some key ideas that you want to remember.

_____

_____

_____

_____

_____

_____

Activities and Exercises

Some of the following activities are appropriate for you to do on your own; others are designed for two people in an intimate relationship to do together. Select the ones that have the most meaning for you, and consider sharing the results with the other members of your class.

1. In your journal, write down some reflections on your parents' relationship. Consider such questions as the following:

   - Would you like to have the same kind of relationship your parents have had? What are some of the things you liked best about their relationship? What are some features of their relationship that you would not want to have in your own marriage?
   - How have your own views, attitudes, and practices regarding marriage and intimacy been affected by your parents' relationship? Discuss the impact of their relationship on your own marriage, intimate relationship, or views about marriage and intimacy.

2. How much self-disclosure, honesty, and openness do you want in your intimate relationships? In your journal, reflect on how much you would share your feelings concerning each of the following with your partner. Then discuss how you would like your partner to respond to this same question.

   - your sexual fantasies about another person
   - your secrets
   - when you feel needy and want support from your partner
   - your angry feelings
   - your dreams
   - your desire for an affair with someone else
   - your behavior if you did decide to have an affair
   - your friendships with persons of the opposite sex

- your ideas on religion and your philosophy of life
- the times when you feel inadequate as a person
- the times when you feel extremely close and loving toward your partner
- the times in your relationship when you feel boredom, staleness, hostility, detachment, and so on

After you've answered this question for yourself, think about how open you want *your partner* to be with *you*. If your partner were doing this exercise, what answers do you wish he or she would give for each of the preceding items?

3. Over a period of about a week, do some writing about the evolution of your relationship, and ask your partner to do the same. Consider issues such as: Why were we initially attracted to each other? How have we changed since we first met? Do I like these changes? What would I most like to change about our life together? What are the best things we have going for us? What are some problem areas we need to explore? If I could do it over again, would I select the same person? What's the future of our life together? What would I like to see us doing differently? After you've each written about these and any other questions that are significant for you, read each other's work and discuss where you want to go from here. This activity can stimulate you to talk more openly with each other and can also give each of you the chance to see how the other perceives the quality of your relationship.

4. Here is another activity for a couple to do together. Select a book dealing with the themes of love, sex, intimacy, or related issues. (See the reading list at the end of the chapter for suggestions.) Read the book separately, and write down some notes about ideas or feelings that have an impact or special meaning. Then get together and share your reactions and notes, and relate them to your own relationship.

5. Make up a list of specific suggestions for ways of experimenting with your intimate relationships. What are some concrete things you'd like to try with another person? If you're presently involved in a couple-type relationship, ask your partner to make up his or her own list; then share your results, and discuss some possibilities for action.

6. Often, we engage in unacknowledged conspiracies with another person in order to keep a relationship secure. For the sake of this exercise, assume that there are some conspiracies going in your intimate relationships, and see whether you can detect them. For instance, does one of you have to be a winner and one of you a loser? Does either of you need to be helpless in order for the other to feel powerful? Are you a mother or father to the other person? Are you the other person's "child"? Are you the other's security blanket? Are you the other's policeman? Try to be as honest as you can. If you're presently involved in a couple-type relationship, ask your partner to do the exercise as well; then share your results.

7. Interview some friends, associates, neighbors, and acquaintances, to determine what their views are concerning intimacy. To get started, you might ask them to respond to some of the specific questions raised in this chapter.

8. As you look at various television shows, keep a record of the kinds of messages you get regarding marriage, family life, and intimacy. What are some common stereotypes? What sex roles are portrayed? What myths do you think are being presented? After you've kept a record for a couple of weeks or so, write down some of the attitudes that you think you may have incorporated from television and other media about marriage, family life, and intimacy.

Suggested Readings

Bach, G., & Wyden, P. *The Intimate Enemy: How to Fight Fair in Love and Marriage.* New York: Morrow, 1969. This book deals with a wide range of marital games and proposes guidelines for "fighting fair."

Bernard, J. *The Future of Marriage.* New York: Bantam, 1973. Bernard discusses many timely issues concerning the present state and the future of marriage, such as: Is marriage obsolete? When is a marriage too secure? What is the relationship like between man and woman traditionally? Will we have group marriages in the future? Are marriage contracts realistic?

DeLora, J. S., & DeLora, J. R. (Eds.). *Intimate Life Styles: Marriage and Its Alternatives* (2nd ed.). Pacific Palisades, Calif.: Goodyear, 1975. This is a book of readings that deal with alternatives to traditional marriage, future intimate life-styles, stresses in a changing society, and sex as a personal and interpersonal concern.

Gibran, K. *The Prophet.* New York: Knopf, 1923. Gibran's poetic book has much to say about the meaning of intimacy.

Herrigan, J., & Herrigan, J. *Loving Free.* New York: Ballantine, 1975. This book tells the story of one couple's marriage and struggles: the problems they faced, how they worked at their own marriage, and how they enhanced their marriage. The authors state: "We're not professionals nor are we psychologists. We're two people who love each other and believe there is something worth fighting for in marriage. After thirteen years of marriage we still believe that love is the best shot we've got. We're still willing to put our all into it, and are more enthusiastic than ever about our life together—in or out of bed."

Lasswell, M., & Lobsenz, N. *No-Fault Marriage: The New Technique of Self-Counseling and What It Can Help You Do.* New York: Ballantine Books, 1976. This book is designed to help couples look at their own marriages and apply some of the counseling and communication skills that they can learn in marriage counseling. The authors point out why "winning" doesn't work in marital situations.

O'Neill, N., & O'Neill, G. *Open Marriage, a New Life Style for Couples.* New York: Avon, 1973. This book recommends a flexible concept of marriage that allows each couple to draw upon their particular qualities as individuals and develop a relationship that is uniquely suited to them. Although it has sometimes been misinterpreted as an endorsement for open sexual relationships, the book is really focused on how two people can grow both individually and as a couple.

Paul, J., & Paul, M. *Free to Love.* New York: Pyramid, 1975. In this book, a husband/wife marriage-counselor team share their personal struggles and joys in their own twelve-year marriage. They discuss what they have learned about marriage counseling through their own courtship, adjustment problems, sex life, child rearing, and efforts to be separate people and at the same time a couple capable of love and intimacy.

Rogers, C. *Becoming Partners.* New York: Dell (Delta), 1973. Rogers describes a number of forms of marriage as seen through the eyes of the participants. This book deals with both traditional marriages and experimental forms of living together.

Shain, M. *Some Men Are More Perfect Than Others.* New York: Bantam, 1976. This is an insightful book that deals with loving, being together and being apart, the meaning of love, and women/men relationships.

Chapter 9

Loneliness
and Solitude

Once we fully accept our aloneness, it can become the source of our strength and the foundation of our relatedness to others. Taking time to be alone gives us the chance to think, plan, imagine, and dream. It allows us to listen to ourselves and to become sensitive to what we are experiencing. In solitude we can come to appreciate anew both our separateness from, and our relatedness to, the important people and projects in our lives.

Pre-Chapter Self-Inventory

For each statement, indicate the response that most closely identifies your beliefs and attitudes. Use this code: A = I strongly agree; B = I slightly agree; C = I slightly disagree; D = I strongly disagree.

_____ 1. Loneliness is a condition that needs to be cured.

_____ 2. Experiencing aloneness gives us a sense of strength and power.

_____ 3. Loneliness is generally intensified during our adolescent years.

_____ 4. Our culture provides many ways of escaping the experience of aloneness.

_____ 5. If we don't feel valuable as persons when we're alone, we probably won't feel valuable when we're with others.

_____ 6. Experiencing solitude is an essential way of rediscovering ourselves.

_____ 7. People who seek to be alone usually are escaping from intimacy with others.

_____ 8. It's very possible to be lonely in a crowd.

_____ 9. The popularity of encounter groups stems from our need to overcome our isolation and alienation.

_____ 10. The experience of loneliness can be a path to personal renewal and self-discovery.

_____ 11. We cannot escape loneliness completely.

_____ 12. Trying to avoid any experience of loneliness can lead to alienation from ourselves and others.

_____ 13. There is little value in experiencing loneliness.

_____ 14. We don't have much control over the circumstances that can cause loneliness; so, if we're lonely, there's not much we can do except suffer through it.

_____ 15. My childhood was a lonely period in my life.

_____ 16. My adolescent years were lonely ones for me.

_____ 17. Older people are necessarily lonely.

_____ 18. Older people, like people of any age, can choose how they will respond to lonely circumstances in life.

_____ 19. Loneliness is a problem for me in my life now.

_____ 20. I generally arrange for time alone so that I can gain some perspective on what is important and what is unimportant in my life.

Introduction

One of the greatest fears many people have is the fear of loneliness. Because we may associate the lonely periods in our lives with pain and struggle, we may think of loneliness only as a condition to be avoided as much as possible. Furthermore, we may identify being alone with being lonely and actively avoid having time by ourselves or else fill such time with distractions and diversions. Paradoxically, out of fear of rejection and loneliness, we may even make ourselves needlessly lonely by refusing to reach out to others or by holding back parts of ourselves in our intimate relationships.

In this chapter, I encourage you to think of loneliness as a natural—and potentially valuable—part of human experience. I also encourage you to distinguish between being lonely and being alone. In a real sense, all of us are ultimately alone in the world, and appreciating our aloneness can actually enable us to enrich our experience of life. Moreover, we can use times of solitude to look within ourselves, renew our sense of ourselves as the centers of choice and direction in our lives, and learn to trust our inner resources instead of allowing circumstances or the expectations of others to determine the course of our lives. Finally, if we fundamentally accept our aloneness and recognize that no one can take away *all* our loneliness, we can deal more effectively with our experiences of loneliness and give of ourselves to our projects and relationships out of our freedom instead of running to them out of our fear.

Our Ultimate Aloneness

With the existentialist thinkers, I believe that, ultimately, we are alone. Although the presence of others can surely enhance our lives, no one else can completely become us or share our unique worlds of feelings, thoughts, hopes, and memories. In addition, none of us knows when our loved ones may leave us or die, or when we will no longer be able to involve ourselves in a cherished activity, or when the forest we love will be burned or destroyed. We come into the world alone, and we will be alone again when the time comes to leave it.

This awareness of our ultimate aloneness—like the awareness of our freedom or of our mortality—can be frightening. Just as we may shrink from recognizing our freedom out of fear of the risks involved or resist thinking about our eventual death, so too we may avoid experiencing our ultimate aloneness. We may throw ourselves into relationships, activities, and diversions and depend on them to numb our sense of aloneness. Certainly, our society provides many distractions and escapes for those who choose to avoid the experience of aloneness. However, I believe that we cannot deny something we deeply feel to be true without becoming alienated from ourselves.

Perhaps we fear our aloneness because we identify it with extreme loneliness. I think it's important to recognize that experiencing our aloneness is not the same as being without friends or loved ones or pondering something depressing or morbid. On the contrary, it can be an invaluable and positive experience. Throughout this book, I have stressed the theme of *choice* and encouraged you to think about ways of

directing your life according to your own inner standards, desires, values, and ethics. My premise has been that each of us is an individual, unique being and that whatever meanings we discover in our lives have their source within our individual selves. This means, in part, that each of us creates a unique world by our own choices and experiences—a world that has never existed before and never will again. If we dare to experience our ultimate aloneness, we can strengthen our awareness of ourselves as the true centers of meaning and direction in our lives. In times of solitude, we can restore our perspective on life and return to our projects and relationships refreshed and renewed. By experiencing our aloneness, we can become more fully aware that, although nothing we cherish is permanent, it is our free choice that makes it valuable and unique. In these ways, our freedom and aloneness come together as the twin sources of meaning in our lives.

Confronting Our Aloneness

Just as we may look to others to make our choices for us, so we may look outside ourselves for rescue from our aloneness. We may become dependent on others for direction and for protection from feelings of loneliness. Instead of confronting the fears we may have of being bored, empty, or lost if we are left to ourselves, we can allow our anxiety to determine the choices we make. In so doing, we risk becoming alienated from our inner selves and thus actually increasing our sense of loneliness.

Some of the ways in which we may try to escape the experience of aloneness include the following:

- We can busy ourselves in work and activities, so that we have little time to think or to reflect by ourselves.
- We can schedule every moment and overstructure our lives so that we have no opportunity to think about ourselves and what we are doing with our lives.
- We can surround ourselves with people and become absorbed in social functions, in the hope that we won't have to feel alone.
- We can try to numb ourselves with television, loud music, alcohol, or drugs.
- We can immerse ourselves in helping others and in our "responsibilities."
- We can eat compulsively, hoping that doing so will fill our inner emptiness and protect us from the pain of being alone.
- We can make ourselves slaves to routine, becoming machines that don't feel much of anything.
- We can find plenty of trivial things to occupy our attention so that we never really have to focus on ourselves.
- We can go to bars and other centers of activity, trying to lose ourselves in a crowd.

Even if we dimly sense a need for solitude, in our society we often have to work at giving ourselves a chance to be alone. Most of us lead hectic lives in crowded, noisy environments. We are surrounded by entertainments and escapes. Paradoxically enough, in the midst of our congested cities and with all the activities available to us, we are often lonely because we are alienated from ourselves. The predicament of many people in our society is that of the alienated man described by the Josephsons in their book, *Man Alone: Alienation in Modern Society:* "The alienated man is everyman and no man, drifting in a world that has little meaning for him and over which he exercises no power, a stranger to himself and to others" (Josephson & Josephson, 1962, p. 11). As the Josephsons argue, too many of us are estranged from ourselves and from nature. We are not close to the sky, the ocean, the mountains, the wind. We have learned to fear solitude instead of welcoming it, and we have become strangers to ourselves as a result.

If we want to get back in touch with ourselves, we can begin by looking at the ways in which we have learned to escape the anxiety of being alone. We can examine the values of our society and question whether they are contributing to our estrangement from ourselves and to our sense of isolation. We can ask whether the activities that fill our time actually satisfy us or whether they leave us hungry and discontented. I believe that we can begin to feel connected with ourselves, others, and nature, but it may take an active effort on our part to resist the pressures of our lives and take the time to be with ourselves.

The Values of Solitude

Loneliness and solitude are different experiences, each of which has its own potential value. Loneliness is an experience that generally results from certain situations that occur in our lives—the death of someone we love, the decision of another person to leave us for someone else, a move to a new city, a long stay in a hospital. Loneliness can occur when we feel set apart in some way from everyone around us. And sometimes feelings of loneliness are simply an indication of the extent to which we've failed to listen to ourselves and our own feelings. However it occurs, loneliness is generally something that happens to us, rather than something we choose to experience; but we *can* choose the attitude we take toward it. If we try to dull or ignore our lonely feelings, we may only become even more alienated from ourselves. If we choose to run from any experience of loneliness, we may become overly dependent on people and things outside ourselves, thus diminishing our freedom and inviting inner resentment over our own dependence. Alternatively, if we allow ourselves to experience our loneliness, even if it is painful, we may be surprised to find within ourselves the sources of strength and renewal.

Unlike loneliness, solitude, or being alone for a time, is something that we often choose for ourselves. In solitude, we make the time to
be with ourselves, to discover who we are, and to renew ourselves. The
point that solitude is not the same as loneliness is well expressed by
Schnitzer (1977), who writes that learning how to live alone and find
contentment in solitude has helped him to preserve a sense of balance in
life:

> I have learned to derive contentment from my own company. To lose
> enjoyment of oneself has always appeared to me one of the great misfor-
> tunes that can befall a man [p. 77].[1]

Schnitzer agrees with Plato's remark that thinking is "a dialogue
within the soul" and believes that "being by oneself does not exclude
company of a special kind." He adds:

> There are two of us, and we can talk together. I have found a companion
> and a confidant, there is a sympathizer as well as a critic living in the
> same body with me. Together we can reach out more fully into the
> stream of life [p. 81].

Let's look more closely at some of the values of loneliness and
solitude. In the first place, unless we can enjoy our own company, we
have little chance of really being vital persons in our relationships with
others. I like the saying "If you can't make it alone, then you can't make it
with anybody else." In her beautiful and poetic book, *Gift from the Sea*,
Anne Morrow Lindbergh (1975) describes her own need to get away by
herself in order to find her center, simplify her life, and nourish herself so
that she would be able to give to others again. She describes how her
busy life, with its many and conflicting demands, had fragmented her, so
that she felt "the spring is dry, and the well is empty" (p. 47).[2] Through
solitude, she found replenishment and became reacquainted with herself:

> When one is a stranger to oneself then one is estranged from others too.
> If one is out of touch with oneself, then one cannot touch others. . . .
> Only when one is connected to one's own core is one connected to
> others. . . . For me, the core, the inner spring, can best be refound
> through solitude [pp. 43–44].

If we don't take time for ourselves but instead fill our lives with
activities and projects, we run the risk of losing a sense of centeredness.
As Lindbergh puts it, "Instead of stilling the center, the axis of the wheel,
we add more centrifugal activities to our lives—which tend to throw us

---

[1]This and all other quotations from this source from *Looking In*, by E. W. Schnitzer.
Copyright 1977. Reprinted by permission.

[2]This and all other quotations from this source from *Gift from the Sea*, by A. M. Lindbergh.
Copyright 1955 by Pantheon Books, a Division of Random House, Inc.

off balance" (Lindbergh, 1975, p. 51). Her own solitude taught her that she must remind herself to be alone each day, even for a few minutes, in order to keep a sense of herself and give of herself to others. I like the way she expressed this thought in words addressed to a seashell she took with her from an island where she had spent some time alone:

> You will remind me that I must try to be alone for part of each year, even a week or a few days; and for part of each day, even for an hour or for a few minutes, in order to keep my core, my center, my island-quality. You will remind me that unless I keep the island-quality intact somewhere within me, I will have little to give my husband, my children, my friends or the world at large [p. 57].

In much the same way as Anne Lindbergh described solitude as a way of discovering her core and putting her life in perspective, Clark Moustakas (1977) relates that a critical turning point in his life occurred when he discovered that loneliness could be a creative experience. Moustakas came to see that his personal growth and changed relationships with others were related to his feelings of loneliness. Accepting himself as a lonely person gave him the courage to face aspects of himself that he had never dared to face before and taught him the value of listening to his inner self. He writes: "In times of loneliness, my way back to life with others required that I stop listening to others, that I cut myself off from others and deliberately go off alone, to a place of isolation" (p. 109). In doing so, Moustakas became aware of how he had forsaken himself and of the importance of returning to himself. This process of finding himself led him to find new ways of relating to others: "In solitude, silent awareness and self-dialogues often quickly restored me to myself, and I was filled with new energy and the desire to renew my life with others in real ways" (p. 109).

Solitude can thus provide us with the opportunity to sort out our lives and gain a sense of perspective. It can give us time to ask significant questions, such as: How much have I become a stranger to myself? Have I been listening to myself, or have I been distracted and overstimulated by a busy life? Am I aware of my sense experiences, or have I been too involved in doing things to be aware of them?

One way to become aware of how much experience you ordinarily shut out is to do the following simple exercise. Choose a relatively quiet place where you can be alone. Close your eyes. Listen carefully to all the sounds about you. What are you aware of hearing? Do you hear sounds you usually don't hear? Become aware of smells. Become aware of touch. Try to experience all your senses. How much do you hear, feel, smell, and see that you ordinarily miss because of the hectic pace of your life?

Another value of taking time to be alone is that solitude can help us find new purpose and meaning when life begins to lose its vitality. As Moustakas (1975) says in *The Touch of Loneliness*, we can contemplate life and discover its meaning for us by experiencing the depths of our own being when the external world fails to alleviate our inner suffering or satisfy our hunger. When life seems empty, we can renew ourselves by taking time alone to look within for our answers, instead of to others. We can realize new dimensions of ourselves and examine the patterns that may be causing our lives to be empty, or at least not as rich as they might be. In Moustakas' words, "In such times it is essential that the person look within, detached and isolated, that he or she be open to the unknown resources of energy in life and in the universe" (Moustakas, 1975, p. 105). According to Moustakas, in order to experience this self-discovery and self-renewal, we must be willing to accept that we are basically alone in our lives, even though we may be comforted by the presence of others. This experience of our aloneness can be a source of power, insight, and creativity. Moustakas adds: "I saw loneliness as a requirement of living no matter how much love and affirmation one receives in work and in relationships with others" (p. 14).

Solitude thus seems to be essential for maintaining our sense of autonomy, especially in times of struggle. Too many of us look to others for direction instead of trusting ourselves at such times. Actually, our best hope for a resolution is to listen to our inner selves during periods of solitude. As Moustakas (1972) puts it:

In times of doubt and conflict there is no other way but to find a way from within. Being a self is a responsibility as well as a right. Thus the person cannot totally destroy his real self, even though this might please others and bring a gentler life [p. 7].

Many of us fail to experience solitude because we allow our lives to become more and more frantic and complicated. Unless we make a conscious effort to be alone, we may find that days and weeks go by without our having the chance to be with ourselves. Moreover, we may fear that we will alienate others if we ask for private time, so we alienate ourselves instead. Perhaps we fear that others will think us odd if we express a need to be alone. Indeed, others may sometimes fail to understand our need for solitude and try to bring us into the crowd or "cheer us up." People who are close to us may feel vaguely threatened, as if our need for time alone somehow reflected on our affection for them. Perhaps their own fears of being left alone will lead them to try to keep us from taking time away from them. Thus, claiming what we need and want for ourselves can involve a certain risk; however, if we fail to take that risk, we give up the very thing solitude could provide—a sense of self-direction and autonomy.

I think that most of us need to remind ourselves that we can tolerate only so much intensity with others and that ignoring our need for distance can breed resentment. For instance, a mother and father who are constantly with each other and with their children may not be doing a service either to their children or to themselves. Eventually they are likely to resent their "obligations." Unless they take time out, they may be there bodily and yet not be fully present to each other or to their children.

In summary, I hope that you will welcome time alone and strive to accept your own aloneness. Once we fully accept it, our aloneness can become the source of our strength and the foundation of our relatedness to others. Taking time to *be* alone gives us the opportunity to think, plan, imagine, and dream. It allows us to listen to ourselves and to become sensitive to what we are experiencing. In solitude we can come to appreciate anew both our separateness from, and our relatedness to, the important people and projects in our lives.

Time Out for Personal Reflection

1. Do you try to escape your loneliness or separateness? In what ways? Check any of the following statements that you think apply to you.

   _____ I busy myself in work.
   _____ I constantly seek to be with others.
   _____ I drink excessively or take drugs.
   _____ I schedule every moment so that I'll have very little time to think about myself.

_____ I attempt to avoid my troubles by watching television or listening to loud music.

_____ I eat compulsively.

_____ I sleep excessively to avoid the stresses in my life.

_____ I become overly concerned with helping others.

_____ I rarely think about anything if I can help it; I concentrate on playing and having fun.

List other specific ways in which you sometimes try to avoid experiencing your aloneness:

_____

_____

_____

_____

2. Would you like to change any of the patterns you've just identified? If so, what are they? What might you do to change them?

_____

_____

_____

_____

_____

3. Would you be willing to devote even ten minutes a day to being alone, without distractions? During these periods you might record in your journal the date, the time, and what you think about. Right now, take the time to list some things that you would like to do or reflect on when you're alone.

_____

_____

_____

_____

4. Do you agree or disagree with the idea that we are ultimately alone in the world? Why?

_____

_____

_____

5. Do you see time alone as being valuable to you? If so, in what ways?

_____

_____

_____

6. Have you experienced periods of creative solitude? If so, what were some of the positive aspects of these experiences?

_____

_____

_____

7. List a few of the major decisions you've made in your life. Did you make these decisions when you were alone or when you were with others?

_____

_____

_____

_____

A journal suggestion: If you find it difficult to be alone, without distractions, for more than a few minutes at a time, try being alone for a little longer than you're generally comfortable with. During this time, you might simply let your thoughts wander freely, without hanging on to one line of thinking. In your journal, describe what this experience is like for you.

Loneliness and Life Stages

How we deal with feelings of loneliness can depend to a great extent on our early experiences of loneliness in childhood and adolescence. Later in life, we may feel that loneliness has no place or that we can and should be able to avoid experiencing it. I think it's important to reflect on our past experiences of loneliness if we're to avoid running from our aloneness because of the anxiety it creates for us. In addition, we may fear loneliness less if we recognize that it is a natural part of living in every stage of life. Once we have accepted our aloneness and the likelihood that we will feel lonely at many points in our lives, we may be better able to take responsibility for our own loneliness and recognize ways in which we may be contributing to needless loneliness.

Reliving some of our childhood experiences of loneliness can help us come to grips with present fears and anxieties about being alone or lonely. The following are some typical memories of lonely periods that people I've worked with have relived in therapy:

- A woman recalls the time her parents were fighting in the bedroom, and she heard them screaming and yelling. She was sure that her parents would divorce, and in many ways she felt responsible. She remembers living in continual fear that she would be deserted.
- A man recalls attempting to give a speech in the sixth grade. He stuttered over certain words, and children in the class began to laugh at him. Afterwards, he developed extreme self-consciousness in regard to his speech, and he long remembered the hurt he had experienced.
- A Black man recalls how excluded he felt in his all-White elementary school, and how the other children would talk about him in derisive ways. As an adult, he can still cry over these memories.
- A woman recalls the fright she felt as a small child when her uncle made sexual advances toward her. Although she hadn't really understood what was happening she remembers the terrible loneliness of feeling that she couldn't tell her parents for fear of what they would do.
- A man recalls the boyhood loneliness of feeling that he was continually failing at everything he tried. To this day, he resists undertaking a task unless he is sure he can handle it, for fear of rekindling those old lonely feelings.
- A woman vividly remembers being in the hospital as a small child for an operation. She remembers the loneliness of not knowing what was going on or whether she would be able to leave the hospital. Since no one talked with her or allowed her to talk out her fears, she was all alone with them.

Experiences such as these can lead us to defend ourselves unnecessarily in later life and thus keep us from experiencing our aloneness in a positive way. As we try to relive these experiences, we should remember that children do not live in a logical, well-ordered world. Our childhood fears may have been greatly exaggerated, and the feeling of fright may remain with us even though we may now think of it as irrational. Unfortunately, being told by adults that we were foolish for having such fears may only have increased our loneliness while doing nothing to lessen the fears themselves.

At this point, you may wonder "Why go back and recall childhood pain and loneliness? Why not just let it be a thing of the past?" I feel convinced that we need to reexperience some of the pain we felt as children to see whether we are still carrying it around with us now. We can also look at some of the decisions we made during these times of extreme loneliness and ask whether these decisions are still appropriate.

Frequently, strategies we adopted as children remain with us into adulthood, when they are no longer appropriate. For instance, suppose your family moved to a strange city when you were 7 years old and that you had to go to a new school. Kids at the new school laughed at you, and you lived through several months of anguish. You felt desperately alone in the world. During this time you decided to keep your feelings to yourself and build a wall around yourself so that others couldn't hurt you. Although this experience is now long past, you still defend yourself in the same way, because you haven't *really* made a new decision to open up and trust some people. In this way, old fears of loneliness might contribute to a real loneliness in the present. If you allow yourself to experience your grief and work it through, emotionally as well as intellectually, you can overcome past pain and create new choices for yourself.

Time Out for Personal Reflection

Take some time to decide whether you're willing to recall and relive a childhood experience of loneliness. If so, try to recapture the experience in as much detail as you can, reliving it in fantasy. Then reflect on the experience, using the following questions as a starting point.

1. Describe in a few words the most lonely experience you recall having as a child.

   _____

   _____

   _____

2. How do you think the experience affected you *then?*

   _____

   _____

3. How do you think the experience may still affect you *now?*

   _____

   _____

Journal suggestions: Consider elaborating on this exercise in your journal. Here are a few questions you might reflect on: How did you cope with your loneliness as a child? How has this influenced the way you deal with loneliness in your life now? If you could go back and put a new ending on your most lonely childhood experience, what would it be? You might also think about times in your childhood when you enjoyed being alone. Write some notes to yourself about what these experiences were like for you. Where did you like to spend time alone? What did you enjoy doing by yourself? What positive aspects of these times do you recall?

Loneliness and Adolescence

For many people, loneliness and adolescence are practically synonymous. Adolescents often feel that they are all alone in their world, that they are the first ones to have the feelings they do, and that in some real way they are separated from others by some abnormality. Bodily changes and impulses are alone sufficient to bring about a sense of perplexity and loneliness, but there are other stresses to be undergone as well. Adolescents are developing a sense of identity. They strive to be successful yet fear failure. They want to be accepted and liked, but they fear rejection, ridicule, or exclusion by their peers. They are curious about sex yet often frightened to experiment or constrained from doing so. Most adolescents know the feeling of being lonely in a crowd or among friends, and many of the young people I've worked with have reported the loneliness they felt as a result of keeping their own convictions private and adopting the views and morals of their group, out of fear of being ostracized. Conformity can bring acceptance, and the price of nonconformity can be steep for those who have the courage to decide for themselves how they will think and behave.

As you recall your adolescent years—and, in particular, the areas of your life that were marked by loneliness—you might reflect on the following questions:

- Did I feel included in a social group? Or did I sit on the sidelines, afraid of being included and wishing for it at the same time?
- Was there at least one person whom I felt I could talk to—one who really heard me, so that I didn't feel desperately alone?
- What experience stands out as one of the most lonely times during these years? How did I cope with my loneliness?
- Did I experience a sense of confusion concerning who I was and what I wanted to be as a person? How did I deal with my confusion? Who or what helped me during this time?
- How did I feel about my own worth and value? Did I believe that I had anything of value to offer anyone or that anyone would find me worth being with?

As you reflect on your adolescence, add your own questions to the list I've suggested. Then try to discover some of the ways in which the person you now are is a result of your lonely experiences as an adolescent. Do you shrink from competition for fear of failure? In social situations, are you afraid of being left out? Do you feel some of the isolation you did then? If so, how do you deal with it?

Time Out for Personal Reflection

1. To facilitate your recollection of your adolescent years, reflect on the following pairs of statements, and check the one that best fits your experience. If neither response fits you, you can write in your own on the line provided.

   a. _____ I felt included in a social group.
   _____ I generally sat on the sidelines and feared being included, while wishing for it at the same time.

   _____

   b. _____ There was at least one person whom I felt I could talk to— someone who really heard me and made me feel less alone.
   _____ I generally felt that there was nobody who really understood or listened to me.

   _____

   c. _____ I felt little value or worth as a person.
   _____ I believed that I had value and that others valued me and wanted to be with me.

   _____

2. Describe the most lonely experience of your adolescent years.

   _____

   _____

   _____

   _____

3. How did you cope with the loneliness you've just described?

   _____

   _____

   _____

   _____

4. What effect do you think the experience you've described has upon you today?

   _____

   _____

   _____

   _____

5. Recall some times as an adolescent when you chose to be alone. What were these times like for you? Were there times when you enjoyed being alone?

_____

_____

_____

_____

Loneliness and Young Adulthood

In our young-adult years, we are engaged in experimenting with ways of being and in establishing life-styles that may remain with us for many years. We may be struggling with the question of what to do with our lives, what kinds of intimate relationships we want to establish, and how we will chart our futures. Dealing with all the choices that face us in this time of life can be a lonely process.

How we come to terms with our own aloneness at this time can have significant effects on the choices we make—choices that, in turn, may determine the course of our lives for years to come. For instance, if we haven't learned to listen to ourselves and to depend on our own inner resources, we might succumb to the pressure to choose a relationship or a career before we're really prepared to do so, or we might look to our projects or partners for the sense of identity that we ultimately can find only in ourselves. Alternatively, we may feel lonely and establish patterns that only increase our loneliness. This last possibility is well illustrated by the case of Larry.

Larry was an exceptionally bright and good-looking 20-year-old who did well in many of the things he tried. In the hope of finding a sense of connectedness or belonging, he enlisted in the military service. He became a sharpshooter and a member of a select group of paratroopers, and he taught scuba diving and other sports. However, when a particular sport didn't go as well as he would have liked, he quickly dropped it and went on to another one. In all his physical activities, he was absolutely fearless and often would tempt fate in regard to risking his life.

Larry is following a hedonistic ideal of a "short but happy" life. His main goal is to acquire all the creature comforts of life as soon as possible. He has a difficult time staying in one place for any length of time, and, even though he says he is extremely lonely, he has an aversion to any kind of committed relationships. He shows little concern for the feelings of others and fears that a long-time relationship would tie him down and restrict his free-wheeling style. However, in choosing this style, Larry is also creating much of his own loneliness. He doesn't realize that his continual rejections of others ultimately result in his own feelings of rejection and loneliness. Rather, he continues to maintain that he doesn't need friends and that expressing tenderness and concern toward others is a sign of weakness. Despite this apparent self-assurance and his natural capabilities, however, Larry seems to have deep feelings of inadequacy and insecurity. This is revealed by the resentment that he directs toward himself and by his remark that it would be easy to turn his gun on himself when he is target-shooting. Larry seems to be well aware of the loneliness of his world, but to this point he isn't willing to change his own behavior, because he isn't convinced that it would be worth it to do so.

The example of Larry illustrates in a dramatic way what many people experience to a lesser degree who are basically ambivalent in their feelings toward themselves. It also illustrates the important point that we often create much of our own loneliness, even though we don't want to be lonely. This point has an application to the experience of many college students I've encountered who talk about the loneliness they experience on the campus. Many students feel isolated and say that the campus is an impersonal place where it is difficult to make contact with others. They come to school, attend class, and go home again, and by the end of the semester they say that they don't know more than a couple of people in a class. As an example, let me briefly describe one such student.

Saul was in his early twenties when he attended the college. He claimed that his chief problem was his isolation, yet he rarely reached out to others. His general manner seemed to say "keep away." Although he was enrolled in a small, informal class of self-awareness and personal growth, he quickly left after each session, depriving himself of the chance to make contact with anyone.

One day, as I was walking across the campus, I saw Saul sitting alone in a secluded spot, while many students were congregated on the lawn, enjoying the beautiful spring weather. Here was a chance for Saul to do something about his separation from others; instead, he chose to seclude himself. Saul continually told himself that others didn't like him and, sadly, made his prophecy self-fulfilling by his own behavior. He made himself unapproachable and, in many ways, the kind of person people would avoid.

In this time of life, we have the chance to decide on ways of being toward ourselves and others as well as on our vocations and future plans. If you feel lonely on the campus, I'd like to challenge you to ask yourself what *you* are doing and can do about your own loneliness. Do you decide in advance that the other students and instructors want to keep to themselves? Do you assume that there already are well-established cliques to which you cannot belong? Do you expect others to reach out to you, even though you don't initiate contacts yourself? What fears might be holding you back? Where do they seem to come from? Are past experiences of loneliness or rejection determining the choices you make now?

Often we create unnecessary loneliness for ourselves by our own behavior. If we sit back and wait for others to come to us, we give them the power to make us lonely. As we learn to take responsibility for ourselves in young adulthood, one area we can work on is taking responsibility for our own loneliness and creating new choices for ourselves.

Loneliness and Middle Age

Many changes occur during middle age that may result in new feelings of loneliness. Although we may not be free to choose some of the things that occur at this time in our lives, we *are* free to choose how we relate to these events. Among the possible changes and crises of middle age are the following:

- Our spouses may grow tired of living with us and decide to leave. If so, we must decide how we will respond to this situation. Will we blame ourselves and become absorbed in self-hate? Will we refuse to see any of our own responsibility for the breakup and simply blame the other person? Will we decide never to trust anyone again? Will we mourn our loss and, after a period of grieving, actively look for another person to live with?
- Our lives may not turn out the way we had planned. We may not have enjoyed the success we'd hoped for, or we may feel disenchanted with our work, or we may feel that we passed up many fine opportunities earlier. Any of these things might be true, but the key point is what we can do about our lives *now*. What choices will we make in light of this reality? Will we slip into hopelessness and berate ourselves endlessly about what we could have done and should have done? Will we allow ourselves to stay trapped in meaningless work and empty relationships, or will we look for positive options for change?
- Our children may leave home, and with this change we may experience emptiness and a sense of loss. If so, what will we do about this transition? Will we attempt to hang on? Can we let go and create a new life with new meaning? Will our will to live leave with our children? Will we look back with regret at all that we could have done differently, or will we choose to look ahead to the kind of life we want to create for ourselves now that we don't have the responsibilities of parenthood?

These are just a few of the changes that many of us confront during the middle years of living. Although we may feel that events are not in our control, we can still choose the ways in which we respond to these life situations. To illustrate, I'd like to present a brief example that reflects the loneliness many people experience after a divorce and show how the two people involved made different decisions with respect to dealing with their loneliness.

Amy and Gary were married for over 20 years before their recent divorce, and they have three children in their teens. Amy is 43; Gary is 41. Although they have both experienced a good deal of loneliness since their divorce, they have chosen different attitudes toward their loneliness. For his part, Gary felt resentful at first and believed that somehow they could have stayed together if only Amy had changed her attitude. He lives alone in a small apartment and sees his teenagers on weekends. He interprets the divorce as a personal failure, and he still feels a mixture of guilt and resentment. He hates to come home to an empty house, with no one to talk to and no one to share his life with. In some ways, he has decided not to cultivate other relationships, because he still bears the scars of his "first failure." He wonders whether women would find him interesting, and he fears that it's too late to begin a new life with someone else.

Gary declines most of his friends' invitations, interpreting their concern as pity. He says that at times he feels like climbing the walls, that he sometimes wakes up at night in a cold sweat and feels real pangs of abandonment and loneliness. He attempts to numb his lonely feelings by burying himself in his work, but he cannot rid himself of the ongoing ache of loneliness. Gary seems to have decided on some level not to let go of his isolation. He has convinced himself that it isn't really possible for him to develop a new relationship. His own attitude limits his options, because he has set up a self-fulfilling prophecy: he convinces himself that another woman would not want to share time with him, and, as a consequence, others pick up the messages that he is sending out about himself.

For her part, Amy had many ambivalent feelings about divorcing. After the divorce, she experienced feelings of panic and aloneness as she faced the prospect of rearing her children and managing the home on her own. She wondered whether she could meet her responsibilities and still have time for any social life for herself. She wondered whether men would be interested in her, particularly in light of the fact that she had three teenagers. She anguished over such questions as "Will I be able to have another life with someone else?" "Do I want to live alone?" "Can I take care of my emotional needs and still provide for the family?" Unlike Gary, Amy decided to date several different people—when she felt like it, and because she felt like it. At first she was pressured by her family to find a man and settle down. She decided, however, to resist this pressure, and she has chosen to remain single for the time being. She intends to develop a long-term relationship only if she feels it is what she wants after she has had time to live alone. Although she is lonely at times, she doesn't feel trapped and resists being a victim of her lonely feelings.

Experiences like those of Gary and Amy are very common among middle-aged persons. Many people find themselves having to cope with feelings of isolation and abandonment after a divorce. Some, like Gary, may feel panic and either retreat from people or quickly run into a new relationship to avoid the pain of separation. If they don't confront their fears and their pain, they may be controlled by their fear of being left alone for the rest of their lives. Others, like Amy, may go through a similar period of loneliness after a divorce, yet refuse to be controlled by a fear of living alone. Although they might want a long-term relationship again some day, they avoid rushing impulsively into a new relationship in order to avoid any feelings of pain or loneliness.

Loneliness and the Later Years

Our society emphasizes productivity, youth, beauty, power, and vitality. As we age, we may lose some of our vitality and sense of power or attractiveness. Many people face a real crisis when they reach retirement, for they feel that they're being put out to pasture—that they aren't needed any more and that their lives are really over. Loneliness and hopelessness are experienced by anyone who feels that there is little to look forward to or that he or she has no vital place in society, and such feelings are particularly common among older adults.

The loneliness of the later years can be accentuated by the losses that come with age. There can be some loss of sight, hearing, memory, and strength. Older people may lose their jobs, hobbies, friends, and loved ones. A particularly difficult loss is the loss of a spouse with whom one has been close for many years. In the face of such losses, a person may ultimately ask what reason remains for living. It may be no coincidence that many old people die soon after their spouses die or shortly after their retirement. However, the pangs of aloneness or the feelings that life is futile reflect a drastic loss of meaning rather than an essential part of growing old. Viktor Frankl has written about the "will to meaning" as a key determinant of a person's desire to live. He noted that many of the inmates in a Nazi concentration camp kept themselves alive by looking forward to the prospect of being released and reunited with their families. Many of those who lost hope simply gave up and died, regardless of their age.

At least until recently, our society has compounded the elderly person's loss of meaning by grossly neglecting the aged population. The number of institutions and convalescent homes in which old persons are often left to vegetate testify to this neglect. It's hard to imagine a more lonely existence than the one many of these people are compelled to suffer.

Despite this societal neglect, those who specialize in the study of aging often make the point that, if we have led rich lives in early adulthood, we have a good chance of finding richness in our later years. Certainly, if we have learned to find direction from within ourselves, we will be better equipped to deal with the changes aging brings. Just this summer, my wife and I had the good fortune to meet an exceptional man, Dr. Ewald Schnitzer, who retired from the University of California at Los Angeles in 1973 and moved to Idyllwild—a place that he considers his last and happiest home. For me, this person provides an outstanding model of the way I hope I face my own old age, for his example demonstrates that one can be old in years and at the same time young and vital in spirit.

Dr. Schnitzer lives alone by preference and continues to find excitement and meaning in his life in art, philosophy, music, history, hiking, writing, and traveling. He believes that his entire life has prepared him well for his later years. He has learned to be content when he is alone, he finds pleasure in the company of animals and nature, and he enjoys many memories of his rich experiences. I respect the way in which he can live fully now, without dreading the future. This spirit of being fully alive is well expressed in his book *Looking In:*

> It would be painful should frailty prevent me from climbing mountains. Yet, when that time comes, I hope I find serenity in wandering through valleys, looking at the realm of distant summits not with ambition but with loving memories [Schnitzer, 1977, p. 88].

Schnitzer is an example of someone who can accept the fact of his aging yet recognize that each stage of life brings its unique challenges and potentialities for creating a meaningful existence. This is how he expresses this thought:

> I am writing this as I stand on the threshold of old age. Like everybody at this stage I have to face the fact of my bodily decline. I am saying this with a tinge of sadness but without a trace of despair. For it has always seemed to me that each age has its own possibilities and challenges, and I have often taken heart from this remark of Roger Fry's: "It is a wonderful thing to recognize the advanced age of a person less by the infirmity of his body than by the maturity of his soul" [p. 87].

I'd like to conclude this discussion of the later years—and, in a sense, this entire chapter on loneliness and solitude—by returning to the example of Anne Morrow Lindbergh. In her later years, her lifelong courage in facing aloneness enabled her to find new and rich meaning in her life. I was extremely impressed with this woman when I first read her book *Gift from the Sea,* but my respect increased when I read the Afterword in the book's 20th-anniversary edition. There, she looks back at the time when she originally wrote the book and notes that she was then deeply involved in family life. Since that time, her children have left and established their own lives. She describes how a most uncomfortable stage followed her middle years—one that she hadn't anticipated when she wrote the book. She writes that she went from the "oyster-bed" stage of taking care of a family to the "abandoned-shell" stage of later life. This is how she describes the essence of the "abandoned-shell" stage:

> Plenty of solitude, and a sudden panic at how to fill it, characterized this period. With me, it was not a question of simply filling up the space or the time. I had many activities and even a well-established vocation to pursue. But when a mother is left, the lone hub of a wheel, with no other lives revolving around her, she faces a total reorientation. It takes time to re-find the center of gravity [Lindbergh, 1975, p. 134].

In this stage, she did make choices to come to terms with herself and create a new role for herself. She points out that all the exploration she did earlier in life paid off when she reached the "abandoned-shell" stage. Here again, earlier choices affect current ones.

Before her husband, Charles, died in 1974, Anne had looked forward to retiring with him on the Hawaiian island of Maui. His death changed her life abruptly but did not bring it to an end. Its continuity was preserved in part by the presence of her five children and twelve grandchildren; moreover, she continued to involve herself in her own writing and in the preparation of her husband's papers for publication. Here is a fine example of a woman who has encountered her share of loneliness and learned to renew herself by actively choosing a positive stance toward life.

Time Out for Personal Reflection

Complete the following sentences by writing down the first response that comes to mind.

1. The most lonely time in my life was when _____

   _____.

2. When I'm alone, I _____.

3. I usually deal with my loneliness by _____.

4. I escape from loneliness by _____.

5. If I were to be left and abandoned by all those who love me, _____

   _____.

6. The place where I most like to be alone is _____.

7. The place where I least like to be alone is _____.

8. One value I see in experiencing loneliness is _____

   _____.

9. My greatest fear of loneliness is _____.

10. To me, solitude means _____.

11. I have felt lonely in a crowd when _____

    _____.

12. When I'm with a person who is lonely, _____

    _____.

13. For me, being with others is _____
_____.

14. I feel most lonely when _____.

15. The thought of living alone the rest of my life _____
_____.

Chapter Summary

In this chapter, I've suggested that experiencing loneliness is part of being human. We can grow from such experience if we understand it and use it to renew our sense of ourselves. Moreover, we don't have to remain victimized by early decisions that we made as a result of past loneliness. Some key points are:

1. Ultimately, we all are alone.
2. Most of us have experienced loneliness during our childhood and adolescent years, and these experiences can have a significant influence on our present attitudes, behavior, and relationships.
3. Times of solitude can give us an invaluable opportunity to gain perspective on the direction and meaning of our lives.
4. We have some choice concerning whether we will feel lonely or whether we will feel in touch with others. We can design our activities so that we reject others before they can reject us, or we can risk making contact with them.
5. We can choose to face our loneliness and deal with it creatively, or we can choose to try to escape from it.

List some other points from this chapter that were significant for you and that you would like to remember.

_____

_____

_____

_____

_____

_____

_____

Activities and Exercises

1. Allocate some time each day in which to be alone and reflect on anything you wish. Note down in your journal the thoughts and feelings that occur to you during your time alone.

2. If you have feelings of loneliness when you think about a certain person who has been or is now significant to you, write a letter to that person expressing all the things you're feeling (you don't have to mail the letter). For instance, tell that person how you miss him or her, or write about your sadness, your resentment, or your desire for more closeness with him or her.

3. Imagine that you are the person you've written your letter to, and write a reply to yourself. What do you imagine that person would say to you if he or she received your letter? What do you fear (and what do you wish) he or she would say?

4. If you sometimes feel lonely and left out, you might try some specific experiments for a week or so. For example, if you feel isolated in most of your classes, why not make it a point to get to class early and initiate contact with a fellow student? If you feel anxious about taking such a step, try doing it in fantasy. What are your fears? What is the worst thing you can imagine might happen? Record your impressions in your journal. If you decide to try reaching out to other people, record what the experience is like for you in your journal.

5. Think about the person that means the most to you. Now let yourself imagine that this person decides to leave you. Imagine what that would be like for you—what you might feel, say, and do. How do you think his or her leaving would affect you?

6. Recall some periods of loneliness in your life. Select important situations in which you experienced loneliness, and spend some time recalling the details of each situation and reflecting on the meaning each of these experiences has had for you. Now you might do two things:
   a. Write down your reflections in your journal. How do you think your past experiences of loneliness affect you now?
   b. Select a friend or a person you'd like to trust more, and share this experience of loneliness.

7. Many people rarely make time exclusively for themselves. If you'd like to have time to yourself but just haven't gotten around to arranging it, consider going to a place you haven't been to before, or to the beach, desert, or mountains. Reserve a weekend just for yourself; if this seems too much, then spend a day completely alone. The important thing is to remove yourself from your everyday routine and just be with yourself without external distractions.

8. Try spending a day or part of a day in a place where you can observe and experience lonely people. You might spend some time near a busy downtown intersection, in a park where old people congregate, or in a large shopping center. Try to pay attention to expressions of loneliness, alienation, and isolation. How do people seem to be dealing with their loneliness? Later, you might discuss your observations in class.

9. Imagine yourself living in a typical rest home—without any of your possessions, cut off from your family and friends, and unable to do

the things you now do. Reflect on what this experience would be like for you; then write down some of your reactions in your journal.

10. Read a book or two on meditation and finding centeredness within yourself. Try doing some of the exercises you come across in these books.

Suggested Readings

Josephson, E., & Josephson, M. (Eds.). *Man Alone: Alienation in Modern Society.* New York: Dell, 1962. This is a book of articles dealing with the theme that the contemporary person—alienated from nature, self, and others—finds it difficult to achieve a sense of identity and relatedness.

Lindbergh, A. *Gift from the Sea.* New York: Pantheon, 1955, 1975. Although this book is over 20 years old, it is still timely for both women and men as a catalyst for thinking about the need for solitude. It is a deep, simply written, and poetic book. The recent edition contains an afterword about the author's life during the past 20 years.

Moustakas, C. *Loneliness.* Englewood Cliffs, N.J.: Prentice-Hall (Spectrum), 1961. In this classic book on loneliness, the central message is that loneliness is a condition of human life and an experience that enables us to realize a deeper meaning in our lives.

Moustakas, C. *Loneliness and Love.* Englewood Cliffs, N.J.: Prentice-Hall (Spectrum), 1972. This insightful book offers a unique approach to the positive dimensions of loneliness and emphasizes individuality, personal honesty, communication, and love in relation to oneself.

Moustakas, C. *The Touch of Loneliness.* Englewood Cliffs, N.J.: Prentice-Hall (Spectrum), 1975. This book contains many letters by the author and by people who have written accounts of their own loneliness.

Moustakas, C. *Turning Points.* Englewood Cliffs, N.J.: Prentice-Hall (Spectrum), 1977. In this book, Moustakas deals with the uncertainty associated with the various transitions in our lives. Its theme is that, by choosing to face these turning points, we can find strength within ourselves and reaffirm our existence.

Schnitzer, E. *Looking In.* Idyllwild, Calif.: Strawberry Valley Press, 1977. This is an inspirational book of essays on such topics as living creatively with solitude and finding meaning in life through travels and encounters with nature. The book has many thoughts on finding meaning in the simple things of life.

Sheehy, G. *Passages: Predictable Crises of Adult Life.* New York: Bantam, 1976. A number of cases described by Sheehy illustrate the loneliness many people experience as they make the passage from one life stage to the next. Some excellent cases depict the challenge of facing loneliness and aloneness and dealing with it creatively.

Stevens, J. *Awareness: Exploring, Experimenting, and Experiencing.* Moab, Utah: Real People Press, 1971. This book discusses how we can deepen and expand our awareness. It contains many exercises and experiments that you can do by yourself or with another person.

Death, Separation, and Loss

The acceptance of death is vitally related to the discovery of meaning and purpose in life. One of our distinguishing characteristics as human beings is our ability to grasp the concept of the future and thus the inevitability of death. Our ability to do so gives meaning to our existence, for it makes our every act and moment count.

Pre-Chapter Self-Inventory

For each statement, indicate the response that most closely identifies your beliefs and attitudes. Use this code: A = I strongly agree; B = I slightly agree; C = I slightly disagree; D = I strongly disagree.

_____ 1. If I'm afraid of dying, then to some degree I'm afraid of living.

_____ 2. I have some irrational fears concerning death.

_____ 3. The fact that I will die makes me take the present moment seriously.

_____ 4. Our culture tends to deny or avoid the reality of death.

_____ 5. When I think about dying, I feel that I'm ultimately alone in life.

_____ 6. If I had a terminal illness, I'd want to know how much time I had left to live, so that I could decide how to spend it.

_____ 7. Because of the possibility of losing those I love, I don't allow myself to get too close to others.

_____ 8. It's best to avoid discussing death and dying with a person who is in danger of death.

_____ 9. I can't really live a meaningful life unless I think about and accept the fact of my eventual death.

_____ 10. Believing in an afterlife is a way of denying the finality of death.

_____ 11. If I live with dignity, I'll be able to die with dignity.

_____ 12. Just as many parents are reluctant to educate their children about sex, many parents are reluctant to educate their children about death.

_____ 13. It's best to take a nonchalant attitude toward death, since thinking seriously about it only makes us morbid.

_____ 14. One of my greatest fears of death is the fear of the unknown.

_____ 15. I've had experiences of loss in my life that in some ways were like the experience of dying.

_____ 16. In a way, the experience of a divorce or separation can be like the experience of dying.

_____ 17. There are some ways in which I'm not really alive emotionally.

_____ 18. I'm not especially afraid of dying.

_____ 19. It's important to allow ourselves to fully mourn the deaths of loved ones and other losses.

_____ 20. I fear the deaths of those I love more than I do my own.

In this chapter, I encourage you to look at your attitudes and beliefs about your own death, the deaths of those you love, and other forms of significant loss. Although the topic of this chapter might seem to be morbid or depressing, I strongly believe that an honest understanding and acceptance of death and loss can be the groundwork of a rich and meaningful life. If we fully accept that we have only a limited time in which to live, we can make choices that will make the most of the time we have.

I also ask you to consider the notion of death in a broader perspective and to raise such questions as: What parts of me aren't as alive as they might be? In what emotional ways am I dead or dying? What will I do with my awareness of the ways in which I'm not fully alive? Finally, I discuss the importance of fully experiencing our grief when we suffer serious losses.

This discussion of death and loss has an important connection with the themes of the preceding chapter on loneliness and solitude. When we emotionally accept the reality of our eventual death, we experience our ultimate aloneness. I believe that this awareness of our mortality and aloneness helps us to realize that our actions do count, that we do have choices concerning how we live our lives, and that we must accept the final responsibility for how well we are living.

This chapter is also a bridge to the next chapter, in which I discuss meaning and values. The awareness of death is a catalyst of the human search for meaning in life. Our knowledge that we will die can encourage us to take a careful and honest look at how we are living now. With a realistic awareness of death, we can ask ourselves whether we're living by values that create a meaningful existence; if not, we have the time and opportunity to change our way of living.

Our Fears of Death

Although a realistic fear of death seems to be a healthy and inevitable part of living, it's possible to become so obsessed with the fear of our own death, or of the deaths of those we love, that we can't really enjoy living. We may be afraid of really getting involved with life, of allowing ourselves to care for others, or of building hopes for the future. On the other hand, we may numb ourselves to the reality of death by telling ourselves there's no point in thinking about it—"When it comes, it comes." Neither of these attitudes permits us to realistically confront death and its meaning. Although I surely don't advocate being excessively preoccupied with the thought of death, I do believe that a conscious acceptance of death and a deliberate reflection about it can help us discover meaning in our lives.

Often, a fear of death goes hand in hand with a fear of life. If we're excessively fearful of death, we'll probably be fearful of investing ourselves in life as well, since nothing we cherish is permanent. By the same token, if we involve ourselves in the present moment as fully as possible, it's unlikely that we'll be obsessed with the thought of life's end.

In *Overcoming the Fear of Death*, Gordon (1972) writes about our refusal to face death because of our fears of it. He contends that we tend to view death as a remote possibility and that we unconsciously repress our fears as well as consciously try to forget about death. The following statement from his book has much meaning for me:

> Most of us are afraid to contemplate our own ending; and when anything reminds us that we too shall die, we flee and turn our thoughts to happier matters. The thought of our finitude and ephemerality is so frightening that we run away from this basic fact of existence, consciously and unconsciously, and proceed through life as though we shall endure forever [p. 13].

There are many aspects of death that we may be fearful of, some of which include: leaving behind those we love, losing our selves, encountering the unknown, coping with the humiliation and indignity of a painful or long dying, losing time in which we could be doing the things we most want to finish, and growing distant in the memories of others. For many people, it's not so much death itself as it is the experience of dying that arouses fears. Here, too, it is well to ask what our fears are really about and to confront them honestly, as Schnitzer (1977) does in *Looking In*:

> Death is feared because it seems to condemn us to utter loneliness and to the loss of identity. But consciousness also vanishes, and what is there to be feared when it is totally gone? "To fear death means pretending to know what we don't know," Plato once said. What we are afraid of is not death but dying, the phase that confronts us with the loss of our world and its familiar beings—the only home we know. And that indeed must be painful. There may be agony, both physical and mental. At that last stage we will be much in need of braveness [p. 89].

In his powerful book, *Facing Death*, Kavanaugh (1972) describes the fears of a woman who was dying of cancer. She related how the fears she actually experienced were not nearly so terrible as the ones she had expected to feel and that any attempt to escape her fears was more painful than the fears themselves. She found that those friends who were not busy running from their own fears were the people who could be the most help and comfort to her as she neared death. The last few lines of her story suggest that, in dying, we may learn important lessons about how to live:

I wish someone had told me that the only impossible fear is the fear to feel and share your feelings with others. Those who love you can understand anything, and all of us are stronger than any of us realize. I think my death will be almost happy, since my one pressing regret is that I cannot live to practice what I learned in dying [p. 57].

We don't have to experience dying to begin learning what it can teach us about life. If we can honestly confront our fears of death, we have a chance to work on changing the quality of our lives and to make real changes in our relationships with others and with ourselves. I agree with Gordon (1972) when he says that, if we could live with the idea that this very moment might be our last, "we would find that many problems and conflicts would evanesce, and life would be simplified and become more satisfying (p. 17)."

At this point, you might pause to reflect on your own fears of death and dying. What expectations seem to arouse the greatest fears in you? Do your fears concern death itself or the experience of dying? In what ways do you think your fears might be affecting how you choose to live now? Have you been close to someone who has died? If so, how did the experience of that person's death affect your feelings about death and dying?

Death and the Meaning of Life

I accept the existentialist view that the acceptance of death is vitally related to the discovery of meaning and purpose in life. One of our distinguishing characteristics as human beings is our ability to grasp the concept of the future and thus the inevitability of death. Our ability to do so gives meaning to our existence, for it makes our every act and moment count.

In his book *Is There an Answer to Death?* Koestenbaum (1976) develops the idea that our awareness of death enables us to have a plan of life. It compels us to see our lives in totality and to seek real and ultimate answers. As Koestenbaum states:

Many people think of death as unreal, as just beyond the horizon, as something they should postpone thinking about—in fact, as an event that is not to be mentioned. As a result, they are incapable of experiencing their lives as a whole, of forming any total life plan [p. 32].

The awareness of death is also related to our ability to form distinctive personal identities. By accepting our mortality, we enable ourselves to define the quality of life we want; as Koestenbaum says, our anticipation of death reveals to us who we are. This anticipation is both an intellectual awareness revelation and an experiential understanding. It puts us in touch with our hopes and our anxieties and gives direction to our lives.

The meaning of our lives, then, depends on the fact that we are finite beings. What we do with our lives counts. We can choose to become all that we are capable of becoming and make a conscious decision to fully affirm life, or we can passively let life slip by us. We can settle for letting events happen to us, or we can actively choose and create the kind of life we want. If we had forever to actualize our potentials, there would be no urgency about doing so. Our time is invaluable precisely because it is limited. Consequently, without living in constant fear of death, it is well for us to dwell on the unique importance of the present moment, for it is all we really have.

Time Out for Personal Reflection

1. What fears do you experience when you think about your own death? Check any of the following statements that apply to you:

   _____ I worry about what will happen to me after death.
   _____ I'm anxious about the way I will die.
   _____ I wonder whether I'll die with dignity.
   _____ I fear the physical pain of dying.
   _____ I worry most about my loved ones who will be left behind.
   _____ I'm afraid that I won't be able to accomplish all that I want to accomplish before I die.

_____ I fear the unknown.
_____ It's difficult for me to think of growing old.

List any other fears you experience in regard to death and dying.

_____

_____

_____

_____

2. How well do you think you're living your life? List some specific things that you aren't doing now but that you'd like to be doing. List some things that you think you'd be likely to do if you knew that you had only a short time to live.

_____

_____

_____

_____

_____

3. In many of my courses, I've asked students to write a brief description of what they might do if they knew they had only 24 hours left to live. If you're willing to, write down what occurs to you when you think about this possibility.

_____

_____

_____

_____

_____

_____

_____

4. In what way does the fact that you will die give meaning to your life now?

_____

_____

_____

_____

5. For many people, it is not so much death itself as it is the experience of dying that arouses fears. Are you more anxious about dying than about death itself? If so, what is it about dying that you're most fearful of?

_____

_____

_____

_____

6. Are there ways in which you avoid facing the inevitability of your own death or the deaths of those you love? If so, in what ways do you try to deny this reality?

_____

_____

_____

_____

_____

7. In what ways do you think your fears about death and dying might be affecting the choices you make now?

_____

_____

_____

_____

8. What have you learned from these exercises?

_____

_____

_____

_____

Freedom in Dying

The process of dying involves a gradual diminishing of the choices available to us. Even in dying, however, we still have choices concerning how we face and deal with what is happening to us.

As I write these words, a friend and student, Jim Morelock, is dying. Jim has permitted me to use his real name and to share some of the significant moments in his dying. I don't know of anyone who shows better than Jim does how we remain free to choose our attitude toward life and toward life's ending.

Jim is 25 years old. He is full of life—witty, bright, honest, and actively questioning. He had just graduated from college as a Human Services major and seemed to have a bright future when his illness was discovered.

About a year and a half ago, Jim developed a growth on his forehead and underwent surgery to have it removed. At that time, his doctors claimed that the growth was a rare disorder but that it was not malignant. Later, more tumors erupted, and more surgery followed. Several months ago, Jim found out that the tumors had spread throughout his body and that, even with cobalt treatment, he would have a short life. Since that time, Jim has steadily grown weaker and has been able to do less and less; yet he has shown remarkable courage in the way he has faced this loss and his dying.

Some time ago, Jim came to Idyllwild and took part in the weekend seminar we had with the reviewers of this book. On this chapter, he commented that, although we may not have a choice concerning the losses we suffer in dying, we do retain the ability to choose our attitude toward our death and the way we relate to it.

Jim has taught me a lot during these past few months about this enduring capacity for choice, even in extreme circumstances, which Viktor Frankl described in connection with his experiences in a concentration camp. Jim has made many critical choices since being told of his illness. He chose to continue taking a course at the university, because he liked the contact with the people there. He worked hard at a boat dock to support himself, until he could no longer manage the physical exertion. He decided to undergo cobalt treatment, even though he knew that it most likely would not result in his cure, because he hoped that it would reduce his pain. It did not, and Jim has suffered much agony during the past few months. He decided not to undergo chemotherapy, primarily because he didn't want to prolong his life if he couldn't really live fully. He made a choice to accept God in his life, which gave him a sense of peace and serenity. Before he became bedridden, he decided to go to Hawaii and enjoy his time in first-class style.

Jim has always had an aversion to hospitals—and to most institutions, for that matter—so he chose to remain at home, in more personal surroundings. As long as he was able, he read widely and continued to write in his journal about his thoughts and feelings on living and dying. With his friends, he played his guitar and sang songs that he had written. He maintained an active interest in life and in the things around him, without denying the fact that he was dying.

More than anyone I have known or heard about, Jim has taken care of unfinished business. He made it a point to gather his family and tell them his wishes, he made contact with all his friends and said everything he wanted to say to them, and he asked Marianne to deliver the eulogy at his funeral services. He clearly stated his desire for cremation;

he wants to burn those tumors and then have his ashes scattered over the sea—a wish that reflects his love of freedom and movement.

Jim has very little freedom and movement now, for he can do little except lie in his bed and wait for his death to come. To this day he is choosing to die with dignity, and, although his body is deteriorating, his spirit is still very much alive. He retains his mental sharpness, his ability to say a lot in very few words, and his sense of humor. He has allowed himself to grieve over his losses. As he puts it, "I'd sure like to hang around to enjoy all those people that love me!" Realizing that this isn't possible, Jim is saying goodbye to all those who are close to him.

Throughout this ordeal, Jim's mother has been truly exceptional. When she told me how remarkable Jim has been in complaining so rarely, despite his constant pain, I reminded her that I've never heard her complain and that she has been on duty constantly for months. I have been continually amazed by her strength and courage, and I have admired her willingness to honor Jim's wishes and accept his beliefs, even though at times they have differed from her own. She has demonstrated her care without smothering Jim or depriving him of his free spirit and independence. Her acceptance of Jim's dying, and her willingness to be fully present to him, have given him the opportunity to express openly whatever he feels. Jim has been able to grieve and mourn, because she has not cut off this process.

This experience has taught me much about dying and about living. Through Jim, I have learned that I don't have to do that much for a person who is dying, other than to be with that person by being myself. So often I felt a sense of helplessness, of not knowing what to say or how much to say, of not knowing what to ask or not to ask, of feeling stuck for words. Jim's imminent death seems such a loss, and it's very difficult for me to accept it. Gradually, however, I have learned not to be so concerned about what to say or to refrain from saying. In fact, in my last visit I said very little, but I feel that we made significant contact with each other. I've also learned to share with Jim the sadness I feel, but there is simply no easy way to say goodbye to a friend.

Jim had been a group leader in several of my personal-growth courses, and I can recall some of the things he confronted others with and what he said to them. Now he is showing me that his style of dying will be no different from his style of living. By his example and by his words, Jim has been a catalyst for me to think about the things I say and do and to evaluate my own life.

Time Out for Personal Reflection

1. If you have been close to someone during his or her dying, how did the experience affect your feelings about your life and about your own dying?

_____

_____

_____

_____

2. How would you like to be able to respond if a person who is close to you were dying?

_____

_____

_____

_____

3. If you were dying, what would you most want from the people who are closest to you?

_____

_____

_____

_____

The Stages of Death and Dying

Within the past decade, death and dying have been topics of widespread discussion among psychologists, psychiatrists, physicians, sociologists, ministers, and researchers. Whereas these topics were once taboo for many people, they have become the focus of seminars, courses, and workshops. A number of recent books, some of which are described in the Suggested Readings section at the end of the chapter, give evidence of the growing interest in the study of death and dying.

Dr. Elisabeth Kübler-Ross is a pioneer in the contemporary study of death and dying. In her widely read books, *On Death and Dying* and *Death: The Final Stage of Growth*, she treats the psychological and sociological aspects of death and the experience of dying. Thanks to her efforts, many people have become aware of the almost universal need dying persons have to talk about their impending deaths and to complete their business with the important people in their lives before they die. She has shown how ignorance of the dying process and the needs of dying persons—as well as the fears of those around them—can rob the dying of the opportunity to fully experience their feelings and arrive at a resolution of them.

A greater understanding of dying can help us to come to an acceptance of death, as well as to be more helpful and present to those who are dying. For this reason, I'd like to describe the five stages of dying that Kübler-Ross (1969, 1975) has delineated, based on her research with terminally ill cancer patients. She emphasizes that these are not neat and compartmentalized stages that every person passes through in an orderly fashion. At times a person may experience a combination of these stages, or perhaps skip one or more stages, or go back to an earlier stage he or she has already experienced. In general, however, Kübler-Ross found this sequence: denial, anger, bargaining, depression, and acceptance.

To make this discussion of the stages of dying more concrete, let me give the example of Ann, a 30-year-old woman dying of cancer. She was married and the mother of three children in elementary school. Before she discovered that she had terminal cancer, she felt that she had much to live for, and she enjoyed life.

The Stage of Denial

Ann's first reaction to being told that she had only about a year to live was shock. At first she refused to believe that the diagnosis was correct, and even after obtaining several other medical opinions, she still refused to accept that she was dying. In other words, her initial reaction was one of *denial*.

However, even though Ann was attempting to deny the full impact of reality, it would have been a mistake to assume that she didn't want to talk about her feelings. Her husband also denied her illness and was unwilling to talk to her about it. He felt that talking bluntly might only make her more depressed and lead her to lose all hope. He failed to recognize how important it would have been to Ann to feel that she *could* bring up the subject if she wished. On some level, Ann knew that she could not talk about her death with her husband.

During the stage of denial, the attitudes of a dying person's family and friends are critical. If these people cannot face the fact of their loved one's dying, they cannot help him or her move toward an acceptance of death. Their own fear will blind them to signs that the dying person wants to talk about his or her death and needs support. In the case of Ann, it would not necessarily have been a wise idea to force her to talk, but she could have been greatly helped if those around her had been available and sensitive to her when *she* stopped denying her death and showed a need to be listened to.

The Stage of Anger

As Ann began to accept that her time was limited by an incurable disease, her denial was replaced by anger. Over and over she wondered why *she*—who had so much to live for—had to be afflicted with this dreadful disease. Her anger mounted as she thought of her children and realized that she would not be able to see them grow and develop.

During her frequent visits to the hospital for cobalt treatment, she directed some of her anger toward doctors "who didn't seem to know what they were doing," toward the "impersonal" nurses, and toward the red tape she had to endure.

During the stage of anger, it's important that others recognize the need of dying persons to express their anger, whether they direct it toward their doctors, the hospital staff, their friends, their children, or God. If this displaced anger is taken personally, any meaningful dialogue with the dying will be cut off. Moreover, persons like Ann have every reason to be enraged over having to suffer in this way when they have so much to live for. Rather than withdrawing support or taking offense, the people who surround a dying person can help most by allowing the person to fully express the pent-up rage inside. In this way, they help the person to ultimately come to terms with his or her death.

The Stage of Bargaining

Kübler-Ross (1969) sums up the essence of the bargaining stage as follows: "If God has decided to take us from this earth and he did not respond to any angry pleas, he may be more favorable if I ask nicely" (p. 72). Basically, the stage of bargaining is an attempt to postpone the inevitable end.

Ann's ambitions at this stage were to finish her college studies and graduate with her bachelor's degree, which she was close to obtaining. She also hoped to see her oldest daughter begin junior high school in a little over a year. During this time, she tried many types of treatment, actively trying anything that offered some hope of extending her life.

The Stage of Depression

Eventually Ann's bargaining time ran out. No possibility of remission of her cancer remained, and she could no longer deny the inevitability of her death. Having been subjected to cobalt treatment, chemotherapy, and a series of operations, she was becoming weaker and thinner, and she was able to do less and less. Her primary feelings became a great sense of loss and a fear of the unknown. She wondered about who would take care of her children and about her husband's future. She felt guilty because she demanded so much attention and time and because the treatment of her illness was depleting the family income. She felt depressed over losing her hair and her beauty.

It would not have been helpful at this stage to try to cheer Ann up or to deny her real situation. Just as it had been important to allow her to fully vent her anger, it was important now to let her talk about her feelings and to make her final plans. Dying persons are about to lose everyone they love, and only the freedom to grieve over these losses will enable them to find some peace and serenity in a final acceptance of death.

The Stage of Acceptance

Kübler-Ross (1969) found that, if patients have had enough time and support to work through the previous stages, most of them reach a stage at which they are neither depressed nor angry. Because they have expressed their anger and mourned the impending loss of those they love, they are able to become more accepting of their death. Kübler-Ross comments:

> Acceptance should not be mistaken for a happy stage. It is almost a void of feelings. It is as if the pain has gone, the struggle is over, and there comes a time for "the final rest before the long journey," as one patient phrased it [p. 100].

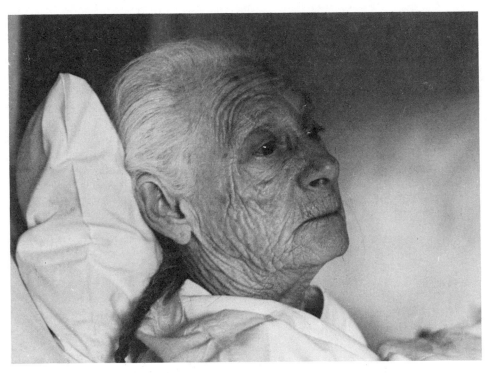

Of course, some people never achieve an acceptance of their death, and some have no desire to. Ann, for example, never truly reached a stage of acceptance. Her final attitude was more one of surrender, a realization that it was futile to fight any longer. Although she still felt unready to die, she did want an end to her suffering. It may be that if those close to her had been more open to her and accepting of her feelings, she would have been able to work through more of her anger and depression.

I want to emphasize again that Kübler-Ross' description of the dying process is not meant to be rigid or definitive; nor is it intended to be a standard by which to judge whether a dying person's behavior is normal or right. The value of the stages is that they describe and summarize in a general way what many patients experience and therefore add to our understanding of the experience of dying.

An Application of the Stages of Dying to Separation and Other Losses

The five stages of dying described by Kübler-Ross seem to have an application to experiences of divorce, separation, and other losses—experiences that bear some similarity to the experience of dying. To illustrate, I'll discuss a divorce in terms of the five stages. Of course, you can broaden this concept and see whether it applies to separation from your parents, your children, or even from an old value system or way of being. Although not all people who divorce go through the stages I'll describe in the same way, I've found that many people do experience similar questions and struggles.

The Stage of Denial

Many people who are divorcing go through a process of denial and self-deception. They may try to convince themselves that the state of their marriage isn't all that bad, that nobody is perfect, and that things would be worse if they did separate. Even after the decision is made to divorce, they may feel a sense of disbelief that this could actually be happening to them. If it was the other person who initiated the divorce, the remaining partner might ask: "Where did things go wrong? Why is she (he) doing this to me? I really don't believe that this is happening to me!"

The Stage of Anger

Once people accept the reality that they are divorcing, they frequently experience anger and rage. They may say "Why did this have to happen? I gave a lot, and now I'm being deserted. I feel as if I've been used and then thrown away." Many people feel cheated and angry over the apparent injustice of what is happening to them. Just as it is very important for dying persons to express any anger they feel over dying, it's also important for people who are going through the grief associated with a divorce or other loss to express any anger they feel. If they keep their anger bottled up inside, it is likely to be turned against themselves and may take the form of depression—a kind of self-punishment.

The Stage of Bargaining

Sometimes people hope that a separation will give them the distance they need to reevaluate things and that they will soon get back together again. Although separations sometimes work this way, often it is futile to wish that matters can be worked out. Nevertheless, during the bargaining stage, one or both partners may try to make concessions and compromises that they hope will make a reconciliation possible.

The Stage of Depression

In the aftermath of a decision to divorce, a sense of hopelessness may set in. As the partners realize that a reconciliation isn't likely, they may begin to dwell on the emptiness and loss they feel. They may find it very difficult to let go of the future they had envisioned. They might spend time wondering what their lives would have been like if they could have made their relationship work. It isn't uncommon for people who divorce to turn their anger away from their spouses and toward themselves. Thus, they may experience much self-blame and self-doubt. They may say to themselves: "Maybe I didn't give our relationship a fair chance. What could I have done differently? I wonder where I went wrong?"

Depression can also be the result of the recognition that a real loss has been sustained. It is vitally important that people fully experience and express the grief they feel over their loss. Too often people deceive themselves into believing that they are finished with their sadness long before they have given vent to their grief. Unresolved grief tends to be carried around within a person, blocking the expression of many other feelings. For instance, if grief isn't worked through, it may be extremely difficult for a person to form new relationships, because in some ways he or she is still holding on to the past relationship.

The Stage of Acceptance

If people allow themselves to mourn their losses, eventually the process of grief work usually leads to a stage of acceptance. In the case of divorce, once the two people have finished their grieving, new possibilities begin to open up. They can begin to accept that they must make a life for themselves without the other person and that they cannot cling to resentments that will keep them from beginning to establish a new life. Although sadness may persist, there can be an acceptance that what has occurred is done with and that brooding won't change things. They can learn from their experience and apply that learning to future events.

In summary, these stages are experienced in different ways by
each person who faces a significant loss. People do not pass through
these stages in neat fashion, and not all people experience all the stages
in working through their losses. Some, for example, express very little
anger; others might not go through a bargaining stage. Nevertheless, the
value of a model such as this one is that it provides some understanding
of how we can learn to cope with the various types of losses in our lives.
Whatever the loss may be, and whatever stage of grieving we may be
experiencing, it seems to be crucial that we freely express our feelings.
Otherwise, we may not be able to achieve acceptance.

For me, the meaning of acceptance is well expressed in the prayer
of Alcoholics Anonymous, and I'd like to close this section by quoting it
here:

> God, grant me serenity to accept the things I cannot change, courage to
> change the things I can change, and wisdom to know the difference.

Time Out for Personal Reflection

1. If you have suffered a serious loss in your life, to what extent did your
   experience correspond to the five stages of dying described by
   Kübler-Ross? In what ways was it different?

   _____

   _____

   _____

   _____

   _____

2. To what extent do you think you've accepted the major losses and
   transitions in your life? Do you sometimes find yourself returning to
   stages you've already experienced in regard to them, such as anger or
   bargaining? Do you have some feelings about these losses that you've
   never really allowed yourself to express?

   _____

   _____

   _____

   _____

   _____

In talking about death in my university courses, I've found it valuable to broaden the conception of death and dying to include being "dead" in a variety of psychological and social ways. What is dead or dying in us may be something we want to resurrect, or it may be something that *should* die in order to make way for new growth. Sometimes growth requires that we be willing to let go of old and familiar ways of being, and we might need to mourn their loss before we can really move on. You may have experienced a letting go of the security of living with your parents, for example, in exchange for testing your independence by living alone and supporting yourself. In the process, you may have lost something that was valuable to you, even if it was incompatible with your further development and growth.

Reflecting on the parts of ourselves that are dead or dying gives us the chance to decide whether we want to try to revitalize them. I'd like to focus now on some ways in which we commonly allow parts of ourselves to die that we might want to bring back into our lives. I hope that the following questions will help you to decide whether you're living as fully as you'd like to be.

Can You Be a Child?

Is the "child" part of you living, or have you buried it away inside? Can you be playful, fun, curious, explorative, spontaneous, inappropriate, silly? As adults, we sometimes begin to take ourselves too seriously and lose the ability to laugh at ourselves. If you find that you're typically realistic and objective to the point that it's difficult for you to be playful or light, you might ask what inner messages block your ability to let go. Are you inhibited by a fear of being wrong? Are you afraid of being called silly or of meeting with others' disapproval? If you want to, you can begin to challenge the messages that say: "Don't!" "You should!" "You shouldn't!" You can experiment with new behavior and run the risk of seeming silly or of "not acting your age." Then *you* can decide whether you like your new behavior and want to be like a child more often. Whatever your decision is, at least it will be your own instead of a command from your past.

Are You Alive to Your Feelings?

We can deaden ourselves to most of our feelings—the joyful ones as well as the painful ones. We can decide that feeling involves the risk of pain and that it's best to *think* our way through life. In choosing to cut off feelings of depression or sadness, we will most likely cut off feelings of joy. Closing ourselves to our lows usually seems to mean closing ourselves to our highs as well.

In my work with people, I sometimes find it difficult to help them even to recognize their flat emotional state, so insulated have they made themselves. To begin assessing how alive you are emotionally, you might ask yourself such questions as the following:

- Do I let myself feel my sadness over a loss?
- Do I try very hard to cheer people up when they're sad or depressed, instead of allowing them to experience their feelings?
- Do I let myself cry if I feel like crying?
- Do I ever feel ecstasy?
- Do I let myself feel close to another person?
- Are there some feelings that I particularly suppress? Do I hide my feelings of insecurity, fear, dependence, tenderness, anger, boredom?

Are You Caught Up in Deadening, Rigid Roles?

Our roles and functions can eventually trap us and keep us from living as *persons*. Instead of fulfilling certain roles while maintaining a separate sense of identity, we may get lost in our roles and in the patterns of thought, feeling, and behavior that go with them. As a result, we may neglect important parts of ourselves and thus limit our options of feeling and experiencing. Moreover, we may feel lost when we're unable to play a certain role. Thus, a supervisor may not know how to behave when he or she isn't in a superior position to others, or an instructor might be at loose ends when he or she doesn't have students to teach, or a parent may find life empty when the children have grown.

At the present time, do you feel caught in certain roles? Do you depend on being able to identify with those roles in order to feel alive and valuable? Are you able to renew yourself by finding innovative ways of being and thinking? At this time in your life, you might find that you're so caught up in the student role that you have little time or energy left for other parts of your life. When our roles begin to deaden us, we can ask whether we've taken on a function or identity that others have defined, instead of listening to our own inner promptings.

Are Your Relationships Vital and Alive?

Our relationships with the significant people in our lives have a way of becoming stale and deadening. It's easy to get stuck in habitual and routine ways of being with another person and to lose any sense of surprise and spontaneity. This kind of staleness is particularly common in long-term relationships such as marriage, but it can afflict our other relationships as well. As you look at the significant relationships in your life, think about how alive both you and the other person in each relationship feel with each other. Do you give each other enough space to grow? Does the relationship energize you, or does it sap you of life? Are you settling into a comfortable, undemanding relationship? If you recognize that you aren't getting what you want in your friendships or intimate relationships, you can ask what *you* can do to revitalize them. You can also consider what specific things you'd like to ask of the other person. Simply asking more from your relationships can do a lot to bring new life into them.

Are You Alive Intellectually?

Children typically display much curiosity about life, yet somehow they often lose this interest in figuring out problems as they grow older. By the time we reach adulthood, we can easily become caught up in our activities, while devoting little time to considering *why* we're doing them and whether we even *want* to be doing them. It's also easy to allow our intellectual potential to shrivel up, either by limiting our exposure to the environment or by failing to follow our curiosity.

How might this apply to you as a student? Have you given up on asking any real and substantive questions that you'd like to explore? Have you settled for merely going to classes and collecting the units you need to obtain a degree? Are you indifferent to learning? Are you open to learning new things?

Are You Alive to Your Senses and Your Body?

Our bodies express to a large degree how alive we are. They show signs of our vitality or reveal our tiredness with life. Since our bodies don't lie, we can use them as an indication of the degree to which we're affirming life. As you look at your body, you can ask: Do I like what I see? Am I taking good care of myself physically, or am I indifferent to my own bodily well-being? What does my facial expression communicate?

We can also become deadened to the input from our senses. We may become oblivious to fragrances or eat foods without tasting or savoring them. We may never stop to notice the details of our surroundings. On the other hand, taking time to be alive to our senses can help us feel renewed and interested in life. You might ask yourself: What sensations have particularly struck me today? What have I experienced and observed? What sensory surprises have enlivened me?

Time Out for Personal Reflection

1. How alive do you feel psychologically and socially? Check any of the following statements that apply to you.

   _____ I feel alive and energetic most of the time.
   _____ My body expresses aliveness and vitality.
   _____ I feel intellectually curious and alive.
   _____ I have significant friendships that are a source of nourishment for me.

_____ I can play and have fun.
_____ I allow myself to feel a wide range of emotions.
_____ I'm keenly aware of the things I see, smell, taste, and touch.
_____ I feel free to express who I am; I'm not trapped by my roles.

2. When do you feel most alive?

_____

_____

3. When do you feel least alive?

_____

_____

4. What specific things would you most like to change about your life so that you could feel more alive? What can you do to implement these changes?

_____

_____

_____

_____

_____

_____

Taking Stock: How Well Are You Living Life?

It seems tragic to me that some people never really take the time to evaluate how well they are living life. Imagine for a moment that you're one of those people who get caught up in the routine of daily existence and never assess the quality of their living. Now assume that you are told that you have only a limited time to live. You begin to look at what you've missed and how you wish things had been different; you begin to experience regrets over the opportunities that you let slip by; you review the significant turning points in your life. You may wish now that you had paused to take stock at many points in your life, instead of waiting until it was too late.

Writing Your Own Eulogy

One way to take stock of your life is to imagine your own death, including the details of the funeral and the things people might say about you. As an extension of this exercise, you might try actually writing down your own eulogy or obituary. This can be a powerful way of summing up how you see your life and how you'd like it to be different. In

fact, I suggest that you try writing three eulogies for yourself. First, write your *"actual"* eulogy—the one you would give at your own funeral, if that were possible. Second, write the eulogy that you *fear*—one that expresses some of the negative things someone could say of you. Third, write the eulogy that you would *hope* for—one that expresses the most positive aspects of your life so far. After you've written your three eulogies, seal them in an envelope and put them away for a year or so. Then do the exercise again, and compare the two sets of eulogies to see what changes have occurred in your view of your life.

I'd like to emphasize that this experience is not meant to be morbid; rather, it is a tool you can use in exploring the meaning of death and in creating a more meaningful life. For me, the exercise of writing my own eulogies was not an easy one. I found it difficult to separate my realistic view of myself from my hoped-for and feared assessments. At times when I was writing what I *feared* could be said about me, I wondered how much of what I was writing was actually true of me. I had much the same feeling as I wrote my hoped-for version—that some of what I wrote is true of me now. And no doubt my "actual" eulogy incorporated some of my hopes and fears as well as a truly objective assessment of my life. Nevertheless, the experience of writing my eulogies helped me to consider how fully I'm living life. It also challenged me to do something concrete about changing those aspects of my life that were reflected in the "feared" eulogy. For instance, in writing this eulogy I became aware of the great difficulty I have in living for the present moment. I tend to hurry about and put unnecessary pressure on myself, instead of allowing myself to be an experiencing, feeling, reflective human being. Of course, what you learn from writing your eulogies will be unique to you, but I believe that this exercise can help most of us see ourselves and our lives in a clearer perspective and challenge us to live more fully *now*.

Time Out for Personal Reflection

Complete the following sentences by writing down the first responses that come to mind.

1. When I think of my own death, _____.

2. My greatest fear of death is _____.

3. One way that I'm now "dead" is _____.

4. I deny the reality of my death by _____.

5. After death, there is _____.

6. If I were to die today, _____.

7. If I knew I were to die soon, I'd _____.

8. If I died now, others would _____.

9. When I think of a loved one's death, _____.

10. To me, death means _____.

11. The worst thing about death is _____.

12. I expect to live until the age _____.

13. The way I expect to die is _____.

14. One thing I'd like to accomplish or do before I die is _____

   _____.

15. If I had to choose one line to be inscribed on my tombstone, it would

   be _____.

16. The line that I would *least* like written on my tombstone is _____

   _____.

Before he died, Jim Morelock gave me a poster showing a man walking in the forest with two small girls. At the top of the poster were the words "TAKE TIME." Jim knew me well enough to know how I tend to get caught up in so many activities that I sometimes forget to simply take the time to really experience and enjoy the simple things in life. As I write this, I'm also remembering what one student wrote to me as we were writing what we hoped and wished for each person in the class. On one of my slips of paper was written "I hope you will take the time to smell a rose." In another class, one student gave each person an epitaph—what he thought could be written on that person's tombstone. Mine read "Here lies Jerry Corey—a man who all his life tried to do too many things at once." I promised myself that I'd make a poster with those words on it and place it on my office wall as a reminder for those times when I would begin to hurry and forget to take time to enjoy life. I think many of us could use reminders like these frequently—especially since it took me almost a semester to get around to putting that poster on my office wall! So I'd like to close this chapter with this simple message: *Take time.*

Chapter Summary

In this chapter, I've encouraged you to devote some time to reflecting on your eventual death, because I'm convinced that doing so can lead you to examine the quality and direction of your life and assist you to find your own meaning in living. I've suggested that the acceptance of death is closely related to the acceptance of life. Recognizing and accepting the fact of death gives us the impetus to search for our own answers to questions such as: What is the meaning of my life? What do I most want from life? How can I create the life I want to live? In addition, I've encouraged you to assess how much you are fully alive right now.

Some of the key ideas presented in this chapter are listed below. As a way of stimulating your own reflections, you might think about each statement and decide how much you agree or disagree with it.

1. Many of us fear death, largely because of the uncertainty that surrounds it.
2. Life has meaning because we are finite beings; thus, death gives life meaning.
3. If we're afraid to die, we may be afraid to live.
4. Our culture makes it easy for us to deny the reality of death.
5. There are many ways of being "dead" psychologically, socially, and intellectually. By recognizing ways in which we're not fully alive, we can make decisions that will lead to richer living.
6. The way in which we view death has much to do with the way in which we view life.

Now list some other ideas from this chapter that you want to remember.

_____

_____

_____

_____

_____

_____

Activities and Exercises

1. For a period of at least a week, take a few minutes each day to reflect on when you feel alive and when you feel dead. Do you notice any trends in your observations? What can you do to feel more alive?
2. If you knew you were going to die within a short time, in what ways would you live your life differently? What might you give up? What might you be doing that you're not doing or experiencing now?
3. Imagine yourself on your deathbed. Write down who you want to be there, what you want them to say to you, and what you want to say to them. Then write down your reactions to this experience.
4. For about a week, write down specific things you see, read, or hear relating to the denial or avoidance of death in our culture.
5. Let yourself reflect on how you imagine the death of those you love might affect you. Consider each person separately, and try to imagine how your life today would be different if that person were not in your life. In your journal, you might respond to such questions as: Do I now have the kinds of relationships with my loved ones that I want to have? What's missing? What changes do I most want to make in my relationships?
6. Consider making some time alone in which to write three eulogies for yourself: one that you think *actually* sums up your life, one that you *fear* could be written about you, and one that you *hope* could be written about you. Write the eulogies as if you had died today; then seal them in an envelope, and do the exercise again sometime in the future— say, in about a year. At that time, you can compare your eulogies to see in what respects your assessment of your life and your hopes and fears have changed.
7. After you've written your three eulogies, you might write down in your journal what the experience was like for you and what you learned from it. Are there any specific steps you'd like to take *now* in order to begin living more fully?

Chapter 10   Friedman, M., & Rosenman, R. *Type A Behavior and Your Heart.* Greenwich, Conn.: Fawcett World, 1976. This is an excellent book that deals with personality types and behavior associated with death from coronary diseases—and, more broadly, with learning to take time to enjoy life. Guidelines are given on how to recognize Type A behavior and what you can do about it.

Gordon, D. *Overcoming the Fear of Death.* Baltimore, Md.: Penguin, 1972. This is a very useful book dealing with the fear of death, the ways we avoid facing this fear, some aspects of dying, the meaning of death.

Kavanaugh, R. *Facing Death.* New York: Nash, 1972; Penguin edition, 1974. Kavanaugh discusses some unrealistic fears and attitudes toward dying and shows that a growing awareness of what we hope to achieve in life can bring about an accepting attitude toward death. Other topics include: cultural expectations concerning dying, coping with tragic death, funerals, life after death, and grief work.

Koestenbaum, P. *Is There an Answer to Death?* Englewood Cliffs, N.J.: Prentice-Hall (Spectrum), 1976. This book discusses how a positive confrontation with death can be a liberating experience, how it can help us develop our individual identity and give us the security we need to live our lives courageously, and how an acceptance of death can bring greater meaning to life.

Kopp, S. *If You Meet the Buddha on the Road, Kill Him!* New York: Bantam, 1976. This insightful book deals with the theme that no meaning we take from outside of ourselves is real. In a moving section, the author describes his own choice between living and dying.

Kübler-Ross, E. *On Death and Dying.* New York: Macmillan, 1969. A thoughtful treatment of attitudes toward death and dying, this book is based primarily on interviews with terminal cancer patients. The author is one of the pioneers in the contemporary study of death and dying.

Kübler-Ross, E. *Death: The Final Stage of Growth.* Englewood Cliffs, N.J.: Prentice-Hall (Spectrum), 1975. This excellent book discusses such questions as: Why is it so hard to die? Are death and growth related? How is death the final stage of growth? What is the significance of death?

Lund, D. *Eric.* New York: Dell, 1975. This touching book demonstrates how a person can live to the fullest even in the face of imminent death. Even though Eric finds out that he has leukemia, he continues to make life-oriented decisions, and he distinguishes himself in sports.

Marris, P. *Loss and Change.* Garden City, N.Y.: Doubleday, 1974. This book discusses what happens to us when we lose someone significant, when we divorce, and when we make changes in our daily lives. It includes a good section on the process of grief and mourning.

Moody, R. *Life after Life.* New York: Bantam, 1975. The author describes case histories that focus on the question of what it is like to die.

Pearson, L. (Ed.). *Death and Dying: Current Issues in the Treatment of the Dying Person.* Cleveland, Ohio: Case Western Reserve Press, 1969. This is an excellent treatment of the situation of the dying patient. The topics discussed include: psychological death, the care of the dying person, effects of a death upon the family, awareness of dying, and psychotherapy and the dying patient.

Ruitenbeek, H. (Ed.). *Death: Interpretations*. New York: Delta, 1969. This is a thought-provoking collection of 21 articles on the topic of death and mourning.

Russell, O. R. *Freedom to Die: Moral and Legal Aspects of Euthanasia*. New York: Dell, 1975. The central issue addressed in this book is our right to die as we choose.

Schnitzer, E. *Looking In*. Idyllwild, Calif.: Strawberry Valley Press, 1977. In this book of essays, Schnitzer shares his personal thoughts about death and life, growing old, and ways of finding meaning in life. The author is a positive example of a person who remains vital and alive by traveling and experiencing many facets of life.

Shneidman, E. (Ed.). *Death: Current Perspectives*. Palo Alto, Calif.: Mayfield, 1976. This book is an excellent collection of edited selections dealing with cultural, societal, interpersonal, and personal perspectives on death.

Chapter 11

Meaning and Values

In order to keep ourselves from dying spiritually, we need to allow ourselves to imagine new ways of being, to invent new goals to live for, to search for new and more fulfilling meanings, to acquire new identities, and to reinvent our relationships with others. In essence, we need to allow parts of ourselves to die in order to experience the rebirth that is necessary for growth.

Pre-Chapter Self-Inventory

For each statement, indicate the response that most closely identifies your beliefs and attitudes. Use this code: A = I strongly agree; B = I slightly agree; C = I slightly disagree; D = I strongly disagree.

_____ 1. At this time in my life, I have a sense of meaning and purpose that gives me direction.

_____ 2. Most of my values are similar to those of my parents.

_____ 3. Without some form of religious belief, we cannot expect to find meaning in life.

_____ 4. Accepting our capacity for freedom of choice is an essential part of finding a sense of purpose in living.

_____ 5. I have challenged and questioned most of the values I now hold.

_____ 6. Religion is an important source of meaning for me.

_____ 7. I generally live by the values I hold.

_____ 8. We must each actively engage in a search for meaning in life, because it is not automatically bestowed upon us.

_____ 9. My values and my views about life's meaning have undergone much change over the years.

_____ 10. We must be willing to look within ourselves to discover how to live.

_____ 11. The meaning of my life is based in large part on my ability to have a significant impact upon others.

_____ 12. Many of the people I encounter seem to be without a clear purpose in living.

_____ 13. The meaning of life can only be understood in terms of the reality of death.

_____ 14. I generally feel clear about what I value.

_____ 15. I let others influence my values more than I'd like to admit.

_____ 16. I sometimes subject my values to challenge from others.

_____ 17. The problem of meaninglessness in living is one of the most pressing problems of our society.

_____ 18. I have a clear sense of who I am and what I want to become.

_____ 19. The expectations and demands of others make it difficult for me to retain a firm sense of my own identity.

_____ 20. "A grown-up can be no man's disciple" (Sheldon Kopp).

Introduction

In this chapter, I encourage you to look critically at the *why* of your existence, to clarify the sources of your values, and to reflect on questions such as these: In what direction am I moving in my life? What steps can I take to make the changes in my life that I decide I want to make? What do I have to show for my years on this earth so far? Where have I been, where am I now, and where do I want to go?

Viktor Frankl (1963) often quotes Nietzsche's saying that "He who has a *why* for living can bear with almost any *how*." Cases of extreme deprivation, such as the concentration-camp experience that Frankl describes, illustrate the human need for a sense of meaning and purpose; those who lost all sense of meaning and gave up hope, he observed, died. Although we are not faced with such extreme conditions, the lack of meaning seems to be a pressing and pervasive problem in our society. Many who are fortunate enough to achieve power, fame, success, and material comfort nevertheless experience a sense of emptiness. Although they may not be able to articulate what it is that is lacking in their lives, they know that something is amiss. The astronomical number of pills and drugs produced to allay the symptoms of this "existential vacuum"— depression and anxiety—are evidences of our failure to find values that allow us to make sense out of our place in the world.

There are other signs of this need for a sense of meaning as well, including the popularity of many different kinds of religious groups and practices, the widespread interest in Eastern and other philosophies, the use of meditation, the number of self-help and inspirational books published each year, the experimentation with different life-styles, and even the college courses in personal adjustment! It seems fair to say that we are caught up in a crisis of meaning and values, and in this situation it's easy to look to some authoritative source for answers to our most deeply felt questions. As I have throughout this book, I want to suggest in this chapter that only the meaning and values we affirm from within ourselves, whatever form they may take, can guide us toward the autonomy and freedom that I believe belong to us as persons.

Time Out for Personal Reflection

1. In the space below, list the things that you most like to do or the activities that have the most meaning for you.

_____

_____

_____

_____

_____

2. How often do you do or experience each of the things you've just listed?

_____

_____

_____

_____

3. Does anything prevent you from doing the things you value as frequently as you'd like? If so, what?

_____

_____

_____

_____

4. What are some specific actions you can take to increase the amount of meaningful activity in your life?

_____

_____

_____

_____

5. Do you experience a deep sense of meaninglessness from time to time? How does it manifest itself? Check any of the following that apply to you.

_____ boredom in work, school, other aspects of life
_____ apathy, lack of interest in life
_____ depression, feeling down much of the time
_____ a vague sense of unease, feeling anxious

Others:

_____

_____

_____

6. If you often feel a sense of inner emptiness, what do you think are some of its causes? Check any of the following that apply to you.

_____ falling into ruts of conformity and routine
_____ giving up old values and having nothing to replace them with
_____ studying to learn facts or skills without being able to raise questions of meaning and value

Others:

_____

_____

_____

7. Are there ways in which you're now searching for meaning in your life? If so, what are they?

_____

_____

_____

Our Search for Identity

I believe that the discovery of meaning and values is essentially related to our achievement of identity as persons. The quest for identity involves a commitment to give birth to our selves by exploring the meaning of our uniqueness and humanness. A major problem for many people is that they have lost a sense of self, because they have directed their search for identity outside themselves. In their attempt to be liked and accepted by everyone, they have become finely tuned to what *others* expect them to do and to be but alienated from their *own* inner desires and feelings. As Rollo May (1973) observes, they are able to *respond* but not to *choose*. Indeed, May sees inner emptiness as the chief problem in contemporary society; too many of us, he says, have become "hollow people" who have very little understanding of who we are and what we feel. May cites one person's succinct description of the experience of "hollow people": "I'm just a collection of mirrors, reflecting what everyone expects of me" (p. 15).

Moustakas (1975) describes the same type of alienation from self that May talks about. For Moustakas, alienation is "the developing of a life outlined and determined by others, rather than a life based on one's own inner experience" (p. 31). If we become alienated from ourselves, we don't trust our own feelings but respond automatically to others as we think they want us to respond. As a consequence, Moustakas writes, we live in a world devoid of excitement, risk, and meaning.

In order to find out who we are, we may have to let parts of us die. We may need to shed old roles and identities that no longer give us

vitality. Doing so may require a period of mourning for our old selves. Most people who have struggled with shedding immature and dependent roles and assuming a more active stance toward life know that such rebirth isn't easy and that it may entail pain as well as joy.

Jourard (1971) makes a point that I find exciting. He maintains that we begin to cease living when meaning vanishes from life. Yet too often we are encouraged to believe that we have only *one* identity, *one* role, *one* way to be, and *one* purpose to fulfill in a lifetime. This way of thinking can be literally deadly, for, when our one ground for being alive is outgrown or lost, we may begin to die psychologically instead of accepting the challenge of reinventing ourselves anew. In order to keep ourselves from dying spiritually, we need to allow ourselves to imagine new ways of being, to invent new goals to live for, to search for new and more fulfilling meanings, to acquire new identities, and to reinvent our relationships with others. In essence, we need to allow parts of us to die in order to experience the rebirth that is necessary for growth.

To me, then, achieving identity doesn't necessarily mean stubbornly clinging to a certain way of thinking or behaving. Instead, it may involve trusting ourselves enough to become open to new possibilities. Nor is an identity something we achieve for all time; rather, we need to be continually willing to reexamine our patterns and our priorities, our habits and our relationships. Above all, we need to develop the ability to listen to our inner selves and trust what we hear. To take just one example, I've known students for whom academic life has become stale and empty and who have chosen to leave it in response to their inner feelings. Some have opted to travel and live modestly for a time, taking in new cultures and even assimilating into them for a while. They may not

be directly engaged in preparing for a career and, in that sense, "establishing" themselves, but I believe they are achieving their own identities by being open to new experiences and ways of being. For some of them, it may take real courage to resist the pressure to settle down in a career or "complete" their education.

At this point, you might pause to assess how you experience your identity at this time in your life. The following Time Out may help you to do so.

Time Out for Personal Reflection

1. Who are you? Try completing the sentence "I am _____" 20 different ways by quickly writing down the words or phrases that immediately occur to you.

   I am:

   _____   _____

   _____   _____

   _____   _____

   _____   _____

_____   _____

_____   _____

_____   _____

_____   _____

_____   _____

2. What does this list tell you about your view of yourself?

_____

_____

_____

_____

3. What are some things about yourself that you think make you unique?

_____

_____

_____

_____

4. What are some of the things that you value the most in life?

_____

_____

_____

_____

5. Do you feel that you can identify in any way with the person who said "I'm just a collection of mirrors, reflecting what everyone expects of me"? In what ways?

_____

_____

_____

_____

6. Have you ever experienced an "identity crisis"? If so, what led up to it? What was the nature of your struggle? How did you deal with it?

_____

_____

Our Quest for Meaning and Purpose

Humans are the only creatures we know of who can reflect upon their existence and, based on this capacity for self-awareness, exercise individual choice in defining their lives. With this freedom, however, come responsibility and a degree of anxiety. If we truly accept that the meaning of our lives is largely the product of our own choosing, and the emptiness of our lives the result of our failure to choose, our anxiety is increased. To avoid this anxiety, we may refuse to examine the values that govern our daily behavior or to accept that we are, to a large degree, what we have chosen to become. Instead, we may make other persons or outside institutions responsible for the direction of our lives. I believe that we pay a steep price for thus choosing a sense of security over our own freedom—the price of denying our basic humanness.

One obstacle in the way of finding meaning is that the world itself may appear meaningless. It's easy to give up the struggle, or to look to some authoritative source of meaning, when we look at the absurdity of the world in which we live. Yet creating our own meaning is, to me, precisely our challenge and task as humans.

Creating meaning in our lives isn't all a somber and serious business, however. We can also find meaning by allowing ourselves to play. It seems unfortunate to me that, as we "mature," so many of us lose the capacity we had as children to delight in the simple things in life. We busy ourselves in so many serious details that we really don't take the time to savor life or avail ourselves of its richness. Thus, we may work hard, maintaining all the while that we'll have time for fun when we retire. Then, when we do retire, we're bored and don't know what to do with ourselves. This kind of continued emphasis on the future can keep us from enjoying both our present and our future—when it, too, becomes present.

Religion and Meaning: A Personal View

Religious faith can be a powerful source of meaning and purpose. For many people, religion helps to make sense out of the universe and the mystery of our purpose in living. Like any potential source of meaning, however, religious faith seems most authentic and valuable to me

when it enables us to become as fully human as possible. By this I mean that it assists us to get in touch with our own powers of thinking, feeling, deciding, willing, and acting. The questions I would put to my religion in order to determine whether or not it is a constructive force in my life are the following:

- Does my religion help me to integrate my experience and make sense of the world?
- Does my religious faith grow out of my own experience?
- Do my religious beliefs assist me to live life fully and to treat others with respect?
- Does my religion encourage me to exercise my freedom and to assume the responsibility for my own life?
- Are my religious beliefs helping me to become more of the person I'd like to become?
- Does my religion encourage me to question life and keep myself open to new learning?

At the present time, there appears to be a resurgence of interest in religion in our society. Increasing numbers of people seem to be deciding that some sort of religious faith is necessary if they are to find an order and purpose in life. At the same time, many others insist that religion only impedes the quest for meaning or that it is incompatible with contemporary beliefs in other areas of life. I know that I was convinced for a time that looking to some higher being for the source of meaning was incompatible with looking within ourselves for our own power, strength, and direction. I'm changing my thinking about this issue, and I've seen how religious faith has helped people endure great suffering. What seems essential to me is that our acceptance or rejection of religious faith come authentically from within ourselves and that we remain open to new experience and learning, whatever points of view we decide on.

It's perhaps worth emphasizing that a "religion" may take the form of a system of beliefs and values concerning the ultimate questions in life, rather than (or in addition to) membership in a church. People who belong to a church may or may not be "religious" in this sense, and the same is true of those who don't follow an organized religion or even profess belief in God. Some of those whom I think of as religious don't believe in the existence of God or else say they simply don't know whether any higher being or force exists. Others who might claim to be religious find no incompatibility in using religious belief as a reason to be cruel, inhumane, or neglectful of others. For these reasons, I don't believe that a profession of religious belief is, in itself, necessarily valuable or harmful. Like almost anything else in human life, religion (or irreligion) can be bent to worthwhile or base purposes.

In my own experience, I've found religion most valuable when it has been a challenge to broaden my choices and potential, rather than a restrictive influence. I find it hard to accept what seems to be the fairly common use of religion as a way of remaining dependent on external guidance or authority. I might add that I didn't always think this way; until I was about 30, I tended to think of my religion as a package of ready-made answers for all the crises of life and was willing to let my church make many key decisions for me. I now think that I experienced too much anxiety in many areas of life to take full responsibility for my choices; it was easier to lean on my religion for my answers. Besides, my religious training had taught me that I should look to the authority of the church for ultimate answers in the areas of morality, value, and purpose. Like many people, I was encouraged to learn the "correct" answers and conform my thinking to them. Now, when I think of religion as a positive force, I think of it as being *freeing,* in the sense that it encourages and even commands me to trust myself, to discover the sources of strength and integrity within myself, and to assume responsibility for my own choices.

Although, as an adult, I've questioned and altered many of the religious teachings with which I was raised, I haven't discarded all my past moral and religious values. Many of them served a purpose earlier in my life and, with modification, are still meaningful for me. However, whether or not I continue to hold the beliefs and values I've been taught, it seems crucial to me that I be willing to subject them to scrutiny throughout my life. If they hold up under challenge, I can reincorporate them; by the same token, I can continue to examine the new beliefs and values I acquire.

A philosophy of life is made up of the fundamental beliefs, attitudes, and values that govern a person's behavior. Many students I've taught, from high school to graduate school, have said that they hadn't really thought much about their philosophies of life. However, the fact that we've never explicitly defined the components of our philosophies of life doesn't mean that we are completely without them. All of us do operate on the basis of general assumptions about ourselves, others, and the world. Thus, the first step in actively developing a philosophy of life is to formulate a clearer picture of our present attitudes and beliefs.

We all have been developing implicit philosophies of life since we first began, as children, to wonder about life and death, love and hate, joy and fear, and the nature of the universe. We probably didn't need to be taught to be curious about such questions; raising them seems to be a natural part of human development. If we were fortunate, adults took the time to engage in dialogue with us, instead of discouraging us from asking questions and deadening some of our innate curiosity.

During the adolescent years, the process of questioning usually assumes new dimensions. Adolescents who have been allowed to question and think for themselves as children begin to get involved in a more advanced set of issues. Many of the adolescents I've encountered in my classes and workshops have at one time or another struggled with questions such as the following:

- Are the values that I've believed in for all these years the values I want to continue to live by?
- Where did I get my values? Are they still valid for me? Are there additional sources from which I can derive new values?
- Is there a God? What is the nature of the hereafter? What is my conception of a God? What does religion mean in my life? What kind of religion do I choose for myself? Does religion have any value for me?
- What do I base my ethical and moral decisions upon? Peer-group standards? Parental standards? The normative values of my society?
- What explains the inhumanity I see in our world?
- What kind of future do I want? What can I do about actively creating this kind of future?

These are only a few of the questions that many adolescents think about and perhaps answer for themselves. However, I don't see a philosophy of life as something we arrive at once and for all during our adolescent years. The development of a philosophy of life seems to me to be an ongoing activity that continues as long as we live. As long as we remain curious and open to new learning, we can continue to revise and rebuild our conceptions of the world. Life may have a particular meaning for us during adolescence, a new meaning during adulthood, and still another meaning as we reach old age. Indeed, if we don't remain open to basic changes in our views of life, we may find it difficult to adjust to changed circumstances.

I'm thinking now of a 37-year-old man who is facing a real crisis of meaning in his life, largely because he has been trying to structure his world and experiences as he did as an adolescent. He has many fixed beliefs about how life should be, and, since his current life seems chaotic by these standards, he is really struggling to find a reason to continue living. What he hasn't realized is that he cannot force his experiences today into the value system he held as an adolescent, for his life has changed since that time.

Keeping in mind that developing a philosophy of life is an ongoing activity of examining and modifying the values we live by, you may find the following suggestions helpful as you go about formulating and reformulating your own philosophy:

- Frequently create time to be alone in reflective thought.
- Consider what meaning the fact of your eventual death has for the present moment.
- Make use of significant contacts with others who are willing to challenge your beliefs and the degree to which you live by them.
- Adopt an accepting attitude toward those whose belief systems differ from yours, and develop a willingness to test your own beliefs.

In concluding this section, I'd like to list some of the values I hope my daughters, Heidi and Cindy, come to share. I find that thinking about what values I'd like to see them choose helps me to focus on the things that are most important to me. If you have children, or expect to have children someday, you might pause to think about the values you would most like to pass on to them.

- I hope that my children will be willing to dare and that they won't always choose caution over risk.
- I hope they form sets of values that are their own, not carbon copies of their parents'.
- I hope they always like and respect themselves and feel good about their abilities and talents.
- I'd like them to be open and trusting rather than fearful or suspicious.
- I hope they will respect and care for others.
- I like the way they can have fun, and I hope they don't lose this ability as they grow older.
- I'd like them to be able to express what they feel, and I hope they'll always feel free to come to Marianne and me and share meaningful aspects of their lives.
- I'd like them to be in touch with the power they have, and I hope they refuse to surrender it.
- I'd like them to be independent and to have the courage to be different from others if they want to be.

Time Out for Personal Reflection

1. What do you think of the statement that the meaning of your life is largely the product of your own choosing and that emptiness in your life is the result of your failure to choose for yourself? How does this statement apply to your own experience?

_____

_____

_____

_____

_____

2. Sheldon Kopp (1972) contends that "A grown-up can be no man's disciple." Have you ever looked to some authority or guru to provide you with answers? What do you think of Kopp's contention?

_____

_____

_____

_____

_____

3. Have there been occasions in your life when you've allowed other people or institutions to make key choices for you? If so, give a couple of examples.

_____

_____

_____

_____

4. Do you consider yourself a religious person? What criteria do you use to determine whether someone is "religious"?

_____

_____

_____

_____

5. What role, if any, has religion played in your life?

_____

_____

_____

_____

6. Where did you acquire your religious beliefs and/or your most important values? From your parents? Friends? Church? School? Work? Personal reflection?

_____

_____

_____

_____

7. In your view, when is religion a constructive force in a person's life?

_____

_____

_____

_____

8. In your view, when is religion a *negative* force in a person's life?

_____

_____

_____

_____

9. If you were to create a new religion, what *virtues* and *values* would you include? What would be the *vices* and *sins*?

_____

_____

_____

_____

_____

_____

_____

10. In the past, what have been some of the principal sources of meaning in your life?

_____

_____

_____

_____

11. At this time, what are some of the principal sources of meaning and purpose in your life?

_____

_____

_____

_____

12. What would you like to be able to say about the meaning in your life ten years from now? What do you hope will bring you meaning then?

_____

_____

_____

_____

13. What are some of the values you'd most like to see your children adopt?

_____

_____

_____

_____

14. The following is a list of some of the things different people value. Rate the importance of each one for you, using a 5-point scale, with "1" meaning "extremely important" and "5" meaning "very unimportant."

_____ companionship
_____ family life
_____ security
_____ being financially and materially successful
_____ enjoying leisure time
_____ work

_____ learning and getting an education
_____ appreciation of nature
_____ competing and winning
_____ loving others and being loved
_____ a relationship with God
_____ self-respect and pride
_____ being productive and achieving
_____ enjoying an intimate relationship
_____ having solitude and private time to reflect
_____ having a good time and being with others
_____ laughter and a sense of humor
_____ intelligence and a sense of curiosity
_____ opening up to new experiences
_____ risk taking and personal growth
_____ being approved of and liked by others
_____ being challenged and meeting challenges well
_____ courage
_____ compassion
_____ being of service to others

Now, go back over your list, and circle the things you'd like to have more of in your life. You might think of what keeps you from having or doing the things that you value most.

Reviewing Some Dimensions of Meaning and Value in Your Life

There are many dimensions to a philosophy of life, and one of the best ways to clarify your own philosophy is to take a careful look at the specific things you value and find meaningful in your life now. In many ways, this entire book has dealt with the various sources of meaning in life, including school and learning, views about human nature, our autonomy as persons, work, loving and being loved, sexuality, intimate relationships, being alone, and death and dying. At this point, I suggest that you review these areas in the light of these questions: What do I value? What values give meaning and substance to my life now? Do my actions reflect what I say I value?

Your Values and Learning

You've probably heard it said that learning is a lifelong enterprise. As you examine yourself as a learner, ask yourself whether you keep yourself open to new learning of all sorts—both in and out of school. You might consider what you've learned about yourself, about others, and about life during the past six months. You can look at what blocks your learning, and think about your fears and resistances toward being open to learning. Are your beliefs and values fixed, or are they open to revision? Do you welcome new ideas as a way of expanding the meaning life has for you, or do new ideas threaten you?

Your View of Human Nature

How do you basically view human beings? Your assumptions about human nature can make a difference with respect to the choices you see yourself as having. If you think that we are determined by our past experiences, you may see yourself as a passive victim of forces that have shaped you and your life. You might dismiss values as being merely the products of conditioning and make little effort to create your own values. If, on the other hand, you believe that we are basically free to choose our stance toward life, even though we are affected by circumstances we haven't chosen, then you may actively seek to create your own basis of action.

Your Values and Your Autonomy

As you look at your own development from early childhood to the present, you can probably find some significant patterns in your choices of values. Some questions you might ask in looking at your own autonomy are: Where did I get my values? Are my values open for modification as I grow toward maturity? Do I insist that the world remain the same for me now as it was during an earlier period of my development? Have I challenged the values I live by and really made them my own, or have I looked to someone else to define what I should value?

The struggle for autonomy is well illustrated by the experience of Carl Rogers, whose theory of personality is based on the idea that we must each trust ourselves and rely on our subjective experience as our ultimate guide in forming our values and making our choices. It's interesting that Rogers' emphasis on the value of autonomy seems to have grown, in part, out of his own struggles to become independent from his parents. As a college student, he took the risk of writing a letter to his parents telling them that his views were changing from fundamentalist to liberal and that he was developing his own philosophy of life. Even though Rogers knew that his departure from the values of his parents would hurt them, he felt that such a move was necessary for his own intellectual and psychological freedom.

As you examine your own values, you might reflect on the value you place on your own autonomy. Is it important to you to feel that you are your own person? Are you satisfied with living by the expectations that others have for you? Do you want to become more independent, even though there are risks involved? Or do you prefer the security of being what others want you to be?

Work can be a major part of your quest for meaning, but it can also be a source of meaninglessness. Work can be an expression of yourself; it can be, as Gibran (1923) says, "love made visible" (p. 27). It can be a way for you to be productive and to find enjoyment in daily life. Through your work, you might be making a significant difference in the quality of your life or the lives of others, and this may give you real satisfaction. But work can also be devoid of any self-expressive value. It can be merely a means to survival and a drain on your energy. Instead of giving life value and meaning, it can actually be a destructive force that contributes to an early death, as Jess Lair (1976) describes in *I Ain't Much, Baby—But I'm All I've Got!* Lair relates that he was so caught up in succeeding in the business world that he had a heart attack. While he was recovering in his hospital bed, he looked at his life and saw that he had made many destructive choices and that his work was killing him. At this time, he made a decision that he has stuck with since: "From this time on I am never again going to do something that I don't deeply believe in" (p. 11). I encourage you to ask yourself: Is my work life-giving? Does it bring meaning to my life? If not, what can I do about it? Is my most meaningful activity—my true work—something I do away from the job?

Love and Meaning

Freud defined the healthy person as one who could work well and love well. Like work, love can make living worthwhile, even during bleak times. We can find meaning in actively caring for others and helping them to make their lives better. Because of our love for others, or their love for us, we may be enabled to continue living, even in conditions of extreme hardship. Thus, Frankl (1963) noted that, in the concentration camp, some of those who kept the images of those they loved and retained some measure of hope survived the ordeal, while many who lost any memories of love perished. From his experiences, Frankl concluded that "the salvation of man is through love and in love" (p. 59).

What place does love have in your life? How is your life different now because of those who love you, or those whom you love? What meaning does love give to your life? What would your life be like if you didn't have love in it?

Your Values and Your Sexuality

Earlier in this book, I encouraged you to look at your identity as a man or a woman and to ask whether there are ways in which you're trapped by others' standards of appropriate sex-role behavior. If you've looked at yourself in this way, perhaps you've discovered that you've been restricting yourself to the narrow range of feelings and behavior prescribed by a male or female stereotype. Deciding what it means for *you* to be a man or a woman is an important part of deciding what kind of person you want to be.

Your sexuality can be an expression of your total self; it can enhance and vitalize you. However, sex can also be a meaningless act or a way of avoiding intimacy with others. Your values will have much to do with how you experience sex and how you choose to act as a sexual person.

It does seem evident to me that being a sexual partner implies valuing one's own sexuality. Thus, one important "value" question is how much you respect your body and your sexuality. What importance do you place on taking care of your body? On developing your sexuality? Do fears, shame, or guilt keep you from experiencing your sexuality and sensuality in the way you'd like to experience them?

Your Values and Your Intimate Relationships

Do your friendships and other relationships contribute to the meaning in your life? Do you have friends with whom you can be completely yourself? Do they challenge or confront you concerning what you value and the degree to which you're living according to your beliefs? In these and many other ways, intimate relationships can be vitally related to our quest for meaning and values. I'm fond of Goethe's observation that, by taking people as they are, we make them worse, but by treating them as if they already were what they ought to be, we help make them better.

Your values have much to do with the kinds of relationships you choose. There are many ways of relating to another person, from a brief and casual encounter to a deep, long-term relationship. You may choose homosexual or heterosexual relationships, conventional marriage or your own variation of it, living with someone as an experiment, a group marriage, communal living, and so on. Whatever styles of relationships you choose, the important question is what values you find in them. What do your relationships bring to your life? Are you living a certain life-style because parents, friends, or others expect you to, or have you selected a life-style that satisfies your own sense of values?

Your Values and Loneliness and Solitude

In *Shifting Gears*, the O'Neills (1975) suggest that many people fear loneliness so much that they will do almost anything to escape it:

> We are afraid to be alone or to feel loneliness because we do not depend on ourselves. We have become so accustomed to depending on others to give pleasure, to fulfill our needs and to give us direction that we are lost when alone. Fearing it, we avoid it, throwing ourselves into random movement, into *anything* that will prevent us from being alone. Fear of loneliness has become a national obsession [pp. 248–249].

What value do you place on the experience of solitude? Have you found meaning in loneliness or in being alone with yourself? Is avoiding loneliness of overriding importance for you? Is it important to you to take time to be with your own thoughts, to see what you really care about, and to discover the things that most give your life meaning?

Death and Meaning

In the preceding chapter, I stressed the idea that our awareness of death enables us to give meaning to our lives. The reality of our finiteness compels us to look at our priorities and to ask what we value most, what brings the most meaning to our lives. I like the way Frankl (1965) expresses the idea:

> In attempting to answer the question of the meaning of life—that most human of all questions—man is thrown back upon himself, must realize that he is questioned by life. That is, he is thrown back upon the primal elements of human existence—being conscious and being responsible [p. 51].

I often think that coming to terms with death can teach us how to really live. I've argued that to run from death is to run from life, for, as Gibran (1923) wrote, "Life and death are one, even as the river and the sea are one" (p. 71).

Time Out for Personal Reflection

Complete the following sentences by writing down the first responses that come to mind.

1. When I feel bored or apathetic, I _____.

2. I feel empty when _____.

3. To me, religion _____.

4. My parents have influenced my values by _____

_____.

5. Life would hardly be worth living if it weren't for _____.

6. One thing that I most want to say about my life at this point is ____

_____.

7. If I could change one thing about my life at this point, it would be

_____.

8. If I had to answer the question "Who am I?" in a sentence, I'd say: _

_____.

9. What I like best about me is _____.

10. I keep myself alive and vital by _____.

11. I'm unique, in that _____.

12. When I think of my future, I _____.

13. I feel discouraged about life when _____.

14. My friends have influenced my values by _____.

15. My beliefs have been most influenced by _____.

16. I feel most powerful when _____.

17. If I don't change, _____.

18. I feel good about myself when _____.

19. To me, the essence of a meaningful life is _____.

20. I suffer from a sense of meaninglessness when _____

_____ .

Chapter Summary

Seeking meaning and purpose in life is an important part of being human. In this chapter, I've suggested that meaning is not automatically bestowed upon us but instead is the result of our active thinking and choosing. I've encouraged you to recognize your own present values and to ask both how you acquired them and whether you can affirm them for yourself out of your own experience and reflection. This task of examining and reexamining our values and purposes is, to me, one that lasts a lifetime.

The following are some of the key ideas in this chapter. I encourage you to think about each idea and to take your own position regarding each one.

1. We need to have a sense of hope and a reason for living.
2. Many people who appear to have achieved success lead empty and unfulfilling lives.
3. When meaning is absent in our lives, we begin to die psychologically.
4. We create meaning by our own choices.
5. Only if we challenge our values and make them truly our own can they give us direction in living.
6. Developing a philosophy of life is a life-long endeavor.

List some additional ideas from this chapter that you'd most like to remember:

_____

_____

_____

_____

_____

_____

Activities and Exercises

Writing Your Philosophy of Life

To integrate your thoughts and reflections on the topics raised in this chapter, and throughout this book, I encourage you to develop, in writing, your philosophy of life. Your paper should represent a critical analysis of who you are now and of the factors that have been most influential in contributing to the person you are now. You should also discuss the person you'd like to become; include your goals for the future and the means by which you think you'll be able to achieve them.

The following outline may be a helpful guide as you write your paper. Feel free to use or omit any part of the outline, and modify it in any way that will help you to write a paper that is personally significant. You might also consider adding poetry, excerpts from other writers, and pictures or art to supplement your writing, if they will contribute to the meaningfulness of your paper.

I. Who are you now? What influences have contributed to the person you are now?
  A. Influences during childhood
    1. Your relationship with your parents
    2. Your relationship with your siblings
    3. Important turning points
    4. Successes and failures
    5. Personal conflicts
    6. Family expectations
    7. Impact of school and early learning experiences
    8. Your relationships with friends
    9. Experiences of loneliness
    10. Other
  B. Influences during adolescence
    1. Impact of your family and your relationship with your parents
    2. School experiences
    3. Personal struggles
    4. Critical turning points
    5. Influence of your peer group
    6. Experiences of loneliness
    7. Successes and failures, and their impact on you
    8. Influential adults, other than parents
    9. Your principal values
    10. Other
  C. Love and sex
    1. Your need for love
    2. Your fear of love
    3. The meaning of love for you
    4. Dating experiences and their effect on you
    5. Your view of sex roles
    6. Expectations of others and their influence on your sex role
    7. Attitudes toward the opposite sex
    8. Meaning of sexuality in your life

      9. Your values concerning love and sex
    10. Other
  D. Intimate relationships and family life
      1. The value you place on marriage
      2. How children fit in your life
      3. The meaning of intimacy for you
      4. The kind of intimate relationships you want
      5. Areas of struggle for you in relating to others
      6. Your views of marriage
      7. Your values concerning family life
      8. How social expectations have influenced your views
      9. Sex roles in intimate relationships
    10. Other
  E. Death and meaning
      1. Your view of an afterlife
      2. Religious views and your view of death
      3. The way death affects you
      4. Sources of meaning in your life
      5. The things you most value in your life
      6. Your struggles in finding meaning and purpose
      7. Religion and the meaning of life
      8. Critical turning points in finding meaning
      9. Influential people in your life
    10. Other
II. Who do you want to become?
  A. Summary of your present position
      1. How you see yourself now (strengths and weaknesses)
      2. How others perceive you now
      3. What makes you unique
      4. Your relationships with others
      5. Present struggles
  B. Your future plans for an occupation
      1. Nature of your work plans and their chances for success
      2. Kind of work that is meaningful to you
      3. How you chose or will choose your work
      4. What work means to you
      5. What you expect from work
  C. Your future with others
      1. The kind of relationships you want
      2. What you need to do to achieve the relationships you want
      3. Plans for marriage or an alternative
      4. Place of children in your future plans
      5. Your fears, hopes, and expectations concerning the future
  D. Future plans for yourself
      1. How you would like to be ten years from now
        a. What you need to do to achieve your goals

   b. What you can do now
   c. What you are doing now
2. Your priorities for the future
   a. Your values
   b. How you arrived at them
3. Your view of the good life
   a. Ways to achieve it
   b. How your view of the good life relates to all aspects of your life
4. Choices you see as being open to you now
   a. Choices in work
   b. Choices in school
   c. Value choices
   d. Other areas of choice in your life
5. Other aspects of your future

Suggested Readings

Deikman, A. *Personal Freedom.* New York: Bantam, 1976. This book is a guide to finding your way to the "real world." It offers a challenging view of reality and shows how we have been deceived and how we deceive ourselves in regard to reality.

Dyer, W. *Your Erroneous Zones.* New York: Avon, 1976. In this popular self-help book, Dyer describes ways of discovering pitfalls that lead to stale living and ways of taking charge of your life.

Fabry, J. *The Pursuit of Meaning.* Boston: Beacon Press, 1969. This book, which is based on Viktor Frankl's logotherapy, treats such topics as meaning in life, values, freedom, religion, and traditions.

Frankl, V. *Man's Search for Meaning.* New York: Washington Square Press, 1963; Pocket Books, 1975. In describing his experiences in a concentration camp, Frankl shows how it is possible to find meaning in life through suffering. His thesis is that we all have a need to discover meaning.

Frankl, V. *The Doctor and the Soul.* New York: Bantam, 1965. This book goes into more detail on how to find meaning in death, suffering, work, and love.

Frankl, V. *The Will to Meaning: Foundations and Applications of Logotherapy.* New York: New American Library, 1969. This book sets forth the basic assumptions underlying logotherapy, which include: the freedom of the will, the will to meaning, and the meaning of life. Frankl also describes in depth the existential vacuum of meaning that many people experience.

Gale, R. *Who Are You? The Psychology of Being Yourself.* Englewood Cliffs, N.J.: Prentice-Hall (Spectrum), 1974. This is a very readable account of a humanistic perspective of human nature and personal identity. There are good chapters on love, meaning, self-actualization, validating your identity, and becoming an authentic person.

Gibran, K. *The Prophet.* New York: Knopf, 1923. A famous book of poetic essays on such topics as religion, death, friendship, self-knowledge, joy and sorrow, and prayer.

Jourard, S. *The Transparent Self* (Rev. ed.). New York: Van Nostrand Reinhold, 1971. This book has a very worthwhile chapter on "the invitation to die."

Koestenbaum, P. *Managing Anxiety: The Power of Knowing Who You Are.* Englewood Cliffs, N.J.: Prentice-Hall (Spectrum), 1974. This useful book deals with pain, consciousness, meaninglessness, death, guilt, and other existential themes.

Kopp, S. *If You Meet the Buddha on the Road, Kill Him!* New York: Bantam, 1972. The message of this powerful book is that no meaning that comes from outside ourselves is real. The book deals with the theme of finding meaning in life by accepting the freedom and responsibility to find our own way.

Lair, J. *I Ain't Much, Baby—But I'm All I've Got!* New York: Fawcett World, 1976. This popular self-help book deals with a range of human-interest topics, including an appraisal of the meaning of life.

Maslow, A. *Toward a Psychology of Being* (2nd ed.). New York: D. Van Nostrand, 1968. This book contains some excellent material on creative values, personal growth, and self-actualization.

May, R. *Man's Search for Himself.* New York: Dell (Delta), 1973. This is a powerful and provocative work that addresses the issues of rediscovering selfhood, freedom and inner strength, becoming a person, meaning and emptiness, and the unique dimensions of being human.

Moustakas, C. *Finding Yourself, Finding Others.* Englewood Cliffs, N.J.: Prentice-Hall (Spectrum), 1975. A book of brief commentaries on topics such as remaining alive as a person, the path of alienation, the search for self, and valuing one's self.

O'Neill, N., & O'Neill, G. *Shifting Gears.* New York: Avon, 1975. This book deals largely with finding values in a changing society. It can inspire reflection on topics such as formulating a philosophy of life in a world of crisis, changing values, and renewal of self.

Perls, F. *Gestalt Therapy Verbatim.* Lafayette, Calif.: Real People Press, 1969. Much of the material in this book deals with autonomy, identity, and the accepting of responsibility for our own lives.

Powell, J. *Why Am I Afraid to Tell You Who I Am?* Niles, Ill.: Argus Communications, 1969. An easy-to-read and popular book of insights concerning self-awareness, personal growth, and the meaning of life. Powell discusses the human condition, interpersonal relationships, dealing with emotions, and methods of ego defense.

Rogers, C. *On Becoming a Person.* Boston: Houghton Mifflin (Sentry), 1961. In this excellent book, Rogers develops the theme that we each have a natural urge to become a "fully functioning person."

Part 3

Where to Go from Here

When you stop to think about it, aren't there choices you could be making right now that would make your life a richer one? What changes are you willing to make today, this week, this month, this year?

A Consumer's Guide
to Resources for Continued
Personal Growth and
Crisis Resolution

*I encourage you to think of professional
assistance as a resource you can use in
increasing your self-understanding and thus
your range of choices, rather than as a place to
turn only when you feel overwhelmed by
problems in living.*

Pre-Chapter Self-Inventory

For each statement, indicate the response that most closely identifies your beliefs and attitudes. Use this code: A = I strongly agree; B = I slightly agree; C = I slightly disagree; D = I strongly disagree.

_____ 1. There is a social stigma attached to going to a counselor or psychotherapist.

_____ 2. Counseling is aimed at producing drastic changes in a person's character and life-style.

_____ 3. Although counseling is an effective way of treating people with emotional problems, it has little to offer people who aren't experiencing some sort of crisis.

_____ 4. Most people experience crises at various times in their lives.

_____ 5. Personal growth requires a willingness to tolerate uncertainty.

_____ 6. Most people who seek counseling or therapy are experiencing some kind of crisis.

_____ 7. Once people achieve insight into their problems, they usually change their behavior.

_____ 8. The experience of pain is an inevitable part of personal growth.

_____ 9. My friends would think that something was wrong with me if I went to a counselor or therapist.

_____ 10. I've experienced personal growth through involvement in intimate relationships.

_____ 11. I want to seek out ways in which I can grow as a person by using my own resources.

_____ 12. Encounter groups and therapy groups are suitable for everyone.

_____ 13. It's important to shop around carefully before selecting a personal counselor or group leader.

_____ 14. The basic goal of counseling and psychotherapy is to teach people how to understand and resolve their own problems.

_____ 15. Counseling is essentially a form of advice giving.

_____ 16. Reading good books is one way to grow as a person.

_____ 17. Personal growth is an ongoing process rather than something that essentially ends when we reach adulthood.

_____ 18. I would be interested in some type of group experience as an avenue to personal growth.

_____ 19. I'd be willing to get involved in some type of individual counseling if I felt the need to do so.

_____ 20. Even as adults, if we're not growing, we're stagnating.

Introduction

Now that you're completing this book and your course, you may want to consider ways of continuing your personal learning. In this final chapter, I describe some ways of expanding your self-awareness, beginning with steps you can take for yourself. I also present a "consumer's guide" to continued personal growth through individual and group counseling. Although counseling is often very helpful in times of crises, I'll be emphasizing the use of counseling as a way of expanding our awareness of ourselves and of others. In other words, I encourage you to think of professional assistance as a resource you can use in increasing your self-understanding and thus your range of choices, rather than as a place to turn only when you feel overwhelmed by problems in living.

Choosing Experiences for Personal Growth

You can deliberately choose experiences for yourself that will enhance your growth as a person. Perhaps you remember reading a book or viewing a film that had a profound impact on you and really seemed to put things in perspective. Certainly, reading books that deal with significant issues in your life can be a growth experience in itself, as well as an encouragement to try new things.

Often, we make all sorts of resolutions about what we'd like to be doing in our lives or about experiences we want to share with others and then fail to carry them out. How much is this true of you? Are there activities you value yet rarely get around to doing? Perhaps you tell yourself that you prize making new friendships; yet, when you stop to think about it, you find that you do very little to actually initiate any contacts. Or perhaps you derive satisfaction from growing vegetables or puttering in your garden and yet find many reasons to neglect this activity. You might tell yourself that you'd love to take a day or two just to be alone and yet never get around to arranging it. When you stop to think about it, aren't there choices you could be making right now that would make your life a richer one? How would you really like to be spending your time? What changes are you willing to make today, this week, this month, this year?

In addition to activities that you enjoy but don't engage in as often as you'd like, there are undoubtedly many new things you might consider trying out as ways of adding meaning to your life and developing your potentials. You might consider making a contract with yourself to start now on a definite plan of action, instead of putting it off until next week or next year. Some of the ways in which many people choose to challenge themselves to grow include the following:

- finding hobbies that develop new sides of themselves
- going to plays, concerts, and museums

- taking courses in pottery-making, wine-tasting, guitar, and innumerable other special interests
- getting involved in exciting work projects, or actively pursuing forms of work that will lead to the development of hidden talents
- spending time alone to reflect on the quality of their lives
- initiating contacts with others and perhaps developing an intimate relationship
- enrolling in continuing-education courses, or earning a degree primarily for the satisfaction of learning
- doing volunteer work and helping to make others' lives better
- experiencing the mountains, the desert, and the ocean—by hiking, sailing, and so on
- becoming involved in religious activities
- traveling to new places, especially to experience different cultures
- keeping a journal

Any list of ways of growing is only a sample, of course; the avenues to personal growth are as various as the people who choose them. What I want to suggest is that growth can occur in small ways and that there are many things that you can do on your own (or with friends or family) to continue your personal development. Perhaps the greatest hindrance to our growth as persons is our failure to allow ourselves to imagine all the possibilities that are open to us.

Time Out for Personal Reflection

1. Check any of the following activities involving professional resources that you think you might like to pursue in the near future as a way of continuing your personal development.

    _____ attend a personal-growth group
    _____ take another psychology course
    _____ become involved in some kind of personal counseling
    _____ seek family counseling
    _____ seek marital or relationship counseling
    _____ take a class in Eastern philosophies
    _____ learn to practice yoga
    _____ attend an assertiveness-training workshop
    _____ join a consciousness-raising group
    _____ get involved in some type of self-control program (for example, to lose weight or stop smoking)
    _____ attend a massage workshop
    _____ learn relaxation exercises

2. List any other activities involving professional resources that you might want to pursue in the near future.

    _____

    _____

    _____

    _____

    _____

3. What are some of the reasons that you haven't previously done the things you've listed? Check any of the following responses that fit you.

    _____ I haven't known about some of the available resources.
    _____ I haven't been able to afford some of the activities I've listed.
    _____ I'm afraid of failing.

_____ I'm hesitant about trying new things.
_____ I haven't had the time.

List any other reasons that apply to you.

_____

_____

_____

4. What are some things you'd like to do more often, or begin doing, that would not demand the use of professional resources? Check any of the following that fit you.

_____ play more often
_____ spend more time alone
_____ exercise more frequently
_____ do more reading
_____ keep a detailed daily journal
_____ attend church more often
_____ be more open in my intimate relationships
_____ take better care of my body
_____ increase my enjoyment of sex and sensuality
_____ do things for other people
_____ cultivate more hobbies

5. List any other things that you'd like to do, either by yourself or with others:

_____

_____

_____

_____

_____

6. What are some of the reasons that you haven't done the things you've listed more often?

_____

_____

_____

7. Review your responses so far, and then write down some specific things you're willing to do for yourself or others within the next month.

_____

_____

Individual and Group Counseling as Avenues to Personal Growth

So far in this chapter, I've encouraged you to think of things that you can do on your own to further your personal growth. As I've stressed throughout this book, there are many practical things we can do to change our lives in the direction that *we* want to move in. In addition to the activities we can pursue on our own, there are also professional resources we can utilize to increase our understanding of ourselves and others. A counselor or psychotherapist can provide a unique relationship by means of which we can gain insight into our early decisions and learn to make new choices for more effective living. The rest of the chapter describes a range of professional resources that you might consider using.

Counseling and Psychotherapy

What are counseling and psychotherapy? How are they alike? How are they different? I use the term *counseling* to refer to the process whereby people are given an opportunity to explore personal concerns with a trained professional. Frequently, this exploration leads to an increased awareness of choice possibilities. Generally speaking, counseling is short-term, focuses on problems, and assists people to remove blocks to their personal growth and to discover their own inner resources. Unlike counseling, *psychotherapy* frequently focuses on unconscious processes and is much more concerned with changes in personality structure. Rather than being aimed merely at the resolution of particular problems, psychotherapy generally is geared toward the development of an intensive self-understanding of the inner dynamics that give rise to these problems.

I want to emphasize that counseling and psychotherapy don't have to be thought of in terms of a medical model, according to which clients are patients who need to be cured of mental illnesses. It's true that psychotherapy is one process used with people who function ineffectively or who have become overwhelmed by stresses and conflicts. However, individual counseling and therapy, as well as group methods, have much to offer those who simply want to increase their self-awareness and more fully develop their personalities. Thus, the therapies and counseling methods presented in this chapter are discussed primarily in terms of their value as resources for personal growth.

The counseling experience is difficult to describe in general, since it varies with the personalities of clients and counselors, the styles and orientations of counselors, and the particular relationships that are established between clients and their counselors. The following general remarks may give you some idea of what the experience of counseling is like; however, you should keep in mind that counseling and psychotherapy are highly subjective and personal experiences.

Most clients enter counseling with definite expectations, although these will be different for each client. Some expect relief from disabling symptoms. Some are searching for an answer to their conflicts from the counselor; others hope that the counselor will help them find their own answers. In addition to their hopes or expectations, most clients have some fears about what counseling will be like or about what they might discover about themselves. During the initial stages of counseling, one of the best ways for a client to establish a trusting relationship with the counselor is to talk about these expectations and fears. Rapport between the client and counselor is a prerequisite of any real progress.

As counseling progresses, clients usually begin to express feelings and thoughts that they formerly kept out of awareness. They become able to talk about themselves in deeply personal ways and to trust that their feelings are accepted. Because of the care and acceptance they receive from the counselor, they are increasingly able to accept themselves. They feel less need to be defensive, and they move in the direction of being open to all the facets of themselves. This openness enables them to achieve a clarity about themselves that they did not have before.

It isn't unusual for clients to feel worse before they feel better, however. As people open up to another human being (and to themselves), they become more vulnerable and exposed. As they shed the defenses that have been shielding them from threat, they experience some anxiety before they develop new resources with which to replace these defenses. Some people may say "Sometimes I wonder whether it was wise to begin therapy, because I *feel* my sadness and fear more now than I ever did before. Maybe I should have stayed less aware and more comfortable." Fortunately, if they have the courage to stay with the counseling process for a time, they generally discover that they have resources within themselves that they can draw upon in making changes.

The expression of feelings, the reliving of past experiences, and the discussion of current struggles are all a part of counseling, but they are not the whole story. As clients express themselves, they begin to see connections between their past and their present, they come to see their own role in creating their own unhappiness or dissatisfaction, and they generally gain new insight into themselves. For most counselors, this achievement of self-awareness is not the end of therapy or counseling but merely the beginning. The crucial issue is what clients choose to do with the awareness they acquire. For this reason, most counseling approaches emphasize that it's very important for clients to work on actively changing their behavior outside of the counseling sessions in ways that accord with their new insights. As they make specific changes in their behavior, they generally feel more in control of their own lives. When a client and counselor decide to discontinue their sessions together, the client takes an important step toward greater autonomy. Ideally, by the time clients come to the end of the counseling process, they have acquired some of the tools they need to continue their own growth and to challenge themselves. They aren't "finished products," any more than anyone else, but they have become able to make clearer, more authentic choices.

This general description of psychological counseling is applicable to both individual and group counseling. Although these two broad types of counseling have much in common, each has its unique features and strengths.

Individual counseling provides an opportunity for an in-depth involvement between clients and counselors. The one-to-one relationship can provide the continuity and trust that enable clients to explore highly personal material. Further, it can give them the opportunity to relive past and present conflicts with the significant individuals in their lives. Through the counseling relationship, clients can come to understand how their other relationships affect them.

In therapeutic groups, the one-to-one relationship is not the primary focus. Generally, a group is a microcosm of society. Group members are able to see a sample of how they relate to others, and, from the feedback they receive, they can begin to appreciate how others perceive them. They can use the group situation to try out new behavior among people who are responsive and accepting. Through this process of experimentation, they can make decisions about what kinds of changes they want to make in their everyday behavior. Groups also give people the chance to learn interpersonal skills. The members open themselves to certain risks; they confront others and are confronted by others; they give and receive support; and they have an opportunity to get a clearer picture of themselves.

In the next few sections, I discuss some general types of groups and then give a brief overview of various systematic approaches to both individual and group counseling. This information should enable you to become a wiser consumer of professional resources in the area of personal growth.

General Types of Groups

The consumer who is interested in groups is faced with an overwhelming variety from which to choose. The purpose of this section is to give you some information about the general types of groups, so that you can decide which ones you might want to investigate further. Most of the groups listed in the following chart are primarily oriented toward personal awareness and growth. At the end of the chapter, I've listed some further sources of information about each of these types of groups.

Encounter Groups

Encounter groups, or personal-growth groups, offer an intense group experience designed to help relatively healthy people gain closer contact with themselves and others. Most people join a personal-growth group with the intention of exploring aspects within themselves that block the realization of their full potential. The thrust of such groups is toward intimacy and sharing, spontaneity, openness, honesty, confrontation, heightened emotional expressiveness, exploration, and intense interpersonal relating.

Marathon Groups

One way to intensify the encounter-group experience is to use the *marathon* format, in which the group meets for a sustained period of time—anywhere from 18 hours to 48 hours. It's not unusual for these groups to function almost nonstop, breaking only for meals and perhaps a short nap. In this format, the process of opening up appears to be accelerated by continuous contact and by fatigue-produced lowering of inhibitions and defenses. Marathon-group members are encouraged to become aware of masks and pretenses and to question their necessity, to experience trust in the unmasking process, to be "real" by taking the risk of showing who they are, and to think about the possibility of giving up their pretenses as they reenter the outside world.

Group Therapy

Whereas encounter groups are generally intended for well-functioning people who wish to enhance their personal growth, group therapy frequently attracts people who want to treat specific symptoms or problems, such as depression, sexual problems, anxiety, psychosomatic disorders, and so forth. Group therapy may be of longer duration than the usual encounter-group experience, and attention is often given to unconscious factors and past experiences. Some therapy groups are primarily designed to correct emotional and behavioral disorders that impede one's functioning. The goal may be a minor or major transformation of personality structure, depending on the theoretical orientation of the group leader.

Group Counseling

Group counseling often has a specific focus, which may be educational, vocational, social, or personal. Counseling groups generally differ from therapy groups in that they stress conscious problems, do not aim at major personality changes, are frequently oriented to the resolution of specific and short-term issues, and are not concerned with the treatment of neurotic or psychotic disorders.

Most colleges and universities that have a counseling center offer various types of counseling groups. Some that are commonly offered include groups for exploring careers and occupational choices, enhancing self-development, and dealing with loneliness and alienation. In addition, groups may be set up for specific kinds of students, such as returning students, middle-aged students who are beginning new careers, and students having academic difficulties.

Self-Help and Peer Groups

Self-directed groups, or peer self-help groups, are becoming increasingly popular. These groups operate on the assumption that the primary resources of healing lie within the group itself, so that a formal leader is unnecessary. The idea is that people who have experienced similar problems and life situations can be of real help to one another.

Two peer-directed groups that rely on leaders drawn from the ranks of former members are Alcoholics Anonymous (AA) and Synanon. The recovery program of AA is based on a twelve-step program that begins with the alcoholic's admission that he or she is powerless in regard to alcohol. The meetings are designed to help the members see what they are doing to themselves and to others and take specific steps to change their lives so that they can live effectively without alcohol. In addition to AA meetings, supportive groups for children and relatives of alcoholics are available.

Synanon is a program for combatting drug addiction. Members live full-time in a community with other drug addicts. Former addicts lead Synanon groups, which are basically confrontation groups in which the drug addict is confronted squarely with his or her games and self-destructive patterns.

Among the many other self-help groups are Weight Watchers, gay-liberation groups, Recovery Incorporated, women's consciousness-raising groups, and parent-effectiveness groups.

Groups for Specific Populations

In addition to the types of groups already described, there are groups designed for various age levels and populations. For example, groups for children are offered in many schools, family-counseling agencies, and other community centers. There are adolescent groups for dealing with the unique needs of this period of life. Workshops and groups for middle-aged persons are available, often through the continuing-education programs in colleges and universities; these groups deal with middle-age life crises, with making new choices, and with learning more effective ways of coping. There are groups for the elderly, focusing on such problems as loneliness, losses, finding meaning in retirement, and so on; these groups are often conducted in day-treatment centers, community mental-health centers, or in homes for the aged. There are also groups available for couples who wish to improve their communication, discover blocks in their relationships, and resolve conflicts that prevent intimacy.

Systematic Approaches to Counseling and Psychotherapy

The consumer who is interested in individual counseling or therapy should have a general understanding of some of the major systematic approaches to the therapeutic process. If you look under "psychologists" in your telephone directory, you might find some therapists listed as "Gestalt therapists," "Transactional Analysis therapists," "behavior therapists," and so on. Although some practitioners follow a particular school of therapy rather faithfully, the majority describe themselves as *eclectic*; in other words, they are not bound by any one therapeutic model but have developed their own styles, which may borrow from several theoretical approaches. These therapists tend to use whatever concepts and techniques suit their own personalities and seem to be best suited to the needs of their clients. In order to give you a basis for choosing among the many types of therapists, as well as an overall grasp of contemporary therapies, I'll briefly describe the major concepts, goals, techniques, and applications of the various systematic approaches.

After you finish reading this section, you might want to refer back to Chapter 3, in which the three broad psychological approaches of psychoanalysis, behaviorism, and existential humanism are described in greater detail. The discussion of these approaches in Chapter 3 is very relevant to this description of therapeutic methods. As with the general types of groups, you'll find additional readings listed at the end of the chapter for each of these approaches.

Psychoanalytic Therapy

Assumptions. Freud developed the first systematic treatment procedure, which was based on the assumption that psychological problems have their roots in the first five years of life and in the unconscious.

Goals. The goal of analytic therapy is to reform the individual's character structure by bringing unconscious material into the client's awareness. The therapeutic process focuses on the reliving of childhood experiences. Past experiences are reconstructed, discussed, analyzed, and interpreted with the aim of reconstructing the client's personality.

Techniques. Since successful treatment requires the exposure and defusing of unconscious impulses and the establishment of more effective coping techniques, clients must be willing to commit themselves to an intensive and long-term therapy process. Typically, clients come to therapy several times a week for a period of three to five years. The sessions usually last an hour. After some sessions face-to-face with the therapist, the client lies on a couch for free-association activity; that is, he or she says whatever comes to mind. This free association provides the basic material of the analysis.

A characteristic of psychoanalysis is that the therapist remains anonymous, engaging in very little sharing of his or her own feelings and experiences. The therapist's role is to become a blank screen onto which clients can project feelings that they have had toward significant people in their lives. This process, known as *transference*, is basic to psychoanalysis. Transference allows clients to attribute to the therapist "unfinished business" from their past relationships. As therapy progresses, childhood feelings and conflicts begin to surface from the depths of the unconscious, and clients regress emotionally. The therapist becomes a substitute for significant others from a client's life, and, for the therapy to effect a cure, a transference relationship must be worked through. Together, client and therapist explore the parallels between the client's past and present experiences. The client has many opportunities to see the variety of ways in which his or her core conflicts and defenses are manifested in daily life. As a result of this long-term intensive regression to the past, the client achieves insight into repressed material.

Analysts use techniques such as diagnosis, questioning, and the gathering of life-history data; they also use procedures such as interpretation, dream analysis, and free association, all of which are tools for bringing the unconscious into conscious awareness and discovering the meaning of symptoms. In the course of therapy, clients ideally move from talk to catharsis (the expression of intense emotion), to insight, to intellectual and emotional understanding—which, it is hoped, will lead to personality change.

Applications. Orthodox psychoanalysis is limited to a few clients who want this kind of experience, who can afford the expense involved, and who will commit themselves to the process for several years. However, many psychotherapists who are not classical Freudians have modified this approach and do use some of its concepts and procedures. Thus, it's very possible that, if you seek therapy, your therapist may be psychoanalytically oriented, even though your therapy is relatively short-term and does not follow the exact process I've described.

Existential Therapy

Assumptions. Existential therapy is based on concepts such as purpose, choice, freedom, and self-awareness. Existential therapists emphasize the way in which we experience the world and choose to relate to it. For existential therapists, our capacity for self-awareness leads to both freedom and responsibility in shaping our destinies, which in turn lead to *existential anxiety*—a condition arising from the necessity to make our own choices and assume responsibility for the outcomes. Existential therapists focus on what they see as the predicament of the contemporary person: the breakdown of traditional values, the absence of viable values to replace the traditional ones, and the sense of emptiness, alienation, and depersonalization that many individuals experience in contemporary society.

Goals. The goals of existential therapy are to maximize growth, spontaneity, and fulfillment, and to assist clients to recognize and exercise their personal freedom to decide what they want to become.

Techniques. Existential therapy is basically an attitude toward persons and an approach to the understanding of human problems, and no clearly defined procedures are spelled out. Although existential therapists may draw upon other therapies for techniques, they generally stress the *encounter* (the person-to-person relationship between the client and the therapist) and the understanding of the client's uniqueness and his or her subjective way of experiencing the world. They also stress the importance of challenging the client to question the purpose of his or her existence and to find a meaning in living.

Applications. Existential therapy is particularly appropriate for clients who struggle with meaninglessness in life, with identity problems, with achieving autonomy, and with deep feelings of alienation, loneliness, and depersonalization.

Client-Centered Therapy

Assumptions. Carl Rogers developed client-centered therapy as a reaction against what he considered the limitations of psychoanalysis. A branch of humanistic therapy, the client-centered approach is essentially directed toward the growth of the self. The main goal of therapy is to assist clients to develop the ability and willingness to be themselves. The therapist mainly tries to help clients discover their own capacities for solving their problems. This approach puts great faith in the capacity of clients to lead the way in their therapy and to find their own direction.

Goals. A major goal of this therapy is to provide a climate of trust and safety in which clients can become aware of inner blocks to personal growth. Client-centered therapists believe that our defenses and pretenses keep us from being real with others and, in the end, from being real with ourselves. When facades are surrendered during the therapeutic process, clients ideally tend to move toward greater openness and self-trust. They display more willingness to be *processes* rather than fixed products and to live more by their internal standards than by external cues.

In client-centered therapy, the relationship between the therapist and client is one of primary importance. The requisite qualities of the therapist include genuineness, warmth, accurate empathy, and unconditional acceptance of, and respect for, the client. The client is then able to carry the learnings achieved by means of the therapeutic relationship to his or her relationships with others.

Techniques. In this type of therapy, techniques are secondary to the therapist's attitudes. Client-centered therapy minimizes directive techniques, interpretation, questioning, probing, diagnosis, and collection of data about the client's past. It maximizes active listening, reflection of feelings, and clarification. Most of all, client-centered therapy emphasizes being fully present with the client.

Applications. Client-centered therapy tends to be short-term and to focus on the client's own resources. Many college students and people who are struggling with vocational, marital, and personal conflicts have found it very helpful. It is most effective with clients who are verbal and who have initiative.

Gestalt Therapy

Assumptions. Developed by Frederick Perls, Gestalt therapy is a form of existential therapy that is based on the premise that individuals must find their own way in life and accept personal responsibility if they hope to achieve maturity. The approach is experiential, emphasizing here-and-now awareness and the integration of the fragmented parts of the client's personality. It focuses on the *what* and *how* of behavior and on the role of unfinished business from the past in preventing effective functioning in the present. The basic assumption of Gestalt therapy is that individuals can themselves deal effectively with their life problems.

Goals. A central aim of Gestalt therapy is to challenge clients to move from environmental support to self-support. Expansion of awareness, which is viewed as being growth-producing in and of itself, is a basic goal. Gestalt therapists believe that, with awareness, clients become able to reconcile the polarities and dichotomies within themselves and thus move toward a reintegration of all the aspects of themselves.

Techniques. Gestalt therapists assist clients to experience more fully all their feelings, which enables them to make their own interpretations. They avoid making interpretations, focusing instead on how a client is behaving. Clients identify their own unfinished business, and they work through impasses or blockages impeding their growth largely by reexperiencing past situations as though they were happening in the present. A Gestalt therapist has many techniques available, all of which are designed to intensify clients' direct experiencing and to help clients integrate conflicting feelings. Gestalt therapy gives much attention to nonverbal and body messages. It also stresses *doing* and *experiencing*, as opposed to merely talking about problems in a detached way.

Applications. Gestalt therapy is particularly well suited for group work, but it also can be used in individual sessions. The therapy is relatively brief, and it tends to become intense and emotional. For this reason, clients who have difficulty in experiencing and expressing feelings, and clients who tend to be "heady" might profit from Gestalt sessions.

Transactional Analysis

Assumptions. Transactional Analysis (TA) is set apart from most other therapies in that it involves a contract, developed by the client, that clearly states the goals and direction of the therapy process. It focuses on a client's early decisions in life and stresses the capacity of a person to make new decisions.

Goals. The basic goal of TA is to assist clients in making new decisions regarding their present behavior and the direction of their lives. Its aims are to foster an awareness of how freedom of choice has been restricted by early decisions clients made about themselves and to provide options to sterile and deterministic ways of living. Clients are encouraged to replace a life-style characterized by manipulative game playing with a more autonomous life-style characterized by awareness, spontaneity, and intimacy.

Techniques. One basic prerequisite for being a TA client is the capacity and willingness to understand and accept a therapeutic contract. The treatment contract contains a concrete statement of objectives and lists the criteria for determining how and when these goals have been met. Any transactions that are not related to the contract between the client and the therapist are excluded. In this way, TA emphasizes an equal relationship between the client and the therapist that is characterized by a joint sharing of responsibility. The client contracts with the therapist for specific desired changes; when the contract is fulfilled, therapy is terminated.

In TA therapy, clients can expect to learn how to identify their own *ego states*. These ego states include: the *Parent* (whereby we imagine what our parents would feel, do, or say in a situation or else act toward others as our parents acted toward us); the *Adult* (whereby we process information and deal with the facts of external reality); and the *Child* (which includes our feelings, impulses, and spontaneous acts). TA therapists assume that, once people learn how to identify what ego states are at work in given situations, they can exercise greater control and choice. For instance, people who are so bound by "oughts" and "shoulds" that they can have fun only rarely can achieve greater freedom when they become aware of their "critical parents" who are inhibiting their spontaneity.

Clients of TA therapists also learn about their *life scripts*, which are made up of parental teachings combined with the early decisions they made about themselves and continue to carry around with them as adults. They focus on the *life positions* they have adopted, which are basically decisions concerning how they relate to others. The possible life positions include: (1)

I'm OK—you're OK; (2) *I'm OK—you're not OK;* (3) *I'm not OK—you're OK;* and (4) *I'm not OK—you're not OK.* TA therapists believe that, once people make one of these four decisions early in life, they generally stay with it unless something intervenes to change matters. TA aims at helping clients develop the tools they need to feel like "winners," which is a feeling of *I'm OK—you're OK.*

TA clients pay attention to their need for "strokes," the kind of strokes they give and receive, and the way in which they ask for the strokes they need. The principles of TA are designed to enable people to become aware of the kinds of strokes they have been raised on and to change the strokes they respond to from negative ones to positive ones. Clients also learn to detect the *games* they play and to recognize the "pay-offs" of these games. Games are characterized as indirect, manipulative, and impersonal ways of avoiding intimacy that lead to the treating of others as objects.

Applications. Besides being a systematic approach to individual therapy, TA is used in marriage and family counseling and is well suited to use in groups. TA may be applied to many types of problems: delinquent behavior, alcoholism, schizophrenia, and interpersonal problems. In addition to being used in the treatment of behavior problems, it can be a valuable tool for increasing self-awareness and can encourage persons to evaluate their early decisions and to redecide their life plans in the present.

Behavior Therapy

Assumptions. The term *behavior therapy* covers the application of a variety of techniques and procedures that are rooted in many different theories of learning. Essentially, behavior therapy involves the systematic application of principles of learning to the task of changing behavior and making it more adaptive. In contrast to most other therapies, behavior therapy is characterized by: (a) a focus on overt and specific behavior, (b) a precise spelling-out of the goals of treatment, (c) a formation of specific procedures appropriate to a particular problem, and (d) an objective assessment of the outcomes of therapy. The approach stresses present behavior and focuses on changes in behavior rather than on the achievement of insight.

Goals. The general goals of behavior therapy are the elimination of maladaptive behavior and the learning of more effective behavior patterns. The client decides upon the goals, but the therapist helps make them specific and concrete. Continual assessment throughout therapy determines the degree to which the goals are being met.

Techniques. Behavior therapists do not emphasize their personal relationships with their clients, but they do see good working relationships as important for the implementation of a plan of treatment. The therapist is active and directive, often functioning as a teacher and director, as well as an expert in the diagnosis of maladaptive behavior and the prescription of corrective procedures. In this type of therapy, clients cannot stop at mere verbalization or intellectual understanding of themselves but must practice different behaviors outside of the therapy sessions.

Many specific techniques based on learning principles and geared to behavioral change are available to the behavior therapist. In addition, there are numerous techniques that clients can practice on their own, such as relaxation training, and many self-control methods are used in behavior therapy.

Applications. This system of therapy has applicability to a wide range of specific behavioral problems. It can be used in either individual or group counseling and is useful for people who want to change such behaviors as excessive smoking, eating, and drinking; sexual problems; phobias and fears; and unassertive behavior.

Rational-Emotive Therapy

Assumptions. Albert Ellis, the founder of Rational-Emotive therapy (RET), holds that human misery and emotional disturbance stem from irrational ideas acquired during childhood but perpetuated through self-indoctrination. Thus, people who are emotionally disturbed make wrong assumptions about themselves and the world. They become anxious, depressed, or guilt-ridden, not necessarily because of events that happen to them, but because of how they interpret these events.

RET stresses the importance of values in human living. It holds that personality is largely the product of beliefs and attitudes. Thus, people function well when their values are rationally based and feel emotionally disturbed when they live by unchallenged values, by untested, irrational beliefs, and by tyrannical *oughts, shoulds,* and *musts.*

Goals. The goal of rational-emotive therapy is to help clients rid themselves of self-defeating outlooks on life and to acquire a more rational and tolerant philosophy.

Techniques. RET therapists tend to borrow diverse techniques from many behavioral approaches. All these techniques are designed to help clients evaluate their self-defeating ideas and verbalizations, understand their role in causing and maintaining their difficulties, and verbalize more constructive beliefs. These techniques may include: persuasion, suggestion, confrontation, challenging, teaching, questioning, probing, interpreting, role-playing, desensitization, behavior rehearsal, coaching, modeling, and assertiveness training. Clients are expected to become active in the therapeutic process by extending their learnings to their everyday lives. Clients are thus expected to formulate contracts, to carry out specific "homework assignments" (things for them to do in daily life that will enable them to challenge their faulty thinking), to read, to listen to tapes, and to practice new behaviors.

Applications. RET can be applied to individual therapy, ongoing group therapy, marathon-encounter groups, brief therapy, marriage and family therapy, and sex therapy. Clients with moderate anxiety, neurotic disorders, character disorders, psychosomatic problems, or sexual dysfunctions may find it useful. It is most effective with people who can reason well.

Reality Therapy

Assumptions. Reality therapy, founded by William Glasser, stresses problem solving and coping with the demands of society. It focuses on the present and on the client's strengths. It does not emphasize the past; nor does it stress awareness of the unconscious. It does stress moral and value judgments and demands that clients judge their own behavior to determine whether it is leading to a constructive life. Reality therapy does not deem insight and attitudinal change crucial but instead focuses on behavioral change.

Goals. The goals of reality therapy are to guide clients toward making value judgments about their present behavior and to help them decide on a plan of responsible action for implementing changes in behavior.

Techniques. In reality therapy, the therapist attempts to get involved with clients and encourage them to face reality and make choices that will fulfill their needs in socially acceptable ways. Clients decide on specific desired changes; then plans are formulated, commitment to follow through is established, and results are evaluated. Reality therapists are active and directive. They often use the contract method; when the contract is fulfilled, therapy is terminated.

Applications. Reality therapy is designed to help people achieve a "success identity," and it is used in individual and group counseling, teaching, social work, marriage counseling, institutional management, and community development. Many different types of people may find it useful, since the therapy is short-term and stresses clear, easily understood concepts.

Primal Therapy

Assumptions. A striking contrast to most traditional therapies is provided by primal therapy, which was developed by Arthur Janov. Primal therapy views all behavior and personality problems as the result of painful emotions that have been held inside; the cure consists of reexperiencing these feelings. This approach focuses on the earliest repressed emotions and the expression in the present of "primal pain" (which is the result of unmet needs of hunger, warmth, love, and security).

Goals. The goal of treatment is to promote the experience of the "primal scream," which occurs when the client vividly visualizes the original scene that was so painful and becomes able to give full expression to the pain by screaming in a way characteristic of the early years of life. The primal scream is considered the curative factor. A cure doesn't involve a complete erasing of the past; individuals can still expect to feel some sadness when they think about their early hurts. However, Janov claims that, once people confront their inner pain and understand its meaning for them, they will never need therapy again.

Techniques. The primal therapist sees clients intensely during a three-week period to promote the expression of the primal pain, at which time the therapist attempts to assist them in uncovering and reexperiencing this repressed pain. These three weeks represent a full-time commitment on the part of both therapist and client. The period of individual therapy is followed by an extended period of weekly group therapy, lasting for about six to nine months. At these weekly sessions the participants continue to experience their "primals." After this time, they do most of their work on their own. Janov believes that therapists do not have to interpret anything for clients, because the truth is locked within the clients themselves. Once they have experienced their primal feelings, no interpretation by anyone else is needed.

Applications. This type of therapy may be of interest to those who want to explore early experiences in an intense, emotional way. The approach has merit for people whose current problems are rooted in their experiences as infants.

Time Out for Personal Reflection

In the next section, I discuss the values and limitations of counseling, some cautions and risks associated with it, and a few common misconceptions about the counseling process. This discussion may help you decide whether some type of counseling would be useful to you. Before going on, however, pause a moment to focus on your own present beliefs and attitudes about counseling.

Mark each of the following statements with a "T" or an "F" to indicate whether you think the statement is true or false.

_____ 1. Therapists generally decide upon the goals a client should have.
_____ 2. Therapeutic groups are artificial and unreal.
_____ 3. Only people who are psychologically disturbed seek individual or group counseling.
_____ 4. It's wise to begin counseling because someone close to you recommends it.
_____ 5. Counseling can be an effective way of resolving crises.
_____ 6. If I become involved in counseling, the counselor or group leader will be able to tell me what I do wrong and how I can correct a troubled situation.
_____ 7. Pursuing either individual or group counseling would be an indication that there was something wrong with me.
_____ 8. If I seek out counseling, things may get worse before they get better.
_____ 9. It's acceptable for a client to disagree with a counselor.
_____ 10. If I join a therapy group, I can expect to like some members more than others.
_____ 11. It can be useful to talk about feelings and problems.

_____ 12. Counseling is really a form of brainwashing.
_____ 13. Most people experience some fear and anxiety when beginning individual or group counseling.
_____ 14. If I'm honest and disclose my true feelings, the counselor or group leader will provide me with answers to my problems.
_____ 15. Counseling may disrupt a person's life.
_____ 16. By participating in a counseling group, I would come to realize that I'm not alone in my struggles.
_____ 17. Going to a counselor or group can be a way of remaining dependent.
_____ 18. Counseling involves risks.
_____ 19. Only counselors can really help people change.
_____ 20. Counseling can teach people that they are responsible for their own problems.

Basic Issues in Individual and Group Counseling

Values of Individual and Group Counseling

Throughout this book, I've stressed that growth is a lifelong process and that we never really arrive at a finished state. In the beginning of this chapter, I suggested that there are many ways of enhancing personal growth, most of which you can do without professional assistance. However, at times in your life you might use professional resources to help you get out of a rut or find new meaning in your life or deal with a crisis. Although they are surely not the only means of growing, individual counseling and personal-growth or therapy groups can help you come to a greater awareness of yourself and lead to greater self-development. The following are some of the values I see in individual and group counseling.

1. Counseling provides a learning situation in which we can openly explore our style of relating with others.
2. Counselors can offer support and encourage us to experiment with new behaviors.
3. Through counseling, we can get feedback concerning how others see us, and we can use this feedback to better understand the impact we have on others.
4. Through counseling we can realize that we're not alone in our struggles and thus come to feel less isolated.
5. Counseling can help us gain insight into the nature of our problems, and it can help us in our decision making by teaching us to look within ourselves for our own answers.
6. Counseling can show us new sides of ourselves. We can discover things about ourselves that are disturbing to us, yet at the same time we can discover latent strengths that we have denied.

Although counseling can have the values I've mentioned, there are also some limitations common to most forms of counseling. The following are some of the most significant of these limitations.

1. Counseling isn't appropriate for everybody at all times. Individuals should decide for themselves whether they want counseling and whether the time is right for them to pursue it. Some people may feel ready for a relationship with an individual therapist but not for a group experience. Others, while not feeling a need for individual counseling, may want to become involved in a short-term personal-growth group. If you consider counseling, it's important that *you* be the one who decides whether you should become involved in it and what type of counseling is right for you.

2. Individuals can use counseling to remain dependent on others for direction. They may look to the expectations and values of the counselor or of the members of a group for guidance, instead of deciding on their own expectations of themselves.

3. Some people become addicted to a group or to their weekly counseling sessions and make the counseling process an end in itself rather than a means to change.

4. Some people use counseling sessions as a forum for venting their misery, in the hope that they will be rewarded for being "open." Although there is a value to expressing our woes, it seems to me that it's important to work on actually changing our situations and that too many people get stuck in the mere expression of problems.

5. Neither individual nor group counseling is a cure-all. A person who looks to the professional for all the answers to his or her problems will be disappointed.

Cautions and Risks in Individual and Group Counseling

When considering counseling, you should be aware of some of the hazards involved and of what you can do to protect yourself from them. The following are a few important guidelines.

1. Keep in mind that either individual or group counseling may lead to a disruption in your life-style. For example, you might have a style of asking for very little for yourself and so tolerate a mediocre marriage. As a result of counseling, you may begin an intense process of searching and questioning that leads to drastic changes in your values and behavior. Of course, these changes may be constructive and lead to a revitalization of your personal life, but the process may also involve crisis and turmoil. Your spouse, for instance, may not welcome or be ready for changes, and this can create a difficulty for you.

2. Be aware of your rights as a client. You can choose whether to enter into individual counseling or try a group. You have the right to disagree with or question the therapist or group leader, as well as the right to terminate your counseling. If you don't feel satisfied with a

therapist, you can select another one. Realistically, in some situations (such as in a community mental-health center), you may not have options presented to you. You may be assigned to a group because groups enable a therapist to see more than one client at a time. However, various resources are usually available in a community, and you should keep in mind that you don't have to be a passive agent in your counseling.

3. There is a risk that you will be turned off to counseling because of a single negative experience with a counselor. Consequently, it's important to recognize that counselors don't all function in the same way and that personality differences among counselors are also significant. Thus, you may have a very positive experience with another counselor even if you're unhappy with your first one.

4. It's important not to quit counseling prematurely. There is a danger of opening up vulnerable areas and then terminating counseling before they are really dealt with. In addition, you should realize that counseling may lead to some changes that affect the people you're close to. For example, you might decide to risk more and to tell a person that you'd like to have his or her support—and then discover that, instead of supporting you, the other person fights your changes. As a result, you may become discouraged and undo the work you began in your counseling. Ideally, you and your counselor will agree on when the time comes to discontinue your sessions together.

5. Keep in mind that you are the one who should decide on the goals of your counseling. Some groups fall into the trap of imposing the values of the group on its members. Of course, the imposition of the counselor's values is a real danger in individual counseling also. Remember that counseling is a tool to help you clarify your own issues and provide you with resources for making choices; it's not a way of having your decisions made for you.

Misconceptions Concerning Individual and Group Counseling

Some common myths and misconceptions concerning counseling may lead you to conclude that the disadvantages of counseling far outweigh the advantages. For this reason, I want to comment briefly on some of these misconceptions.

1. *Counseling is a form of brainwashing.* On the contrary: counseling should assist you to look within yourself for your own answers to present and future problems in your life. Counseling is not synonymous with advice giving; nor does it involve the indoctrination of a "correct" philosophy of life.

2. *Only sick people seek individual or group counseling.* Although some forms of counseling are specifically aimed at helping people in crises or assisting people who are psychologically disturbed, many people utilize individual and group counseling to come to a fuller recognition of their potential and to remove blocks to personal growth.

3. *People in counseling become more unhappy, because their problems come to the surface.* There is some truth in this statement. Conflict *can* arise if you face painful truths about yourself, but it's important to realize that this increased awareness can lead to decisive steps toward change. Once you accept that you contribute to your own unhappiness or dissatisfaction, you have the choice of doing something to change your life.

4. *Counseling leaves a person defenseless.* People frequently express the fear that counseling will only rob them of defenses and that they won't have the resources to cope successfully without them. In fact, many people learn through counseling that rigid defenses aren't always necessary and that they can decide to shed unnecessary defenses that seal them off from others.

5. *Fear of counseling isn't normal.* On the contrary: most people who enter individual counseling or join a group do experience some anxiety. The important thing is how we deal with the fears we experience as we confront ourselves.

Some Consumer Guidelines for Use in Selecting a Group or a Counselor

With the range of professional services that are available, the consumer is sometimes at a loss in making a decision and knowing what to look for. Although there are no assurances that the group or counselor you pick will be the right one for you, the following suggestions may be helpful in making your selection.

1. It's generally unwise to initiate private counseling or to join a group simply because someone else thinks you should. Instead, decide for yourself whether you want to be a client of a particular kind of group or of a particular counselor.

2. Try to check with others who know the counselor or group leader before you make your decision. Although some reports may be biased (either positively or negatively), feedback from people who have worked with a counselor or group leader can be valuable.

3. Before you begin counseling or join a group, interview the counselor or group leader. For example, suppose that you're considering joining a group. Many group leaders will want a private session with a prospective member to determine the person's readiness for the group. By the same token, you have a right to know about the personal and professional qualifications of the person who leads the group. If the group leader resists such a request, you should probably avoid this person's group. If you do speak with the leader, try to decide the degree to which he or she inspires trust in you.

4. Learn to be an intelligent consumer of psychological services.

After all, if you were interested in buying a car or a house you would probably shop around and make some comparisons. Since the selection of a therapist that you will want to trust with intimate aspects of yourself is a crucial decision, devote the necessary time to looking for the type of service and the kind of person that will best fit your needs. In making your selection, you might consider some of the following questions:

- What are the responsibilities of the therapist and of the client?
- What are the expectations of the therapist or group leader?
- What are some of the psychological risks involved in participating in this type of counseling?
- What are the desired outcomes, and what measures are taken to achieve them? What kinds of techniques does the therapist use?
- What are the fees? Will insurance cover a portion of them?
- What background, training, and experience does the therapist have? What is his or her specialty? What degrees and licenses does he or she possess?

As you consider the selection of a counselor, keep in mind that this is a highly personal decision. Consequently, even though you want to select a qualified person, one of the most important aspects of your decision is your degree of trust in that person.

5. If you have any reservations about your own readiness to enter individual counseling or to participate in a group, I suggest discussing them with the counselor or group leader prior to making a commitment. For example, you may have some anxiety concerning your readiness for counseling, or you may wonder whether a group is really what you need, or you may have fears about participating. Any of these matters could be productively explored in a pre-counseling interview.

6. Be very cautious about responding to advertisements or to brochures and pamphlets circulated in the mail. Referrals from agencies, from professionals, and most of all from clients who have worked with a counselor can more appropriately guide you in your selection.

7. Check with your college or university counseling center to find out what kind of professional services they offer. These counseling services are generally offered free to students and are designed especially for the needs of college students of all ages.

8. Look into the continuing-education or extension programs and summer sessions of the community colleges and other colleges and universities in your area. Increasingly, departments of psychology, education, and counseling are offering many types of experiential courses, personal-growth groups, weekend workshops, and special-interest programs. For instance, most college-extension programs offer several types of workshops or groups, such as groups for the divorced, assertiveness-training groups, groups for professionals, couples' workshops, and consciousness-raising groups for both men and women.

9. Check out the resources for individual counseling, marriage and family counseling, and groups available at community mental-health centers. Many local agencies provide counseling services on an ability-to-pay basis.

Counseling for Crisis Resolution

This discussion of individual and group counseling has focused primarily on the use of these resources as aids in personal growth. However, the same guidelines apply if you find yourself in some type of crisis at any time in your life. For example, a divorce can precipitate a crisis in an entire family, or an adolescent son or daughter who gets heavily involved in drugs can cause a crisis that involves every person in the family. You may experience a crisis if you fail to get a promotion or if you lose a job. Many people experience a mid-life crisis when they begin to realize that many of their dreams and hopes will not be fulfilled. Loss of a loved one through death or separation can also lead to a crisis. In short, there are many sources of minor or major disruptions in our lives, and at times you may want to seek some form of counseling to help you get through a crisis more effectively than you would by coping with the problems yourself.

Deciding Whether You Need Professional Services

Often people are really unclear about whether or not they need or want to get involved in psychological counseling. How can you know whether you have a need for psychological services? This is an extremely difficult question to answer in general, but I'll give as examples some reasons that clients typically seek professional assistance. *Some* people initiate personal therapy because:

- they are facing a situational crisis in which they feel their subjective world (or some part of it) is collapsing.
- they have been unable to get free from a prolonged period of depression, anxiety, or guilt.
- they find that their work is no longer meaningful and that they want to explore other options.
- they are hurting over some particular situation and want help in understanding how to deal with their hurt.
- they find their marriage intolerable and want to resolve their conflicts by discovering more constructive ways of living together.
- they feel a deadness and lack of meaning in their lives.
- they have certain symptoms that interfere with their functioning, such as being overweight, frequently getting sick, having exaggerated fears, and so forth.

No set of guidelines concerning whether or not you need psychotherapy can be complete, of course, because so much depends on how much you want for yourself. Some people are satisfied as long as they are relatively comfortable. Some seek therapy only when they are in emotional turmoil; as soon as they begin to feel less emotionally upset, or as soon as the crisis passes, they terminate their counseling. Some people hope that a counselor will take away all their problems. Others who feel they have grown stale want to do something to get out of a rut they're in. Thus, the decision to seek professional help depends greatly on whether you want what you have now or want to risk doing whatever is necessary to make greater progress in your life.

You may be hesitant to initiate personal therapy because you feel that there is a stigma attached to being in therapy. Many people feel that it is a sign of weakness or inadequacy to need help from others, and they believe that they should be able to resolve any crisis by themselves. However, it takes courage to recognize things about yourself that you want to change and then to follow through by actually doing something to change. This may involve trusting a therapist to challenge you and assist in your learning, and doing so is hardly a confession of weakness.

Where to Go for Professional Assistance

If you decide that you want to use professional resources, where can you go for help, and how can you find out what resources are available? In most communities, there are mental-health centers and free clinics that offer a variety of services. These agencies can also give you leads on where to go for assistance with particular types of problems. You can check with friends to see whether any of them have been involved in counseling and, if so, what their impression of the counselor was. The university or college counseling center is another place to look. If you're enrolled in the college, the services may be free or available on an ability-to-pay basis. If you aren't enrolled, the center can probably give you a list of professionals in private practice or in community clinics. Ministers and physicians can also refer you to counseling professionals.

You should also have some understanding of the different types of mental-health professionals. There are several types of professionals who work with people experiencing psychological, interpersonal, and behavioral problems. Each of these types has its own strengths, but they all have much in common. Members of the helping professions generally try to minimize or eliminate the environmental conditions that may be causing and maintaining behavioral problems. They all are concerned with developing therapeutic (growth-producing) relationships with clients, and many of them use similar techniques.

In practice, the lines between the various kinds of professionals and professional services are not always clearly drawn, and there may be considerable overlap in functions. With this in mind, let's look at the various kinds of personnel who offer these human services.

Members of the Helping Professions

Clinical psychologists. Clinical psychologists have Ph.D.s in psychology and have had a year or two of supervised clinical practice (internship). They deal with psychological testing, psychotherapy, and research. Clinical psychologists are usually trained in both individual and group therapy; in most states, they must also possess a license to engage in private practice.

Counseling psychologists. Counseling psychologists hold doctoral degrees, either a Ph.D. or an Ed.D., from a counseling program at a university. They have had essentially the same kind of training as clinical psychologists, although their internships are with clients who have problems related to educational, vocational, and personal/social matters. Counseling psychologists often work in college counseling centers or for community mental-health agencies. They might also have a private practice in which they perform individual and group counseling or therapy, in which case they must be licensed by the state.

Educational psychologists and *school psychologists*. Educational and school psychologists specialize in learning, problems in learning, and testing and evaluation. Some school psychologists, who usually hold a master's degree, do some counseling with parents, families, or children, but they are more likely to do testing and make referrals to other professionals if treatment is indicated.

Psychiatrists. Psychiatrists are trained doctors (M.D.s) who have had specialized training in psychiatry in mental hospitals or clinics. In addition to practicing verbal therapy, psychiatrists can prescribe medication and may use various types of drugs in conjunction with therapy. Psychiatrists often perform the same services as clinical psychologists, except that they tend to specialize in cases of more severe disturbances or of psychosomatic disorders, such as high blood pressure, migraine headaches, respiratory problems, skin disorders, and so on. Many psychiatrists are oriented toward the psychoanalytic approach to therapy originated by Freud.

Psychoanalysts. Psychoanalysts are usually psychiatrists who have had extensive training in the theory and practice of intensive psychotherapy founded by Freud. Although psychiatrists may also make use of psychoanalytic techniques, psychoanalysts base their treatment procedure on the lengthy process of analysis described earlier in this chapter.

Behavior therapists. Behavior therapists are psychologists who specialize in behavior modification—that is, in the use of learning principles in eliminating maladaptive behavior and shaping more effective behaviors. Behavior therapy was described earlier in the chapter.

Psychiatric social workers. Psychiatric social workers have master's degrees in social work and have had supervised internships in psychiatric settings. They may work in clinics, in private practice as psychotherapists, or in social-service agencies. Their training makes them especially qualified to

work with families of clients in treatment, with social and cultural realities
that cause personal stress, with community groups, and with individuals.

Psychiatric nurses. Psychiatric nurses have had specialized education
and training in work with emotionally disturbed patients. They often work in
conjunction with psychiatrists; they may also practice individual and group
therapy with supervision or work with families.

Marriage, family, and child counselors. These counselors hold master's
or doctoral degrees in a behavioral-science field (usually counseling or psychology) or in marriage, family, and child counseling. They specialize in
problems in relationships and often help couples with their sexual conflicts.

Paraprofessionals. In addition to the professionals who work in the
mental-health field, there are increasing numbers of paraprofessionals who
perform many of the same psychological services. Paraprofessionals usually
have A.A. degrees in human services from a community college or B.A.
degrees in human services from a college or university. There are also paraprofessionals who are serving internships as part of their master's degree
programs; these people work under supervision and have an opportunity to
meet with their supervisors and other interns. Many paraprofessionals are
both talented and qualified for the work they do with clients—a fact that
clients may not appreciate who are disappointed when they have their first
session with an intern or a paraprofessional. Sometimes clients ask to see the
''real doctor'' or have reservations about trusting a person who has not had
advanced professional training. You should know that much more than training goes into the making of a sensitive and helpful counselor, and many
paraprofessionals have had life experiences that are most advantageous to
them in their work with clients.

Evaluating Members of the Helping Professions

To maximize your chances of benefiting from any form of psychological services, you should apply some of the guidelines given in this
chapter and realize that you must ask questions if you're to become an
intelligent consumer of these services. Some questions to consider are:
Do I feel a need for professional help? Am I willing to invest the necessary energy, time, and money? Am I prepared to develop a set of goals
that I want to achieve through counseling? What do I hope to get from
the process? Once you've decided that you want professional help and
determined what you want from the counselor, you can consider the
range of professionals to see who might best meet your needs.

In evaluating different counselors, a crucial issue is how to determine their level of competence. Degrees and licenses ensure a
minimum level of competence, but there are qualitative differences
among those who hold these credentials. Moreover, many qualified persons who work in institutions such as schools and churches are not
required to have licenses yet may be very effective counselors. Ulti-

mately, after you have consulted others and considered a counselor's qualifications, you still need to trust your own feelings and judgment concerning whether to work with a particular person.

Chapter Summary

In this chapter, I've emphasized that counseling is one resource we can turn to in expanding our awareness and discovering possibilities for change. Thus, counseling and psychotherapy should not be viewed merely as methods of treating people who have emotional and behavioral disorders.

There are any number of reasons why people who might benefit from counseling never make use of it, some of which are: they don't recognize their need for professional help; they are frightened of getting involved in therapy; they accept certain misconceptions about therapy; they don't know where to look for professional assistance; they think they should be able to deal with their difficulties without help from others.

When people do decide to become involved in the experience of therapy, they should be aware that it is a highly personal process and that many factors influence the results achieved. For counseling or therapy to be helpful, clients must be motivated to change and willing to become actively involved. Therapy is not something that is done *to* clients or *for* them; rather, they are partners with their therapists in a joint undertaking. For this reason, clients should select their therapists wisely, for the client/therapist relationship is of central importance in determining the outcomes of therapy.

There is a very wide range of therapeutic styles, ranging from psychoanalysis to primal therapy. However, most therapists develop their own therapeutic styles and use methods drawn from various approaches. More important than theoretical orientation is what kind of person a counselor is; hence, prospective clients need to pay attention to how much trust they feel in the person and should avoid selecting a counselor or therapist merely on the basis of what "school" of therapy he or she belongs to. Moreover, no therapeutic approach has a monopoly on truth or value; each has something valuable to offer. Some approaches may work well for certain people and yet be inappropriate for others.

Although I've presented a great deal of information about counseling in this chapter, my primary purpose has been to encourage you to continue your growth and to consider ways of realizing your potential more fully, whether on your own or with professional assistance. You can decide for yourself whether you want to take the time to decide on your priorities and actually begin to do for yourself and others some of the things you want to do. You can assume control of your life by choosing your direction rather than merely waiting for good things to happen to you. Once you fully recognize that you *do* have a choice, you have a gift that no one can take from you.

Activities and Exercises

1. Consider asking some friends, acquaintances, or fellow students to respond to the statements in this chapter's Self-Inventory or Time Out. What are their views of counseling and therapy?
2. If you've had any contact with professionals in the mental-health field, describe what your experience was like. Based on this experience, would you recommend psychological assistance to a friend?
3. List the criteria *you* would most look for in selecting a therapist for individual counseling. Would your list include fees? Degrees and credentials? Type of specialization? Recommendations from those who have worked with the professional? Your own impressions? The theoretical approach used? The techniques used?
4. List any factors that might keep you from seeking some form of counseling even if you felt a need and desire to do so. For example, would the possible reactions of your family or friends keep you from getting involved in counseling?
5. Look in your telephone directory under the listings "Psychologists" and "Marriage and Family Counselors." What different types of counselors or agencies are available in your area?
6. If you know people who have been involved in either individual or group counseling, ask them to talk with you about what the experience has meant to them. How did they feel when they first began?

What is it like to be in counseling? What do they think they've derived from the experience?

7. Describe what you would want to derive from the experience if you were to become involved in group or individual counseling. What conflicts and problems would you want to gain a fuller understanding of? What kinds of decisions would you want to make?

8. Check with the counseling center at your college or university (or at a local mental-health clinic) to find out what types of psychological services are available. Is crisis counseling available? Is long-term individual counseling available? How about other services, such as: therapy groups, personal-growth groups, vocational counseling, psychological and vocational testing, family counseling, marriage counseling, groups for couples, assertiveness training, and relaxation training? Once you've looked into the available resources, you might consider whether you'd want to take advantage of any of these services at some time.

Suggested Readings

If you wish to explore one or more of the types of counseling and therapy described in this chapter, you might want to select a few books dealing with general types of counseling or with specific approaches, philosophies, and techniques. For this reason, I've compiled a list of helpful books and grouped them according to whether they discuss counseling in general or particular systematic approaches or methods.

General Readings in Counseling

Adams, S., & Orgel, M. *Through the Mental Health Maze.* Washington, D.C.: Health Research Group, 1975. Available from the publisher, 2000 P Street N.W., Washington, D.C. 20036.

Binder, V., Binder, A., & Rimland, B. *Modern Therapies.* Englewood Cliffs, N.J.: Prentice-Hall (Spectrum), 1976.

Corey, G. *Theory and Practice of Counseling and Psychotherapy.* Monterey, Calif.: Brooks/Cole, 1977.

Corey, G. *Manual for Theory and Practice of Counseling and Psychotherapy.* Monterey, Calif.: Brooks/Cole, 1977.

Heck, E. *A Guide to Mental Health Services.* Pittsburgh: University of Pittsburgh Press, 1973.

Kopp, S. *If You Meet the Buddha on the Road, Kill Him!* New York: Bantam, 1972.

Ruitenbeek, H. *Psychotherapy: What It's All About.* New York: Avon, 1976.

Systematic Approaches

Psychoanalytic Therapy
Baruch, D. *One Little Boy.* New York: Dell (Delta), 1964.

Green, H. *I Never Promised You a Rose Garden*. New York: New American Library (Signet), 1964.

Existential Therapy

Frankl, V. *Man's Search for Meaning*. New York: Washington Square, 1963 (Pocket Books edition, 1975).

May, R. *Man's Search for Himself*. New York: Dell (Delta), 1973.

Client-Centered Therapy

Rogers, C. *On Becoming a Person*. Boston: Houghton Mifflin, 1970.

Rogers, C. *Carl Rogers on Encounter Groups*. New York: Harper and Row, 1973.

Gestalt Therapy

Perls, F. *Gestalt Therapy Verbatim*. New York: Bantam, 1971.

Polster, E., & Polster, M. *Gestalt Therapy Integrated*. New York: Brunner/Mazel, 1973.

Transactional Analysis

Harris, T. *I'm O. K.–You're O. K.* New York: Avon, 1976.

James, M., & Jongeward, D. *Born to Win: Transactional Analysis with Gestalt Experiments*. Reading, Mass.: Addison-Wesley, 1971.

Steiner, C. *Scripts People Live*. New York: Bantam, 1975.

Behavior Therapy

Sherman, A. *Behavior Modification: Theory and Practice*. Monterey, Calif.: Brooks/Cole, 1973.

Watson, D., & Tharp, R. *Self-Directed Behavior: Self-Modification for Personal Adjustment* (2nd ed.). Monterey, Calif.: Brooks/Cole, 1977.

Williams, R., & Long, J. *Toward a Self-Managed Life-Style*. Boston: Houghton Mifflin, 1975.

Rational-Emotive Therapy

Ellis, A. *Humanistic Psychotherapy: The Rational-Emotive Approach*. New York: McGraw-Hill, 1974.

Ellis, A., & Harper, R. *A New Guide to Rational Living*. Hollywood: Wilshire, 1975.

Reality Therapy

Glasser, W. *Reality Therapy: A New Approach to Psychiatry*. New York: Harper & Row, 1975.

Glasser, W. *Positive Addiction*. New York: Harper & Row, 1976.

Primal Therapy

Janov, A. *The Primal Scream*. New York: Dell, 1971.

Janov, A. *The Primal Revolution*. New York: Simon and Schuster, 1974.

Group Counseling

Alberti, R., & Emmons, M. *Stand Up, Speak Out, Talk Back*. New York: Pocket Books, 1975.

Blank, L., Gottsegen, G., & Gottsegen, M. *Confrontation: Encounter in Self and Interpersonal Awareness.* New York: Macmillan, 1971.

Brown, G. *Human Teaching for Human Learning: An Introduction to Confluent Education.* New York: Viking, 1971.

Burton, A. (Ed.). *Encounter: The Theory and Practice of Encounter Groups.* San Francisco: Jossey-Bass, 1969.

Corey, G. *Teachers Can Make a Difference.* Columbus, Ohio: Charles E. Merrill, 1973.

Corey, G., & Corey, M. *Groups: Process and Practice.* Monterey, Calif.: Brooks/Cole, 1977.

Egan, G. *Encounter: Group Processes for Interpersonal Growth.* Monterey, Calif.: Brooks/Cole, 1970.

Egan, G. *Face to Face: The Small Group Experience and Interpersonal Growth.* Monterey, Calif.: Brooks/Cole, 1973.

Egan, G. *Interpersonal Living.* Monterey, Calif.: Brooks/Cole, 1976.

Egan, G. *You and Me.* Monterey, Calif.: Brooks/Cole, 1977.

Fagen, J., & Shepherd, I. *Gestalt Therapy Now: Theory, Techniques, and Applications.* New York: Harper & Row, 1971.

Fensterheim, H., & Baer, J. *Don't Say Yes When You Want to Say No.* New York: Dell, 1975.

Harper, R. *The New Psychotherapies.* Englewood Cliffs, N.J.: Prentice-Hall, 1975.

Johnson, D., & Johnson, F. *Joining Together: Group Theory and Group Skills.* Englewood Cliffs, N.J.: Prentice-Hall, 1975.

Johnson, D. W. *Reaching Out: Interpersonal Effectiveness and Self-Actualization.* Englewood Cliffs, N.J.: Prentice-Hall, 1972.

Katz, R. *Preludes to Growth: An Experiential Approach.* New York: Free Press, 1973.

Lewis, H., & Streitfeld, H. *Growth Games.* New York: Bantam, 1972.

Lieberman, M. A., Yalom, I., & Miles, M. *Encounter Groups: First Facts.* New York: Basic Books, 1973.

Lowen, A. *The Betrayal of the Body.* New York: Macmillan, 1969.

Lowen, A. *The Language of the Body.* New York: Macmillan, 1971.

Mann, J., & Otto, H. (Eds.). *Ways of Growth.* New York: Viking, 1969.

Mintz, E. *Marathon Groups: Reality and Symbol.* New York: Avon, 1972.

Napier, R., & Gershenfeld, M. *Groups: Theory and Experience.* Boston: Houghton Mifflin, 1973.

O'Banion, T., & O'Connell, A. *The Shared Journey: An Introduction to Encounter.* Englewood Cliffs, N.J.: Prentice-Hall, 1970.

Otto, H. *Group Methods to Actualize Human Potential—A Handbook.* Beverly Hills, Calif.: Holistic Press, 1970.

Passons, W. *Gestalt Approaches in Counseling.* New York: Holt, Rinehart and Winston, 1975.

Rogers, C. *Carl Rogers on Encounter Groups.* New York: Harper & Row, 1973.

Ruitenbeek, H. *The New Group Therapies.* New York: Discus/Avon, 1970.

Schutz, W. *Joy: Expanding Human Awareness.* New York: Grove Press, 1967.

Schutz, W. *Here Comes Everybody: Body-Mind and Encounter Culture.* New York: Harper & Row, 1972.

Schutz, W. *Elements of Encounter.* New York: Bantam, 1975.

Shaffer, J., & Galinsky, M. D. *Models of Group Therapy and Sensitivity Training.* Englewood Cliffs, N.J.: Prentice-Hall, 1974.

Smith, M. *When I Say No, I Feel Guilty*. New York: Bantam, 1975.
Stevens, J. *Awareness: Exploring, Experimenting, Experiencing*. New York: Bantam, 1973.
Verny, T. *Inside Groups: A Practical Guide to Encounter Groups and Group Therapy*. New York: McGraw-Hill, 1975.
Yalom, I. *The Theory and Practice of Group Psychotherapy* (2nd ed.). New York: Basic Books, 1975.

Index